Beyond Good and Evil /

On the Genealogy of Morality

Volume Eight

Based on the edition by
Giorgio Colli & Mazzino Montinari

First organized in English by Ernst Behler

The Complete Works of Friedrich Nietzsche

EDITED BY ALAN D. SCHRIFT AND DUNCAN LARGE

Friedrich Nietzsche

Beyond Good and Evil /
On the Genealogy of Morality

Translated, with an Afterword,
by Adrian Del Caro

STANFORD UNIVERSITY PRESS
STANFORD, CALIFORNIA

Stanford University Press
Stanford, California

Translated from Friedrich Nietzsche, *Sämtliche Werke: Kritische Studienausgabe*, ed. Giorgio Colli and Mazzino Montinari, in 15 vols. This book corresponds to Vol. 5, pp. 9–421.

Critical edition of Friedrich Nietzsche's *Sämtliche Werke* and unpublished writings based on the original manuscripts.

Contents

Reference Matter

A Note
on This Edition

This is the first English translation of all of Nietzsche's writings, including his unpublished fragments, with annotation, afterwords concerning the individual texts, and indexes, in nineteen volumes. The aim of this collaborative work is to produce a critical edition for scholarly use. Volume 1 also includes an introduction to the entire edition, and Volume 19 will include a detailed chronology of Nietzsche's life. While the goal is to establish a readable text in contemporary English, the translation follows the original as closely as possible. All texts have been translated anew by a group of scholars, and particular attention has been given to maintaining a consistent terminology throughout the volumes. The translation is based on *Friedrich Nietzsche: Sämtliche Werke. Kritische Studienausgabe in 15 Bänden* (1980), edited by Giorgio Colli and Mazzino Montinari. The still-progressing *Nietzsche Werke: Kritische Gesamtausgabe,* which Colli and Montinari began in 1963, has also been consulted. The Colli-Montinari edition is of particular importance for the unpublished fragments, comprising more than half of Nietzsche's writings and published there for the first time in their entirety. Besides listing textual variants, the annotation to this English edition provides succinct information on the text and identifies events, names (except those in the index of persons), titles, quotes, and biographical facts of Nietzsche's own life. The notes are numbered in the text and are keyed by phrase. The afterword presents the main facts about the origin of the text, the stages of its composition, and the main events of its reception. The index of persons includes mythological figures and lists the dates of birth and death as well as prominent personal characteristics. Since the first three volumes appeared, important corrections to the 1980 edition of the *Kritische Studienausgabe* have been noted, and these corrections have been incorporated into the translation that appears here.

ERNST BEHLER AND ALAN D. SCHRIFT

Beyond Good and Evil

Prelude to a Philosophy of the Future[1]

Preface

Supposing that truth is a woman — well? is the suspicion not founded that all philosophers, insofar as they were dogmatists, poorly understood women? that the ghastly earnest and the clumsy obtrusiveness with which they tended to approach truth so far were inept and indecent[1] means for nothing more than charming a female[2] for themselves? What is certain is that she has not allowed herself to be charmed: — and every kind of dogmatism stands there today with a gloomy and despondent look. *If* it stands at all anymore! For there are scoffers who claim it has fallen, that all dogmatism is lying on the ground or even worse, all dogmatism is in its last throes. Seriously speaking, there are good reasons for hoping that all philosophical dogmatizing, however solemnly, however definitively and conclusively it has behaved, has in fact been only a noble childishness and noviceness. And perhaps the time is very near when it will be understood again and again *what* has actually sufficed to serve as the cornerstone of such sublime and unconditional philosophical edifices as the dogmatists have constructed to date — some popular superstition from time immemorial (like the superstition of the soul, which, as the superstition of the subject and the ego, to this day has not ceased to cause mischief), some play on words perhaps, a seduction on the part of grammar or a daring generalization of very narrow, very personal, very human-all-too-human facts. The philosophy of the dogmatists was hopefully only a promise spanning the millennia, as in still earlier times astrology was, in whose service perhaps more work, money, ingenuity and patience were expended so far than for any real science: — we owe the grand style of architecture in Asia and Egypt to its "superterrestrial" claims. It seems that all great things, in order to inscribe themselves with eternal demands upon the heart of humanity, must first stalk the earth as colossal and fear-inducing masks; dogmatic philosophy was such a mask, for instance the Vedanta doctrine in Asia, and Platonism in Europe. Let us not be ungrateful to it, even as surely as it must be admitted that the worst, longest lasting and most dangerous of all errors so far has been the dogmatist's error, namely Plato's invention of pure spirit and of good in itself. But now that it has been overcome, now that Europe breathes freely after this nightmare and can enjoy at least a healthier — sleep, we *whose task is wakefulness itself* are the heirs to all the strength that the struggle against this error has cultivated to maturity.[3] This meant of course that truth had to be stood on its head and the *perspectival*, the basic condition of all life, had to be denied in order to speak about spirit and good as Plato did; indeed, one is allowed to ask, as a physician: "What explains such a disease on the most beautiful plant of antiquity, on Plato? did the evil Socrates corrupt him? was Socrates the corrupter of youth after all? and did he deserve his hemlock?" — But the struggle against Plato or, to put it more plainly and for the "people," the struggle against the Christian-ecclesiastical pressure of millennia — for Christianity is Platonism for the "people"[4] — has created a magnificent tension of the spirit in Europe, such as never existed on earth; with such a tense bow we can now shoot for the most distant goals. Indeed, the European human being regards this tension as a state of emergency,[5] and already it has been attempted twice in grand style to slacken the bow, once through Jesuitism, a second time through the democratic Enlightenment: — which with the help of freedom of the press and the reading of newspapers may in fact succeed in persuading the spirit itself that it is no longer so obviously a "need."[6] (The Germans invented gun powder—hats off! but they canceled it out—they invented the printing press.) But we who are neither Jesuits nor democrats nor even sufficiently German, we *good Europeans* and free, *very* free spirits—we still have it, the entire need of the spirit and entire tension of its bow! And perhaps too the arrow, the task, who knows? the *goal* . . . . .[7]

Sils-Maria, UPPER ENGADINE,
IN JUNE 1885.

Part One

On the Prejudices of Philosophers

1[1]

The will to truth that will yet seduce us to many a risk, that famous truthfulness of which all philosophers so far have spoken with deference: what questions this will to truth has already laid before us! What strange, wicked, questionable questions! That is already a long story—and yet it seems it has scarcely begun? No wonder if we finally just become suspicious, lose our patience, turn around impatiently? That *we* for our part should also learn from this sphinx how to ask questions? *Who* is it, really, who asks questions of us here? *What* in us really wants "the truth"?—Indeed, we stopped for a long time before the question about the cause of this will—before we, finally, stopped completely before an even more thorough question. We asked about the *value* of this will. Suppose we want truth: *why not rather* untruth? And uncertainty? Even ignorance?—The problem of the value of truth stepped before us—or was it we who stepped before the problem? Who of us here is Oedipus? Who the sphinx? It is a rendezvous, so it seems, of questions and question marks.—And can you believe it, it finally seems to us as if the problem had never even been posed before—as if it were seen, looked in the eye, *risked* by us for the first time? For there is a risk involved, and perhaps there is none greater.

2

"How *could* something originate from its opposite? For example, truth from error? Or the will to truth from the will to deception? Or the selfless deed from self-interest? Or the pure sunny gaze of the wise man from greed? Such origins are impossible; whoever dreams of them is a fool, even worse; the things of highest value must have a different origin, *their own*—they are not derivable from this transitory, seductive, deceptive, meager world, from this chaos of delusion and craving! On the contrary, in the lap of being, in the everlasting, in the hidden god, in the 'thing in itself'—*there* must their ground lie, and nowhere else!"[2] —This kind of judging constitutes the typical prejudice by which the metaphysicians of all times can be recognized; this kind of valuation stands in the background of all their logical procedures; from this their "faith" they strive for their "knowledge," for something that in the end is solemnly christened as "the truth." The grounding faith[3] of metaphysicians is *the faith in the opposition of values*. Not even to the most cautious among them did it occur to doubt already here at the threshold, where it was after all most necessary; even when they vowed themselves to "*de omnibus dubitandum.*"[4] For one may doubt first whether there are oppositions at all, and second whether those populist valuations and value oppositions upon which the metaphysicians have pressed their seal are not perhaps mere foreground valuations, mere provisional perspectives, even more, perhaps from an angle, perhaps from below, frog perspectives as it were, to borrow an expression familiar to painters? For all the value that may be attributed to the true, the truthful, the selfless,[5] it would be possible that a higher and more fundamental value for all life would have to be ascribed to appearance, to the will to deceive, to self-interest and craving. It might even be possible that *what* constitutes the value of those good and honored things consists precisely in their being insidiously related, allied, linked, perhaps even essentially identical to those wicked, seemingly opposing things. Perhaps!—But who has the will to be concerned with such a dangerous Perhaps! For this, one really has to await the arrival of a new species of philosopher, those who have some other kind of reverse taste and inclination from their predecessors—philosophers of the dangerous Perhaps in every sense. —And in all earnestness: I see such new philosophers emerging.[6]

3

After looking long enough between the lines the philosophers write, and having kept my eye on them, I say to myself: one must still count the greatest part of conscious thinking among the instinctive activities, and even in the case of philosophical thinking; here we must rethink as we have re-thought with respect to heredity and what is "innate." Just as the act of birth is given little consideration in the whole process and progress of heredity: so too "consciousness" is in no decisive sense *opposed* to the instinctive—most conscious thinking of a philosopher is secretly guided by his instincts and forced into certain channels. Behind all logic and its seeming tyranny of movement there also stand valuations, or more plainly spoken, physiological demands for the preservation of a certain type of life. For instance, that the definite is worth more than the indefinite, or appearance worth less than "truth": such estimations could still be mere foreground-estimations, despite all their regulative importance to *us*, a certain kind of *niaiserie*[7] as may be necessary precisely for the preservation of beings like us. Supposing, of course, that it is not exactly mankind who is the "measure of things" . . . . .[8,9]

4

The falseness of a judgment[10] is for us not yet an objection to a judgment; perhaps our new language sounds strangest in this respect. The question is how far it is life-promoting, life-preserving, species-preserving, perhaps even species-cultivating; and we are fundamentally inclined to assert that the falsest[11] judgments[12] (among which synthetic judgments *a priori* belong) are the most indispensable to us, that without an acceptance of logical fictions, without a measuring of reality against the purely invented world of the absolute and the self-identical, without a constant falsification of the world through numbers mankind could not live—that renouncing false judgments would be a renunciation of life, a denial of life. Acknowledging untruth as a condition of life: this truly means offering resistance in a dangerous way to the accustomed value-emotions; and a philosophy that dares this already places itself, solely by those means, beyond good and evil.

§13

What prompts us to regard all philosophers half suspiciously, half mockingly is not that we figure out time and again how innocent they are—how often and easily they err and stray, in short, their childishness and childlikeness—but instead that among them there is not sufficient honesty: whereas they all raise a great and virtuous racket as soon as the problem of truthfulness is touched upon even from a distance. They all act as if they had discovered and reached their real opinions through the self-development of a cold, pure, divinely unconcerned dialectic (as opposed to mystics of every rank, who are more honest than philosophers and clumsier—they speak of "inspiration"—): whereas at bottom they are defending some anticipated proposition, a notion, an "intuition," most often a fervent desire rendered abstract and sifted for reasons they seek after the fact:—they are all advocates who do not wish to be called that, and in fact most often they are even sly spokesmen of their prejudices, which they christen "truths"—and *very* distant from the courage of conscience that acknowledges this, this very fact; very distant from the good taste of courage which lets this be known, whether in order to warn an enemy or friend, whether from impiety or in order to mock themselves. The tartuffery[14] of the old Kant, as stiff as it was demure and with which he lures us onto secret dialectical paths leading or better yet misleading to his "categorical imperative"—this spectacle makes us pampered viewers smile, we who take no small pleasure in keeping an eye out for the subtle tricks of old moralists and preachers of morals. Or even that hocus pocus of mathematical form with which Spinoza heavily armored and masked his philosophy — "love for *his* wisdom" ultimately, to use the term properly and fairly — in order to intimidate from the start the courage of the attacker who would dare to cast a glance at this unconquerable virgin and Pallas Athena: — how much personal timidity and vulnerability is revealed by this masquerade of a reclusive, sick man!

6[15]

Gradually it has occurred to me what every great philosophy has been so far: namely the personal confession of its author and a kind of involuntary and unnoticed *mémoires*; likewise that the moral (or immoral) intentions in every philosophy constitute the actual living seed from which the entire plant has grown every time. In fact, one always does well (and wisely) to first ask oneself, in explaining how the most far-fetched metaphysical claims of a philosopher came about: at what morality is it (or is *he* —) aimed? Accordingly I do not believe that a "drive for knowledge" is the father of philosophy, but that a different drive, here as elsewhere, has merely used knowledge (and misjudgment!)[16] as a tool. But whoever examines the basic human drives with an eye toward how far they may have played their game right here as *inspiring* geniuses (or demons and kobolds —), will find that they all have done philosophy at some time — and that every single one of them would too gladly wish to present *itself* as the ultimate purpose of existence and as the rightful *master* of all other drives. For every drive is bent on ruling: and as *such* it attempts to philosophize. — Indeed: things might be different among scholars, the real scientific people — "better" if you will — there might really be something like a knowledge-drive there, some small independent clockwork that, once properly wound, bravely ticks and ticks *without* all the other drives of the scholar coming into play. For this reason the real "interests" of the scholar usually lie somewhere else entirely, perhaps with his family, or earning money or in politics; in fact, it makes precious little difference whether his little machine is placed on this or that scientific location, and whether the "hopeful" young worker makes a good philologist or fungi specialist or chemist of himself: — it does not *characterize* him if he becomes this or that. Conversely, in the philosopher there is absolutely nothing that is impersonal; and in particular his morality provides decided and decisive testimony to *who he is*— meaning in what order of rank the innermost drives of his nature stand in relation to each other.

7

How malicious philosophers can be! I know of nothing more poisonous than the joke Epicurus[17] allowed himself against Plato and the Platonists: he called them *Dionysiokolakes*. This means according to the wording and in the foreground "syco-phants of Dionysios," thus tyrant paraphernalia and lickspit-tles; but in addition to all this it also means "they are all *actors*, there is nothing genuine about them" (for *Dionysokolax* was a popular designation for an actor). And the latter meaning is actually the malice that Epicurus fired at Plato: he was an-noyed by the grand manner, the self-dramatizing that Plato and his disciples were so good at— that Epicurus was not good at! he, the old school master from Samos, who sat holed up in his little garden in Athens and wrote three hundred books, who knows? maybe out of rage and ambition against Plato? — It took hundreds of years before Greece figured out who this gar-den deity Epicurus was. — Did it ever figure it out? —

8[18]

In every philosophy there is a point where the "conviction" of the philosopher steps onto the stage, or to put it in the words of an ancient mystery:

> *adventavit asinus,*
> *pulcher et fortissimus.*[19]

9[20]

You want to *live* "according to nature"? Oh you noble Stoics, what a fraud of words! Imagine a being such as nature, wasteful without measure, indifferent without measure, without purpose and consideration, without mercy and justice, fertile and barren and uncertain at the same time, imagine indifference itself as power—how *could* you live according to this indifference? Living—is that not precisely wanting to be different than this nature? Is living not assessing, preferring, being unjust, being limited, wanting to be different? And supposing your imperative "live according to nature" means at bottom nothing more than "live according to life"—then how could you *not*? Why make a principle of that which you yourselves are and must be?—In truth things are quite different: in gleefully alleging to read the canon of your law out of nature, you really want the reverse, you strange actors and self-deceivers! Your pride wants to prescribe and incorporate your morality and your ideal onto nature, onto nature itself; you demand that it be nature "according to the Stoa" and want to make all existence conform only to your own image of existence—as a monstrous eternal glorification and universalization of Stoicism! For all your love of truth you force yourselves so long, so persistently, so hypnotically and rigidly to see nature *falsely*, namely stoically, that you're no longer able to see it any other way—and some kind of abysmal arrogance finally implants the madhouse hope in you that *because* you are good at tyrannizing yourselves—Stoicism is self-tyranny—nature too can be tyrannized: after all, isn't the Stoic a *piece* of nature? . . . . .But this is an old, eternal story: what happened back then with the Stoics still happens today just as soon as a philosophy begins to believe in itself. It always creates the world in its own image, it cannot do otherwise; philosophy is this tyrannical drive itself, the most spiritual will to power, to "world creation," to the *causa prima*.[21]

10

The eagerness and subtlety, indeed I am almost tempted to
say: the slyness with which everywhere in Europe the problem "of the real and the apparent world" is tackled nowadays,
makes us think and listen; and whoever hears only a "will to
truth" in the background here certainly does not enjoy the
sharpest of ears. In a few rare cases such a will to truth might
actually be involved, some extravagant and adventurous act of
courage, a metaphysician's ambition for a lost cause, which in
the end still prefers a handful of "certainties" to a whole wagon
full of beautiful possibilities; there may even be puritanical
fanatics of conscience who would rather lie down and die on a
definite nothing than on an uncertain something, but this is
nihilism and the sign of a desperate, dead-tired soul: no matter how brave the gestures of such a virtue may seem.[22] In the
stronger thinkers who are more full of life and still thirsty for
it, however, things appear to be different, insofar as they side
against appearance and speak even the word "perspectival" with
arrogance, and insofar as they trust the credibility of their own
bodies about as little as the credibility of appearance that says
"the earth stands still," and though they let go of their most
certain possession seemingly in good cheer (for what does anyone believe in today more firmly than in the body?), who knows
whether deep down they want to reconquer something they
had once possessed even *more certainly*, some thing or some
piece of the old property of a bygone faith, maybe "the immortal soul," maybe "the old God," in short, ideas on which people could live better, that is, heartier and more cheerfully than
on "modern ideas"? There is a *mistrust* of modern ideas in this,
a disbelief in all that was built yesterday and today; perhaps a
slight disgust and scorn is mixed in, which no longer tolerates
the bric-a-brac of concepts of the most diverse lineage, with
which so-called positivism brings itself to market these days, a
disgust on the part of the more pampered taste at the fairground
motleyness and patches of all these reality-philosophasters[23] in

whom there is nothing new and genuine but this motleyness. On this matter we should, it seems to me, acknowledge
that these skeptical anti-realists and knowledge-microscopists
are right: their[24] instinct, which drives them away from *modern* reality, is not refuted—what do we care about their retro-
grade secret paths! What is essential in them is *not* that they
want to go "back": but that they—want to go *away*. A bit *more*
strength, flight, courage, artistry: and they would want to get
out—and not back!—

11[25]

It seems to me that people everywhere now are making an
effort to divert attention from the actual influence Kant exerted
on German philosophy, and especially to wisely sidestep the
value he attributed to himself. Kant was above all and chiefly
proud of his table of categories, saying with this table in his
hands: "this is the most difficult task that ever could be undertaken for the benefit of metaphysics."—Let us make sure we
understand this "could be"! he was proud of having *discovered*
a new faculty in human beings, the faculty for synthetic judgments *a priori*. Suppose he deceived even himself about this:
but the development and rapid blossoming of German philosophy depended on this pride and on the rivalry of all the younger
generation to possibly discover something even prouder—and
in any case "new faculties"!—But let us stop and think: it is
high time we did. How are synthetic judgments *a priori possible*, Kant asked himself—and what did he answer really? *By
virtue of a faculty:*[26] but unfortunately not in five words but so
ceremoniously, reverentially, and with such a dose of German
profundity and flourish that people failed to hear the amusing
niaiserie allemande[27] that lies in such an answer. People were in
fact beside themselves over this new faculty, and the jubilation
reached its peak when Kant discovered an additional moral
faculty in human beings:—for back then Germans were still
moral, and not yet "real-political"[28] by any means.—Then
came the honeymoon of German philosophy; all the young

theologians of the Tübingen seminary[29] rushed into the
bushes — they all searched for "faculties." And what didn't
they find — in those innocent, rich, still youthful times of the
German spirit, into which Romanticism, the malicious fairy,
breathed her magic and sang her songs, back then when they
still did not know how to distinguish "finding" from "inventing"![30] Above all a faculty for the "supersensible": Schelling
christened it intellectual intuition and thus accommodated
the heartiest cravings of his fundamentally piety-craving Germans. We can do no greater injustice to this entire emboldened
and enthusiastic movement, which was only youthfulness, however boldly it disguised itself in gray and hoary concepts, than
to take it seriously and even perhaps treat it with moral indignation; enough, people got older — the dream vanished. A time
came when they scratched their heads: we are still scratching
our heads today. People had dreamed: first and foremost — old
Kant. "By virtue of a faculty" — he had said, or at least meant.
But is that really — an answer? An explanation? Or on the
contrary only a repetition of the question? How does opium
make you sleepy? "By virtue of a faculty," namely the *virtus
dormitiva* — replies the physician in Molière:

> quia est in eo virtus dormitiva,
> cujus est natura sensus assoupire.[31]

But those kinds of answers belong to comedy, and it is finally
time to replace the Kantian question, "how are synthetic judgments *a priori* possible" with another question, "why is the
belief in such judgments *necessary*?" — that is, to comprehend
that for the purpose of preserving beings of our kind such
judgments must be *believed* to be true; which is why they
could naturally still be *false* judgments! Or, to be clearer and
crude and complete: synthetic judgments *a priori* should not
"be possible" at all: we have no right to them, in our mouths
they are nothing but false judgments. Only the belief in their
truth is necessary, to be sure, as a foreground belief and visual
evidence belonging to the perspectival optics of life. — Finally,

in order to give due consideration to the tremendous effect that "German philosophy" — I hope its right to be in quotation marks is understood? — has had on all of Europe, let no one doubt that a certain *virtus dormitiva* played a part: there was delight among the noble idlers, the virtuous, mystics, artists, three-fourths-Christians and political obscurantists of all nations in having an antidote, thanks to German philosophy, to the still overpowering sensualism that gushed over from the previous century into this one, in brief — *"sensus assoupire"*. . . . .

12^{32}

As concerns materialistic atomism: this is among the best-refuted things there are, and perhaps today in Europe no scholar is unscholarly enough to still allot it major significance, except for convenient and handy household purposes (namely as an abbreviated figure of speech) — thanks first to that Pole, Boscovich,[33] who along with the Pole Copernicus was the greatest and most victorious opponent of visual evidence so far. For while Copernicus persuaded us to believe counter to all our senses that the earth does *not* stand still, Boscovich taught us to abjure faith in the last thing about the earth that "stood still," the belief in "matter," in "material," in the earth-residuum and particle-atom: it was the greatest triumph over the senses ever achieved on earth. — But we must go still further and declare war on the "atomistic need" that still leads a dangerous afterlife in regions where no one suspects it, like that more famous "metaphysical need" — a ruthless war to the finish: but we must also first dispatch that other and more disastrous atomism that Christianity has taught best and longest, the *soul-atomism*. Allow me to use this word to characterize the belief that holds the soul to be something ineradicable, eternal, indivisible, a monad, an *atomon*: it is *this* belief that we should banish from science! But just between you and me, in doing so it is not necessary in the least to get rid of "the soul" itself, and thereby relinquish one of our oldest and most venerable hypotheses, as tends to be the case with the clumsiness of the naturalists who scarcely touch "the soul" before losing it. But the way to new conceptions and refinements of the soul-hypothesis stands open; and concepts like "mortal soul" and "soul as subject-multiplicity" and "soul as social structure of drives and affects" want henceforth to have their citizens' rights in science. Insofar as the *new* psychologist is preparing to put an end to the superstition that has so far proliferated around the idea of the soul with almost tropical luxuriance, he has of course banished himself as it were into a new wasteland and a new suspicion—it may be that the older psychologists were better off in terms of comfort and entertainment—: ultimately, however, he knows himself in this very way to be condemned to *inventing*—and who knows? maybe to *finding.*—[34]

13

The physiologists should stop and think before positing the drive for self-preservation as the cardinal drive of an organic being. Anything that lives wants above all to *discharge* its strength—life itself is will to power—: self-preservation is only one of the indirect and most frequent *consequences* of this.—In brief, here as everywhere beware of *superfluous* teleological principles!—such as the drive for self-preservation (for which we have Spinoza's inconsistency to thank—). This is demanded by method after all, which must essentially be the economy of principles.

14

It is dawning now on perhaps five or six minds that physics too is only a world interpretation and arrangement (by us! if I may say so) and *not* a world explanation: however, insofar as it relies on belief in the senses, it passes for more and must continue for a long time to come to pass for more, namely for an explanation. It has eyes and ears going for it, it has visual evidence and tangibility going for it: the effect this has on a fundamentally plebeian age is bewitching, persuasive, *convincing*—it even instinctively follows the truth-canon of eternally populist sensualism. What is clear, what "clarifies"? First that which can be seen and touched—every problem has to be pursued this far. Conversely: it was in the opposition *against* obviousness that the magic of the Platonic way of thinking resided, which was a *noble* way of thinking—and perhaps among people who enjoyed even stronger and more demanding senses than our contemporaries, but who knew how to find a higher triumph in maintaining their mastery over these senses: this they did using pale, cold, gray nets of concepts which they cast over the motley whirlwind of the senses—the rabble of the senses as Plato[35] called it. There was a different kind of *enjoyment* in this overpowering of the world and interpreting of the world in the manner of Plato, than the one offered us by the physicists of today, likewise the Darwinists and anti-teleologists among the physiological laborers, with their principle of "the smallest possible force" and the biggest possible stupidity. "Where someone has nothing more to see and to grasp, then he also has nothing more to do"—this of course is a different imperative than the Platonic, but in fact may be exactly the right imperative for a tough, hard-working species of machinists and bridge-builders of the future who have nothing but *rough* work to take care of.

15[36]

In order to pursue physiology in good conscience we must insist that the sense organs are *not* appearances in the sense of idealistic philosophy: as such they simply could not be causes! Sensualism then at least as a regulative hypothesis, if not as a heuristic principle. — What? and others even say the external world is supposed to be the work of our organs? But then even our body, as a piece of this external world, would be the work of our organs! And then even our organs themselves would be—the work of our organs! To me this appears to be a thorough *reductio ad absurdum*:[37] supposing that the concept *causa sui*[38] is something thoroughly absurd. Consequently the external world is *not* the work of our organs—?

There are still some harmless self-observers who believe that
there are "immediate certainties," for instance "I think," or
in the case of Schopenhauer's superstition, "I will": just as if
here knowledge got to grasp its object purely and nakedly, as
"thing in itself," and no falsification took place either on the
part of the subject or on the part of the object. But I will repeat a hundred times that "immediate certainty," and likewise
"absolute knowledge" and "thing in itself" contain a *contradictio
in adjecto*:[39] we really ought to free ourselves finally of the
seduction of words! Let the people believe that knowing involves knowing something to the end,[40] the philosopher has to
say to himself: "when I dissect the event expressed in the proposition 'I think,' then I get a series of audacious claims whose
proof is difficult, perhaps even impossible — for instance, that
it is *I* who thinks, that it must even be a something that thinks,
that thinking is an activity and effect on the part of a being that
is thought of as the cause, that there is an 'I' and finally, that it
is already firmly established what is meant by thinking — that
I *know* what thinking is. For if I had not already decided
this on my own, what would I use to gauge whether what is happening right now might not be 'willing' or 'feeling'? Enough,
this 'I think' presupposes that I *compare* my momentary state
with other states I know to be mine, in order to determine
what it is: because of this retrospective reference to other
'knowledge' it has no immediate certainty at least for me." — In
place of this "immediate certainty" in which the people in
this case might believe, the philosopher is handed a veritable
bundle of metaphysical questions, truly genuine intellectual
questions of conscience such as: "Where do I get the concept
of thinking? Why do I believe in cause and effect? What gives
me the right to speak of an ego, let alone of an ego as cause,
and finally of an ego as the cause of thought?" Whoever ventures
to answer these metaphysical questions at once with an appeal

to a kind of *intuition* of knowledge, as does someone who says: "I think, and I know that this at least is true, real, certain"—he would find the philosopher of today ready with a smile and two question marks. "Sir," the philosopher might give him to understand, "it is improbable that you are not mistaken: but does it absolutely have to be truth?"[41]—

17

As concerns the superstition of the logicians: I will never tire of emphasizing one short, sweet fact, which is not gladly conceded by these superstitious people—namely that a thought comes when "it" wants,[42] and not when "I" want; so that it is a *falsification* of the facts to say: the subject "I" is the condition of the predicate "think." It thinks: but that this "it" is precisely that old famous "ego" is only an assumption, an assertion, to put it mildly, and by no means an "immediate certainty." In fact too much is already claimed with this "it thinks": even this "it" contains an *interpretation* of the process and doesn't belong to the process itself. Here the concluding is done according to grammatical habit, namely "thinking is an activity, to every activity belongs something that is active, therefore—." Following basically the same scheme, the older atomism looked at every effective "force" for that little particle of matter in which it resides, and from which it produces effects, that is, the atom; more rigorous minds finally learned to do without this "earth residuum," and perhaps someday we will even accustom ourselves, logicians included, to doing without this little "it" (into which the honest old ego has vanished).

18[43]

It is truly not the least appealing aspect of a theory that it is refutable: this is precisely how it attracts the more refined intellects. It seems that the theory of "free will," refuted a hundred times, owes its longevity only to this appeal—: someone always come along and feels strong enough to refute it.

19

Philosophers tend to speak of the will as if it were the best-known thing in the world; indeed, Schopenhauer gave us to understand it is the will alone that is really known to us, known through and through, known without adding or subtracting. But more and more it seems to me that Schopenhauer in this case did what philosophers just tend to do: that he adopted a *popular prejudice* and exaggerated it. Willing to me seems above all to be something *complicated*, something that is a unity only in word—and it is precisely one word that contains the popular prejudice that has triumphed over the habitually minimal caution of philosophers. Let us for once be more cautious, let us be "unphilosophical"—let's say: first of all in every willing there is a plurality of sensations, namely the sensation of the state *away from which*, the sensation of the state *toward which*, the sensation itself of this "away" and "toward," then an accompanying sensation in the muscles that comes into play through a kind of habit as soon as we "will," even without our having to move our "arms and legs." Secondly therefore, just as sensation and in fact many kinds of sensations are to be recognized as ingredients of the will, so too thinking: in every act of will there is a commanding thought;—and we had better not believe that this thought can be separated from the "willing" as if will would still be left over! Thirdly the will is not only a complex of sensation and thinking, but above all an *affect*: and specifically that affect of command. What we call "freedom of the will" is essentially the affect of superiority with respect to the one who must obey; "I am free, 'he' must obey"—this consciousness lies in every will, and likewise that straining of attention, that straight focus that fixes on one thing exclusively, that unconditional valuation "now this is essential and nothing else," that inner certainty that something will be obeyed, and whatever else belongs to the disposition of the commander. Someone who *wills*—commands something in himself that obeys or that he believes obeys. But now let us observe what is the most wondrous thing about the will—about this very multifarious thing for which the people have only one word; insofar as in this case we are simultaneously the commanders *and* the obeyers, and as obeyers we know the sensations of forcing, pushing, pressing, resisting, moving, that usually begin immediately after the act of willing; and insofar as, on the other hand, we have a habit of disregarding and deceiving ourselves about this duality by virtue of the synthetic concept "I," a whole chain of erroneous conclusions and consequently of false valuations has attached itself to willing—to such an extent that the willing individual believes in good faith that willing *suffices* for action. Because in most cases by far there has only been willing where the effect of command, therefore obedience, therefore action could be *expected*, the *appearance* has translated into sensation, as if there were a *necessity of effect* there. Enough, someone who wills believes with a considerable degree of certainty that will and action are somehow one—he attributes the success, the execution of willing to the will itself and in doing so enjoys an increase in that feeling of power that comes with all success. "Freedom of the will"—that is a word for the multifarious state of pleasure of the one who wills, who commands and simultaneously identifies himself as the executor—who as such also enjoys the triumph over obstacles but thinks to himself that it is his will alone that really overcomes the obstacles. In this manner the one who wills adds the pleasurable sensations of the executing, successful tools, the useful "sub-wills" or sub-souls—our body is after all only a society constructed of many souls—to his feeling of pleasure as commander. *L'effet c'est moi*:[44] what happens here is what happens in every well constructed and happy community, namely the ruling class identifies itself with the successes of the community. With all willing we are dealing simply with commanding and obeying, on the foundation, as mentioned earlier, of a social structure of many "souls," which is why a philosopher should exercise the right to conceive willing itself under the horizon of morality: that is, morality understood

as a doctrine of the power relations under which the phenomenon "life" emerges. —[45]

20

That individual philosophical concepts are not something
arbitrary, not something growing on their own but grow in relation and kinship to one another, that as suddenly and randomly
as they appear to sprout in the history of thought, in fact they
belong just as firmly to a system as all the members of the fauna
of a continent: this is ultimately revealed by how certainly the
most diverse philosophers always fill out a definite basic scheme
of *possible* philosophies. Under an invisible spell they constantly
start anew and repeat the same orbit: however independent of
one another they might feel with their critical or systematic will:
something in them guides them, something drives them in a
specific order one after the other, namely that innate systemat-
ics and kinship of concepts. Their thinking in fact is not so
much a discovering as a recognizing, remembering, a return
and homecoming to a distant, primordial, overall economy of
the soul, from which those concepts once sprouted — philosophizing is in this sense a kind of atavism of the highest order.
The peculiar family resemblance of all Indian, Greek, and
German philosophizing is explained easily enough. Precisely
where linguistic kinship is present it cannot be avoided at all
that, thanks to the common philosophy of grammar — I mean
thanks to the unconscious rule and leadership of the same
grammatical functions — everything lies ready from the beginning for a similar development and sequence of philosophical systems: just as the route to certain other possibilities of
interpreting the world seems almost barred. Philosophers of the
Ural-Altaic language group (in which the subject-concept is
least developed) will with great probability look differently
"into the world" and will be found on different routes than
Indo-Germans or Muslims: the spell of specific grammatical
functions is in the final analysis the spell of *physiological* value

judgments and racial conditions.—This much by way of refuting Locke's superficiality with respect to the origin of ideas.

21

The *causa sui* is the best self-contradiction thought of to date, a kind of logical rape and violation of nature: but humanity's excessive pride has succeeded in deeply and horribly entangling itself in this very nonsense. The desire for "freedom of the will," in the superlative metaphysical sense, as it unfortunately still reigns in the minds of the semi-educated, the desire to bear on your own the entire and ultimate responsibility for your actions, and to absolve God, the world, ancestors, chance, and society of them is really nothing less than being just this *causa sui*, and it amounts to pulling yourself up by the hair out of the swamp of nothingness into existence, with an audacity exceeding that of Münchhausen.[46] Supposing someone sees through the boorish simplicity of this famous concept of "free will" and manages to strike it from his mind, I would then ask him to take his "enlightenment" one step further and also strike the reverse of that absurd concept of "free will" from his mind: by which I mean the "unfree will," which amounts to an abuse of cause and effect. "Cause" and "effect" should not be erroneously reified, as the natural scientists do (and whoever else today thinks in terms of naturalizing—) according to the prevailing mechanistic buffoonery that has the cause pressing and pushing until it "effects";[47] "cause" and "effect" should only be used as pure *concepts*, that is as conventional fictions for the purpose of characterization, of communication, *not* of explanation. In the "in-itself" there is nothing of "causal connections," of "necessity," of "psychological unfreedom," there the "effect" does *not* "follow from the cause," this is not governed by any "law." It is *we* alone who have invented causes, succession, for-each-other, relativity, compulsion, numbers, law, freedom, grounds and purpose; and when our imaginations impose and mix this sign-world into things as an "it-itself," we're still doing things

as we've always done them, namely *mythologically*. The "unfree
will" is mythology: in real life it is a matter of *strong* and *weak*
wills. — It is almost always a symptom of what a thinker is
lacking when he senses some kind of compulsion,[48] need, being forced to follow, pressure, unfreedom in all "causal connection" and "psychological necessity": it is revealing to feel this
way in particular — the person betrays himself. And if I have
observed correctly, generally it is the "unfreedom of the will"
that is conceived as a problem, from two entirely opposing
sides but always in a deeply *personal* manner: one side doesn't
want to relinquish their "responsibility" at any price, their faith
in *themselves*, the personal right to *their* merit (the vain races
belong to this group —); the others conversely, motivated by
inner self-contempt, want to be responsible for nothing and
guilty of nothing, and wish they were able to *shift responsibility*
for themselves to some other place. The latter when they write
books tend to sympathize with criminals; their most appealing disguise is a kind of socialist compassion. And indeed, the
fatalism of the weak-willed embellishes itself amazingly when
it knows how to pass for "*la religion de la souffrance humaine*":[49]
this is *its* "good taste."[50]

22

I should be forgiven as an old philologist who cannot forgo
the malice of putting his finger on bad tricks of interpretation:
but that "conformity of nature to law" spoken of so proudly by
you physicists, as if — — it exists only thanks to your interpretation and bad "philology" — it is not a fact, not a "text,"
but on the contrary only a naïvely humanitarian justification
and distortion of meaning with which you appease and accommodate the democratic instincts of the modern soul! "Everywhere equality before the law — nature is no different and no
better off than we are in this regard": a nice example of ulterior motives, disguising once again the plebeian hostility
against everything privileged and autocratic, likewise a second
and more refined atheism. "*Ni dieu, ni maître*"[51] — that is how

you want it: and so "long live natural law!"—right? But like I said, this is interpretation, not text; and someone could come along with the opposite intention and mode of interpretation, who was able to infer from the same nature and with respect to the same phenomena instead a tyrannically ruthless and relentless imposition of power claims—an interpreter who so convincingly opened your eyes to the "will to power" with its lack of exceptions and its unconditional nature, that nearly every word and even the word "tyranny" itself would ultimately appear useless or as weakening and mitigating metaphor—as too human—; yet he would still end up claiming the same thing about this world that you claim, namely that it has a "necessary" and "calculable" course, but *not* because laws govern in it but because the laws are absolutely *lacking*, and every power draws its final consequence in every moment. Supposing this too is only interpretation—and you will be eager enough to make this objection?—well then, so much the better.—

23

All psychology so far has gotten stuck in moral prejudices and fears: it has not dared to enter the depths. To conceive it as morphology and *doctrine of the development of the will to power* as I conceive it—no one yet has touched this even in thought: that is, to the extent it is permitted to recognize in that which has been written so far a symptom of that which has so far remained unsaid. The power of moral prejudices has penetrated deeply into the most spiritual world, into the seemingly coldest world most devoid of presuppositions—and it goes without saying that it has been damaging, inhibiting, blinding, distorting. A real physio-psychology has to contend with[52] unconscious obstacles in the heart of the researcher, it has "the heart" against it: even a doctrine of the reciprocal dependence of the "good" and the "bad" drives, as a more refined morality, causes distress and revulsion in a still strong and hearty conscience—and even more so a doctrine of the derivation of all good drives from bad ones. But suppose someone were to take even the affects hatred, envy, greed, and lust to rule as conditions of life, as something whose presence is fundamental and absolutely essential to the overall economy of life, and therefore must even be enhanced if life is to be enhanced — he would suffer from such a turn in his thinking as if from seasickness. And yet even this hypothesis is by far not the most distressful and foreign in this vast, almost new realm of dangerous knowledge: — and in fact there are a hundred good reasons for everyone to keep their distance from it, if they — *can*! On the other hand: if you happen to be driven off course here in your ship, well then, so be it! Now's the time to just clench your teeth! open your eyes! hold on tight to the helm! — we're sailing straight over and *away* from morality, we're smashing, maybe we're crushing our own remnant of morality by daring to travel there — but what do *we* matter! Never before has a *deeper world* of insight opened up to bold travelers and adventurers: and the psychologist who "makes a sacrifice" in this way — it is *not* the *sacrifizio dell'intelletto*,[53] on the contrary! — will at least be allowed to demand in exchange that psychology again be recognized as the ruler of the sciences, for whose service and preparation the remaining sciences exist. For psychology is now once again the way to the fundamental problems.

Part Two

The Free Spirit

24[1]

O sancta simplicitas![2] In what a strange simplification and falsification human beings live! We cannot cease to wonder as soon as we develop an eye for this wonder! How we've made everything around us bright and free and easy and simple! how we have been able to give our senses a free pass for everything superficial, and our thinking a divine craving for impudent leaps and false conclusions!—how we have known from the start to preserve our ignorance in order to enjoy a scarcely comprehensible freedom, thoughtlessness, carelessness, heartiness, cheerfulness in life, in order to enjoy life! And only on this now solid and granite foundation of ignorance could science raise itself up until now, the will to knowledge on the foundation of a much more powerful will, the will to not know, to the uncertain, to the untrue! Not as its opposite but—as its refinement! Even if here as elsewhere *language* cannot get past its clumsiness and continues to speak of opposites where there are only degrees and many subtleties of levels; even if likewise the entrenched tartuffery of morality, which now belongs to our invincible "flesh and blood," twists the words in our mouths, though we know better: here and there we comprehend it and laugh about how precisely the best science tries best to keep us in this *simplified*, thoroughly artificial world that we have composed and forged into shape,[3]

how it involuntarily-voluntarily loves error because this lively
one — loves life!

25

After such a cheerful entrance a serious word does not wish
to go unheard: it is directed at the most serious. Watch out,
you philosophers and friends of knowledge, and beware of
martyrdom! Of suffering "for the sake of truth"! Even of defending yourselves! It will ruin all the innocence and delicate
neutrality of your conscience, it will make you stiff-necked
against objections and red flags, it will stupefy, animalize and
brutalize you when in struggling with danger, slander, suspicion, expulsion and even cruder consequences of animosity you
even have to pose as a defender of truth on earth: — as if "the
truth" were such a harmless and awkward person that it needed
defenders! and you of all people, you Knights of the Mournful
Countenance,[4] Messrs. Do-little and Webspinner of the Spirit!
In the end you know well enough that it is not supposed to
matter whether *you* are right, and likewise that until now no
philosopher has been right, and that a more praiseworthy truth
could be in every little question mark you put behind your
choice words and favorite doctrines (and occasionally behind
yourselves) than in all the solemn gestures and trumps put before prosecutors and courts of law! Rather step aside! Go into
hiding! And have your mask and subtlety so that you will be
mistaken for something, or feared a bit! And do not forget the
garden, the garden with golden trelliswork! And have people
around you who are like a garden — or like music over waters
at evening time, when the day fades into memories: — choose
the *good* solitude, the free, mischievous, light solitude that also
gives you the right in some sense to remain good yourselves!
How poisonous, how sneaky, how bad every long war makes
us, that cannot be waged with open force! How *personal* a long
fear makes us, a long focus on enemies, on possible enemies!
These outcasts of society, these long-persecuted, badly-
harassed — also the forced hermits, the Spinozas or Giordano

Brunos—always become ingenious avengers and mixers of poison in the end, even under the most spiritual masquerade and perhaps without their even knowing it (just try digging up the foundation of Spinoza's ethics and theology!)—not to mention the silliness of moral indignation that in a philosopher is the infallible sign that his philosophical humor has abandoned him.[5] The martyrdom of a philosopher, his "sacrifice for the truth" forces into the light all that is agitator and actor in him, and supposing he has been viewed up till now only with an artistic curiosity, then with respect to many philosophers we certainly understand the dangerous desire to see him for once in his degeneration (degenerated to a "martyr," to a screamer of the stage and the soapbox). Only we have got to be clear with such a desire about *what* we will get to see in any case:—only a satyr play, only an epilogue farce, only the continuing proof that the long, real tragedy *is over*: assuming that every philosophy in its origins was a long tragedy.—

26[6]

Every choice human being strives instinctively for his fortress and secrecy, where he is *redeemed* from the crowds, the many, the great majority, where he can forget the rule among "humans," as their exception:—with the one exception that he is driven by an even stronger instinct straight toward this rule, as a knowing one in the great and exceptional sense. It is certainly not a person of elevated taste who does not occasionally glisten in all the colors of distress while interacting with people, green and gray with disgust, satiety, sympathy, gloominess, and isolation; but supposing he does not voluntarily take all this burden and aversion on himself, but constantly avoids it and as I said earlier stays quietly and proudly hidden in his fortress, then one thing is clear: he is not made for knowledge, not predestined for it. For if he were, he would one day have to say to himself: "To hell with my good taste! but the rule is more interesting than the exception—than I, who am the exception!"—and he would start going *downward*, and most

importantly, "inwards." The study of the *average* human being, long, serious, and to this end requiring much disguise,
self-overcoming, intimacy, bad company—any company is bad
company except with one's equals—: this makes up a necessary part of the life story of every philosopher, perhaps the
most unpleasant, foul-smelling and richest in disappointments.
But if he is lucky, as befits a favorite child of knowledge, then
he will encounter real abbreviators and alleviators of his task—
I mean so-called cynics, hence those who simply acknowledge
the animal, the vulgarity, the "rule" in themselves and yet
at the same time have that degree of spirituality and yearning
that compels them to talk about themselves and their kind *in
front of witnesses*: — sometimes they will even wallow in books
as if in their own filth. Cynicism is the only form in which
vulgar souls come in contact with what honesty is; and the
higher human being has to open his ears to every cruder and
finer cynicism and congratulate himself each time the shameless jester or the scientific satyr speaks up right in front of him.
There are even cases where enchantment is mixed with disgust: namely where by a whim of nature genius is united with
such an indiscreet billy-goat and ape as the Abbé Galiani, the
profoundest, most insightful and perhaps also filthiest man
of his century—much profounder than Voltaire and consequently also a good deal more taciturn. It happens even more
often that, as indicated already, a scientific head is mounted
on an ape's body, a subtle, exceptional understanding on a base
soul—especially not a rare occurrence among doctors and
physiologists of morals. And wherever even one person speaks
without bitterness, or even just innocuously about mankind
as of a belly with two different needs and a head with one;
wherever someone seeks and *wants to* see only hunger, sexual
lust and vanity as if they were the actual and sole incentives
of human behavior; in short, where anyone speaks "badly" of
humanity—and not even *wickedly*—there the lover of knowledge should listen subtly and studiously, he should generally
keep his ears open wherever people speak without indigna-

tion. For the indignant person, and whoever tears and mangles himself (or, as a substitute, the world, God, or society) with his own teeth may indeed be higher morally speaking than the laughing and self-satisfied satyr, but in every other sense he is the more ordinary, more indifferent and less instructive case. And nobody *lies* as much as the indignant.—

27[7]

It is hard to be understood: especially if you think and live *gangasrotogati*[8] among nothing but people who think and live differently, namely *kurmagati*[9] or at best "in the manner of the frog," *mandeikagati*—am I just doing everything to be hard to understand myself?—and we should cordially acknowledge the good will to a modicum of subtlety in interpretation. But as concerns "the good friends" who always want to have it too easy and think they have a right to easiness just because they are friends: you do best at the outset to grant them some room to play and a playground for misunderstanding:—then you can still laugh;—or just get rid of them completely, these good friends—and laugh then too!

28[10]

What is hardest to translate from one language to another is the *tempo*[11] of its style: which is grounded in the character of the race or, physiologically speaking, in the average *tempo* of its "metabolism." There are well-intentioned translations that are nearly falsifications, being involuntary vulgarizations of the original, merely because the bold and joyful *tempo* that leaps over and helps us out of everything dangerous in things and words could not be captured in translation. The Germans are practically incapable of a *presto*[12] in their language: and thus, it is fair to conclude, also incapable of many of the most delightful and daring nuances of the free, free-spirited thought. As surely as the *buffo*[13] and satyr are foreign to him in body and conscience, just as surely Aristophanes and Petronius are untranslatable to him. Everything ponderous, lethargic and

pompously awkward, all wordy and boring genres of style are
developed with excessive diversity in Germans—forgive me
for stating the fact that even Goethe's prose with its mixture of
stiffness and grace is no exception, as a mirror image of the
"good old time" to which it belongs and an expression of German taste at a time when there still was a "German taste,"
namely a rococo taste *in moribus et artibus*.[14] Lessing is an exception, thanks to his thespian nature, which understood much
and knew many things so well: he who was not by accident
the translator of Bayle and gladly took refuge in the company
of Diderot and Voltaire, even more gladly among the Roman
comedy writers:—Lessing even in *tempo* loved free-thinking
and fleeing from Germany. But how could the German language, even in the prose of a Lessing, imitate the *tempo* of
Machiavelli who in his *Prince* gives us the dry, refined air of
Florence and cannot resist presenting the most serious matters
in an unruly *allegrissimo*:[15] perhaps not without the malicious
artist's sense for the kind of contrast he dares—thoughts that
are long, difficult, hard, dangerous and yet in a gallop *tempo*
and the very best, most defiant mood. Who, finally, would
venture a German translation of Petronius, who more than
any other great musician to date was a master of the *presto* in
inventions, insights, words:—in the end what do all the swamps
of the sick, wicked world matter, of the "ancient world" too, if
someone has feet of wind, like him, the force, breath and liberating scorn of a wind that makes everything healthy by
making everything *run*! And as concerns Aristophanes, that
transfiguring, complementary spirit for whose sake we *forgive*
the entire Greek world for having existed, supposing that we
have grasped in its full profundity exactly *what* needs transfiguring and forgiving here:—then I know of nothing that has
made me puzzle more about *Plato's* secrecy and sphinx nature
than the fortunately preserved *petit fait*:[16] that under the pil-
low of his death bed no "Bible" was found, nothing Egyptian,
Pythagorean, Platonic—but instead Aristophanes. How could

even Plato have endured life—a Greek life to which he said No—without an Aristophanes!—

29

Being independent is a matter that concerns the fewest people:—it is a privilege of the strong. And whoever tries it, even with the best right but without *having to*, proves that he is probably not only strong but daring to the point of abandon. He enters into a labyrinth, he multiplies by a thousand the dangers that life already brings with it; not the least of which is that no one will witness how and where he gets lost, isolated, and torn to pieces by some cave Minotaur of conscience.[17] Supposing such an individual were to perish, it happens so far from the understanding of human beings that they can neither feel it nor feel for him:—and he can no longer return![18] nor can he return anymore to the compassion of human beings!——

30[19]

Our highest insights must—and should!—sound like follies, and in some cases like crimes when heard without permission by those who are not cut out and predestined for them. The exoteric and the esoteric, a distinction formerly used by philosophers, as it is found in the Indians, Greeks, Persians and Muslims, in short wherever people believed in an order of rank and *not* in equal rights—is based not only on the exoteric standing outside and seeing, valuing, measuring, judging from the outside as opposed to from the inside: what is more essential is that he sees things from below—but the esoteric looks *down from above*! There are heights of the soul from which viewing even tragedies ceases to have a tragic effect; and bundling together all the miseries of the world, who would dare to decide whether the sight of it would *necessarily* seduce and compel us to compassion and therefore to compounding the misery? . . . What serves the higher type of human being as nourishment or refreshment has to be nearly

poison to a very different and lesser type. The virtues of a
common man would probably signify vices and weaknesses in
a philosopher; it would be possible that a higher type of human being, supposing he were to degenerate and perish,
would only then acquire qualities for whose sake people in the
lower world into which he descended would now be compelled to venerate him as a saint. There are books that have an
inverse value for souls and health depending on whether a lower
soul, a lower life force or a higher and more powerful one makes
use of them: in the first case they are dangerous, deteriorating
and disintegrating books, while in the second they are heralds' calls summoning the bravest to *their* bravery. Books for
all the world are always foul-smelling books: the odor of little
people clings to them. Where the common people[20] eat and
drink, even where they worship, it tends to stink. You should
not go into churches if you want to breathe *clean* air.[21] — —

31[22]

In our youth we still admire and despise without that art of
nuance that constitutes the greatest benefit of life, and so it is
only fair that we have to pay dearly for having assaulted people
and things like this with a Yes or a No. Everything is arranged
so that the worst of all tastes, the taste for the unconditional,
is cruelly fooled and abused until someone learns to put a little
art in their feelings and risk the attempt using the artificial instead: the way the real artists of life do. The anger and reverence
suited to youth seem unwilling to rest until they have falsified
people and things into such shape that they can vent themselves on them: — youth in itself is already something falsifying and deceiving. Later on, tortured by sheer disappointments,
the young soul finally turns suspiciously on itself, still hot and
wild even in its suspicion and pangs of conscience: how furious it makes itself now, how impatiently it tears itself apart,
how it avenges itself for its long self-blinding, as if it had been
a voluntary blindness! In this transition we punish ourselves
by distrusting our feelings; we torture our enthusiasm with

doubts, indeed we feel even a good conscience to be a danger, as self-veiling and weariness of more subtle honesty, as it were; and above all, we take sides, fundamentally take sides *against* "youth."—One decade later: we understand that all this too was still—youth!

32[23]

Throughout the longest period of human history—we call it prehistoric times—the value or lack of value of an action was derived from its consequences: the action in itself was given just as little consideration as its origin,[24] and instead, similar to how today in China a distinction or disgrace of the child still reaches back to the parents, it was the retroactive force of the success or failure which prompted people to think well or ill of an action. Let us call this period the *premoral* period of mankind: the imperative "know thyself!" was still unknown then. In the last ten millennia, on the other hand, in some major regions of the earth people have step by step reached the point of no longer allowing the consequences but the origin of an action to decide its value: on the whole a great event, a considerable refinement of view and standard, the unconscious aftereffect of the rule of aristocratic values and faith in "origin," the sign of a period that we may call *moral* in a narrow sense, and it represents the first attempt at self-knowledge. Origin instead of consequences: what a reversal of perspectives! And certainly a reversal reached only after long struggles and vacillations! Of course: a fatal new superstition, a peculiar narrowness of interpretation came to power in this way: the origin of an action was interpreted in the most definitive sense as origin of an *intention*; people became unified in the belief that the value of an action was exemplified by its intention. Intention as the entire origin and prehistory of an action: under this prejudice we have morally praised, blamed, judged and philosophized almost to the present day on earth.—But shouldn't we have arrived at the necessity of resolving ourselves once more to a reversal and fundamental shift of values, thanks to having come to our senses again and to a deepening of mankind—shouldn't we be standing today on the threshold of a period that would be characterized at first negatively as *extramoral*: today after all, when at least we immoralists harbor the suspicion that the decisive value of an action is exemplified precisely by what is *unintentional* in it, and that all its intentionality, everything about it that can be seen, known, "conscious" belongs to its surface and skin—which like any skin reveals something but *conceals* even more? In short, we believe that the intention is only a sign and symptom requiring interpretation, moreover a sign that means too many things and consequently means almost nothing in and of itself—that morality as understood up till now, hence morality of intentions, has been a prejudice, a precipitousness, perhaps a preliminary thing, something along the lines of astrology and alchemy perhaps, but in any case something that must be overcome. The overcoming of morality, in a certain sense even the self-overcoming of morality: let this be the name for that long, secretive work that was reserved for the most subtle and honest, and also the most malicious consciences of today, as the living touchstones of the soul.—

33

There is no way around it: our feelings of devotion, of sacrifice for our neighbor, and the whole morality of self-renunciation must be mercilessly called to account and taken to court; and likewise the aesthetics of "disinterested contemplation" under which the emasculation of art today seductively tries to create a good conscience for itself. There is much too much allure and sugar in those feelings of "for others," of "*not* for me," for us not to need to be doubly suspicious here and to ask: "are these not perhaps—*seductions*?"—That they are *pleasing*—to someone who has them and to someone who enjoys their fruits, even to the mere spectator—still does not serve as an argument *for* them, but demands caution instead. So let's be cautious!

34

Whatever standpoint of philosophy someone might adopt today: the surest and firmest thing our eyes can grasp, from any point of view, is the *erroneousness* of the world in which we think we are living: — we find reasons upon reasons for this, that would like to lure us into speculations about a deceptive principle in the "essence of things." But whoever makes our thinking itself, hence "the mind" responsible for the falseness of the world — an honorable way out, taken consciously or unconsciously by every *advocatus dei*[25] — : whoever takes this world along with space, time, form, motion to be falsely *inferred*: that person would at least have good cause in the end to learn to be suspicious of thinking altogether: would it not have played the greatest practical joke of all time on us? and what guarantee would there be that it would not continue to do what it has always done? In all seriousness: the innocence of thinkers has something touching and awe-inspiring that allows them even today to walk up to consciousness with the request that it give them *honest* answers: for instance, whether it is "real" and why after all does it so resolutely keep the world at arm's length, and more questions of the sort. The belief in "immediate certainties" is a *moral* naïveté that brings honor to us philosophers: but — we should try for once to not be "*merely* moral" human beings! Aside from morality, this belief is a stupidity that brings us little honor! In bourgeois life it may be regarded as a sign of "bad character" and therefore as unwise to constantly be prone to suspicion: here among us, beyond the bourgeois world and its Yeses and Nos — what is stopping us from being unwise and saying: a philosopher practically has a *right* to "bad character" as the creature on earth who has so far been duped the most — today he has a *duty* to be suspicious, to squint maliciously from every abyss of suspicion. — Forgive me the joke of this gloomy grimace and expression: for I myself have long since learned to think and to evaluate differently about deceiving and being deceived, and I am ready with at least a couple of digs in the ribs for the blind rage with which philosophers strain against being deceived. Why *not*? It is nothing more than a moral prejudice that truth is worth more than appearance; in fact, it is the most poorly proven assumption in the world. This much really has to be admitted: no life would exist if not on the basis of perspectival valuations and appearances; and if, with the virtuous enthusiasm and ineptness of some philosophers, we wanted to abolish altogether the "apparent world," supposing now that *you* could do that—then at the very least there would be nothing left of your "truth" either! Indeed, what is it anyway that compels us to assume there is an essential opposition between "true" and "false"? Doesn't it suffice to assume stages of apparentness and brighter and darker shades and overall tones of appearance, so to speak—different *valeurs*,[26] to use the language of painters? Why shouldn't the world *that concerns us*—be a fiction? And whoever were to ask: "but doesn't an author belong with a fiction?"—could we not flatly respond: *Why*? Does this "belong" perhaps also belong to fiction? Is it not permitted by now to be a bit ironic toward the subject, as we are toward the predicate and the object? Shouldn't the philosopher be permitted to rise above faith in grammar? With all due respect for the governesses: isn't it time that philosophy renounced its governess-faith?—[27]

35[28]

Oh Voltaire! Oh humanity![29] Oh nonsense! There is something to "truth," to the *search* for truth; and when a human being is just too humane about it—"*il ne cherche le vrai que pour faire le bien*"[30]—I bet he finds nothing!

36[31]

Supposing nothing were "given" as real besides our world of desires and passions, that we could go down or up to no other "reality" than simply the reality of our drives—since thinking is only a relation of these drives to one another—: is it not permissible to make the attempt and to ask the question whether this given or something like it is not *sufficient* for understanding even the so-called mechanistic (or "material") world? I do not mean as a deception, an "appearance," a "representation" (in the Berkeleyan and Schopenhauerian sense), but instead as something on the same rank of reality as our affect itself—as a more primitive form of the world of affects in which everything is still locked within a powerful unity, which then branches off in the organic process and takes shape (even becomes tender and weak, as is only fair—), as a kind of life of the drives in which all the organic functions are still synthetically bound to each other with self-regulation, assimilation, nutrition, excretion, metabolism—as a *pre-form* of life?—In the end it is not only permitted to make this attempt: it is demanded on the basis of the conscience of *method*. Do not assume several types of causality as long as the attempt to suffice with a single one has not been pushed to its outermost limit (—to the point of nonsense if you will): this is a morality of method that cannot be evaded today;—it follows "from its definition," as a mathematician would say. Ultimately the question is whether we actually acknowledge the will as *effective*, whether we believe in the causality of the will: if we do—and at bottom the belief in *it* is our belief in causality itself—then we *must* make the attempt hypothetically to posit will-causality as the only one. "Will" naturally can only have an effect on "will"—and not on "matter" (not on "nerves" for instance—): enough, we have to venture the hypothesis that wherever "effects" are recognized, will is affecting will—and all mechanical occurrences, insofar as a force is active in them, are nothing but will-force and will-effect.—Supposing finally that we were to succeed in explaining our entire life of drives as the taking shape and ramification of a basic form of the will—namely of the will to power, as *my* proposition has it—; supposing that we could trace all organic functions to this will to power and were able to find in it the solution to the problem of reproduction and nutrition—which is one problem—then we would have earned the right to unequivocally determine *all* effective force as: *will to power.* The world seen from inside, the world determined and characterized on the basis of its "intelligible character"—it would be precisely "will to power" and nothing else.—

37[32]

"What? Does this not mean, using a popular expression: God is refuted but the devil is not—?" On the contrary! On the contrary, my friends! And who the devil is forcing you to use popular expressions anyway!—

38[33]

Just as happened ultimately in the broad daylight of recent times with the French Revolution, that horrific and, on closer examination, superfluous farce into which noble and impassioned spectators from the whole of Europe so passionately interpreted their own indignations and enthusiasms from a distance and for so long, *until the text disappeared under the interpretation*: so too a noble posterity could once again misunderstand the whole past and perhaps make the sight of it bearable only by doing so.—Or rather: has this not already happened? were we not ourselves—this "noble posterity"? And insofar as we grasp this, is now not the precise moment—when it is over?

39

No one would go so far as to consider a doctrine true just because it makes people happy or virtuous: except maybe the precious "idealists" who gush about the Good, the True, the Beautiful and allow all kinds of motley, clumsy and good-natured desiderata to swim around willy-nilly in their pond. Happiness and virtue are not arguments. But it is easy to forget, even for thoughtful spirits, that making people unhappy and evil likewise are not counter-arguments. Something could be true: whether it were harmful and dangerous in the highest degree; indeed it could be part of the fundamental character of existence that someone would perish from complete knowledge of it—such that the strength of a spirit would be measured by just how much he could still endure of the "truth," or more precisely, to what extent he would *need* it to be diluted, shrouded, sweetened, blunted, falsified. But there is no doubt that evil and unhappy people are more favored for the discovery of certain *parts* of the truth and have a greater probability of success; not to mention those who are evil and happy—a species about whom the moralists remain silent. Perhaps hardness and cunning represent more favorable conditions for the emergence of a strong, independent spirit and philosopher than that gentle, refined, yielding good-naturedness and art of taking things easy that are valued and rightly valued in a scholar. Assuming what is most important here, that the concept "philosopher" is not restricted to the philosopher who writes books—or worse puts *his* philosophy into books!—One last feature in the image of the free-spirited philosopher is conveyed by Stendhal, which I can not resist emphasizing for the sake of German taste:—because it goes *against* German taste. "*Pour être bon philosophe,*" says this last great psychologist, "*il faut être sec, clair, sans illusion. Un banquier, qui a fait fortune, a une partie du caractère requis pour faire des découvertes en philosophie, c'est-à-dire pour voir clair dans ce qui est.*"[34]

40

All that is profound loves a mask; the very profoundest things even have a hatred for images and likenesses. Shouldn't the *opposite* be the only proper disguise to accompany the shame of a god? A questionable question: it would be odd if some mystic had not already risked something like this with his own person. There are events of such a delicate nature that we do well to bury them under something crude and make them unrecognizable; there are acts of love and extravagant generosity following which nothing is more advisable than to take a stick and beat up on the eyewitness: that is how to dim his memory of it. Some know how to dim their own memory and to abuse it, in order to have their revenge on at least this one initiate: — shame is inventive. It is not the worst things that make someone most ashamed: it is not only guile that hides behind a mask — there is so much goodness in cunning. I could imagine that someone who had something precious and vulnerable to hide would roll through life rough and round like an old green cask of wine with thick hoops: the delicate nature of his shame wants it like this. Someone who has profundity in his shame also encounters his destinies and delicate decisions along paths few ever reach, and of whose existence his closest and most trusted friends must not know: his mortal danger is hidden to their eyes and likewise his regained mortal safety. Such a secretive person, who instinctively uses speech for being and keeping things silent and is inexhaustible in evading communication, *wants* and promotes that a mask of himself wanders around in place of him in the hearts and minds of his friends; and supposing he did not want it, some day it will dawn on him that a mask of him is there nonetheless — and this is good. Every profound spirit needs a mask: even more, a mask is continuously growing around every profound spirit thanks to the constantly false, that is *shallow* interpretation of every word, every step, every sign of life he gives. — [35]

41[36]

We must test ourselves to determine whether we are destined for independence and commanding; and this at the right time. We should not sidestep our tests, even though they are probably the most dangerous game that can be played, and are ultimately tests witnessed only by ourselves and taken before no other judge. Do not become hung up on a person: even if they were the most beloved — every person[37] is a prison, a corner too. Do not become hung up on a fatherland: even if it were the most suffering and the neediest — it is not as hard to unbind your heart from a victorious fatherland. Do not become hung up on some compassion: even when it applies to higher human beings into whose rare agonies and helplessness chance has allowed us to glimpse. Do not become hung up on a science: even if it were to lure us with the most precious discoveries seemingly reserved just for *us*. Do not become hung up on your own detachment, on that rapturous distance and alienation of a bird who flies ever deeper into the heights in order to see ever more below him: — the danger of a flier. Do not become hung up on our own virtues and fall victim as a whole to some detail of ourselves, for instance to our "hospitality": as it constitutes the danger of dangers among superior and rich souls who spend themselves extravagantly and almost indifferently and push the virtue of liberality to the point of vice. We must know how *to preserve ourselves*: the strongest test of independence.

42[38]

A new species of philosophers is emerging: I dare to christen them with a name that is not without its dangers. As I guess them to be, as they allow themselves to be guessed—for it belongs to their nature to *want* to remain riddles in some respects—these philosophers of the future might have a right, maybe even a wrong to be characterized as *tempters*.[39] This name itself is only an attempt and, if you will, a temptation.

43[40]

Are they new friends of "truth," these philosophers to come? This is probable enough: since all philosophers to date loved their truths. But they certainly will not be dogmatists. It has to offend their pride, and also their taste, for their truth to also be a truth for everyone: which so far has been the secret wish and background of all dogmatic endeavors. "My judgment is *my* judgment: no one else easily has a right to it" — this is perhaps what such a philosopher of the future says. We have to divest ourselves of the bad taste of wanting to agree with many people. "Good" is no longer good if it is on the lips of your neighbor. And how could there ever be a "common good"! The word contradicts itself: whatever can be common always has only little value. Ultimately it will have to be as it always is and always was: great things are reserved for the great, abysses for the profound, delicacy and awe[41] for the subtle, and all in all, everything rare for those who are rare. —

44[42]

After all this do I still need to expressly say that they will also be free, *very* free spirits, these philosophers of the future — just as surely as they will not be merely free spirits, but something more, higher, greater and fundamentally different, that does not want to be misunderstood and mistaken for something else? But now, in saying this, I feel almost as much toward them as toward us, we who are their heralds and precursors, we free spirits! — the *responsibility* to blow away an old stupid prejudice and misunderstanding for all our sakes, that has far too long made the concept of "free spirit" opaque as a fog. In all the countries of Europe and likewise in America there is now something that perpetrates an abuse of this name, a very narrow, restricted kind of spirit, on a chain, that wants just about the opposite of what lies in our intentions and instincts — not to mention that they turn out to be fully shut windows and bolted doors to those *new* philosophers who are emerging. Briefly and brutally, they belong to the *levelers*, these wrongly designated "free spirits" — as eloquent and scribble-fingered slaves of democratic taste and its "modern ideas": all of them people without solitude, without their own solitude, clumsy nice fellows whose courage and respectable morals are not to be denied, only they are quite unfree and ridiculously superficial, especially with their fundamental tendency to more or less see the cause of *all* human misery and failure in the forms of the previous old society: which means standing truth happily on its head![43] What they want to strive for with all their might is the universal green pasture happiness of the herd, with security, freedom from danger, comfort, and easy living for everyone; the two songs and doctrines they sing most often are called "equal rights" and "sympathy for all that suffers" — and suffering itself is construed by them as something that must be *abolished.* We contrarians meanwhile, we who have opened an *eye* and a conscience for the question of where and how the plant "human being"[44] has so far grown most robustly, we surmise that this has happened each time under the reverse conditions, that for this to happen first the dangerousness of his situation had to grow immensely, his power of invention and dissimulation (his "spirit"—) had to develop under long pressure and compulsion into subtlety and audacity, his life-will had to be intensified to the point of unconditional power-will:—we surmise that harshness, violence, slavery, danger in the streets and in the heart, concealment, stoicism, the art of seduction[45] and devilry of every kind, that everything evil, horrible, tyrannical, predatory and snakelike in human beings serves to elevate the species "human being" as well as its opposite:—in fact we do not even say enough when we only say this much, and in any case with our saying and our silence at this point we find ourselves on the *other* end of all modern ideology and herd desire: maybe as their antipodes? Is it any wonder that we "free spirits" are not exactly the most communicative spirits? that we do not wish to reveal in every detail what a spirit can free himself *from* and *where* he might then be driven? And as far as concerns that dangerous formula "beyond good and evil," with which we at least guard against being mistaken for others: we *are* something different than "*libres penseurs*," "*liberi pensatori*," "*Freidenker*"[46] and whatever else all these respectable advocates of "modern ideas" love to call themselves. At home in many countries of the spirit, or at least a guest there; forever slipping away from the musty, cozy corners into which we seem to have been banished by our preferences and prejudices, youth, background, chance people and books, or even the exhaustion of wandering; full of malice for the lures of dependency that lie hidden in honors, or money, or offices, or enthusiasms of the senses; grateful even for adversity and on-and-off illness because they always freed us from some rule and its "prejudice," grateful for the god, devil, sheep and worm in us, curious to a fault, researcher to the point of cruelty, with uninhibited fingers for the unfathomable, with teeth and stomachs for the indigestible, ready for every piece of work that demands shrewdness and shrewd senses, ready for every risk, thanks to an excess of "free will," with fore and back souls whose ultimate aims no one easily sees, with fore- and backgrounds no foot is allowed to walk to the end, con- cealed under the cloaks of light, conquerors though we look like heirs and spendthrifts, arrangers and collectors from morning till night, misers of our wealth and our overflowing drawers, economical in learning and forgetting, inventive in schemata, sometimes proud of tables of categories, sometimes pedants, sometimes night owls of work even in broad day- light; indeed, when necessary even scarecrows — and today it is necessary: namely insofar as we are the born and sworn jealous friends of *solitude*, our ownmost, deepest, most mid- nocturnal, most noon-diurnal solitude: — this is the kind of human being we are, we free spirits! And maybe *you* too are something of this, you coming ones? you *new* philosophers? —

Part Three

The Religious Character

45

The human soul and its borders, the entire scope of human inner experiences reached so far, the heights, depths and distances of these experiences, the whole history of the soul *so far* and its untapped possibilities: this is the predestined hunting ground for a born psychologist and friend of the "great hunt." But how often must he say to himself in despair: "Just one! oh just one! and this huge forest, this primeval forest!" And so he wishes himself a few hundred hunting aids and well-trained bloodhounds, which he could drive into the history of the human soul to round up *his* game there. In vain: he tries and learns again and again, thoroughly and bitterly, how hard it is to find aids and hounds for all the things that pique his curiosity. The drawback of sending scholars into new and dangerous hunting grounds, where courage, cleverness, and subtlety of all the senses are needed, is that they are no longer useful precisely where the "*great* hunt" but also the great danger begins: — it is in this very place that they lose their keen eye and their keen nose. For instance, in order to unravel and determine what kind of history the problem of *science and conscience*[1] has had so far in the soul of *homines religiosi*,[2] we would[3] possibly need someone who was himself as profound, as wounded, and as monstrous as the intellectual conscience of Pascal: — and then we would still need that gaping sky of bright, malicious spirituality from on high that is capable of surveying, ordering,

and forcing into formulas this throng of dangerous and painful experiences. — But who could provide me this service! But
who would have time to wait for such servants! — clearly they
grow too rarely, they are so improbable in all times! Ultimately you have to do everything *yourself*, in order to know
a few things yourself: that means you have *much* to do! — But
my kind of curiosity simply remains the most pleasant of
vices — excuse me! I meant to say: the love of truth has its reward in heaven and already on earth. —

46

The faith demanded and not infrequently attained by early
Christianity, in the midst of a skeptical and southerly, free-
spirited world that had a centuries-long struggle of philosophical schools behind and in it, plus the training in tolerance
provided by the *imperium Romanum*[4] — this faith is *not* that
ingenuous and gruff faith of the loyal subject with which a
Luther or a Cromwell or some other northern barbarian of
the spirit would have clung to their God and Christianity; far
more likely the faith of Pascal, which in a terrifying manner
looks more like the protracted suicide of reason — of reason
that is tough, long-lived and wormlike and cannot be killed
all at once with a single stroke. From the outset Christian faith
is sacrifice: sacrifice of all freedom, all pride, all self-assurance
of the spirit; enslavement and self-derision, self-mutilation at
the same time. There is cruelty and religious Phoenicianism
in this faith expected of an over-ripe, multifarious and multi-
pampered conscience: its presupposition is that the subjugation of the spirit *hurts* indescribably, that the entire past and
habit of such a spirit resist the *absurdissimum*[5] that presents
itself as "faith." Modern people, desensitized to all Christian
nomenclature, no longer have any feeling for how the grisly
superlative "God on the cross" affected ancient taste with its
paradoxical formula. Until now there has never been anything
equal in boldness to this formula anywhere, anything equally
horrible, questioning and questionable: it promised a revalua-

tion of all the values of antiquity. — It is the orient, the *deep* orient, the oriental slave who in this manner took revenge on Rome and its more noble and frivolous tolerance, on the Roman "Catholicism" of faith: — and always what infuriated the slaves about and against their master was not faith itself, but the freedom from faith, that half stoic and smiling, carefree attitude about the seriousness of faith. "Enlightenment" infuriates: the slave wants the unconditional, he understand only the tyrannical, even in morality, he loves as he hates, without nuance, to the depths, to the point of pain, to the point of illness, — his abundant *hidden* suffering is infuriated by the noble taste that seems to *deny* suffering. Skepticism toward suffering, at bottom only an affectation of aristocratic morality, also played its proper role in the emergence of the last great slave revolt which began with the French Revolution.

47[6]

Wherever on earth the religious neurosis has appeared so far, we find it connected with three dangerous dietary restrictions: solitude, fasting, and sexual abstinence — but of course without distinguishing here between what is cause and what is effect, and *whether* a cause and effect relationship is present here at all. The latter doubt is justified because among its most regular symptoms, in both wild and tamed peoples, there is also the most precipitous, dissolute lasciviousness, which then just as suddenly transforms into penitential cramps and denial of the world and the will: both perhaps capable of being interpreted as masked epilepsy? But nowhere should interpretations be resisted more: around no type to date has there grown such a profusion of nonsense and superstition, and no one to date has been of greater interest to people, even to philosophers — it would be high time to become a bit cooler right here, to learn caution, or better: to look away, *to go away*. — Even in the background of the most recent philosophy, Schopenhauer's, stands this grisly question mark of religious crisis and revival, nearly as the problem in itself. How is denial of the will *possible*? how

is the saint possible? this really seems to be the question with
which Schopenhauer became a philosopher and started out.
And so it was a genuinely Schopenhauerian consequence that
his most devoted follower (maybe even his last, as far as Germany is concerned —), namely Richard Wagner, finished his
own life's work at just this point and in the end produced that
horrible and eternal type as Kundry[7] on the stage, *type vécu*,[8]
and as it lives and breathes; this at the same time that the psy-
chiatrists of almost all the countries in Europe had good reason to study it up close, wherever the religious neurosis — or as
I call it, "the religious character" — had its last epidemic outbreak and pageant as the "Salvation Army." — But if one were
to ask himself what was so tremendously interesting to people
of all kinds and times, even to philosophers, about the whole
phenomenon of the saint: then without any doubt it was the
semblance of the miraculous associated with it, specifically the
immediate *succession of opposites*, of states of the soul evaluated
in morally opposite ways: here people believed they could
grasp with their own two hands how a "bad human being" all
at once turned into a "saint," a good human being. Psychology as practiced up till now suffered shipwreck at this point:
could this not have happened primarily because it had placed
itself under the rule of morality, because it itself *believed* in
moral value-opposites, and it saw, read, and *interpreted* these
opposites into the text *and* into the facts? — What? "Miracles"
only an error of interpretation? A lack of philology? —

48

It seems that Catholicism belongs to the Latin races much
more intimately than does the whole of Christianity generally
to us northerners: and that consequently the lack of faith in
Catholic countries means something quite different than in
Protestant lands — that is, a kind of indignation toward the
spirit of the race, whereas among us it is more likely a return
to the spirit (or non-spirit) of the race. We northerners undoubtedly stem from barbarian races, even with respect to our

talent for religion: we are *poorly* equipped for it. We can make
an exception of the Celts, who therefore also represented
the best soil for the contraction of the Christian infection in
the north:—in France the Christian ideal blossomed, to the
extent allowed by the pale sun of the north.[9] How strangely
pious to our taste are even these recent French skeptics, insofar as any Celtic blood is in their background! How Catholic,
how un-German Auguste Comte's sociology smells to us, with
its Roman logic of the instincts! How Jesuitical is that endearing and clever Cicero of Port-Royal, Sainte-Beuve, despite all
his hostility toward the Jesuits! And especially Ernest Renan:
how inaccessible the language of such a Renan sounds to us
northerners, insofar as every now and then his soul, lascivious
in a finer sense and normally at ease with itself, loses its balance on account of some nothing of religious tension! Let's
repeat these beautiful sentences after him—and see what kind
of malice and insolence immediately stirs in our probably
less beautiful and harder, that is more German soul as a response!—"*disons donc hardiment que la religion est un produit
de l'homme normal, que l'homme est le plus dans le vrai quand
il est le plus religieux et le plus assuré d'une destinée infinie . . . .
C'est quand il est bon qu'il veut que la vertu corresponde à un
ordre éternel, c'est quand il contemple les choses d'une manière
désintéressée qu'il trouve la mort révoltante et absurde. Comment
ne pas supposer que c'est dans ces moments-là, que l'homme voit
le mieux*? . . . ."[10] These sentences are so very *antipodal* to my
ears and habits that when I found them, my first anger wrote
in the margins "*la niaiserie religieuse par excellence*!"[11]—until
my last anger even began to like them, these sentences with
their truth stood on its head! It is so nice, so distinguishing to
have one's own antipodes!

49

What amazes us about the religiosity of the ancient Greeks
is the tremendous abundance of gratitude it exudes:—it is a
very noble kind of human being that stands *thus* before nature

and life! — Later on when the rabble rose to dominance in Greece, even religion became overgrown with *fear*; and Christianity began to rear its head. —

50

The passion for God: there is the peasant-like, ingenuous and obtrusive kind, like Luther's — the whole of Protestantism lacks a southern *delicatezza*.[12] There is an oriental way of being beside oneself[13] to it, like with a slave who is undeservedly pardoned or promoted, for instance in Augustine, who in an offensive manner lacks all nobility of demeanor and desire. There is a womanly tenderness and lust to it, which bashfully and unknowingly presses toward an *unio mystica et physica*:[14] as in Madame Guyon. In many cases, amazingly enough, it appears as the disguise for the puberty of a girl or a boy; here and there even as the hysteria of an old maid, also as her final ambition: — in such cases the church has more than once declared a woman to be holy.

51

Up till now the most powerful human beings have still bowed respectfully before the saint, as the riddle of self-mastery and intentional, ultimate renunciation: why did they bow? They intuited in him — and likewise behind the question mark of his frail and pathetic appearance — the superior force that wanted to test itself on such a conquest, the strength of will in which they again recognized and honored their own strength and dominating lust: they honored something in themselves when they honored the saint. In addition, the sight of the saint planted a suspicion in them: such a monstrosity of renunciation, of anti-nature will not have been desired for nothing, thus they told and asked themselves. Maybe there is a reason for it, some very great danger that the ascetic knows more about thanks to his secret interlocutors and visitors? Enough, the powerful of the world learned a new fear before him, they intuited a new power, a foreign, not yet

vanquished enemy:—it was the "will to power" that compelled them to stop in front of the saint. They had to ask him——

52

In the Jewish "Old Testament," the book of divine justice,
there are people, things and speeches in such a grand style that
Greek and Indian writing has nothing to compare with it. We
stand in horror and awe before these prodigious remnants of
what human beings used to be, and we have gloomy reflections
about ancient Asia and its little protruding peninsula, Europe,
that wants more than anything to upstage Asia and represent
the "progress of humanity." Indeed: whoever is only a skinny,
tamed house pet himself, and knows only the needs of house
pets (like our educated people of today, the Christians of "educated" Christianity included—) should neither be amazed nor
too melancholy among those ruins—the taste of the Old Testament is a touchstone for the "big" and the "small"—: maybe
he will still be likely to find the New Testament, the book of
mercy, more to his liking (it reeks of really tender, musty bigots
and small souls). To have glued this New Testament, a kind of
rococo of taste in every sense of the word, to the Old Testament to form one book, as "the Bible," as "the book in itself":
this is possibly the greatest audacity and "sin against the spirit"
that literary Europe has on its conscience.

53

Why atheism today?—"The father" in God has been
soundly refuted; likewise "the judge" and "the rewarder." The
same for his "free will": he doesn't listen—and if he listened, he
wouldn't know how to help anyway. What's worst is: he seems
incapable of communicating distinctly: is he unclear?—On
the basis of all kinds of conversations, and by asking and listening, these are the causes I have found for the decline of European theism; to me it seems that the religious instinct is indeed growing powerfully—but that it rejects theistic satisfaction
in particular with deep mistrust.

54

What at bottom is the whole of modern philosophy doing? Since Descartes — and this more out of spite toward him than on the basis of his precedent — an assassination attempt has been made by all philosophers against the old concept of the soul, under the pretext of a critique of the concept of the subject and predicate — that is: an assassination attempt on the fundamental prerequisite of the Christian doctrine. Modern philosophy, as a form of epistemological skepticism, is covertly or overtly *anti-Christian*: even though, for the sake of finer ears, it is by no means anti-religious. Formerly we believed in "the soul" as we believed in grammar and the grammatical subject: we said "I" is the condition, "think" is the predicate and the conditioned — thinking is an activity for which a subject *must* be thought as the cause. Now people tried with admirable tenacity and cunning to see whether they could escape from this net — whether perhaps the opposite might be true: "think" is condition, "I" conditioned; therefore "I" is only a synthesis that is *made* by thinking itself. *Kant* wanted at bottom to prove that the subject could not be proven from the standpoint of the subject — nor could the object: the possibility of an *illusory existence* of the subject, hence of "the soul," might not have always been foreign to him, a thought that has already been on earth before with tremendous force as Vedanta philosophy.

55

There is a great ladder of religious cruelty with many rungs; but three of them are most important. Once people sacrificed a human being to their god, maybe even those who were best loved — this is where the sacrifice of first-borns of all prehistoric religions belongs, as well as the sacrifice of Emperor Tiberius in the Mithras grotto on the isle of Capri, that most gruesome of all Roman anachronisms. Then, in the moral epoch of humanity, people sacrificed to their god the strongest instincts they possessed, their "nature"; *this* festive joy gleams in the cruel gaze of the ascetic, the enthusiastic "anti-natural one." Finally: what remained to be sacrificed? Didn't people have to ultimately sacrifice all solace, holiness, salvation, all hope, all faith in a secret harmony, in future bliss and justice? didn't they have to sacrifice their very God and, out of cruelty against themselves, worship stones, stupidity, gravity, fate, nothingness? To sacrifice God for nothingness—this paradoxical mystery of the ultimate cruelty was reserved for the generation that is now emerging: all of us already know something of this. —

56[15]

Whoever, like me, has long exerted himself with some enigmatic desire to think pessimism through to the bottom and to free it from the half-Christian, half-German narrowness and naïveté with which it last presented itself to this century, namely in the form of Schopenhauerian philosophy; whoever has actually looked with an Asian and super-Asian eye into and down at the most world-negating of all possible modes of thought—beyond good and evil, and no longer like Buddha and Schopenhauer under the spell and delusion of morality— by doing so he has possibly opened his eyes to the inverse ideal, without really intending to do so: to the ideal of the most exuberant, lively and world-affirming human being who has learned to reconcile and come to terms with not only what was and is, but also wants to have it again *as it was and is*, for all eternity, insatiably shouting *da capo*[16] not only to himself but to the whole play and performance, and not only to a performance, but at bottom to the one who needs this performance—and makes it necessary: because he needs himself again and again—and makes himself necessary——What? And this wouldn't be—*circulus vitiosus deus*?[17]

57

With the force of their intellectual gaze and insight, the distance and as it were the space around human beings are growing:

their world is becoming deeper, ever newer stars, ever newer riddles and images come into view. Maybe everything on which the eye of the spirit practiced its acumen and profundity was only just a chance to practice, a matter of play, something for children and childish minds. Maybe someday the most solemn concepts, those for which we have fought and suffered most, the concepts of "God" and "sin," will seem no more important to us than a child's toy and a child's pain seem to an old man—and maybe then "the old man" will need a different toy and a different pain—still child enough, an eternal child!

58

Has it been duly noted to what extent extreme idleness or semi-idleness is necessary for a truly religious life (as much for its microscopic favorite activity of self-examination as for that tender composure that calls itself "prayer" and is a constant readiness for the "coming of God"), I mean idleness with a good conscience, from ancient times, of the blood, which is not entirely foreign to the aristocratic feeling that work *disgraces*[18]—that is, makes the soul and the body common? And that consequently our modern, noisy, time-consuming industriousness, that is so proud, so stupidly proud of itself, trains and prepares us more than anything else for "unbelief"? For instance, among those who now live apart from religion in Germany, I find people from many different kinds and backgrounds of "free thinking," but above all a majority for whom industriousness has dissolved their religious instincts from generation to generation, so that they no longer know at all what religions are good for, and only register, so to speak, their existence in the world with a kind of dull amazement. They feel themselves abundantly put upon, these good people, whether by their businesses, or their pleasures, not to speak at all of their "fatherland" and the newspapers and the "responsibilities to the family": it seems they have no time at all left over for religion, especially since it remains unclear to them whether it is a matter of a new business or a new pleasure—for it is impossible, they tell themselves, for someone to go to church purely to spoil a good mood. They are not enemies of religious customs; if in certain cases, say on the part of the state, participation in such customs were demanded of them, then they do what's called for as people tend to do so many things—with a patient and modest earnestness and without much curiosity and discontent:—they simply live too much apart and outside to find even a pro or contra in such matters necessary for themselves. The great majority of German Protestants in the middle class belong to this indifferent group, especially in the industrious, major centers of trade and transportation; likewise the great majority of industrious scholars and the whole university apparatus (except for the theologians, whose existence and possibility there give a psychologist ever more and ever subtler riddles to figure out). On the part of pious or even just church-going people there is seldom an inkling of *how much* good will, one could say arbitrary will is now required for a German scholar to take the problem of religion seriously; from the standpoint of his entire craft (and, as mentioned before, from the standpoint of the craft-like industriousness to which his modern conscience obligates him) he is inclined toward a superior, almost good-natured cheerfulness toward religion, in which occasionally a mild disdain is mixed, directed at the "uncleanliness" of the spirit which he presupposes wherever people still support the church. The scholar only succeeds in achieving a respectful earnestness and a certain reserved consideration toward religion with the help of history (therefore *not* on the basis of his personal experience); but even if he has elevated his feeling toward it to the point of gratitude, still he has not come a single step closer in his own person to what still exists as church or piety: perhaps on the contrary. The practical indifference toward religious things, in which he was born and raised, tends to sublimate in him into caution and hygiene that shy away from contact with religious people and things; and it can be precisely the depth of his tolerance and humanity that prompts him to turn away from the subtle distress that tolerating brings with it. — Every age has its own divine kind of naïveté, for whose invention other ages may envy it: — and how much naïveté, venerable, childish and boundlessly clumsy naïveté lies in the scholar's belief in his own superiority, in the good conscience of his tolerance, in the clueless, simple certainty with which his instinct treats the religious individual as an inferior and lesser type, which he himself has grown beyond, away from, and *above*—he, the presumptuous little dwarf and rabble man, the busy-whizzy mental-manual laborer of "ideas," of "modern ideas"!

59

Whoever has looked deeply into the world surely will guess how much wisdom lies in the fact that human beings are superficial. It is their preserving instinct that teaches them to be flighty, light, and false. Here and there we find a passionate and exaggerated worship of "pure forms," among philosophers as well as artists: let no one doubt that whoever *needs* the cult of surface to this degree at some time or another reached *beneath* it with disastrous results. Maybe there is even an order of rank among these burned children, these born artists, who are able to still find pleasure in life only by purposely *falsifying* its image (as it were in a protracted revenge on life—): we can deduce the degree to which life has been spoiled for them by how far they wish to see its image falsified, diluted, transcendentalized, deified—we could count the *homines religiosi*[19] among the artists as their *highest* rank. It is the deeply suspicious fear of an incurable pessimism that compels entire millennia to sink their teeth into a religious interpretation of existence: the fear of that instinct that intuits that people could gain possession of the truth *too early*, before they have become strong enough, hard enough, artist enough.[20] . . . Seen from this view, piety, "the life in God," would appear as the most subtle and ultimate spawn of *fear* of truth, as artistic worship and intoxication before the most consequential of all falsifications, as the will to the reversal of truth, to untruth at any price. Maybe up till now there has been no stronger method to beautify human beings than this very piety: through it human beings can become art, surface, play of colors, goodness to such an extent that we no longer suffer at the sight of them. —

60

To love human beings *for God's sake* — so far this was the noblest and most alienating feeling achieved among human beings. That love for human beings without a sanctifying ulterior motive is just one *more* stupidity and animality, that the tendency toward this love of human beings must first receive its measure, its subtlety, its grain of salt and dash of ambergris from a higher tendency: — whoever it may have been who first sensed and "experienced" this, however much his tongue may have stumbled as it tried to express such a delicate idea, let him be forever holy and venerable to us as the human being who up till now has flown highest and has gotten lost most beautifully!

61[21]

The philosopher, as *we* understand him, we free spirits — as someone of the most comprehensive responsibility who has the conscience for the overall development of humanity: this philosopher will use religion for his works of cultivation and education just as he will use the respective political and economic conditions. The selecting, cultivating influence which can be wielded with the help of religions, which is always just as much a destroying as it is a creative and shaping influence, is manifold and different depending on the kind of people who are placed under its sway and protection. For those who are strong, independent, ready and predestined for commanding, in whom the reason and art of a governing race are embodied, religion is another means of overcoming obstacles, of being able to rule: as a bond that binds ruler and subjects together and betrays and delivers the consciences of the latter, their hidden and innermost aspects which would like to escape obedience, over to the former; and if a few natures of such noble descent incline to a more withdrawn and contemplative life through their higher spirituality, and reserve for themselves only the most subtle variation of ruling (over selected disciples or brothers of an order), then religion can even be used as a means to secure peace from the noise and toil of *cruder* forms of ruling, and purity from the *necessary* dirt of all political dealings. That is how the Brahmins understood it, for example: with the help of a religious organization they gave themselves the power to appoint kings for the people, while they themselves kept and felt apart and removed, as men of higher and super-royal tasks. Meanwhile religion also gives guidance and opportunity to some of the ruled to prepare themselves for future ruling and commanding, in particular those slowly ascending classes in which, through fortunate marriage customs, the strength and joy of the will, the will to self-mastery, is always on the rise: — religion offers them sufficient occasions and temptations to walk the paths of higher spirituality and to test the feelings of great self-overcoming, of silence and solitude: — asceticism and Puritanism are almost indispensable means of educating and ennobling when a race wants to rise above its descent from the rabble and work its way up to future rule. Finally, for ordinary people, the vast majority who exist for service and the general good, and are *allowed* to exist only to this extent, religion provides an invaluable contentment with their situation and kind, manifold peace of the heart, an ennoblement of obedience, another happiness and sorrow to share with their peers and something transfiguring and beautifying, something that justifies the whole commonplace, the whole baseness, the whole semi-bestial poverty of their souls. Religion and the religious meaning of life spread sunshine on such eternally tormented people and make them bearable in their own sight, it usually affects as an Epicurean philosophy affects those who suffer in the higher ranks, refreshing, refining, simultaneously *exploiting* suffering and ultimately even sanctifying and justifying it. Perhaps nothing is as venerable in Christianity and Buddhism as their art of teaching even the lowliest to place themselves into a higher illusory order of things through piety, and to firmly embrace their contentment with the real order — in which they have a hard enough life — and it is this very hardness that is needed!

62[22]

Finally, of course, in order to also present the negative counter-claim of such religions and to shed light on their uncanny dangerousness: — we always pay dearly and terribly when religions are *not* a means of cultivation and education in the hands of the philosopher, but rule *sovereignly* and in their own right, when they themselves want to be the ultimate goal and not a means beside another means. In human beings as in every other species of animal there is a surplus of failures, of the diseased, degenerating, frail, and those who necessarily suffer; the successful cases are always the exception even among human beings, and in view of the fact that the human being is the *as yet undetermined animal*, they are the rare exception. But even worse: the higher the type of human being, the greater the improbability that he will *turn out well*: chance, that law of nonsense in the overall economy of humanity reveals itself most horribly in its destructive effect on the higher human beings whose conditions for life are delicate, manifold and difficult to calculate. Now how do both the above-mentioned religions, the greatest ones, relate to this *surplus* of failed cases? They try to preserve and keep alive anything at all that can be kept alive, in fact, they fundamentally take their side, as religions *for the suffering*, they give rights to all who suffer from life as if from a disease, and they want to ensure that any other perception of life be regarded as false and rendered impossible. However highly we might praise this merciful and preserving care, directed as it is and has been also to the highest, and so far almost always most suffering type of human being, along with all the others: considered overall the religions we have had so far, namely the *sovereign* religions belong to the major causes that have kept the type "human being" on a lowly level—they preserved too much of *what should have perished*. What we owe them in terms of gratitude is inestimable; and who has such a wealth of gratitude that he does not grow poor, for instance, in the face of what the "spiritual people" of Christianity have done so far for Europe! And yet, when they gave comfort to the suffering, courage to the oppressed and desperate, a staff and support to the dependent and lured the internally devastated and those who had gone wild away from society and into monasteries and psychic prisons: what did they have to do besides, in order to work in good conscience in such a categorical fashion on the preservation of everything that is sick and suffering, that is, in fact and in truth on the *worsening of the European race*? Stand all valuations *on their head—that's* what they had to do! And smash the strong, poison the great hopes, cast suspicion on the happiness of beauty, twist everything that is autocratic, manly, conquering, domineering, all the instincts that belong to the highest "human" type who has turned out best, into insecurity, crisis of conscience, self-annihilation, indeed invert the whole love of the earthly and all dominion over the earth into hatred for the earth and the earthly—*that* is what the church set as its task, and had to set, until in the end, in its estimation, "anti-worldliness," "desensualizing," and "higher human being" all melted into one feeling. Supposing we were capable of surveying the oddly painful and crude yet refined comedy of European Christianity with the mocking and disinterested eye of an Epicurean god, I believe our amazement and laughter would never end: does it not seem as though a single will dominated Europe for eighteen centuries for the purpose of making human beings into a *sublime abortion*? But if someone with opposite needs, no longer Epicurean but with a divine hammer in hand approached this almost willful degeneration and atrophy of the human being that is the Christian European (Pascal for example), would he not have to cry out with rage, compassion, and horror: "Oh you clumsy oafs, you presumptuous pitiful oafs, what have you

done! Was this a job for your hands! Look how you've bat-
tered and botched my beautiful stone! How could *you* presume!" — What I meant to say: Christianity has been the most
disastrous kind of arrogance to date. People not high and
hard enough to shape *human beings* as artists; people not
strong and far-sighted enough to stand with a sublime self-
discipline and *allow* the foreground law of thousandfold failure and ruin to simply run its course; people not noble enough
to see the abysmally different order of rank and chasm of rank
between one human being and another: — *such* people with
their "equal before God" have so far ruled over Europe's fate,
until finally a shrunken, almost laughable species, a herd animal, something well-meaning, sickly and mediocre has been
bred, the European of today . . . .

Part Four

Epigrams and Interludes

63[1]

Whoever is a teacher through and through takes all things seriously only in relation to his pupils — even himself.

64[2]

"Knowledge for its own sake" — this is the last snare set by morality: with it we again become completely entangled in morality.

65[3]

The charm of knowledge would be meager if there were not so much shame to overcome on the way to it.

65a[4,5]

People are most unfair toward their God: he is not *allowed* to sin!

66[6]

The tendency to let ourselves be disparaged, robbed, lied to and exploited could be the shame of a god among human beings.

67[7]

Love of one person is a barbarism: since it is practiced at the expense of all others. Love of God also.

68[8]

"I did that" says my memory. I could not have done that—says my pride, and refuses to yield. Finally—memory gives in.

69[9]

You've only been a poor observer of life if you haven't also seen the hand that indulgently—kills.

70[10]

If you've got character, then you also have your typical experience that always recurs.

71[11]

The sage as an astronomer.—As long as you still feel the stars as something "above you," you lack the vision of a knower.

72[12]

It is not the strength but the duration of a lofty sentiment that makes for higher human beings.

73[13]

Whoever reaches their ideal surpasses it for the very same reason.

73a[14]

Many a peacock hides his tail from all eyes—and calls that his pride.

74[15]

Someone endowed with genius is unbearable without at least two more things: gratitude and cleanliness.

75[16]

The degree and kind of a person's sexuality reaches up into the ultimate pinnacle of their spirit.

76[17]

Under peaceful conditions warlike human beings will attack themselves.

77[18]

With our principles we want to tyrannize or justify or honor or insult or hide our habits: — two people with the same principles probably want something fundamentally different with them.

78[19]

Whoever despises himself still respects himself as a despiser.

79[20]

A soul that knows it is loved but does not itself love reveals its sediment: — its lowermost rises to the top.

80[21]

An issue that is clarified ceases to concern us. — What did that god mean who counseled: "Know thyself!"[22] Was it perhaps: "stop being of concern to yourself! become objective!" — And Socrates? — And the "scientific human being"? —

81[23]

It is terrible to die of thirst in the ocean. So do you have to go and salt your truth so much that it no longer even — quenches a thirst?

82[24]

"Compassion for all" — would be harshness and tyranny for *you*, my dear neighbor! —

83[25]

Instinct. — When the house is burning you even forget about lunch. — Yes: but you make up for it in the ashes.

84

Woman learns to hate to the extent that she unlearns — how to charm.

85[26]

The same affects have a different tempo in men and women: this is why men and women do not cease to misunderstand one another.

86[27]

Women themselves still have in the background of all personal vanity their impersonal contempt — for "woman."

87

Bound heart, free spirit. — If someone harshly binds their heart and makes it a captive, he can give his spirit many freedoms: I have said this once before. But no one believes me, unless they already know it themselves. . . . .

88[28]

You begin to mistrust very clever people when they become embarrassed.

89[29]

Terrible experiences invite speculation on whether the one who has them is not something terrible.

90[30]

Heavy, heavy-hearted people are made lighter by the very things that make others heavy, by hate and love, and they temporarily rise to their surface.

91[31]

He's so cold, so icy that you burn your fingers on him! Any hand that touches him is shocked!—And that's exactly why many people consider him red hot.

92[32]

Who for the sake of his own good reputation has never once—sacrificed himself?—

93[33]

In affability there is no misanthropy, but for this very reason all too much contempt for human beings.

94[34]

Maturity in a man: this means rediscovering the seriousness we had as children, when we played.

95[35]

Being ashamed of your immorality: that is one step on the stairway, at the end of which you are ashamed of your morality too.

96[36]

We should depart life the way Odysseus departed Nausicaa[37]—more blessing than in love.

97[38]

What? A great man? All I ever see is the actor of his own ideal.

98[39]

When we break in our conscience, it kisses at the same time it bites us.

99[40]

The disappointed one speaks. — "I listened for an echo and heard only praise — "

100[41]

Before ourselves we all pose as more naïve than we are: this is how we rest from our peers.

101[42]

A knowing one today could easily feel like God become animal.

102[43]

Discovering that love is requited should really disenchant the lover about the beloved. "What? someone is modest enough to love even me? Or stupid enough? Or — or — "

103[44]

The danger in happiness. — "Now everything turns out best for me, now I love every fate: — who wants to be my fate?"

104[45]

It is not their love of human beings, but rather the impotence of their love of human beings that prevents Christians of today from — burning us.

105[46]

For the free spirit, the "pious man of knowledge" — the *pia fraus*[47] offends taste (offends *his* "piety") even more than the *impia fraus*.[48] Hence his deep lack of understanding for the church, as befits the type "free spirit" — as *his* unfreedom.

106[49]

By virtue of music even the passions enjoy themselves.

107[50]

Once the decision has been made, close your ears to even the best counterargument: sign of strong character. Therefore an occasional will to stupidity.

108[51]

There are no moral phenomena at all, but only a moral interpretation of phenomena. . . . .

109[52]

The criminal is often enough not equal to his deed: he diminishes and slanders it.

110

The attorneys of a criminal are rarely artist enough to turn the beautiful horror of the deed to the perpetrator's advantage.

111[53]

Our vanity is hardest to wound just when our pride has been wounded.

112[54]

Whoever feels predestined to see and not to believe finds all believers too noisy and obtrusive: he will fight them off.

113[55]

"You want to win him over? Then pretend to be embarrassed in front of him—"

114[56]

For women the enormous expectation regarding sexual love and the shame involved with this expectation ruin all perspective from the start.

115

Where neither love nor hate play a role, a woman's playing is mediocre.

116[57]

The great epochs of our life are to be found where we summon the courage to rechristen our evils as our best.

117[58]

The will to overcome an affect is still in the end only the will of another or of several different affects.

118[59]

There is an innocence of admiration: it is possessed by those who have not yet realized that they too could be admired someday.

119[60]

Disgust at filth can be so great that it prevents us from cleaning ourselves — from "justifying" ourselves.

120[61]

Sensuality often hastens the growth of love so that the root stays weak and is easy to tear out.

121[62]

There was subtlety in God learning Greek when he wanted to become a writer — and in his not having learned it better.

122[63]

For some people the enjoyment of praise is only a courtesy of the heart — and the very opposite of vanity of the spirit.

123[64]

Even concubinage has been corrupted: — by marriage.

124

Whoever rejoices even while burning at the stake is not triumphing over pain but over not feeling pain where he expected it. A parable.

125[65]

When we have to change our mind about someone, we hold it against him that he has caused us such an inconvenience.

126[66]

A people is nature's detour to arrive at six or seven great men. — Indeed: and then to get around them.

127

Science makes all real women feel ashamed. To them it seems as if someone were trying to peek under their skin — even worse! under their dress and finery.

128[67]

The more abstract the truth you want to teach, the more you must seduce the senses to it.

129[68]

The devil has the broadest perspectives for God, which is why he keeps so far away from God: — the devil, that is, as the oldest friend of knowledge.

130[69]

What someone *is* begins to reveal itself when his talent diminishes — when he ceases to show what he *can do*. Talent is also finery; finery is also a hiding place.

131

The sexes deceive themselves about one another: this is because at bottom they honor and love only themselves (or their own ideal, to put it more politely—). Thus man wants woman peaceful—but it is precisely woman who is *essentially* unpeaceful, like a cat, however much she has trained herself to appear peaceful.

132[70]

People are punished best for their virtues.

133[71]

Whoever does not know the way to *his* ideal lives more carelessly and impudently than someone without an ideal.

134

All credibility, all good conscience, all appearance of truth come only from the senses.

135[72]

Pharisaism is not a degeneration in a good human being: rather, a good part of it is the condition of being good at all.

136[73]

One seeks a midwife for his thoughts, the other someone whom he can help: and so a good conversation arises.

137[74]

In dealing with scholars and artists we easily miscalculate in the opposite direction: behind a remarkable scholar we will not infrequently find a mediocre human being, and behind a mediocre artist often—a very remarkable human being.

138[75]

Even when we're awake we do things as in dreams: we first invent and create the person with whom we are dealing—and forget it right away.

139[76]

In revenge and in love[77] woman is more barbaric than man.

140[78]

Counsel as conundrum.[79] — "If the bond won't burst—you must bite on it first."

141[80]

The lower body[81] is the reason why human beings do not so easily take themselves for gods.

142

The chastest words I have ever heard: "*Dans le véritable amour c'est l'âme, qui enveloppe le corps.*"[82]

143[83]

Our vanity wants to regard what we do best as the very thing that is hardest for us. On the origin of many a morality.

144

When a woman has scholarly inclinations, then usually something is wrong with her sexuality. Even infertility predisposes us to a certain masculinity of taste; for it is the man, if I may say so, who is "the sterile animal."

145

Comparing man and woman on the whole, one may say: woman would not have the genius for finery if she did not have the instinct for a *secondary* role.

146

Whoever battles monsters should take care that he doesn't become one in the process. And if you stare for a long time into an abyss, the abyss looks into you, too.

147[84]

From old Florentine novellas, moreover—from life: *buona femmina e mala femmina vuol bastone*.[85] Sacchetti, Nov. 86.[86]

148[87]

To seduce your neighbor into a good opinion and afterward believing piously in this opinion of your neighbor's: who is the equal of women in this trick?—

149[88]

What an age perceives as evil is usually an untimely afternote of what was formerly perceived as good—the atavism of an older ideal.

150[89]

Around the hero everything becomes tragedy, around the demigod everything becomes a satyr play; and around God everything becomes—what? maybe the "world"?—

151[90]

Having a talent is not enough: we must also have your permission for it—right? my friends?

152[91]

"Where the tree of knowledge stands, paradise is always found": that is what the oldest and the youngest serpents say.

153

What is done out of love always happens beyond good and evil.

154[92]

Objections, wayward strokes, cheerful mistrust, and delight in mockery are signs of health: everything unconditional belongs to pathology.

155[93]

Our sense for the tragic declines and grows with our sensuality.

156[94]

Insanity is something rare in individuals — but in groups, parties, peoples, and ages it is the rule.

157[95]

The thought of suicide is a strong consolation: it's a good way to survive many an evil night.

158[96]

Not only our reason, but also our conscience subjects itself to our strongest drive, to the tyrant in us.

159[97]

We *have to* repay good and ill: but why specifically to the person who did us good or ill?

160[98]

We no longer love our knowledge enough as soon as we communicate it.

161[99]

Poets are shameless toward their experiences: they exploit them.

162[100]

"Our fellow-man[101] is not our neighbor, but someone else's neighbor" — this is how all peoples think.

163[102]

Love brings to light the lofty and hidden qualities of a lover — what is rare and exceptional in him: to this extent it easily deceives concerning what is the rule in him.

164[103]

Jesus said to his Jews: "The law was for servants—love God as I love him, as his son! What do we sons of God care about morality!"—

165[104]

Regarding all parties.—A shepherd always needs a bell-wether too—or he must occasionally be a wether himself.

166[105]

We may lie through the mouth, but with the face we make when doing it, we end up telling the truth.

167[106]

In harsh people intimacy is a shameful thing—and something precious.

168[107]

Christianity gave Eros poison to drink:—although he didn't die from it, he degenerated into a vice.

169[108]

Talking a lot about yourself can also be a means of hiding.

170[109]

There is more obtrusiveness in praise than in reproach.

171[110]

In a knowledgeable human being compassion seems almost laughable, like delicate hands on a cyclops.

172[111]

Love of human beings occasionally inspires us to randomly embrace someone (because we cannot embrace everyone): but

that is precisely what we must not reveal to the random someone. . . . .

173[112]

We do not hate as long as we still disdain, but only when we
regard someone to be equal or higher.

174[113]

You utilitarians, even you love everything utile only as a *ve-
hicle* for your inclinations — even you really find the noise of
its wheels unbearable?

175[114]

Ultimately we love our desire, and not the desired.

176[115]

The vanity of others offends our taste only when it offends
our vanity.

177

Perhaps no one yet has been truthful enough about what
"truthfulness" is.

178[116]

We don't believe that clever people commit follies: what a
loss of human rights!

179[117]

The consequences of our actions grab us by the scruff, quite
indifferent to the fact that we have "improved" ourselves in
the meantime.

180[118]

There is an innocence in lying that is the sign of good faith
in a cause.

181[119]

It is inhuman to bless where you are being cursed.[120]

182[121]

We are embittered when a superior confides in us, because it cannot be reciprocated. —

183[122]

"I am shaken not by the fact that you lied to me, but that I no longer believe you." —

184[123]

There is a spirited kind of goodness that resembles malice.

185[124]

"I don't like him." — Why? — "I am not his equal." — Has anyone ever answered this way?

Part Five

On the Natural History of Morality

186

Moral sentiment in Europe now is just as refined, late, multifarious, irritable, and cunning as the "science of morality"
that belongs to it is still young, neophyte, clumsy and ham-
fisted: — an attractive contrast that occasionally becomes
visible and incarnate in the person of the moralist himself.
Considering what they refer to, even the words "science of morality" are much too arrogant and offensive to *good* taste: which
always tends to prefer more modest words. We should admit
to ourselves here with complete discipline *what* will be necessary for a long time to come, and *what* alone is correct for the
time being: namely collecting material, conceptual formulation and arrangement of an immense realm of tender value-
emotions and value-differences that live, grow, beget and
perish — and, perhaps, attempts to make clear the returning
and more frequent forms of these living crystallizations — as
preparation for a *typology* of morals. Of course: so far we have
not been this modest. With a stiff seriousness that is comical,
all the philosophers demanded of themselves something much
more exalted, pretentious, solemn, as soon as they took up morality as a science: they wanted the *foundation* of morality — and
up till now every philosopher has believed he has founded
morality; but morality itself was regarded as "given." How distant from their clumsy pride was that seemingly improbable

task of a description, left behind in the dust and mold, even though the finest hands and senses could scarcely be fine enough for it! Precisely because moral philosophers only knew the moral *facta*[1] crudely from arbitrary excerpts and random abbreviations, for instance as the morality of their environment, their class, their church, their spirit of the age, their climate and region — precisely because they were poorly informed and even minimally curious about peoples, ages, and the past, they never got to see the real problems of morality: — that only surface in a comparison of *many* moralities. As strange as it may sound, in all previous "science of morality" the problem of morality itself was *missing*: the suspicion was lacking that there was anything problematic here. What the philosophers called "foundation of morality" and demanded of themselves was, viewed in the proper light, only a scholarly form of good *faith* in the prevailing morality, a new means of its *expression*, thus a fact itself within a certain morality, indeed, in the final analysis a kind of denial that this morality *could* be considered a problem: — and in any case it was the opposite of an examination, dissection, interrogation, vivisection of this very faith. For instance, let us listen to the almost venerable innocence with which even Schopenhauer presents his own task, and then make our conclusions about the scientific standing of a "science" whose ultimate masters still talk like children and little old ladies: — "the principle," he says (p. 136 of *Prize Essay on the Basis of Morals*[2]), "the basic proposition about whose content all ethicists *really* are united: *neminen laede, immo omnes, quantum potes, juva*[3] — this is *really* the claim all ethical theorists labor to ground . . . . . the *proper* foundation of ethics, which people have been seeking like the philosopher's stone, for millennia."[4] — The difficulty of grounding the cited claim may of course be great — it is well known that Schopenhauer himself did not succeed — : and whoever has thoroughly sensed how insipidly false and sentimental this claim is, in a world whose essence is will to power — might allow

himself to be reminded that Schopenhauer, although a pessimist, *actually*—played the flute. . . . Daily, after dinner:
just read his biographer on this point. And incidentally: a pessimist, a denier of God and the world who *stops* before morality—who says Yes to morality, to the morality of *laede nemi-
nem* and plays the flute: what? is this really—a pessimist?

187

Aside from the value of such claims as "there is in us a categorical imperative," we can still ask: what does such a claim
say about the one who claims it? There are moralities that are
supposed to justify their creator before others; other moralities are supposed to calm him and put him at peace with
himself; with others he wants to nail himself to a cross and
humiliate himself; with others he wants to exact revenge, with
others hide, with others transfigure himself and position himself way out into the heights and distance; one morality is used
by its creator to forget, another to let him or something about
him be forgotten; many a moralist wants to impose his power
and creative whim on humanity; many others, perhaps Kant
in particular, use their morality to indicate: "what is respectable in me is that I can obey—and for you it *should not* be any
different than for me!"—in short, even moralities are only a
sign language of the affects.

188

Every morality, as opposed to *laisser aller*,[5] is a piece of tyranny against "nature," also against "reason": but this is still not
an objection to it, since we ourselves would have to decree again
from the standpoint of some morality that every manner of
tyranny and unreason is forbidden. What is essential and inestimable in every morality is that it is a long compulsion: in order
to understand Stoicism or Port-Royal or Puritanism, we need to
recall the compulsion under which so far every language has
achieved strength and freedom—the compulsion of meter, the
tyranny of rhyme and rhythm. How much trouble the poets and

orators of every people have been through!—including a few
prose writers of today, in whose ear an unrelenting conscience
dwells—"for the sake of foolishness," as utilitarian dolts say,
who think they're being smart—"out of submissiveness to arbitrary laws," as the anarchists[6] say, imagining themselves to be
"free," even free-spirited. The odd fact, however, is that everything there is or has been on earth by way of freedom, refinement, boldness, dance and masterly assurance, whether in
thinking itself, or in ruling, rhetoric or persuasion, in the arts
as well as in ethics, only developed by virtue of the "tyranny of
such arbitrary laws"; and in all seriousness, the probability is
not small that precisely this is "nature" and "natural"—and
not that *laisser aller*! Every artist knows how distant the
feeling of letting go is from his "most natural" state, the free
ordering, positing, disposing and shaping in moments of
"inspiration"—and how strictly and subtly he obeys thousand-
fold laws at this very time, which defy all formulation through
concepts precisely on the basis of their harshness and exacti-
tude (even the firmest concept, by contrast, has something
floating, multifarious and ambiguous about it—). I will repeat: what is essential "in heaven and on earth," as it seems, is
that *obedience* exists for a long time in one direction: this way
in the long term something was and is produced for whose
sake it is worthwhile to live on earth, for instance virtue, art,
music, dance, reason, spirituality—something transfiguring,
refined, mad and divine. The long unfreedom of the spirit, the
mistrustful constraint in the communicability of thoughts,
the discipline a thinker imposed upon himself in order to
think within ecclesiastical and courtly guidelines or under
Aristotelian presuppositions, the long spiritual will to interpret everything that happens according to a Christian scheme
and to rediscover and justify the Christian God in every chance
event—all these violent, arbitrary, harsh, grisly, anti-rational
things have turned out to be the means by which strength,
ruthless curiosity and subtle mobility have been cultivated in
the European spirit: admittedly, in the process much energy

and spirit were likewise irreplaceably crushed, stifled and ruined (for here as everywhere "nature" reveals itself as it is, in all its wasteful and *indifferent* magnificence, which is outrageous but noble). That for thousands of years European thinkers only thought in order to prove something—today conversely we suspect every thinker who "wants to prove something"—that the results that were *supposed* to be produced by their most rigorous meditating were always firmly established beforehand, perhaps as formerly in Asian astrology, or even like today's harmless Christian-moral interpretation of the closest personal events "to the glory of God" and "for the salvation of the soul":—this tyranny, this arbitrariness, this strict and grandiose stupidity has *trained* the spirit; slavery, it seems, in the cruder and finer sense of the word, is also an indispensable means of spiritual discipline and cultivation.[7] We should regard every morality with this in mind: it is the "nature" in it that teaches us to hate the *laisser aller,* the all-too-great freedom, and sows our need for limited horizons and the closest tasks—and that teaches the *narrowing* of *perspective,* and thus in a certain sense stupidity, as a condition for life and growth. "Thou shalt obey, anybody at all, and for a long time: *otherwise* you will perish and lose all respect for yourself"—this seems to me to be nature's moral imperative, which of course is neither "categorical," as the old Kant demanded (hence the "otherwise"—), nor addressed to the individual (what does it care about individuals!), but rather to peoples, races, ages, classes, but primarily to the whole animal "human," to *the* human being.

189

The industrious races find it extremely troubling to tolerate idleness: it was a masterpiece of *English* instinct to render Sunday so holy and boring that the English would unconsciously lust for their week- and workdays:—as a kind of cleverly invented and cleverly inserted *fasting,* the like of which is also abundantly visible in the world of antiquity (even though not exactly with respect to work, in fairness to the southern peoples—). There must be fasting of many kinds; and wherever powerful drives and habits prevail, the lawmakers must see to it that leap days are added, on which such a drive is put in chains and learns again how to hunger. Viewed from a higher vantage point, entire generations and ages, emerging with the infection of some kind of moral fanaticism, seem like such interposed periods of compulsion and fasting during which a drive learns to cower and submit, but also to *purify* and *sharpen* itself; even some philosophical sects permit such an interpretation (for instance the Stoa in the midst of Hellenic culture, whose atmosphere had become lascivious and overcharged with aphrodisiac fragrances).— Here we also have a clue for explaining the paradox of why it was precisely in Europe's Christian period and generally only under the pressure of Christian value-judgments that the sex drive sublimated itself into love (*amour-passion*[8]).

190[9]

There is something in Plato's morality that does not really belong to Plato, but only exists[10] in his philosophy despite Plato, so to speak: namely Socratism, for which he was really too noble. "No one wants to do harm to himself, therefore everything bad happens involuntarily. For the bad man inflicts harm on himself: he would not do this if he knew that the bad is bad. Accordingly the bad man is only bad through error; if we remove his error, then we necessarily make him—good."—This kind of inference stinks of the *rabble*, who only focus on the unpleasant consequences of bad actions and in fact judge "it is *stupid* to act badly"; whereas they blithely take "good" and "useful and pleasant" to be identical. We can surmise from the start that this is the same origin of every utilitarianism of morality, and follow our nose: we will seldom go astray.— Plato did everything to interpret something subtle and noble into the proposition of his teacher, above all himself—he, the most daring of all interpreters, who took the whole Socrates like a popular theme and folksong from the streets in order to vary it infinitely and impossibly, specifically into all his own masks and

multiplicities. Spoken in jest, and moreover Homerically: just
what is the Platonic Socrates if not

πρόσΘε Πλάτων ὄπιΘέν τε Πλάτων μέσσῃ τε
Χίμαιρα.[11]

191

The old theological problem of "faith" and "knowledge"—or,
more clearly, of instinct and reason—thus the question of
whether with respect to the valuation of things instinct deserves more authority than rationality, which wants us to evaluate and act according to grounds, according to a "why?", and
on the basis of expediency and utility—this is still that old
moral problem as it first appeared in the person of Socrates
and already divided minds long before Christianity. Socrates
himself of course, with the taste of his talent—that of a superior dialectician—at first took the side of reason; and in truth,
what else did he do his whole life long than laugh at the clumsy
ineptitude of his noble Athenians, who were men of instinct
like all noble human beings and could never provide sufficient
information about the reasons for their actions? Ultimately,
however, silently and secretly he laughed about himself too:
faced with his more refined conscience and self-interrogation,
he found the same difficulty and ineptitude in himself. But why
for this reason, he told himself, should we let go of the instincts!
We must help them and reason *also* to get their fair share—we
must follow the instincts but persuade reason to support them
with good grounds. This was the actual *falseness* of that great
secretive ironist; he managed to satisfy his conscience with a
kind of self-deception, while at bottom he had seen through the
irrationality in moral judgments.—Plato, much more innocent
in these matters and lacking the craftiness of a plebeian, wanted
to apply all his strength—the greatest strength a philosopher so
far has had available!—to prove to himself that reason and instinct by themselves head for a single goal, for the good, for

"God"; and since Plato all theologians and philosophers have been on the same track—that is, in matters of morality so far either instinct, or "faith" as Christians call it, or "the herd" as I call it, has triumphed. But Descartes would have to be an exception, this father of rationalism (and consequently the grandfather of the Revolution), who granted authority to reason alone: but reason is only a tool, and Descartes was superficial.

192[12]

Whoever has investigated the history of a single science discovers in its development a clue to understanding the most ancient and common processes of all "knowing and cognition": there as here the hasty hypotheses, fictions, the good stupid will to "believe," and lack of mistrust and patience develop first—our senses only learn late, and never entirely, to be subtle, faithful, and careful organs of knowledge. In response to a given stimulus our eyes find it more comfortable to reproduce an image they have frequently produced before, as opposed to registering what differs and is new in an impression: the latter requires more energy, more "morality." It is awkward and difficult to the ears to hear something new; we are bad at listening to foreign music. When listening to a different language, we involuntarily try to form the sounds we hear into words that sound more familiar and at home to us: so for instance Germans long ago devised the word *Armbrust* when they heard *arcubalista*.[13] What is novel is also greeted with hostility and reluctance by our senses; and generally speaking even the "simplest" processes of sensation are *ruled* by affects like fear, love and hate, including the passive affects of laziness. — Just as little as a reader today completely reads off the individual words (let alone syllables) on a page—instead randomly taking about five words out of twenty and "guessing" the probable meaning of these five words— just as little do we see a tree accurately and completely with respect to its leaves, branches, color, and shape; it is so much easier for us to fantasize an approximation of a tree. Even in the middle of the strangest experiences we do the same thing: we make up the bigger part of the experience and can barely be forced *not* to observe some event as its "inventor." All this is to say: from the ground up and from time immemorial we are — *in the habit of lying*. Or, to say it more virtuously and hypocritically, in short, more pleasantly: we are much more artist than we know. — In an animated conversation I often see the face of the person with whom I am talking with such clarity and detail, adapting to each thought he expresses or which I have produced in him, that this degree of clarity far exceeds the *power* of my capacity to see: — the subtlety of muscle movement and the expression of the eyes *must* therefore have been made up by me. The person probably made quite a different face or none at all.

193

Quidquid luce fuit, tenebris agit:[14] but also vice versa. What we experience in dreams, provided that we experience it often, belongs in the end just as much to the total economy of our soul as anything we "really" experienced: by virtue of it we are richer or poorer, have one need more or less, and finally in broad daylight and even in the most cheerful moments of our waking spirit we are led by the hand somewhat by the habits of our dreams. Supposing someone has often flown in their dreams and finally, as soon as he starts dreaming, becomes aware of a power and art of flying as his privilege, even as his very own enviable happiness: such a person, who believes he is able to realize every manner of curve and angle with the slightest impulse, who knows the feeling of a certain divine levity, an "upward" without tension and compulsion, a "downward" without condescension and degradation — without *gravity!* — how could a human being of such dream experiences and dream habits in the end not find that the word "happiness" is differently colored and defined even for his waking day! how could he not demand — a *different* kind of happiness? "Soaring inspiration," as described by poets, would have to be too earthly, muscular, violent, too "heavy" for him compared to this "flying."[15]

194[16]

The diversity of mankind is demonstrated not only in the diversity of their tablets of goods, hence in the fact that they consider different goods to be worth striving for and also disagree on the more and less of a value, and on the order of rank of the goods they recognize in common:—it is demonstrated even more in what they regard to be really *having* and *possessing* a good. With respect to a woman, for instance, to a more modest man disposing over her body and sexual pleasure already qualifies as an adequate and satisfying sign of having and possessing; another man with his more suspicious and demanding thirst for possession sees the "question mark," the mere semblance of such having, and wants more subtle tests, above all in order to know whether the woman not only gives herself to him, but also for his sake gives up what she has or would like to have—: only *this* will he regard as "possessing." A third man, however, is not at the end of his suspicion and possessiveness even here: he asks whether the woman who gives up everything for him is not perhaps doing so for the sake of a phantom of him, he wants to be known deep down, indeed abysmally deep down before he can be loved at all, he dares to let himself be figured out—. He only feels his beloved to be fully in his possession when she no longer deceives herself about him, when she loves him just as much for the sake of his devilishness and hidden insatiability as for his goodness, patience and spirituality. One type would like to possess an entire people: and all the higher Cagliostro and Catiline[17] arts are fine with him. Another with a more refined thirst for possession tells himself "it's not right to deceive when you want to possess"—he is irritated and impatient at the idea that a mask of him commands the hearts of the people: "therefore I must *allow* myself to be known and above all know myself!" Among helpful and benevolent people we almost routinely find that clumsy ruse that gets someone ready to be helped: as if for instance he "deserved" help, or was in need of precisely *their* help, and would prove to be deeply grateful, obliged, and obsequious for all help — with these conceits they dispose of the needy as if of property, since they are generally benevolent and helpful people out of a craving for property. We find them jealous if we cross them or beat them to it when they are being helpful. Parents involuntarily make their children into something like themselves — they call it "upbringing" — no mother doubts at the bottom of her heart that the child she has borne is her property, and no father disputes his right to subject the child to *his* notions and value-judgments. Indeed, there was a time when it seemed fair to a father to decide on the life or death of a newborn as he saw fit (as among the ancient Germans). And like the father, today the teacher, the social class, the priest and the ruler still see in every new human being an unobjectionable opportunity for a new possession. From which follows. . . . .

195[18]

The Jews — a people "born to slavery," as Tacitus[19] and the entire ancient world say, "the chosen people among peoples," as they themselves say and believe — the Jews have succeeded in that miraculous feat of inversion of values thanks to which life on earth obtained a new and dangerous charm for a couple of millennia: — their prophets fused together "rich," "godless," "evil," "violent," and "sensual" and for the first time used the word "world" as an opprobrium. In this inversion of values (which includes using the word for "poor" as synonymous with "holy" and "friend") lies the significance of the Jewish people: with them begins the *slave revolt in morality.*

196

There are countless dark bodies to be *inferred* near the sun — those we will never see.[20] This is, between you and me, a parable; and[21] a psychologist of morality reads the whole astral text only as a parable- and sign-language, with which much can be left unsaid.[22]

197

We thoroughly misunderstand predatory animals and predatory human beings (for instance Cesare Borgia), we misunderstand "nature" as long as we look for a "pathology" at the bottom of these most healthy of all tropical monsters and growths, or even for some "hell" innate to them —: as almost all moralists so far have done. It seems that among the moralists there is a hatred for the primeval forest and the tropics? And that the "tropical human being" has to be discredited at any cost, whether as disease and degeneration of the human being, or as his own hell and self-torture? But why? In favor of the "temperate zones"? In favor of temperate human beings? Of "moral people"? Of mediocre people? — This for the chapter "Morality as Timidity." —

198

All these moralities that address themselves to the individual person with the aim of his "happiness" — what else are they but recommendations for behavior in relation to the degree of *danger* in which the individual person lives with himself; recipes against his passions, his good and bad inclinations insofar as they have the will to power and wish to play the master; small and large acts of cleverness and artifices that carry the musty odor of old household remedies and the wisdom of old wives; all of them are baroque in form and unreasonable — because they address themselves to "everyone," because they generalize where there should be no generalizing — all of them speaking unconditionally, taking themselves unconditionally, all of them flavored with not only one grain of salt but tolerable only and sometimes even seductive when they learn to be over-spiced and to smell dangerous, and above all to smell "like the other world": measured intellectually all of this has little value and is not "science" by a long shot, let alone "wisdom," but instead, to say it once more and three more times, cleverness, cleverness, cleverness mixed with stupidity, stupidity,

stupidity—whether as that indifference and statue coldness
against the overheated foolishness of the affects, that the Stoics
prescribed and administered; or as that no-more-laughing and
no-more-weeping of Spinoza, his so naïvely championed destruction of the affects through analysis and vivisection; or as
that tuning down of the affects to a harmless mean with which
they could be satisfied, the Aristotelianism[23] of morality; even
morality as enjoyment of the affects in a deliberate dilution and
spiritualization through the symbolism of art, for instance as
music, or as love for God and for human beings for the sake of
God—since in religion the passions have their citizens' rights
again, provided that. . . . .; finally even that accommodating
and mischievous surrender to the affects taught by Hafiz and
Goethe,[24] that bold dropping of the reins, that spiritual-physical
licentia morum[25] in the exceptional case of old wise eccentrics
and drunkards, in whom it "has little danger anymore." This
too for the chapter "Morality as Timidity."

199

Inasmuch as at all times, since there have been human beings, there have also been human herds (clans, communities,
tribes, peoples, countries, churches) and always many more
who obey in relation to the small number of those who command—hence in light of the fact that among human beings
obedience has so far been practiced and cultivated best and
longest, it is fair to assume that the need for obedience is now
innate in the average person as a kind of *formal conscience* that
commands: "Thou shalt unconditionally do something, and
unconditionally not do something," in short, "thou shalt."
This need seeks to satisfy itself and to fill its form with content; proportionate to its strength, impatience and tension, it
therefore indiscriminately latches onto and adopts like a crude
appetite whatever kind of commands—by parents, teachers,
laws, class prejudices, public opinion—are screamed into its
ears. The strange limitation of human evolution, its hesitating,

long-lasting, and often backsliding and self-reversing nature is based on the fact that the herd instinct of obedience is inherited best and at the expense of the art of commanding. If we imagine this instinct ever advancing to its ultimate excesses, then in the end the commanders and those who are independent are the very ones who will be lacking; or they will suffer inwardly from bad conscience and first need to deceive themselves in order to command, that is, by pretending as if they too were merely obeying. This is in fact the situation that exists in Europe today: I call it the moral hypocrisy of those who command. The only way they know to protect themselves from their own bad conscience is to act as though they were the executors of more ancient or higher commands (of their forefathers, the constitution, justice, laws or even God), or even to borrow herd maxims from the herd's way of thinking, for instance "first servants of the people" or "instruments of the common weal." On the other side, the herd man in Europe today gives himself the appearance of being the only permissible kind of human being and glorifies his qualities, by virtue of which he is tame, peaceable and useful to the herd, as the authentically human virtues: hence communal spirit, benevolence, consideration, industriousness, moderation, modesty, indulgence, and compassion. For those cases, however, in which we believe we cannot get by without leaders and bellwethers, today we launch experiment upon experiment to replace commanders by adding together clever herd people instead: all representative constitutions share this origin, for example. What a boon, what[26] a relief was provided for these herd-animal Europeans from a pressure that was becoming unbearable, when despite everything an unconditional commander did make his appearance, for which the effect of Napoleon's emergence was the last great testimony: — the history of Napoleon's impact is nearly the history of the higher happiness achieved by this entire century in its most worthwhile human beings and moments!

200

Someone from an age of disintegration, in which races are
mixed together, who as such embodies the heritage of multiple
origins,[27] that is, conflicting and often not only conflicting
drives and value-standards that fight one another and rarely
give each other any peace—such a human being of late cultures and refracted lights will on average be a weaker human
being: his most basic longing is that the war that he *is* simply
come to an end; to him happiness, in keeping with a tranquil-
izing medicine and way of thinking (for instance the Epicurean or Christian), seems primarily the happiness of resting, of
being undisturbed, of satiety, of unity finally attained, as the
"Sabbath of Sabbaths," to use an expression of the rhetorician
Augustine, who was himself such a human being.—But if opposition and war in such a nature function as one *more* stimulus and spur to life—and if on the other hand the genuine
mastery and subtlety of waging war with oneself, in other
words, self-mastery and outwitting oneself are added through
inheritance and cultivation to their powerful and irreconcil-
able drives, then those magically incomprehensible and unthinkable human enigmas develop, those who are predestined
for victories and for seduction, whose most beautiful expression are Alcibiades and Caesar (—to whose company I would
like to add that *first* European after my taste, the Hohenstaufen Frederick II), and among artists perhaps Leonardo da
Vinci. They appear in exactly the same ages when that weaker
type with his longing for peace steps to the fore: both types
belong together and stem from the same causes.[28]

201

As long as the only utility that governs in moral value judgments is the utility of the herd, as long as our gaze is directed
solely at the preservation of the community, and what is immoral is sought precisely and exclusively in whatever seems

dangerous to the survival of the community: there cannot
yet be a "morality of neighbor love." Supposing that even here
there was a consistent minor exercising of consideration, compassion, fairness, mildness, reciprocity of rendering assistance;
supposing that even in this state of society all those drives
were active that later will be distinguished with honorable
names, as "virtues," and in the end practically coincide with
the concept of "morality": in that period they still do not at all
belong to the realm of moral valuations — they are still *extramoral*. In the finest period of Rome, for instance, an act of pity
was not called either good or evil, moral or immoral; and if
it was praised in its own right, then the praise was perfectly
compatible with a kind of annoyed disdain as soon as it was
compared to any kind of action that served to promote the
whole, the *res publica*.[29] Ultimately "love of the neighbor" is
always something incidental, partly conventional and will-
fully specious in relation to *fear of the neighbor*. After the structure of society on the whole has been established and appears
secure against external dangers, it is this fear of the neighbor
that again creates new perspectives of moral valuation. Certain strong and dangerous drives, such as an enterprising nature, recklessness, vindictiveness, cunning, rapacity, and lust
to rule, which up till now had to be not only honored in a
communally useful sense — under different names than those
used here, of course — but even nurtured and cultivated to
greatness (because given the danger to the whole they were
constantly needed against the enemies of the whole), now are
perceived as twice as dangerous — now that they lack chan-
neling mechanisms — and step by step they are branded as
immoral and exposed to slander. Now the opposite drives and
inclinations receive moral honors; the herd instinct draws its
conclusions, step by step. Now the moral perspective is how
much or how little danger there is to the community, danger
to equality in an opinion, in a condition and affect, in a will,
in a talent: here too fear is the mother of morality. It is the

highest and strongest drives, when they passionately break out and drive the individual far beyond and above the average and the lowlands of the herd conscience, that bring about the destruction of the community's sense of self, their belief in themselves, breaking their spine, so to speak: consequently these very drives will be branded and slandered most. High, independent spirituality, the will to stand alone, even superior reason are perceived as danger; everything that elevates the individual beyond the herd and causes fear in neighbors is called *evil* from now on; the fair, modest, conforming, leveling mentality, the *mediocrity* of desires acquires moral names and honors. Finally, under very peaceful conditions, the opportunity and need continually decrease for training one's emotions to be severe and harsh, and now every kind of severity, even in just circumstances, troubles the conscience; a high and harsh nobility and self-reliance is almost offensive and arouses suspicion, the "lamb," or even more "the sheep" gains in stature. There is a point of pathological softening and tenderizing in the history of a society, where it even sides with those who do harm to it, the *criminals*, and does so quite seriously and honestly. Punishment: somehow that seems unfair to it—and it is certain that the concept "punishment" and "should punish" hurts it and causes fear. "Does it not suffice to render him *no longer dangerous*? Why still punish? Punishment itself is terrible!"—with this question herd morality, the morality of timidity, draws its ultimate consequence. Supposing we could eliminate danger itself, the reason for fear, then we would have eliminated this morality as well: it would no longer be necessary, it would no longer *consider itself* to be necessary!—Whoever examines the conscience of today's European will always have to pull the same imperative from a thousand moral folds and hiding places, the imperative of herd timidity: "we want that some day there should be *nothing more to fear*!" Some day—everywhere in today's Europe the will and way *there* is called "progress."

202

Let us immediately say once more what we already have said a hundred times: since today the ears for such truths—for *our* truths—are not well disposed. We know well enough how offensive it sounds when someone dares openly and without metaphor to count human beings among the animals; but we will almost be charged with a *crime* for constantly using expressions like "herd," "herd instinct" and so on with respect to people of "modern ideas." What good is it! We cannot do otherwise: since this is precisely where our new insight lies. We found that in all major moral judgments[30] Europe has become unanimous, including those countries where Europe's influence dominates: in Europe they clearly *know* what Socrates believed he did not know, and what that famous old snake once promised to teach—they "know" today what good and evil is. Now it has to sound harsh and grate on the ears when we repeatedly insist: what thinks it knows here, what glorifies itself here with its praise and blame, and pronounces itself good, is the instinct of the herd-animal human: which has achieved a breakthrough, a preponderance, a supremacy over other instincts and increasingly does so according to the growing physiological approximation and assimilation whose symptom it is. *Morality in Europe today is herd-animal morality*: — thus as we understand matters only one kind of human morality, beside which, before which, after which many other, above all *higher* moralities are possible or should be. But this morality resists such a "possibility," such a "should be" with all its might: it says stubbornly and ruthlessly "I am morality itself, and nothing besides is morality!"—indeed, with the help of a religion that indulged and flattered the most sublime herd-animal desires, it has gotten to the point where we find an ever more visible expression of this morality even in political and social institutions: the *democratic* movement is the heir of the Christian movement.[31] But that its tempo is much too slow and sleepy for the more impatient, for the sick and those addicted to the instinct in question, is dramatized by the increasingly rabid howling and the increasingly open snarling of the anarchist dogs who now roam the streets of European culture: apparently in contrast to the peaceful, industrious democrats and ideologists of revolution, even more to the clumsy philosophasters[32] and brotherhood zealots who call themselves socialists and want a "free society," but in truth they are all one and the same with their thorough and instinctive hostility toward every form of society other than that of the *autonomous* herd (even to the point of rejecting the concepts "master" and "servant" — *ni dieu ni maître*[33] reads a socialist formula —); they are all one and the same in their tough resistance to every special claim, special right and privilege (that means in the final analysis they are opposed to *any* right: because when all are equal, no one needs "rights" anymore —); one and the same in their mistrust of punitive justice (as if it were a violation of the weaker, an injustice to the *necessary* consequences of all earlier society —); but likewise united in the religion of compassion, in sympathy, wherever there is feeling, experiencing, suffering (down to animals and up to "God": — the excess that is "compassion for God" belongs in a democratic age —); all one and the same in their cries and impatience of compassion, in lethal hatred for suffering generally, in their almost feminine inability to remain spectators and to *let* suffering be; united in embracing the involuntary gloom and tenderness under whose spell Europe seems to be threatened by a new Buddhism;[34] united in their faith in the morality of *shared* compassion, as if it were morality in itself,[35] the height, the *achieved* height of humanity, the sole hope of the future, the solace of the present, the great absolution of all guilt from times past:[36] — all one and the same in their faith in community as the *redeemer*, thus in the herd, in "themselves"[37]. . . . .

203[38]

We who are of a different faith — we who consider the democratic movement not merely as a declining form of political organization, but as a declining, moreover diminishing form of the human being,[39] as his mediocritization and debasement in value: where do *we* have to reach with our hopes? — For *new philosophers*, there is no choice; for spirits who are strong and original enough to stimulate opposing valuations and to revalue "eternal values"; for forerunners, for human beings of the future who in the present will forge the ties and tie the knot that forces the will of millennia onto *new* rails. To teach human beings the future of humanity as its *will*, as dependent on a human will to prepare great risks and overall experiments of culture and cultivation,[40] in order to make an end to that grisly reign of nonsense and accident that has been known as "history" so far — the nonsense of the "greatest number" being only its latest form — : for this some day a new kind of philosopher and commander will be needed, whose image will make pale and dwarf everything that has ever existed on earth in the form of concealed, terrible and benevolent spirits. It is the image of such leaders that hovers before *our* eyes: — may I say it out loud, you free spirits? The conditions that we would have to partly create and partly exploit for their emergence; the probable ways and tests whereby a soul would grow high and powerful enough to perceive the *compulsion* to assume these tasks; a revaluation of values under whose new pressure and hammer a conscience could be steeled and a heart transformed to bronze, so that it could withstand the weight of such responsibility; on the other hand the necessity of such leaders, the terrible danger that they could fail to appear or turn out badly and degenerate — these are *our* genuine worries and dark thoughts, you know this, you free spirits? these are the heavy distant thoughts and thunder that pass over the sky of *our* lives. Few pains are as poignant as having once seen, realized, and sympathized with how an extraordinary human being went off track and degenerated: but whoever has a rare eye for the overall danger that "the human" itself *degenerates*, whoever like us has recognized the monstrous fortuity that has so far played its game with respect to the future of humanity — a game in which no hand and not even a "finger of God" played along!—whoever fathoms the disaster that lies in the dimwitted guilelessness and blissful credulity of "modern ideas," still more in the whole Christian-European morality: *he* suffers from an anxiety with which no other can be compared—he sees at a single glance everything that could yet *be cultivated in human beings* given a favorable accumulation and intensification of strengths and tasks, he knows with all the science of his conscience how humanity is still unexhausted for the greatest possibilities, and how often the type human being has already faced mysterious decisions and new paths:—he knows even better from his own most painful recollection what kind of pitiful things have so far generally contributed to the crushing, breaking, sinking and pitiful downfall of a developing spirit of the highest rank. The *total degeneration of human beings* down to what appears to the socialist clowns and flatheads of today as their "human of the future"—as their ideal!—this degeneration and diminution of the human to the perfect herd animal (or, as they say, to the humans of "free society"), this animalization of human beings to dwarf animals of equal rights and claims is *possible*, there is no doubt! Anyone who has ever thought this possibility through to the end knows one more nausea than other human beings—and perhaps also a new *task*! . . . .

Part Six

We Scholars

204

At the risk that here too moralizing turns out to be what it always was — namely an undaunted *montrer ses plaies*,[1] according to Balzac — I would like to venture to speak out against an indecent and harmful shift in rank that today threatens to establish itself, completely unnoticed and with the best conscience, between science and philosophy. In my opinion we need to speak from our *experience* — experience it seems to me always means bad experience? — to have the right to speak out on such a higher question of rank: or else we speak like the blind about colors or like women and artists *against* science ("oh, this nasty science!" their instinct and their shame sighs, "it always *finds out*!" —). The declaration of independence of the scientific person, his emancipation from philosophy, is one of the more subtle aftereffects of democratic doings and undoings: the self-glorification and self-aggrandizing of scholars stand in full bloom everywhere today and in their finest spring — by which I do not mean to say that in this case self-praise smells lovely. "Free of all masters!" — this is how the rabble man's instinct wants it here too: and now that science has been so utterly successful in warding off theology, whose "handmaid" it was for too long, it is now aiming with complete overconfidence and lack of understanding to dictate laws to philosophy and for its part to play the "master" for once — what am I saying! to play the *philosopher*. My memory — the memory of a scientific human, if I may!—is bristling with naïvetés of arrogance about philosophy that I have heard from the mouths of young natural scientists and old physicians (not to mention the most studious and snootiest of all scholars, the philologists and schoolmen who are both these things only by profession—). Sometimes it was the specialist and the loafer who instinctively resisted all synthetic tasks and abilities generally: sometimes the industrious worker who caught a whiff of the otiosity and noble opulence in the psychic economy of the philosopher and so felt hampered and belittled. Sometimes it was that color blindness of the utilitarian person who sees nothing in philosophy but a series of *refuted* systems and a wasteful expenditure that does no one "any good." Sometimes fear arose of disguised mysticism and corrections to the limits of knowledge: sometimes disdain for certain philosophers, which involuntarily became generalized into disdain for philosophy. In the end, what I found most often behind the arrogant contempt of young scholars for philosophy was the nasty aftereffect of a philosopher himself, although he had been denied allegiance on the whole, people failed to step clear of the spell of his dismissive valuations of other philosophers:—with the result being an overall souring against all philosophy. (Schopenhauer's aftereffect on our most recent German past strikes me as an example:—with his unintelligent rage against Hegel he managed to break away the whole last generation of Germans from the context of German culture, a culture which, all things considered, was a[2] high point and divinatory refinement of the *historical sense*: but Schopenhauer himself was poor, unreceptive, and un-German on this very issue.) On the whole, it may have been primarily the human, all-too-human nature, in short, the wretchedness of our more recent philosophy itself that most thoroughly damaged respect for philosophy generally and opened the gates to the rabble man's instinct. We should just admit the extent to which our modern world is lacking any kind of Heraclitus, Plato, Empedocles, and whatever else all these royal and magnificent hermits of the spirit might have been called; and how it is quite justifiable that, given the kind of representatives of philosophy who are as done-up as they are done-in today thanks to fashion — in Germany for instance the two lions of Berlin, the anarchist Eugen Dühring and the amalgamist Eduard von Hartmann[3] — a solid man of science *should* feel himself to be of a better kind and lineage —. Especially the sight of those mish-mash philosophers who call themselves "philosophers of reality" or "positivists" is capable of planting a dangerous mistrust into the soul of a young, ambitious scholar: those are at best scholars and specialists themselves, it is palpable! — those are all defeated spirits *brought back* under the dominion of science, who at some remote time wanted *more* of themselves without having had a right to this "more" and its responsibility — and who now honorably, angrily, and vengefully represent in word and deed their *unbelief* in the ruler-task and the notion that philosophy should rule. In the end: how could it be otherwise! Today science is blossoming and its good conscience is written all over its face, whereas the depths to which all recent philosophy has gradually sunk, this leftover philosophy of today, arouses mistrust and displeasure, if not mockery and pity.[4] Philosophy reduced to "epistemology," in fact nothing more than a timid epochism and doctrine of abstinence; a philosophy that does not even cross the threshold and scrupulously *denies* itself the right to enter — this is philosophy in its last throes, an end, an agony, something that arouses compassion. How could such a philosophy — *rule*!

205

Today the dangers to the development of a philosopher are in truth so manifold that we could doubt whether this fruit can even ripen anymore. The circumference and the height of the tower of science have grown colossally, with them the probability that a philosopher will already grow weary at the learning stage or allow himself to be held back somewhere and "specialize": and so he no longer reaches his full height, from which he looks over, looks around, and *looks down*. Or he arrives too late at the top, after his best time and strength are already gone; or damaged, coarsened, degenerated, so that his gaze, his overall value-judgment means little anymore. Precisely the fineness of his intellectual conscience perhaps has him hesitating along the way and slowing down; he fears the seduction of becoming a dilettante, a millipede and a milli-antennae, he knows too well that someone who has lost respect for himself no longer commands and no longer *leads* in matters of knowledge either: unless he wanted to become a great actor, a philosophical Cagliostro and pied piper of spirits, in short a seducer. Ultimately this is a question of taste: if it were not even a question of conscience. In addition, to double again the difficulty of the philosopher, he demands a judgment of himself, a Yes or a No, not on the sciences but on life and the value of life — he reluctantly learns to believe that he has a right or even a duty to have this judgment, and so he must seek his way to that right and that belief, often hesitating, doubting and falling silent, drawing only from the most extensive — perhaps most disruptive and most destructive — experiences. Indeed, the masses have misjudged and mistaken the philosopher for a long time, whether for the scientific human and ideal scholar, whether for the religiously elevated, desensualized, "desecularized" zealot and drunkard of God; if we even hear someone praised today for living "wisely" or "as a philosopher," then it practically means nothing more than "cleverly and off to the side." Wisdom: to the rabble this seems like a kind of escape, a means and a trick to effectively extricate themselves from a dicey game; but the real philosopher — so it seems to *us*, my friends? — lives "unphilosophically" and "unwisely," above all *uncleverly*, and feels the burden and duty of a hundred experiments and temptations of life: — he constantly risks *himself*, he plays *the* dicey game. . . . .

206

Compared to a genius, that is to a being that either *begets* or *bears*, both words taken in their highest sense — the scholar, the scientific average human being always has something of the old maid about him: since like her he has no expertise in the two most valuable functions of human beings. Indeed, as compensation to both of them, so to speak, to scholars and to old maids, we concede respectability—in these cases we underscore respectability—and yet under the pressure of this concession we have the same admixture of annoyance. When we look closer: what is the scientific human? First of all an ignoble kind of human, with the virtues of someone who is not dominating, not authoritative and not even self-sufficient: he has industriousness, patient compliance with his rank and file, evenness and moderation in his capabilities and needs, the instinct for his kind and for what his kind needs, for instance that patch of independence and green pasture without which there is no quiet for working, that claim to honor and acknowledgment (which presupposes recognition and being recognizable first and foremost—), that sunshine of a good name, that constant reaffirmation of his value and his utility with which he must overcome again and again the inner *mistrust* lying at the bottom of the hearts of all dependent people and herd animals. The scholar also has, as is only fair, the illnesses and bad habits of an ignoble type: he[5] is rich in petty jealousies and has lynx eyes for what is lowly in the natures of those whose heights he cannot reach. He is trusting, but only like someone who lets himself go without letting himself *flow*; and it is right here, in the presence of someone who flows greatly that he stands there all the more cold and reserved—then his eyes are like a smooth and unwilling lake in which no delight, no sympathy ripples anymore. The worst and most dangerous thing of which a scholar is capable comes from the instinct of mediocrity of his type, from that Jesuitism of mediocrity that instinctively works on the annihilation of the extraordinary human being and tries to break or—better yet!—slacken every taut bow. Slackening after all, with a merciful hand of course—*slackening* with intimate compassion: that is the genuine art of Jesuitism, which has always known how to introduce itself as a religion of compassion.—

207

However gratefully we might approach the *objective* spirit—and who has not been sick to death at least once of everything subjective and its damned *ipsissimosity*![6]—in the end we still have to learn to be cautious of our gratitude and put a stop to the exaggeration with which the de-selfing and de-personalizing of the spirit is being celebrated recently as if it were a goal in itself, as redemption and transfiguration: this is what tends to happen, for example, within the pessimists' school, which also has good reasons of its own to give highest honors to "disinterested knowledge." The objective human who no longer curses and scolds like the pessimist, the *ideal* scholar in whom the scientific instinct suddenly blossoms and blooms out after things have failed entirely or partially a thousand times, is surely one of the most precious tools there is: but he belongs in the hands of someone more powerful. He is only a tool, or let us say: he is only a *mirror*—he is not an "end in itself." In fact the objective human is a mirror: in the face of everything that wants to be known, accustomed to subservience, without any other desire than that provided by knowing, by "mirroring"—he waits until something comes along, and then he gently spreads himself out so that even the light footsteps and the slipping by of ghostly beings are not lost on his surface and skin. Whatever remains of "person" in him seems accidental to him, often arbitrary, even more often disturbing: that is how much he has become a passage and reflection to himself of strange shapes and events. With effort he recollects "himself," often mistakenly; he easily confuses himself with others, he errs in relation to his own basic needs and only here is he crude and negligent. Perhaps he is tormented by his health or the pettiness and stale air of wife and friend, or the lack of companions and companionship—indeed, he forces himself to reflect on his torments: in vain! Already his thoughts are wandering off, to some more *general* case, and tomorrow he will know as little as he knew yesterday how to help himself.

He has lost the ability to take himself seriously, and the time
as well: he is cheerful *not* from an absence of distress but from
a lack of fingertips and handiness for *his* distress. The accommodating manner he has for every thing and experience, the
sunny and impartial hospitality with which he adopts everything that bumps into him, his kind of reckless benevolence,
of dangerous indifference about Yes and No: oh, there are
enough cases where he has to pay for these virtues of his!—and
as a human anyway he all too easily becomes the *caput mortuum*[7]
of these virtues. If someone wants love and hate from him, I
mean love and hate as God, woman and animal understand
them—: he will do what he can and give what he can. But we
should not be surprised if it is not much—if precisely here he
shows how fake, fragile, questionable and brittle he is. His love
is forced, his hate artificial and more *un tour de force*,[8] a small
vanity and exaggeration. He is indeed only genuine to the extent he can be objective: only in his cheerful totality is he still
"nature" and "natural." His mirroring soul, forever smoothing
itself out, no longer knows how to affirm, how to deny; he does
not command, neither does he destroy. "*Je ne méprise presque
rien*"[9]—he says along with Leibniz: we should not overlook and
underestimate the *presque*! Nor is he a model human; he is neither out in front of anyone, nor behind; he positions himself too
far away to have any reason for taking sides between good and
evil. If people have mistaken him all this time for a *philosopher*,
for the Caesarian cultivator and brute of culture: then he has
been given too much honor and what is essential in him has
been overlooked—he is a tool, a piece of slave, even if certainly
the most sublime kind of slave, but in himself he is nothing—
presque rien! The objective human is a tool, a costly, easily damaged and clouded measuring tool and mirroring work of art,
that we should protect and honor; but it is no goal, no exit and
ascent, no complementary human in whom the *rest* of existence
justifies itself, no conclusion—and even less a beginning, a begetting and first cause, he is nothing sturdy, powerful, self-reliant
who wants to rule: rather only a cleaned-up, delicate, fine,

flexible pot of forms who first has to wait for some kind of
content and substance in order "to shape" himself accordingly—ordinarily a human without content and substance,
a "selfless" human. Consequently nothing for women either,
in parenthesi. —

208[10]

When today a philosopher makes it known that he is not a
skeptic—I hope this was heard clearly enough in the account
of the objective spirit just given?—then nobody likes to hear
it; they look at him with a certain apprehension, there is so
much they would like to ask, to ask . . . indeed, among the
fearful eavesdroppers who now exist in droves, from now on
he will be known as dangerous. To them it is as if they had
heard some evil threatening sound from the distance when he
rejected skepticism, a dynamite of the spirit, perhaps a newly
discovered Russian *nihilin*,[11] a pessimism *bonae voluntatis*,[12]
that does not only say No, and want No, but—horrible
to think!—*does* No. Against this kind of "good will"—a
will to the actual, active denial of life—it is well known today
that there is no better soporific and tranquilizer than skepticism, the gentle, lovely, lulling poppy of skepticism; and *Hamlet* itself is prescribed by physicians of the day as a remedy for
"spirit" and its underground rumblings. "Aren't everybody's
ears full enough as it is with wicked noises?" says the skeptic, as
a friend of quiet and nearly as a kind of security police: "This
underground No is horrible! Be quiet already, you pessimistic
moles!" The skeptic, you see, this delicate creature, startles all
too easily; his conscience has been trained to twitch with every No, indeed even with a decisively firm Yes, and to feel it as
some kind of bite. Yes! and No!—that goes against morality
for him; conversely he loves to treat his virtues to a feast of
noble abstinence, perhaps by quoting Montaigne: "what do I
know?" Or with Socrates: "I know that I know nothing." Or:
"I don't trust myself here, there is no door open to me here."

Or: "supposing it were open, why enter right away!" Or: "what good are all hasty hypotheses? Making no hypotheses at all could easily belong to good taste. Do you absolutely have to straighten right away whatever is crooked? Absolutely plug every hole with some kind of putty? Isn't there time for that? Doesn't time have time? Oh you devilish rogues, can't you just *wait* a bit? What is uncertain also has its charms, the Sphinx too is a Circe, even Circe was a philosopher." — Thus a skeptic consoles himself; and it is true that he needs some consolation. Skepticism, after all, is the most spiritual expression of a certain complex physiological condition that in common language is called weakness of the nerves and sickliness; it emerges every time races or classes that have long been separated interbreed decisively and suddenly. In the new generation, whose blood inherits as it were different standards and values, everything is unrest, disruption, doubt, experiment; the best powers have an inhibiting effect, the virtues themselves do not let one another grow and become strong, in body and soul balance, center of gravity, and perpendicular stability are lacking. But what gets sickest and degenerates most in such hybrids is the *will*: independence in decisions is no longer known to them at all, nor the valiant sense of joy in willing — they doubt in the "freedom of the will" even in their dreams. Our Europe of today, the showplace of an absurdly sudden experiment of radical class mixing and *consequently* race mixing, is therefore skeptical high and low, sometimes with that mobile skepticism that leaps impatiently and lasciviously from one branch to another, sometimes gloomy as a cloud overloaded with question marks — and often sick to death of its will! Paralysis of the will: where do we not find this cripple sitting today! And often even all dressed up! How seductively dressed up! This illness has the prettiest pomp outfits and liars' clothes; and most of what displays itself today in the shop windows as for instance "objectivity," "scientism," "*l'art pour l'art*,"[13] "pure will-less knowing" is only dressed-up

skepticism and paralysis of the will—I will vouch for this diagnosis of the European disease.—The disease of the will is
unevenly spread across Europe: it reveals itself to be strongest
and most multifaceted where culture has been at home for a
long time, and it disappears to the extent that "the barbarian" still—or again—asserts his rights under the loose gar-
ments of Western culture. Accordingly, in contemporary
France, we can conclude just as easily as we can grasp with our
own two hands that the will is sickest of all; and France,
which has always had a masterful talent for reversing even the
most disastrous turns of its spirit into something charming
and seductive, today really demonstrates its cultural superiority over Europe by being the school and showcase of all the
magic of skepticism. The strength to will, and indeed to will
for the span of a will, is somewhat stronger in Germany, and
in the German north stronger again than in the center; it is
considerably stronger in England, Spain and Corsica, there
bound up with apathy, here with hard heads—not to mention
Italy, which is too young to know what it wants and first has
to prove whether it can will—but strongest of all and most
amazing in that vast empire in-between, where Europe flows
back into Asia, as it were, in Russia. There the strength to will
has long been set aside and stored up, there the will is waiting—uncertain whether as the will of denial or affirmation—poised menacingly to be discharged, to borrow a favorite expression from today's physicists. It may require not only
Indian wars and entanglements in Asia to relieve Europe of its
greatest danger, but internal upheavals, the bursting of the
empire into small bodies and above all the introduction of
parliamentary nonsense, including the obligation for everyone
to read his newspaper at breakfast. I do not say this as someone who wishes it: the opposite would be more to my liking—I
mean such an increase in the menace of Russia that Europe
would have to resolve to become menacing to the same extent, that is, *to acquire one will* by means of a new caste that

would rule over Europe, a long, terrible will of its own, which could establish goals for millennia: — that way finally the drawn-out comedy of its small scattered states and likewise its dynastic as well as democratic practice of scattered willing would come to an end. The time for petty politics is over: already the next century will bring the struggle to rule the earth — the *compulsion* to grand politics.

209[14]

For the time being, I would like to express myself only in a parable as to the extent to which the new warlike age that we Europeans have obviously entered might be favorable for the development of a different and stronger kind of skepticism, and friends of German history will already understand it. That unscrupulous enthusiast for handsome, tall grenadiers, who as king of Prussia called into existence a military and skeptical genius — and thus in the deepest sense that new type of German that has just arrived triumphantly — the questionable, mad father of Frederick the Great, on one point himself had the knack and the lucky claw of a genius: he knew what Germany was lacking back then, and which lack was a hundred times more frightening and urgent than perhaps the lack of education and social decorum — his aversion to the young Frederick stemmed from the fear of a deep instinct. *Men were lacking*; and he suspected to his most bitter dismay that his own son was not man enough. In this he deceived himself: but who in his place would not have deceived himself? He saw his son fall victim to the atheism, the *esprit*, the hedonistic high-life of witty Frenchmen: — in the background he saw the great bloodsucker, the spider of skepticism, he suspected the incurable misery of a heart that is no longer hard enough for good or evil, a broken will that no longer commands, no longer *can* command. But meanwhile in his son that more dangerous and harsher kind of skepticism grew tall — who knows *how much* it was aided by precisely the hate of the father and by the icy melancholy of a will rendered solitary? — the skepticism of audacious manliness that is closely related to the genius of war and to conquest, and first entered Germany in the shape of the great Frederick. This skepticism despises and nevertheless lays hold of things; it undermines and takes into possession; it does not believe, but it does not lose itself on that account; it gives the spirit a dangerous freedom, but it keeps the heart severe; it is the *German* form of skepticism that, as the continuation and most spiritual intensification of Frederickianism, for a long time brought Europe under the dominion of the German spirit and its critical and historical mistrust. Thanks to the indomitably strong and tough masculine character of the great German philologists and critical historians (who, properly viewed, were all artists of destruction and disintegration as well), gradually and despite all romanticism in music and philosophy a *new* concept of the German spirit established itself, in which the tendency toward manly skepticism prominently emerged: whether for instance as an intrepid gaze, as the courage and hardness of the dissecting hand, as the tenacious will to dangerous voyages of discovery, to spiritual North Pole expeditions under desolate and dangerous skies. It may be with good reasons that warm-blooded and superficial humanitarians make the sign of the cross before this very spirit: *cet esprit fataliste, ironique, méphistophélique*[15] as Michelet[16] calls it, not without shuddering. But if we really want to empathize with how distinctive is this fear of the "man" in the German spirit, whereby Europe was awakened from its "dogmatic slumber,"[17] then we would have to recall the former conception that it had to overcome — and how it has not been that long since a masculinized woman[18] dared with unbridled presumption to commend Germans to the sympathies of Europe as gentle, good-hearted, weak-willed and poetic oafs. Finally we should be able to grasp deeply enough the astonishment of Napoleon when he caught sight of Goethe: it reveals what people had thought about "German spirit" for centuries. "*Voilà un homme!*" — meaning: "Now that's a *man!* And I had only expected a German!" —[19,20]

210[21]

Supposing then, that in the image of the philosophers of the future some trait were to suggest whether perhaps they might not be skeptics in the sense just mentioned, then it would only characterize something about them — and *not* who they themselves are. With the same right they could be called critics; and certainly they will be experimenting people. Using the name with which I dared to christen them, I have already expressly underscored attempting and the joy of attempting: did this happen because, as critics in body and soul, they love to partake of experiments in a new, perhaps broader, perhaps more dangerous sense? Must they, in their passion for knowledge, go further in audacious and painful experiments than the fainthearted and pampered taste of a democratic century can condone? — There is no doubt: these coming philosophers will be least able to dispense with those serious and not harmless qualities that distinguish the critic from the skeptic, I mean the certainty of value-standards, the conscious application of a unity of method, shrewd courage, the ability to stand alone and answer to oneself; indeed, to themselves they confess a *delight* in saying No, and to dissecting, and to a certain level-headed cruelty that knows how to wield the knife surely and subtly, even when the heart is bleeding. They will be *harder* (and maybe not always toward themselves only) than humane people might wish, they will not deal with "truth" in such a way that it "pleases" or "elevates" or "inspires" them: — instead, their faith will be small that precisely *truth* entails any such amusements for the feelings. They will smile, these severe spirits, if someone were to say in front of them "that idea elevates me: how could it not be true?" Or: "that work delights me: how could it not be beautiful?" Or: "that artist makes me greater: how could he not be great?" — and perhaps they are ready with not only a smile, but a genuine disgust for everything that is fanatical, idealistic, feminine, and hermaphroditic, and whoever was able to follow them into their secret heart chambers would hardly discover there any intention to reconcile "Christian feelings" with "antiquity's taste" or even "modern parliamentarianism" (though such reconciliation is said to occur even among philosophers in our very insecure and consequently very conciliatory century). These philosophers of the future will not only demand of themselves critical discipline and every habit that leads to cleanliness and rigor in matters of the spirit: they could even wear them as their kind of jewelry—nevertheless they still do not want to be called critics. To them it seems no minor disgrace to philosophy when people decree, as they are so fond of doing today: "Philosophy itself is criticism and critical science—and nothing at all besides!" This evaluation of philosophy may enjoy the approbation of all the positivists in France and Germany (—and it is possible that it might even have flattered the heart and taste *of Kant*: recall the titles of his major works—): nevertheless our new philosophers will say: critics are tools of the philosopher and for that very reason, as tools, are by no means philosophers themselves! Even the great Chinese of Königsberg[22] was only a great critic. —

211

I insist that we finally stop mistaking the philosophical laborers and scientific people generally for philosophers—that precisely here we strictly give "to each his own" and not too much to the former, and much too little to the latter. It may be necessary for the education of the genuine philosopher that he himself has once stood on all these steps where his servants, the scientific laborers of philosophy, remain standing—*must* remain standing; he himself will have to have been a critic and skeptic and dogmatist and historian and moreover poet and collector and traveler and riddle-guesser and moralist and seer and "free spirit" and nearly everything, in order to traverse the circumference of human values and value-feelings and in order to *be able* to gaze with many kinds of eyes and consciences from the heights into every distance, from the depths into every height, and from the corner into every expanse. But all these are only preconditions of his task: this task itself wills something else—it demands that he *create values*. Those philosophical laborers after the noble model of Kant and Hegel have to establish and press into formulas a huge body of valuations—that is, former value-*positings* and value-creations that have become dominant and are called "truth" for a time—whether in the realm of *logic* or *politics* (morality) or *art*.[23] It is up to these researchers to make everything that has so far happened, everything that has been esteemed surveyable, ponderable, graspable and manageable, to abbreviate everything long, even "time" itself, and to *overwhelm* the whole past: a tremendous and wonderful task in whose service every fine pride, every tenacious will can certainly be satisfied. *But the genuine philosophers are commanders and legislators*: they say "thus it *shall* be!", they first determine the where to? and what for? of humanity and in so doing deploy the preliminary labor of all philosophical laborers, all who overwhelm the past—they reach with creative hands for the future, and so everything that is and was becomes for them a means, a tool, a hammer. Their "knowing" is *creating*, their creating is a legislation, their will to truth is—*will to power*.—Are there such philosophers today? Have there ever been such philosophers? *Must* there not be such philosophers? . . . .

212

It seems more and more to me that the philosopher as *necessarily* a human of tomorrow and the day after tomorrow has always found himself to be in contradiction to his today and *must* be: his enemy has always been the ideal of today. So far all these extraordinary promoters of humanity who are called philosophers, and who rarely felt themselves to be friends of wisdom so much as disagreeable fools and dangerous question marks—have found their task, their hard, unwanted, unavoidable task, but in the end the greatness of their task in being the bad conscience of their time. Insofar as they applied their vivisecting knife to the very chest of the *virtues of the age*, they revealed what their own secret was: to know of a *new* greatness of humanity, of a new, untrodden path to making it greater. Each time they uncovered how much hypocrisy, indolence, letting oneself go, letting oneself fall, how much lying was hidden beneath the most revered exemplar of their contemporary morality, how much virtue was *outdated*; each time they said: "we have to go there, out there, where *you* are least at home today." In the face of a world of "modern ideas" that wishes to banish everyone to a corner and "specialty," a philosopher, if there could be philosophers today, would be forced to posit the greatness of humanity, the concept of "greatness" precisely in its extensiveness and multiplicity, in its wholeness in plurality: he would even determine value and rank according to how much and how many different things someone could carry and take upon himself, how *far* someone could extend his responsibility. Today the taste and virtue of the age weaken and dilute the will, nothing is more timely than weakness of the will: this is why the ideal of the philosopher must include precisely this strength of will, and the hardness and ability for long-range decisions in its concept of "greatness"; with the same legitimacy as the opposite doctrine and the ideal of an idiotic, renunciatory, humble, and selfless humanity was suitable for an opposite age, one that suffered like the sixteenth century from its accumulated energy of the will and from the most savage floods and storm tides of selfishness. At the time of Socrates, surrounded entirely by people of exhausted instincts, by conservative, ancient Athenians who let themselves go—"for happiness," as they said, for pleasure as they did—and who still mouthed the old pompous words to which their lifestyle long ago gave them no more right, perhaps *irony* was necessary for greatness of the soul: that Socratic, malicious certainty of the old physician and rabble man who mercilessly cut into his own flesh, as into the flesh and heart of the "noble," with a gaze that said clearly enough: "don't pretend in front of me! Here—we are all equal!" Today conversely, when in Europe only the herd animal receives and dispenses honors, when the "equality of rights" could all too easily turn into the equality of being wrong: I mean into waging war in common on all that is rare, foreign, privileged, the higher humans, the higher souls, the higher duty, the higher responsibility, the creative abundance of power and masterfulness—belonging to the concept of "greatness" today are being noble, wanting to be for oneself, being able to be different, standing alone and having to make it on one's own; the philosopher will reveal something about his own ideal when he posits: "the greatest should be the one who can be most solitary, most hidden, most deviating, the human who is beyond good and evil, the master of his virtues, the one whose will is superabundant; precisely this should be called *greatness*: being able to be just as manifold as whole, just as broad as full." And to ask again: today is—greatness *possible*?[24]

213[25]

It is hard to learn what a philosopher is because it cannot be taught: one has to "know" it, from experience—or one should have the pride *not* to know it. But that the whole world these days talks about things of which they *can* have no experience, applies most and worst to philosophers and philosophical circumstances:—a rare few know them, are allowed to know them, and all popular opinions about them are false. So for instance that genuine philosophical pairing of a bold, exuberant spirituality that runs *presto*[26] and a dialectical rigor and necessity that take no false steps is unknown to most thinkers and scholars from their experience, and therefore unbelievable to them if someone were to bring it up in their presence. They imagine every necessity as a need, as a painstaking having-to-follow and being-forced; and they regard thinking itself as something slow, hesitating, almost as a drudgery and often enough as "worthy of the *sweat* of the noble"—but not at all as something light, divine and most closely related to dance and high spirits! "Thinking" and "taking it seriously" or "treating it gravely"—to them it is all the same: only then have they "experienced" it.—Artists may have a finer nose here: they who know all too well that precisely when they no longer do anything "voluntarily" and everything necessarily, their feeling of freedom, subtlety, full power, of creative positing, disposing, and shaping reaches its height—in short, that necessity and "freedom of the will" become one in them. In the end there is an order of rank to states of the soul, which corresponds with the order of rank of problems; and the highest problems mercilessly repel anyone who gets too close to them without being predestined for their solution by the height and power of their spirituality. What good does it do when nimble but ordinary minds or clumsy but sturdy mechanics and empiricists crowd around them, as happens so often these days, trying with their plebeian ambition to get close to them and into the proverbial "court of courts"! But crude feet should never be allowed to tread such carpets: this is already taken care of by the primordial law of things; the doors remain closed to these obtrusive ones, even if they pound and pulverize their heads against them! For every high world one must be born; or spoken more clearly, one must be *cultivated* for it: the right to philosophy—this word taken in its broad sense—is conferred only by one's origins, and ancestors and "bloodlines" are decisive here. Many generations must have done the preliminary work for the origin of a philosopher; each of his virtues has to have been individually acquired, nurtured, passed on, embodied, and not only the bold, light, delicate gait and course of his thoughts, but above all his willingness for great responsibilities, the elevation of his ruling gazes and gazing down, the feeling of being separate from the crowd and its duties and virtues, the affable protection and defense of what is misunderstood and slandered, whether god or devil, the joy and exercise of great justice, the art of commanding, the broadness of the will, the slow eye that rarely admires, rarely looks up, rarely loves . . . .

Part Seven

Our Virtues

214

Our virtues? — It is probable that we too still have our virtues, though it is only fair that they will not be those ingenuous and foursquare virtues for whose sake we hold our grandfathers in honor but also a bit at arm's length. We Europeans of the day after tomorrow, we first-born of the twentieth century — with all our dangerous curiosities, our multiplicity and art of disguise, our mellow and as it were sweetened cruelty in spirit and in senses — presumably we, *if* we are to have virtues, will have only those that learned to get along best with our most secret and cordial inclinations, with our most fervent needs: well then, let us look for them in our labyrinths! — where, as is well known, so many different things lose themselves, so many different things get totally lost. And is there anything more beautiful than *looking for* one's own virtues? Does this not practically mean: *believing* in one's own virtue? But this "believing in one's virtue" — is this not at bottom the same as what we used to call one's "good conscience," that venerable, long-tailed pigtail of a concept that our grandfathers would hang behind their heads, and often enough behind their understanding too? Accordingly it seems that however little we might otherwise regard ourselves to be old-fashioned and grandfatherly honorable, in one sense we are still the worthy grandchildren of these grandfathers, we last Europeans with a good conscience: we too still wear their pigtail. — Oh! If only you knew how soon, how very soon—it will be different! . . .

215

Just as in the realm of stars sometimes two suns determine the orbit of one planet, as in certain cases suns of a different color shine near a single planet, sometimes with red light, sometimes with green light, and then again striking it simultaneously and flooding it with color: so we modern human beings, thanks to the complicated mechanics of our "astral sky"—are determined by *different* moralities; our actions shine alternately in different colors, they are rarely unequivocal—and there are enough cases in which we perform *multi-colored* acts.

216

Love one's enemies? I believe this has been well taught: it happens today thousands of times, on a small and a large scale; indeed, occasionally something higher and more sublime happens—we learn to *despise* when we love, and precisely when we love best:—but all this unconsciously, without noise, without pomp, with that modesty and concealed goodness that forbids the mouth solemn words and virtuous formulas. Morality as posing—offends our taste today. This too is progress: just as it was the progress of our fathers when finally religion as posing offended their taste, including the hostility and Voltairean bitterness against religion (and whatever else formerly belonged to the sign-language of free thinkers). It is the music in our conscience, and the dance in our spirit with which all puritanical litany, all moral homilies and bourgeois respectability fail to accord.

217

We should watch out for those who place a high value on being credited with moral tact and subtlety in moral distinctions! They never forgive us if they ever make a mistake in front of us (or even *against* us)—they instinctively become our slanderers and detractors, even when they remain our "friends." — Blessed are the forgetful: for they "get over" even their stupidities.

218

The psychologists of France — and where else today are there psychologists? — still have not exhausted their bitter and manifold delight in the *bêtise bourgeoise*,[1] just as if . . . enough, this reveals something about them. Flaubert, for instance, the solid citizen of Rouen, saw, heard and tasted in the end nothing else: it was his brand of self-torment and subtler cruelty. Now for variety's sake — since this gets boring — I recommend something different for our amusement: this is the unconscious craftiness with which all good, fat, solid spirits of mediocrity relate to higher spirits and their tasks, that subtle interwoven Jesuit craftiness, that is a thousand times subtler than the understanding and taste of this middle class in its best moments — even than the understanding of its victims — : this once more as proof that "instinct" is the most intelligent of all the different kinds of intelligence discovered so far. In short, you psychologists should study the philosophy of the "rule" in its struggle with the "exception": there you have a spectacle good enough for gods and godlike malice! Or, spoken more contemporarily: practice vivisection on the "good man," on "*homo bonae voluntatis*"[2] . . . . . on *yourselves!*

219[3]

Moral judgment and condemnation is the favorite revenge of the intellectually limited on those who are less so, also a kind of compensation for the fact that they were poorly endowed by nature, and finally an opportunity to acquire spirit and to *become* refined: — malice spiritualizes. At the bottom of their hearts it does them good that there is a standard before which even those who are overflowing with the abundance and privileges of spirit are on equal footing with them: — they fight for "equality of all before God" and for this practically *need* to believe in God. Among them we find the strongest opponents of atheism. Anyone who said to them "high spirituality is beyond comparison with any kind of proper behavior and respectability of a person who is merely moral" would drive them mad: — I will beware of doing so myself. I would rather like to flatter them with my proposition that high spirituality itself exists only as the last spawn of moral qualities; that it is a synthesis of all those states attributed to "merely moral" human beings after they have been acquired individually, through long cultivation and practice, perhaps over entire series of generations; that high spirituality is simply the spiritualization of justice and of that kindly severity that knows it is charged with preserving the *order of rank* in the world among things themselves — and not only among human beings.[4]

220

With praise of the "disinterested" being so popular now, we must bring to consciousness, perhaps not without a certain danger, *what* exactly the people do take an interest in, and generally what are the things about which the common man is thoroughly and deeply concerned: including the educated, even the scholars, and unless all appearances are deceiving, well-nigh the philosophers as well. Then the fact emerges that most of what interests and attracts finer and more pampered tastes as well as every higher nature seems totally "uninteresting" to the average person: — if he nevertheless notices a devotion to it, then he calls it "*désintéressé*" and wonders how it is possible to act "disinterestedly." There have been philosophers who even knew how to impart a seductive and mystical-transcendental expression to this popular wonder (— perhaps because they did not know the higher nature from experience?) — instead of positing the naked and abundantly plain truth that the "disinterested" action is a *very* interesting and interested action, assuming . . . . . "And love?" — What! Even an action out of love is supposed to be "unegoistic"? But you oafs — ! "And the praise of someone who sacrifices?" — But

anyone who really made sacrifices knows that he wanted and
received something for it—maybe something of himself in
exchange for something of himself—that he gave up something here in order to have more there, maybe even in order to
be more or to feel himself to be "more." But this is a realm of
questions and answers in which a more pampered spirit is reluctant to dwell: even truth finds it necessary here to suppress
a yawn when she's called upon to answer. After all she is a
woman: we should not do violence to her.

221

It happens, said a moral pedant and purveyor of trivia, that
I honor and distinguish a selfless man: but not because he is
selfless, but because to me he seems to have a right to be helpful to someone else at his own expense. Enough, the question
is always who is *he* and who is *that other*. For instance, in someone who was destined and made for commanding, self-denial
and modest stepping aside would not be a virtue but the waste
of a virtue: so it seems to me. Every unegoistic morality that
takes itself unconditionally and addresses itself to everyone
sins not only against taste: it is a provocation to sins of omis-
sion, one *more* seduction under the mask of philanthropy—and
precisely a seduction and injury of the higher, rarer, more
privileged. The moralities must be forced to bow first of all to
the *rank order*, their presumption must be imposed on their
consciousness—until they finally agree with one another that
it is *immoral* to say: "what is right for one is fair for another."—Thus my moral pedant and *bonhomme*:[5] did he deserve to be laughed at when he admonished morals to be
moral like this? But one should not be too right if he wants to
have the laughers on *his* side; a grain of wrong belongs even to
good taste.

222

Where compassion is preached today—and if you listen properly, no other religion is preached now—psychologists should

open their ears: through all the vanity, through all the noise that characterizes these preachers (like all preachers) they will hear a hoarse, groaning, genuine sound of *self-contempt*. It belongs to that darkening and turning ugly in Europe that has been growing now for a hundred years (and whose first symptoms were already documented in a thoughtful letter from Galiani to Madame d'Epinay): *if they are not its cause!* The human being of "modern ideas," this proud ape, is boundlessly satisfied with himself: this much is certain. He suffers: and his vanity wants him only to "show compassion" . . . . .[6]

223

The European hybrid human—all in all a fairly ugly plebeian—simply needs a costume: he needs history as the storage room of costumes. Of course he notices that nothing quite fits him—he changes and changes. Just look at the nineteenth century for these rapid preferences and changes of the style masquerade; also for the moments of despair when "nothing becomes" us—. It is useless to parade as romantic or classical or Christian or Florentine or baroque or "national" *in moribus et artibus*:[7] it "doesn't look good"! But the "spirit," especially the "historical spirit," sees its advantage even in this despair: time and again a new piece of antiquity and foreign country is tried on, put on, taken off, packed away and above all *studied*: —we are the first studied period *in puncto*[8] "costumes," by which I mean moralities, articles of faith, tastes for art and religion, prepared as no period before us for the carnival of great style, for spiritual carnival laughter and high spirits, for transcendental heights of the highest nonsense and Aristophanean mockery of the world. Perhaps we will discover right here the realm of our *invention*, that realm where even we can still be original, perhaps as parodists of world history and buffoons of God—perhaps, even if nothing else of today has a future, our *laughter* still has a future!

224[9]

The *historical sense* (or the ability to quickly guess the rank order of valuations according to which a people, a society, an individual has lived, the "divinatory instinct" for the relations of these valuations, for the relation of the authority of values to the authority of active forces): this historical sense, to which we Europeans lay claim as our specialty, has come to us as a result of the enchanting and crazy *semi-barbarism* into which Europe has been plunged by the democratic mingling of classes and races—only the nineteenth century knows this sense, as its sixth sense. The past of every form and lifestyle, of cultures that earlier lay right next to each other, on top of each other, flows into us "modern souls" thanks to that mixture, our instincts now run back everywhere and we ourselves are a kind of chaos—: finally "the spirit," as mentioned earlier, sees its advantage in this. Through our semi-barbarism in body and desires we have secret passages everywhere, as a noble age has never possessed them, especially passages to the labyrinth of unfinished cultures and to every semi-barbarism that ever existed on earth; and insofar as the most considerable part of human culture so far was semi-barbarism, this "historical sense" almost means the sense and instinct for everything, the taste and tongue for everything: whereby it immediately proves to be an *ignoble* sense. For instance we enjoy Homer again: perhaps it is our most fortunate advantage that we know how to taste Homer, whom people of a noble culture (say the French of the seventeenth century, like Saint-Évremond,[10] who reproaches him for *esprit vaste*,[11] and even its conclusion, Voltaire) do not and did not easily assimilate—whom they scarcely allowed themselves to enjoy. The very definite Yes and No of their palate, their ever-ready nausea, their hesitating reserve toward everything foreign, their fear of the poor taste of even a lively curiosity, and generally that unwillingness of every noble and self-sufficient culture to admit to itself a new desire, a dissatisfaction with its own, an admiration of something foreign: all this positions and disposes them unfavorably toward even the best things in the world that are not their property or *could* not become their spoils—and no sense is less incomprehensible to such people than just this historical sense and its obsequious plebeian curiosity. It is no different with Shakespeare, this amazing Spanish-Moorish-Saxon synthesis of tastes at whom an ancient Athenian friend of Aeschylus would have laughed or angered himself half to death: but we—embrace precisely this wild profusion of colors, this confusion of what is most delicate, most crude and most artificial with a secret familiarity and cordiality, we enjoy him as the artistic refinement saved up just for us, and so we do not allow the repulsive odors and the proximity of the English rabble in which Shakespeare's art and taste dwell to bother us any more than on the Chiaja of Naples: where we make our way with all our senses, enchanted and willing, however much the sewer stench of the rabble neighborhoods is in the air.[12] We human beings of "historical sense": we also have our virtues as such, it cannot be denied—we are unpretentious, selfless, modest, courageous, full of self-overcoming, full of devotion, very grateful, very patient, very accommodating:—for all that perhaps we are not very "tasteful." Let us finally admit to ourselves: what is hardest for us human beings of the "historical sense" to grasp, to feel, to taste again and love again: what at bottom finds us prejudiced and almost hostile is precisely that perfection and recent ripening of every culture and art, that which is genuinely noble in works and human beings, their moment of smooth sea and halcyon self-sufficiency, the gold and coldness shown by all things that have perfected themselves. Perhaps our great virtue of the historical sense is necessarily opposed to *good* taste, at least to the very best taste, and we are able to reproduce in ourselves only poorly, only haltingly, only by force these small, brief and highest serendipities and transfigurations of human life, as they light up occasionally here and there:

those moments and marvels when a great force voluntarily halted in front of the immeasurable and the boundless—when a superabundance of subtle delight in sudden restraint and petrifaction, in standing still and placing oneself firmly on still trembling ground was enjoyed. *Moderation* is foreign to us, let us admit it to ourselves; our thrill is this very thrill of the infinite, the unmeasured. Like the rider on a steed champing to move on, we drop the reins before the infinite, we modern human beings, we semi-barbarians—and are only in *our* bliss, where we also most of all—*are in danger.*

225

Whether hedonism, or pessimism, or utilitarianism, or eudaimonism: all these ways of thinking that measure the value of things according to *pleasure* and *pain*, that is according to concomitant states and secondary factors, are foreground ways of thinking and naïvetés on which anyone who is conscious of *formative* forces and an artist's conscience will look down not without scorn, nor without compassion. Compassion for *you!* of course that is not compassion as you mean it: this is not compassion for social "plight," for "society" and its sick and injured, for the depraved and the broken from the start as they lie on the ground around us; still less is it compassion for the grumbling, oppressed, rebellious slave strata who yearn for dominance—which they call "freedom." *Our* compassion is a higher, more farsighted compassion:—we see how *the human* is becoming smaller, how *you* are making it smaller!—and there are moments when we regard precisely *your* compassion with an indescribable anxiety, when we resist this compassion—when we find your seriousness more dangerous than any kind of frivolity. You want, if possible—and there is no "if possible" more insane than this—*to abolish suffering*; and we?—it seems as though *we* would prefer to have it even higher and worse than it ever was! Well-being as you understand it—that is not a goal, to us it seems like the *end!* A state that immediately makes humans ridiculous and contemptible—that makes their destruction *desirable!* The discipline of suffering, of *great* suffering — do you not know that only *this* discipline so far has created all the enhancements of humans? That strength-cultivating tension of the soul in misfortune, its shudder at the sight of great ruin, its inventiveness and courage in endur-ing, surviving, interpreting, exploiting misfortune, and whatever it was granted in terms of profundity, mystery, mask, spirit, cunning and greatness: — has all this not been granted through suffering, through the discipline of great suf-fering? In humans *creature* and *creator* are one: in humans there is material, fragment, excess, clay, mud, nonsense, chaos; but in humans there is also creator, shaper, hammer-hardness, spectator-divinity and seventh day: — do you understand this contrast? And that *your* compassion targets the "creature in humans," that which must be formed, broken, forged, torn, burned, melted and purified — that which must necessarily *suffer* and *should* suffer? Whereas *our* compassion — do you not grasp whom our inverse compassion targets, when it resists your compassion as the worst of all pamperings and weak-nesses? — So it's compassion *against* compassion! — But to say it again, there are higher problems than all problems of plea-sure and pain and compassion: and every philosophy that ends up only with these is a naïveté. —

226[13]

We immoralists! — This world that concerns *us,* in which *we* have to fear and to love, this almost invisible, inaudible world of subtle commanding, subtle obeying, a world of "almost" in every respect, intricate, tricky, barbed, delicate: indeed, it is well defended against clumsy spectators and intimate curios-ity! We are spun into a harsh yarn and shirt of duties and *can-not* get out — in this we are "human beings of duty," we too! Occasionally, it is true, we dance in our "chains" and between our "swords"; more often, no less true, we gnash our teeth and feel impatient about all the mysterious harshness of our fate. But do what we will: the oafs and appearances speak against

us, "those are human beings *without* duty"—we always have
the oafs and appearances against us!

227[14]

Honesty, supposing that this is our virtue from which we cannot get away, we free spirits—well then, we want to work on it
with all our malice and love and never tire of "perfecting"
ourselves in *our* virtue, the one that is left us: may its glow
someday lie upon this aging culture and its dull, dismal seriousness like a gilded blue mocking evening light! And if someday our honesty grows tired and sighs and stretches her limbs
and finds us to be too hard and wants to have it better, lighter,
tenderer, like a pleasant vice: we will stay *hard*, we last Stoics!
and to help we will send her every manner of devilry we have
in us—our disgust with clumsiness and what is not-quite, our
"*nitimur in vetitum*,"[15] our adventurer's courage, our sly and
pampered curiosity, our finest, stealthiest, most spiritual will
to power and world-overcoming that greedily roams and rev-
els throughout all the realms of the future—let us come to
the aid of our "God" with all our "devils"! It is probable that
in doing so we will be misjudged and mistaken: what does it
matter! People will say: "their 'honesty'—that is their devilry
and nothing more!" what does it matter! And even if they
were right! Were not all gods hitherto rechristened devils who
were later pronounced holy in this way? And ultimately what
do we know about ourselves? And what the spirit that leads us
wants to be *called*? (it is a matter of names.) And how many
spirits we harbor? Our honesty, we free spirits—let us make
sure it does not become our vanity, our finery and pomp, our
limit, our stupidity! Every virtue tends toward stupidity, every
stupidity toward virtue; "stupid to the point of holiness" they
say in Russia—let us make sure that in the end we do not
turn into saints and bores out of honesty! Is life not a hundred
times too short—to be bored with it? We would have to believe in eternal life in order to . . .

228

I will have to be forgiven for discovering that all moral philosophy so far has been boring and belongs among the soporifics—and that "virtue" for me has been hampered by nothing so much as by this *boringness* of its advocates; although I do not mean to deny their general utility. It matters much that as few people as possible think about morality—consequently it matters *very* much that morality not become interesting someday! But no need to worry! Today things are still the same as always: I see no one in Europe who would have (or *give*) the sense that thinking about morality could be done in a way that is dangerous, tricky, and seductive—that *disaster* could be involved! Just look, for example, at the indefatigable, unavoidable English utilitarians as they clumsily and honorably wander around here and there in the footsteps of Bentham (a Homeric simile says it more clearly), even as he himself had wandered in the footsteps of the honorable Helvétius (no, this was not a dangerous man, this Helvétius![16]). No new thought, nothing by way of a subtle version and wrinkle of an old thought, not even a real history of what had been thought before: an *impossible* literature on the whole, unless one knew how to sour the dough with a bit of malice. You see, that old English vice called *cant*,[17] which is *moral tartuffery*, crept into these moralists as well (they simply have to be read with ulterior thoughts, if they even *have* to be read—), this time in the new form of scientism; nor is there any lack of secret resistance to bites of conscience, from which, as is only fair, a race of former Puritans will suffer whenever it engages scientifically with morality. (Is a moralist not the opposite of a Puritan? That is, a thinker who treats morality as questionable, as worthy of question marks, in short as a problem? Shouldn't moralizing be—immoral?) In the end they all want *English* morality to be right: insofar as then humanity, or "the general utility" or "the happiness of the majority," no! the happiness *of England* is best served; they want to prove to themselves with

all their might that the striving for *English* happiness, I mean
for *comfort* and *fashion* (and in the highest instance a seat in
Parliament) is simultaneously also the right path of virtue, indeed that whatever virtue has existed in the world so far, it has
consisted in precisely such a striving. None of all these ponderous herd animals with their upset consciences (who under-
take to champion the cause of egoism as the cause of the general welfare—) wants to know or smell anything of the fact
that the "general welfare" is no ideal, no goal, no in any way
graspable concept, but only an emetic—that what is fair for
one absolutely *cannot* be fair for another, that the demand for
one morality for everyone is an impairment of precisely the
higher human beings, that there is a *rank order* between human beings and consequently between moralities as well. This
is a modest and thoroughly mediocre kind of human being,
this Englishman, and as I said: insofar as they are boring we
cannot think highly enough of their utility. We should even
encourage them: as has been attempted in part by the following rhymes.

> Hail you sturdy push-cart drivers,
> "Give us more, we like it" strivers,
> Ever stiff in mind and knee,
> Uninspired, all humor lacking,
> Mediocre beyond tracking,
> *Sans genie et sans esprit!*[18,19]

229[20]

In those late ages that have a right to be proud of their humanity there is so much fear, so much *superstition* remaining of the
"wild cruel beast" whose conquest constitutes the very pride of
that more humane age, that even palpable truths go unspoken
for centuries, as if by conspiracy, because they have the appearance of helping to bring back to life that wild beast that
was finally killed off. Maybe I am risking something when I
allow such a truth to escape me: may others recapture it and

give it enough "milk of the pious way of thinking"[21] that it lies
still and forgotten in its old corner. —We should rethink cruelty and open our eyes; we should finally learn to be impatient,
so that such immodest, fat errors no longer wander around virtuously and impudently, like those for instance that have been
nurtured about tragedy by ancient and modern philosophers.
Almost everything we call "higher culture" is based on the
spiritualization and deepening of *cruelty*—this is my proposition; that "wild beast" has not been killed off at all, it lives, it
thrives, it has merely—deified itself. What constitutes the
painful lust of tragedy is cruelty; what has a pleasing effect in
so-called tragic pity,[22] and at bottom even in everything sublime all the way up to the highest and most tender shudders of
metaphysics, gets its sweetness only when the ingredient of
cruelty is mixed in. The Roman in the arena, the Christian in
the raptures of the cross, the Spaniard at the sight of auto-da-fés
and bullfights, today's Japanese who flock to tragedy, the Parisian suburban laborer who is homesick for bloody revolutions,
the lady Wagnerian who abandons her will and lets *Tristan
and Isolde* "wash over her" —what they all enjoy and are eager to drink up with mysterious ardor are the spicy potions of
the great Circe "cruelty." Here of course we must chase away
the clumsy psychology of days gone by, that knew nothing better to teach about cruelty than that it originated at the sight of
another's suffering: there is an abundant, superabundant pleasure
also in one's own suffering, in making oneself suffer—and
wherever someone lets himself be persuaded to self-denial in
the *religious* sense or to self-mutilation, as among Phoenicians
and ascetics, or generally to desensualization, decarnalization,
contrition, to Puritanical spasms of penitence, to vivisections
of the conscience and to Pascalian *sacrifizio dell'intelletto*,[23]
then he is secretly lured and pushed forward by his cruelty, by
that dangerous awe of cruelty directed *against oneself*. Finally
let us consider that even the knowing one, by forcing his spirit
to know *against* the inclination of his spirit and often enough
also against the wishes of his heart—namely by saying No

when he would like to affirm, love, adore—is reigning as an artist and a transfigurer of cruelty; indeed, every time we take something deeply and thoroughly it is a violation, a wanting-to-hurt the fundamental will of the spirit, that incessantly strives for appearances and surfaces—even in every wanting-to-know there is a drop of cruelty.

230[24]

Perhaps what I mean here by a "fundamental will of the spirit" is not readily understood: permit me an explanation.—The commanding something that is called "the spirit" by the people wants to be master in and around itself and to feel like the master: it has the will to simplicity out of multiplicity, a binding, subduing, dominating and truly masterful will. Its needs and capacities here are the same as those physiologists posit for everything that lives, grows and multiplies. The power of the spirit to appropriate the foreign reveals itself in a strong inclination to assimilate the new to the old, to simplify the manifold, and to overlook or repulse whatever is utterly contradictory: just as it arbitrarily stresses, selects and forges into shape certain features and lines of the foreign, of every piece of "external world." Its intention in all this is to incorporate new "experience," to classify new things under old classifications—thus growth itself; more specifically, the *feeling* of growth, the feeling of increased power. An apparently opposite drive serves this same will, a suddenly erupting resolution to ignorance, to arbitrary locking up, a closing of its windows, an inner No-saying to this or any thing, a do-not-approach-me, a kind of defensive state against much that is knowable, a complacency with darkness, with the closed-in horizon, a Yes-saying and approval of ignorance: as all this is necessary depending on the degree of its appropriating force, its "digestive force" to speak meta-phorically—and indeed "the spirit" most resembles a stomach. What belongs here likewise is the occasional will of the spirit to deceive itself, perhaps with a bold hunch to the effect that things are thus and *not* thus, that people just accept things to be this way or that, a pleasure in all uncertainty and ambiguity, a jubilating self-enjoyment of the arbitrary narrowness and secrecy of a corner, of what is all too close, of the foreground, of things magnified and made smaller, of things shifted and embellished, a self-enjoyment of the arbitrariness of all these expressions of power. Finally what belongs here is that not inconsiderable readiness of the spirit to deceive other spirits and to pretend in front of them, that constant pressure and stress of a creating, shaping, and malleable force: in this the spirit enjoys its multiplicity of masks and craftiness, it also enjoys the feeling of its security in them — it is in fact best defended and hidden by precisely these Protean arts! — *This* will to appearance, to simplification, to masks, to cloaks, in short to the surface — since every surface is a cloak — is *countered* by that sublime inclination of the knowing one who treats and *wants* to treat things profoundly, manifoldly, thoroughly: as a kind of cruelty of the intellectual conscience and taste that every brave thinker will recognize in himself assuming, as it should be, that he has hardened and sharpened his eye for himself long enough, and that he is also accustomed to harsh discipline and harsh words. He will say "there is something cruel in the tendency of my spirit": — just let the virtuous and the kindly try to talk him out of it! In fact, it would sound nicer if instead of cruelty people would just accuse us of "extravagant honesty," and whisper about us and eulogize us for that instead — we free, *very* free spirits: — and maybe someday *this* will be our — posthumous fame? Meanwhile — for this will still take some time — we ourselves surely are least inclined to don such moral word tinsel and tassels: our entire work so far spoils precisely this taste and its merry opulence for us. These are beautiful, gleaming, clinking, festive words: honesty, love of truth, love of wisdom, sacrifice for knowledge, heroism of truthfulness — there is something in them that makes a person swell with pride. But we hermits and marmots have long ago persuaded ourselves in the complete secrecy of our hermit conscience that even this worthy word-pomp belongs to the old finery, flotsam and gold dust of lies of unconscious human vanity, and that even beneath such flattering colors and painting-over, the terrible basic text of *homo natura*[25] must be recognized again. To translate humankind back into nature; to master the many vain and gushing interpretations and connotations that have so far been scribbled and painted over that eternal basic text *homo natura*; to ensure that the human being hence-forth stands before human beings even as it stands today, hard-ened by the discipline of science, before the *other* nature, with undaunted Oedipus eyes and sealed Oedipus ears, deaf to the luring songs of old metaphysical bird-catchers who have all too long fluted in their ears: "you are more! you are higher! you are of a different descent!" — that may be a strange and insane task, but it is a *task* — who would deny it! Why did we choose it, this insane task? Or to ask differently: "why knowl-edge at all?" — Everyone will ask us about that. And we, pressed in this manner, we who have already asked ourselves the same question hundreds of times — we have found and find no bet-ter answer . . . .

231[26]

Learning transforms us, it does what all nourishment does that also does not merely "preserve" — : as physiologists know. But at the bottom of us, way "down there," there is in-deed something unteachable, a granite of spiritual *fatum*,[27] of predetermined decision and answer to predetermined selected questions. In every cardinal problem an immutable "this is I" can be heard; about man and woman, for instance, a thinker cannot relearn but only finish learning — only discover to the end what about this is "established" in him already. At times we find certain solutions to problems that inspire strong faith even in *us*; perhaps henceforth we call them our "convictions." Later on — we see in them only the footsteps of our self-knowledge, signposts to the problem that we *are* — more cor-rectly to the great stupidity that we are, to our spiritual *fatum*, to what is *unteachable* way "down there." — After the abundant niceness I have just extended to myself, perhaps I will more easily be permitted to announce a few truths about "woman in itself,"[28] assuming that it is known from the outset now how very much these are only — *my* truths. —

232[29]

Women want to become independent: and so they are beginning to enlighten men about "woman in itself" — *this* belongs among the worst advances in the general increasing *ugliness* of Europe. After all, who knows what all these clumsy attempts of female scientism and self-exposure will have to bring to light! Woman has so much reason for shame; in woman there is hidden so much that is pedantic, superficial, schoolmarmish, such petty arrogance, petty licentiousness and immodesty — just study her interaction with children! — and so far this was at bottom best repressed and restrained by her *fear* of man. Woe to us when the "eternally-boring in woman"[30] — she has a wealth of it! — finally ventures forth! when she thoroughly and fundamentally begins to unlearn her prudence and art, that of grace, play, chasing away worries, lightening burdens and taking things lightly, and her subtle talent for pleasant desires! Even now female voices are being heard that, holy Aristophanes! are frightening, threatening with medical explicitness what first and last women *want* from men. Is it not in the worst taste when women embark on being scientific in this manner? We were fortunate that so far enlightenment has been a man's concern, a man's talent — we remained "among ourselves" in this; and whatever women have written about "woman," in the end we should reserve a healthy suspicion as to whether they actually *want* enlightenment about themselves — and *can* want it . . . . When a woman does this, if she is not looking for some new *finery* for herself — I do think that dressing up is part of the Eternal Feminine? — well then, she is trying to arouse fear of herself: — perhaps she wants to dominate. But she does not *want* truth: what do women care about truth! From the start nothing is more foreign, repulsive,

and hostile to woman than truth — her great art is the lie, her
highest concern is appearance and beauty. Let us admit it, we
men: we honor and love precisely *this* art and *this* instinct in
women: we who have it hard like to get some relief by associating with beings under whose hands, looks and tender follies
our own seriousness, our gravity and profundity almost seem
like foolishness to us. Finally I pose the question: has a woman
herself ever acknowledged the profundity of a female mind, or
the justice of a female heart? And is it not true on the whole
that "woman" so far has been despised most by women themselves — and not in the least by us? — We men wish that
woman would not continue to compromise herself by enlightenment: just as it was male care and consideration of women
when the Church decreed: *mulier taceat in ecclesia!*[31] It happened for the good of women when Napoleon made it clear to
the all-too-eloquent Madame de Staël: *mulier taceat in politicis!*[32] — and I think it is a real friend of women who today
calls out to women:[33] *mulier taceat de muliere!*[34]

233[35]

It betrays corruption of the instincts — not to mention
that it betrays bad taste — when a woman falls back on Madame Roland or Madame de Staël or Monsieur George Sand,
as if this proved anything in *favor* of "woman in itself."
Among men the aforementioned are the three *comical* women
in themselves — nothing more! — and precisely the best involuntary *counter-arguments* against emancipation and female
self-aggrandizement.

234[36]

Stupidity in the kitchen: woman as cook: the horrifying
thoughtlessness that accompanies the feeding of the family
and the master of the house! Woman does not understand what
food *means*: and yet she wants to be the cook! If woman were
a thinking creature, then as cook for thousands of years she
would have had to discover the greatest physiological facts, as

well as gain possession of the art of healing! Because of bad cooks—and the complete lack of reason in the kitchen, the development of human beings has been delayed longest and impaired most: even today things are scarcely better. A speech for young ladies.

235

There are locutions and coups of the spirit, there are epigrams, a small handful of words in which an entire culture, an entire society is suddenly crystallized. Madame de Lambert's[37] casual remark to her son is one of these: *"mon ami, ne vous permettez jamais que de folies, qui vous feront grand plaisir"*:[38] —incidentally the most maternal and prudent word ever addressed to a son.

236

What Dante and Goethe believed about woman—the former when he sang *"ella guardava suso, ed io in lei,"*[39] the latter when he translated it "the Eternal Feminine lifts us *on high*"[40] —: I do not doubt that any nobler woman would resist this belief, for *this* is exactly what she believes about the Eternal Masculine . . .

237

SEVEN LITTLE MAXIMS ABOUT WOMEN[41]

Deepest boredom too takes flight, once a man crawls to our side!

* *

Age, alas! and science give weaker virtue strength to live.

* *

Dress in black and say no word makes a woman seem —assured.

* *

Whom to thank for my success? God!—and tailoring finesse.

* *

Young: a blossom-covered lair. Old: you'll find a dragon
   there.

* *

Noble name, upright carriage, man as well: *there's* my[42]
   marriage!

* *

Where meaning's rich, words are poor—she-mule walks a
   slippery floor!

237{a}[43]

Women have so far been treated by men like birds that strayed
down to them from some height: like something finer, more
vulnerable, wilder, stranger, sweeter and more soulful—but
like something that has to be locked up so that it does not fly
away.

238

To be mistaken about the fundamental problem of "man and
woman," to deny the most abysmal antagonism and the necessity of an eternally hostile tension between them, to perhaps
dream here of equal rights, equal education, equal claims and
obligations: this is a *typical* sign of shallow-mindedness, and
a thinker who[44] has proven to be shallow in this dangerous
place—shallow in instinct!—deserves to be seen as altogether
suspicious, even more, as exposed, as revealed: he will probably be too "short" for all the fundamental questions of life,
future life as well, and not be able to achieve *any* depths. On
the other hand, a man of depth in his spirit and in his desires, who also has that depth of benevolence that is capable of
strictness and harshness and that is easily mistaken for them,
can only ever think about woman in an *oriental* manner: he
must conceive of woman as possession, as property that can be
locked up, as something predestined for service and fulfilling
itself as such—for this he must base himself on Asia's tremendous reason, on Asia's superiority of instinct: just as the Greeks

did in the past, these best heirs and disciples of Asia who, as is well known, during a period of *increasing* culture and expansiveness of power from Homer to the time of Pericles became gradually *stricter* toward woman, in brief, more oriental. *How* necessary, *how* logical, even *how* humanly desirable this was: we should privately reflect on this!

239[45]

In no age more than our age has the weaker sex been treated with such respect on the part of men — this belongs to our democratic tendency and basic taste, just like disrespect for the elderly —: is it any wonder that this respect is immediately abused? People want more, they learn to make demands, in the end they find that obligatory modicum of respect nearly insulting, and they would prefer competition for rights, indeed even an all-out fight: enough, woman is losing her shame. Let us immediately add that she is also losing her taste. She is unlearning her *fear* of man: but the woman who "unlearns fearing" sacrifices her most feminine instincts. Fair enough that woman dares to step up when the fear-inspiring quality of man or, more precisely, the *man* in man is no longer wanted and cultivated, and also understandable enough; what is harder to grasp is that precisely in so doing — woman degenerates. This is happening today: make no mistake about it! Wherever the industrial spirit has triumphed over the military and aristocratic spirit, woman now strives for the economic and legal self-sufficiency of a clerk: "woman as clerk" is inscribed on the gate of emerging modern society. By seizing new rights, striving to be "master" and writing "progress" for woman on her flags and banners in this way, she succeeds with terrifying clarity in the opposite: *woman is regressing*. Since the French Revolution the influence of woman in Europe has *decreased* in proportion to the increase in her rights and claims; and the "emancipation[46] of woman," to the extent that it is demanded and promoted by women themselves (and not by shallow-minded males) turns out to be an odd symptom of the increased weakening and blunting of the most feminine instincts. There is *stupidity* in this movement, an almost masculine stupidity of which a well-adjusted woman—who is always a prudent woman—should be thoroughly ashamed. To lose one's sense for the ground on which becoming victorious is most certain; to neglect practicing one's genuine skill in weaponry; letting oneself go in front of men, perhaps even "to the point of writing books," when earlier one acted with discipline and subtle, cunning humility; to work with virtuous audacity against a man's belief in a *hidden*, fundamentally different ideal in woman, in some kind of Eternal-and-Necessary-Feminine; to emphatically and loquaciously talk men out of the fact that woman should be kept, maintained, protected, and indulged like a delicate, strangely wild and often pleasant pet; the clumsy and indignant gathering together of everything slave-like and serf-like that the position of woman has had so far in the order of society, and still has (as if slavery were a counter-argument and not instead a condition of every higher culture, every elevation of culture):—what does all this mean if not a disintegration of feminine instincts, a defeminization? Of course there are enough idiotic friends of females and corrupters of women among the scholarly asses of the male sex, who advise women to defeminize themselves in this manner and to imitate all the stupidities that afflict the "man" in Europe, and European "manliness"—those who would bring woman down to the level of "universal education," perhaps even to reading newspapers and to politicking. Here and there people even want to make freethinkers and literati out of women: as if a woman without piety were not something totally repugnant or ridiculous to a profound and godless man—; almost everywhere her nerves are being ruined by the most pathological and dangerous of all kinds of music (our most recent German music), and every day she is being made more hysterical and less capable of her first and ultimate calling, that of bearing strong children. Generally speaking people want to "cultivate" her more and, as they say, make the "weaker sex" *strong* through culture: as if history did not teach us as urgently as possible that "cultivation" of humanity and weakening—that is weakening, splintering, afflicting of the *strength of will* always go hand in hand, and that the most powerful and most influential women in the world (most recently even the mother of Napoleon) owed their power and ascendancy over men to their strength of will—and not to their school teachers!—What inspires respect and often enough fear of woman is her *nature*, which is "more natural" than that of man, her genuine predatory, cunning suppleness, her tiger claws beneath the glove, her naïveté in egoism, her ineducability and inner savageness, the incomprehensibility, vastness, and roaming of her desires and virtues . . . . . . Despite all fear, what arouses compassion for this dangerous and beautiful cat "woman" is that she seems to be more suffering, more vulnerable, more in need of love and more doomed to disappointment than any animal. Fear and compassion: so far men have stood before women with these emotions, always with one foot in tragedy that tears to pieces while it delights—. What? And this is now supposed to come to an end? And the *disenchanting* of woman is in the works? Rendering woman boring is slowly coming to pass? Oh Europe! Europe! We know the animal with horns that has always been most attractive to you, that threatens you with danger again and again![47] Your old fable could one day become "history"—one day a tremendous stupidity could assume mastery over you and carry you away! And beneath it no god is concealed, no! only an "idea," a "modern idea"! . . . . .

Part Eight

Peoples and Fatherlands

240[1]

I heard it again for the first time — Richard Wagner's overture to the *Meistersinger*: this is a magnificent, ornate, heavy and late art that has the pride of presupposing two centuries of music as still living in order to be understood: — it does honor to the Germans that such pride did not miscalculate! What morsels and forces, what seasons and climates are not mixed together here! First it strikes us as old-fashioned, then foreign, harsh and overly young, it is just as capricious as pompously traditional, it is not seldom roguish, and more often rude and crude — it has fire and bravado and at the same time the loose, dun skin of fruits that ripen too late. Broad and full it flows: and suddenly a moment of inexplicable hesitation, like a gap springing up between cause and effect, a pressure that makes us dreamy, almost a nightmarish pressure — but already the old stream of contentment spreads itself wide once more, contentment of every kind, with happiness old and new, *very much* including the happiness of the artist with himself, that he does not wish to conceal, his astonished, happy sharing of his knowledge of the mastery of the methods he applies here, new and newly acquired, untested artistic methods, as he seems to reveal to us. All in all no beauty, no south, nothing of the southern refined brightness of the sky, nothing of grace, no dance, scarcely a will to logic; even a certain clumsiness that is underscored as if the artist wanted to say to us: "that is part of

my intention"; a clumsy costume, something arbitrarily barbarian and solemn, a flurry of scholarly and venerable treasures and lace; something German in the best and worst sense
of the word, something manifold, amorphous and inexhaustible in a German way; a certain German powerfulness and
superabundance of the soul which is not afraid to conceal itself beneath the refinement of decline — that perhaps only
feels most comfortable there; a real, genuine token of the
German soul, that is simultaneously young and outdated,
over-ripe and still overly rich in future. This kind of music
best expresses what I think of the Germans: they are of the
day before yesterday and the day after tomorrow — *they still
have no today.*

241

We "good Europeans": even we have hours when we permit
ourselves a hearty dose of fatherlandishness, a stumble and
relapse into old favorites and parochialisms — I just provided a
sample of this — hours of national flushes,[2] patriotic palpita-
tions and all manner of other old-fashioned emotional overflows. Clumsier spirits than we might take longer periods of
time to finish what for us is limited to hours and plays out in
hours, it might take some a half year, others half a lifetime
depending on the speed and power with which they digest
and "metabolize." Indeed, I could imagine dull, sluggish races
that even in our speedy Europe would require a half century
to overcome such atavistic attacks of fatherlandishness and
sod-hugging and return to reason, that is to say, to "good Eu-
ropeanism." And while I am digressing on this possibility, it so
happens that I become an ear-witness to a conversation between two old "patriots" — apparently they were both hard of
hearing and therefore spoke all the louder. "*That one* thinks
and knows as much about philosophy as a farmer or a frater-
nity student" — said the first — : "he's still innocent. But what
does it matter today! This is the age of the masses: they lie on
their bellies before everything that's massive. And the same

goes *in politicis*.[3] To them a statesman is 'great' if he builds them a new Tower of Babel, or some monstrosity of empire and power: — what does it matter that those of us who are more cautious and reserved won't let go yet of the old belief that it's the great thought alone that gives greatness to a deed and a cause. Suppose a statesman put his people in the position of having to conduct 'great politics'[4] from now on, for which they are by nature poorly equipped and prepared: so that for the sake of a new dubious mediocrity they had to sacrifice their old and secure virtues — suppose a statesman condemned his people generally to 'politicizing,' whereas up until now they had better things to do and think about, and deep down in their souls they couldn't rid themselves of a cautious disgust for the unrest, emptiness and noisy, infernal quarreling of the genuinely politicizing peoples:[5] — suppose such a statesman were to goad the slumbering passions and cravings of his people, to make their former shyness and enjoyment of standing aside into a stain, to make their cosmopolitanism and secret infinity into a fault, devalue their most heartfelt inclinations, turn their conscience inside out, make their spirit narrow, their taste 'national' — what! a statesman who would do all this, for whom his people would have to atone for all future time, if they had any future, such a statesman is supposed to be *great*?" "Without a doubt!" replied the other old patriot emphatically: "otherwise he would not have been *able to do it*! Maybe it was madness to want something like this? But maybe everything great was only madness in the beginning!" — "Abuse of words!" his interlocutor shouted back at him: — "strong! strong! strong and mad! *Not* great!" — The old men had become visibly heated as they yelled their "truths" into each other's faces; but I, in my happiness and Beyond, considered how someone stronger will soon become master over the strong; and also that there is a compensation for the spiritual flattening of one people, namely in the deepening of another. —[6]

242[7]

Call it "civilization"[8] or "humanization" or "progress," with
which we try today to identify what is distinctive about Europeans; or without praising or blaming call it simply by a political
formula and say the *democratic* movement of Europe: behind all
the moral and political foregrounds to which such formulas
point a tremendous *physiological* process is taking place and
increasingly gaining momentum — the process whereby Europeans are becoming similar, their growing detachment from
the conditions under which climate- and class-bound races
originate, their increasing independence from every *determi-
nate* milieu, that for centuries has attempted to inscribe itself
with the same demands into souls and bodies — hence the
slow rise of an essentially supra-national and nomadic type
of human being that, physiologically speaking, possesses a
maximum of skill and power for adaptation as its typical distinction. This process of the *developing European*, which can
be retarded by great relapses in tempo but perhaps for the
same reason gains and grows in terms of vehemence — the
storm and stress[9,10] of the "national feeling" that is still raging
today belongs here, likewise the anarchism that is just coming
up —: this process probably leads to results that its naïve sup-
porters and eulogists, the apostles of "modern ideas," would
have least expected. The same new conditions under which on
average a leveling and mediocritization of humanity will
emerge — a useful, industrious, multi-purpose and skillful
herd animal human — are suited in the highest degree to give
rise to exceptional humans of the most dangerous and charis-
matic quality. That is, whereas the power of adaptation that
tries out ever-changing conditions and begins a new work
with each generation, almost with each decade, does not at
all make possible the *powerfulness* of the type; whereas the
overall impression of such future Europeans will be that of
diverse, garrulous, weak-willed and extremely deployable
workers who *require* a master and a commander as much as

their daily bread; whereas therefore the democratization of
Europe is leading to the production of a type that is prepared
in the subtlest sense for *slavery*: therefore in individual and
exceptional cases the *strong* human being will have to turn
out stronger and richer than he has perhaps ever turned
out—thanks to the absence of prejudice in his schooling,
and thanks to the tremendous variety of practice, art and
mask. What I mean is: the democratization of Europe is simultaneously an involuntary arrangement for the cultivation
of *tyrants*—that word understood in every sense, including
the most spiritual.

243

I hear with pleasure that our sun has embarked on a rapid
course toward the constellation of *Hercules*: and I hope that
the human beings on this earth will do the same as the sun.
And we at the forefront, we good Europeans!—

244[11]

There was a time when people were accustomed to calling the
Germans "profound" as a distinction: now, when the most successful type of the new Germanity lusts after quite different
honors and perhaps misses the "dashingness" of everything
that has profundity, the doubt is almost timely and patriotic
as to whether people may have deceived themselves in the past
with that praise: specifically, whether German profundity at
bottom is not something different and worse—something
that, thank God, we are on the verge of successfully getting
rid of. So let us make an attempt to rethink German profundity: we need nothing more for this than a bit of vivisection of
the German soul.—Above all the German soul is manifold,
of different origins, more pieced together and piled on than
actually built: this is because of its descent. A German who
had the temerity to exclaim "two souls, alas! are dwelling in
my breast"[12] would seriously violate the truth or, more cor-
rectly, would fall short of the truth by many souls. As a people

of the most monstrous mixing and blending of races, perhaps even with a preponderance of the pre-Aryan element, as "people of the middle" in every sense of the word, the Germans are more incomprehensible, comprehensive, contradictory, unknown, unpredictable, surprising, even more horrifying than other peoples are to themselves:—they elude *definition* and already for that reason are the despair of the French. It characterizes the Germans that the question "what is German?" never dies out for them. Kotzebue certainly knew his Germans well enough: "we've been recognized!" they cried out to him jubilantly—but *Sand* also thought he knew them.[13] Jean Paul[14] knew what he was doing when he angrily denounced Fichte's mendacious but patriotic flatteries and exaggerations—but it is probable that Goethe[15] thought otherwise about the Germans than Jean Paul[16] did, even if he acknowledged that he was right with respect to Fichte.[17] What did Goethe really think about the Germans?[18]—But there were many things around him that he never spoke to clearly, and his life long he knew how to maintain a subtle silence:—he probably had good reasons to do so. What is certain is that it was not the "Wars of Liberation" that caused him to perk up, no more so than the French Revolution—no, the event for whose sake he *rethought* his *Faust* and in fact the whole problem of being human was the appearance of Napoleon. There are words of Goethe in which he denounces as if from abroad, with impatient harshness, what Germans embrace with pride: the famous German *Gemüt*[19] he once defined as "indulgence toward the weaknesses of others and oneself."[20] Was he wrong?—what distinguishes Germans is that people are seldom completely wrong about them. The German soul contains passages and inter-passages, there are caves, hideouts and dungeons in it; its disorder has much of the charm of mystery about it; and Germans know the secret paths to chaos. And just as every thing loves its likeness, so too Germans love the clouds and all that is unclear, becoming, twilit, damp and overcast: whatever is uncertain, unformed, shifting, growing in any way they feel to be "profound." Germans themselves *are* not, they *become*, they "develop." "Development" is therefore the real German find and coup in the great realm of philosophical formulas: — a ruling concept that, allied with German beer and German music, is working on Germanizing all of Europe. Foreigners stand amazed and enthralled before the riddles posed to them by the contradictory nature at the bottom of the German soul (which Hegel put into systematic form and Richard Wagner ultimately even set to music). "Good-natured and devious" — such a pairing, though nonsensical applied to any other people, is unfortunately too often justified in Germany: just try living for a time among Swabians! The ponderousness of the German scholar, his social boorishness corresponds alarmingly well with an inner tightrope-walking and easy boldness that all gods have learned to fear by now. Anyone who wants a demonstration of the "German soul" *ad oculos*[21] need only look into German taste, German arts and customs: what boorish indifference to "taste"! How the noblest and the vilest stand next to each other there! How disorderly and rich is this entire household of the soul! The German *drags* his soul; he drags everything he experiences. He digests his events badly, he is never "finished" with them; German profundity is often only a hard and sluggish "digestion." And just as all the chronically ill, all dyspeptics have a tendency to seek comfort, Germans love "frankness" and "uprightness": how *comfortable* it is to be frank and upright! — Today it is possibly the most dangerous and successful disguise known by Germans, this confiding, accommodating, cards-on-the-table aspect of German *honesty*: it is their actual Mephistophelian art, and with it they can "still go far"![22] The German lets himself go, looks at you with those true, blue, vacant German eyes — and right away foreigners mistake him for his dressing gown! — What I mean is: let "German profundity" be what it may — entirely between us we perhaps allow ourselves to laugh about it? — we do well to honor its appearance and good name into the future, and not trade our old reputation as a people of profundity too cheaply for Prussian "dashingness" and Berlin wit and sand. It is prudent for a people to make themselves seem profound, awkward, good-natured, honest and imprudent, to *allow* themselves to seem so: it could even be—profound! Finally: one should live up to one's name—we are not for nothing called the "*tiusche*" folk, the *Täusche*-folk . . .[23]

245

The "good old" days are gone, they sang themselves out with Mozart:—how fortunate are *we* that his rococo still speaks to us, that his "good company," his tender enthusiasms, his childish delight in things Chinese and in frills, his courtesy of the heart, his longing for delicate, enamored, dancing and blissfully tearful people, his faith in the south may still appeal to some *vestige* in us! Oh, this too will be gone someday!—but who could doubt that our understanding and taste for Beethoven will be gone even sooner!—he who was after all only the fading of a transitional style and a stylistic breech and *not*, like Mozart, the fading of a great centuries-long European taste. Beethoven is the interim episode of an old brittle soul that is constantly breaking and a future overly young soul that is constantly *arriving*; that twilight of eternal loss and eternally extravagant hope lies on his music—the same light in which Europe was bathed when it dreamed with Rousseau, when it danced around the freedom tree of the Revolution and finally almost came to worship Napoleon. But how quickly now precisely *this* feeling pales, how difficult even *knowledge* of this feeling is today—how foreign to our ears sounds the language of Rousseau, Schiller, Shelley, Byron, in whom *together* the same destiny of Europe found its way into words that in Beethoven knew how to sing!—Whatever German music came afterward belongs in Romanticism, that is, measured historically, in an even briefer, more fleeting, more superficial movement than was that great interlude, that transition of Europe from Rousseau to Napoleon and to the rise of democracy. Weber[24]: but today what are *Freischütz* and *Oberon to us*! Or Marschner's[25] *Hans Heiling* and *Vampyr*! Or even Wagner's *Tannhäuser*! That is music that has died out, even if it is not yet forgotten music. This entire music of Romanticism incidentally was not noble enough to assert itself anywhere except in the theater and before crowds; from the start it was second-class music of little regard among real musicians. It was different with Felix Mendelssohn, that halcyonic master who was quickly revered and just as quickly forgotten on account of his lighter, purer, more favored soul: as a beautiful *interlude* of German music. But as concerns Robert Schumann, who took things seriously and from the start also was taken seriously — he was the last to found a school — : is it not a good fortune among us today, and a relief and a liberation, that precisely this Schumann romanticism has been overcome? Schumann, who fled into the "Saxon Switzerland" of his soul, half Wertherish, half Jean Paulish in disposition, certainly not Beethovenish! certainly not Byronish! — his *Manfred* music is a mistake and a misunderstanding to the point of being an injustice — Schumann with his taste, that was at bottom a *small* taste (namely a dangerous tendency, doubly so among Germans, toward quiet lyricism and drunkardliness of feeling), always off to one side, shyly withdrawing and retreating, a noble sissy who wallowed in all kinds of anonymous happiness and pain, a kind of girl and *noli me tangere*[26] from the start: this Schumann was already a mere *German* event in music, no longer a European one, as Beethoven was, as Mozart had been to an even more encompassing extent — with him German music was threatened by its greatest danger, that of losing *the voice for the soul of Europe* and sinking to a mere fatherlandishness. —

246

— What torture are books written in German for someone who has a *third* ear! How reluctantly he stands beside the slowly revolving swamp of sounds that do not sound, of rhythms without dance that pass for a "book" among Germans! And especially the German who *reads* books! How lazily, how reluctantly, how badly he reads! How many Germans know and demand it of themselves to know that there is *art* in every good sentence — art that wants to be figured out insofar as the sentence wants to be understood! A misunderstanding about its tempo, for instance: and the sentence itself is misunderstood! To not be in doubt about the rhythmically decisive syllables, to feel the break with the all-too-rigid symmetry as deliberate and attractive, to hold up a subtle and patient ear to every *staccato* and *rubato*,[27] to guess the meaning in the sequence of vowels and diphthongs and how tenderly and richly they can color and recolor each other in succession: who among book-reading Germans has enough good will to acknowledge duties and demands such as these and to listen carefully for so much art and intention in language? In the end people simply do not "have the ear for it": and so the strongest contrasts of style go unheard and the finest artistry is *wasted* as if on the deaf. — These were my thoughts as I noticed how clumsily and cluelessly two masters in the art of prose were mistaken for one another, one whose faltering words dripped down coldly as if from the ceiling of a damp cave — he is counting on their dull sound and resounding — and another who wields his language like a flexible rapier, and from his arm to his toes feels the dangerous joy of a quivering super-sharp blade that wants to bite, hiss and slice. —

247[28]

How little German style has to do with sound and with the ears is shown by the fact that precisely our good musicians write poorly. Germans do not read aloud, for the ear, but merely for the eyes: meanwhile they have put their ears away in a drawer. Ancient people read, if they read — it happened rarely enough — aloud to themselves, and even in a loud voice; people would be surprised if someone read softly and they would secretly look for reasons. In a loud voice: that is to say, with all the swells, inflections and reversals of tone and changes in tempo in which the ancient *public* world took delight. Back then the rules of written style were the same as those of spoken style; and its rules depended in part on the amazing development and the refined requirements of the ear and the larynx, partly on the strength, endurance and power of the ancient lung. A period in the sense of the ancients is above all a physiological whole, insofar as it is encompassed in a single breath. Such periods as are found in Demosthenes and Cicero, swelling twice and subsiding twice and all within a single breath: those were pleasures for *ancient* people who knew from their own training to appreciate the rare and difficult virtue of performing such a period: — *we* really have no right to the *great* period, we moderns who are short of breath in every sense! Indeed, all of these ancients were themselves dilettantes in rhetoric, hence connoisseurs, hence critics — that is how they spurred their orators to their utmost; in the same way, in the previous century when all Italian men and women knew how to sing, virtuosity in singing (and therewith also the art of the melodic —) reached its zenith among them. In Germany, however, there was really (until quite recently, when a kind of rostrum eloquence timidly and clumsily stirred its young wings) only one genre of public and *approximately* artistic rhetoric: that which came down from the pulpit. In Germany the preacher alone knew the weight of a syllable and a word, and to what extent a sentence kept time, leapt, plunged, ran and ran out, he alone had conscience in his ears, and often enough a bad conscience: for there is no lack of reasons why Germans in particular rarely achieve excellence in rhetoric, and almost always too late. The masterpiece of German prose is therefore, viewed fairly, the masterpiece of its greatest preacher: the *Bible* has so far been the best German book. Compared with Luther's Bible almost everything else is mere "literature" — a thing that did not grow up in Germany and therefore also did not and does not grow into German hearts: the way the Bible did.

248

There are two kinds of genius: one that primarily begets and wants to beget, and another that likes to get impregnated and to give birth. And likewise there are among the peoples of genius those to whom has fallen the woman's problem of pregnancy and the secret task of forming, ripening, and completing—the Greeks for instance were a people of this kind, as were the French—; then there are others who must fertilize and become the cause of new orders of life—like the Jews, the Romans and, asking in all modesty, the Germans?—Peoples tormented and thrilled by unknown fevers and irresistibly pressed beyond themselves, enamored of and lusting after foreign races (after those that "allow" themselves "to be fertilized"—) and in the process domineering like everything that knows itself to be full of procreative forces and consequently knows "of God's grace." These two kinds of genius seek each other like man and woman; but they also misunderstand each other—like man and woman.

249

Every people has its own tartuffery and calls it its virtues.—The best that we are we do not know—we cannot[29] know.

250

What does Europe owe to the Jews?—Many things, good and bad, and above all one thing that is simultaneously of the best and worst: the grand style in morality, the terribleness and majesty of infinite demands, infinite interpretations, the whole romanticism and sublimity of what is morally questionable—and so precisely the most appealing, insidious and choicest part of those plays of color and seductions to life in whose afterglow the sky of our European culture today, its evening sky, smolders—perhaps smolders out. For this we artists among the spectators and philosophers owe the Jews our—gratitude.[30]

251[31]

We have to take it in our stride if various clouds and disturbances, in brief, small fits of stupidity—drift over the spirit of
a people that suffers and *wants* to suffer from nationalistic nervous fever and political ambition: for instance with the Germans of today there is now the anti-French stupidity, now the
anti-Jewish, now the anti-Polish, now the Christian-romantic,
now the Wagnerian, now the Teutonic, now the Prussian (just
look at these poor historians, these Sybels[32] and Treitzschkes[33]
with their thickly bandaged heads—), and whatever else they
might be called, these little befoggings of the German spirit. It
might be forgiven that I too was not completely spared of this
illness during a brief risky sojourn on very infected turf, and
like everyone else I started to have thoughts about things that
do not concern me: the first symptom of the political infection. For example about the Jews: listen now.—I have yet to
meet a German who was well disposed toward Jews; and
though the rejection of actual anti-Semitism on the part of all
who are cautious and political is unconditional, still this
caution and politics is not directed against the species of
the feeling itself, but only against its dangerous immodera-
tion, particularly against the insipid and disgraceful expression of this immoderate feeling—there is no deceiving ourselves about this. That Germany has abundantly *enough*
Jews, that the German stomach and German blood have
problems (and will have problems for a long time) even digest-
ing this existing quantum of "Jew"—as the Italians, French
and English have already done as a result of their stronger digestion—: this is the clear testimony and language of a general instinct to which we should listen and according to which
we must act. "Admit no more Jews! And bar the doors especially to the East (Austria too)!"—thus commands the instinct of a people whose type is still weak and indeterminate,
so that it could be easily blurred and easily extinguished. But
the Jews are without a doubt the strongest, most tenacious and

purest race[34] now living in Europe; they know how to assert themselves even under the worst conditions (better even than under favorable ones), by means of some kinds of virtues that people today would like to label as vices—thanks above all to a resolute faith that need not be ashamed before "modern ideas"; they change, *if* they change, always only as the Russian empire makes its conquests—as an empire that has time and is not of yesterday—: namely according to the principle "as slowly as possible!" A thinker who has the future of Europe on his conscience will reckon with the Jews as with the Russians for every scenario he drafts of this future, as the most certain and probable factors in the great play and struggle of forces at this time. What is today called a "nation" in Europe and is really more a *res facta* than *nata* (indeed sometimes looks indistinguishable from a *res ficta et picta*—)[35] is in any case something becoming, young, easily displaced, and still not a race, let alone such an *aere perennius*[36] as is the Jewish type: these "nations" should really beware of any hot-headed rivalry and hostility! That the Jews if they wanted—or if they were forced, as the anti-Semites seem to want—even now *could* have the upper hand, indeed quite literally mastery over Europe, is certain: that they are *not* working toward it and planning for it is likewise certain. For the time being they want and desire on the contrary, even with some importunity, to be absorbed and assimilated into and by Europe, they thirst to finally be stable, permitted, respected and to put an end to the nomadic life, to the "Wandering Jew"—; and we should note well and accommodate this urge and impulse (which itself possibly expresses a mitigation of Jewish instincts): for which it would perhaps be useful and fair to expel the anti-Semitic screamers from the country. Accommodate with every caution, selectively; more or less as the English nobility does.[37] It is plain as day that the easiest involvement with them could be undertaken by the stronger and already more firmly defined types of the new Germany, for instance the officers of the nobility of the Mark:[38] it would be of manifold interest to see whether the genius of money and patience (and above all some spirit and spirituality, in which the place in question is seriously lacking—) could not be added and cultivated into the hereditary art of commanding and obeying—the region in question is classical today in both.[39] But here it behooves me to break off my cheerful Germanifications and banquet speech: since I am already touching on what is *serious* to me, on the "European problem," as I understand it, on the cultivation of a new caste that will rule over Europe.—

252[40]

This is no philosophical race—these English: Bacon signifies an *attack* on the philosophical spirit generally, Hobbes, Hume and Locke a debasement and decline in value of the concept "philosopher" for more than a century. Kant arose and rose up *against* Hume; it was Locke of whom Schelling *was able* to say: "*je méprise Locke*";[41] Hegel and Schopenhauer (with Goethe) were of one mind in the struggle against the English-mechanistic nitwitization of the world, those two hostile brother geniuses in philosophy who strove apart along the opposite poles of the German spirit and in doing so wronged each other as only brothers do.—What is lacking and has always been lacking in England was known well enough by that half actor and rhetorician, that insipid muddle-head Carlyle, who tried to conceal beneath passionate grimaces what he knew about himself: namely what was *lacking* in Carlyle—real *power* of spirituality, real *depth* of intellectual vision, in short, philosophy.—It is characteristic of such an unphilosophical race that it adheres rigidly to Christianity: it *needs* Christianity's discipline in order to become "moralized" and more humanized. The English: gloomier, more sensual, more strong-willed and brutal than the Germans—are for precisely that reason, as the meaner of the two, also more pious than the Germans: they simply *need* Christianity more. To finer nostrils even this English Christianity still has a genuinely English odor of spleen and alcoholic dissipation, against which it is used as a remedy, for good reasons—the subtler poison against the cruder: a subtler poisoning is indeed already progress among clumsy peoples, a step toward spiritualization. English clumsiness and peasant earnestness are most tolerably dressed up, or more correctly explained and reinterpreted, by Christian gestures, by praying and by singing psalms; and for those cattle-like drunkards and dissipaters who formerly learned to grunt morally under the sway of Methodism and recently once more as the "Salvation Army," a spasm of penitence might actually be the relatively highest achievement of "humanity" to which they can be elevated: this much we should in fairness confess. But what is offensive in even the most humane Englishman is his lack of music, to speak metaphorically (and without metaphors—): he has no rhythm and dance in the movements of his soul and his body, indeed not even the desire for rhythm and dance, for "music." Just listen to him speak; watch the most beautiful Englishwomen *walk*—in no country on earth are there more beautiful doves and swans—finally: listen to them sing! But I am asking for too much . . . . .[42]

253[43]

There are truths known best by mediocre minds, because they are best suited for such minds: there are truths that have charm and seductive power only for mediocre spirits:—we are just now bumping up against this perhaps unpleasant proposition, since the spirit of respectable but mediocre Englishmen—I will name Darwin, John Stuart Mill and Herbert Spencer—is on the verge of becoming predominant in the middle regions of European taste. Indeed, who would question the utility of *such* spirits occasionally ruling? It would be a mistake to regard the highly developed and solo-flying spirits as particularly skilled in determining, collecting and drawing conclusions from many common little facts:—on the contrary as exceptions they are from the outset in no favorable position vis-à-vis "rules." Ultimately they have more to do than merely to know—namely to *be* something new, to *mean* something new, to *represent* new values! The chasm between knowing and being able to do something is perhaps greater, and also uncannier than we think: the capable man of the grand style, the creative one, will possibly have to be ignorant—whereas on the other hand a certain narrowness, dryness and industrious attention to detail, in short something English might not be a bad thing to have at our disposal for discoveries like those of Darwin.—In the end we should not forget about the English that already once before they caused an overall depression of the European spirit with their deep ordinariness: what people call "modern ideas" or "the ideas of the eighteenth century" or also "French ideas"—hence that against which the *German* spirit rose up in profound disgust—that was of English origin, of this there is no doubt. The French have only been the apes and actors of these ideas, also their best soldiers, and likewise unfortunately their first and most thorough *victims*: for on this damnable Anglomania of "modern ideas" the *âme française*[44] has become so skinny and emaciated that today we recall its sixteenth and seventeenth centuries, its deep, passionate power, its inventive nobility almost with disbelief. But we must hang on to this proposition of historical fairness with our teeth, and defend it against the moment and appearances: European *noblesse*—of feeling, of taste, of custom, in short, taking the word in every elevated sense—is *France's* work and invention, while European vulgarity, the plebeianism of modern ideas—is *England's*.—

254

Even now France is still the seat of the most spiritual and sophisticated culture in Europe and the preeminent school of taste: but one has to know where to find this "France of taste." Whoever belongs to it keeps himself well hidden:—it may be a small number in whom it actually lives, and what's more, these are perhaps people who do not stand on the strongest of legs, some are fatalists, dark souls, and the sick, some are pampered and affected, those who have the *ambition* to hide. All of them have something in common: they close their ears to the raving stupidity and the noisy gab of the democratic bourgeois. Indeed it is a dumbed-down and coarsened France that wallows in the foreground today — recently at the funeral of Victor Hugo[45] it celebrated a veritable orgy of bad taste and self-admiration at the same time. There is something else they have in common: the good will to resist spiritual Germanization — and an even better inability to do so! Perhaps Schopenhauer even now is more at home and familiar in this France of the spirit, which is also a France of pessimism, than he ever was in Germany; not to mention Heinrich Heine, who long ago was adopted into the flesh and blood of the subtler and more demanding lyric poets of Paris, or Hegel, who in the form of Taine — that is, the *foremost* living historian — exerts a nearly tyrannical influence. But as concerns Richard Wagner: the more French music learns to shape itself according to the real needs of the *âme moderne*,[46] the more it will "Wagnerize," this is predictable — it is already doing it enough! Still there are three things that the French even today can point to with pride as their heritage and their property, and as the enduring mark of an old cultural superiority over Europe, despite all voluntary or involuntary Germanization and vulgarizing of taste: the first is their capacity for artistic passions, for the devotion to "form" for which the term *l'art pour l'art*[47] was invented, along with a thousand others: — things like this have not been missing in France for three centuries, and thanks to their respect for the "small number" they have repeatedly made possible a kind of chamber music of literature that is not to be found in the rest of Europe —.[48] The second thing, on which the French can ground their superiority over Europe, is their old diverse *moralistic* culture, which allows on average that even in the case of little *romanciers*[49] of newspapers and chance *boulevardiers de Paris*[50] we find a psychological irritability and curiosity of which Germans for instance have no idea (let alone the thing itself!). For this the Germans are lacking a couple of centuries of a moralistic kind, which as I have said France did not spare itself; whoever calls the Germans "naïve" for this would be praising them for a defect. (As the opposite of German inexperience and innocence *in voluptate psychologica*,[51] which is not too distantly related to the tedium of German company—and as the most successful expression of a genuine French curiosity and inventiveness for this realm of delicate awe there is Henri Beyle,[52] that remarkable, anticipatory forerunner who ran with Napoleonic speed through *his* Europe, through several centuries of the European soul, as a pathfinder and discoverer of this soul:—it took two generations to halfway *catch up* with him, to figure out a few of the riddles that tormented and delighted this odd epicurean and question mark of a human being who was France's last great psychologist—.) There is still a third claim to superiority: in the nature of the French there is a halfway successful synthesis of north and south which allows them to comprehend many things and enables them to do others that the English never will comprehend; their temperament, periodically turning toward and away from the south, in which from time to time the Provençal and Ligurian blood foams over, protects them from the horrific northern gray on gray and the sunless conceptual spookiness and anemia[53]—our *German* sickness of the taste, against whose excesses people at the moment have with great resolve prescribed blood and iron:[54] that is, "great politics" (in keeping with a dangerous medical practice that teaches me to wait and wait but so far not to hope—). Even now in France there is still a predisposition and an accommodation for those rarer and rarely satisfied people who are too comprehensive to be content with any kind of fatherlandishness and in the north know how to love the south, in the south the north—for the born midlanders, the "good Europeans."—*Bizet* made his music for them, this last genius who saw a new beauty and seduction—who discovered a piece of *music's southernness.*

255

I think it is necessary to be cautious of German music in many ways. Suppose someone who loves the south as I do, as a great school of convalescence in the most spiritual and sensual sense, as a boundless fullness and transfiguration of sun that spreads itself over an overbearing existence that believes in itself: well now, someone like this would have to learn to be a bit wary of German music, because as it ruins his taste it also ruins his health again. Such a southerner, not by birth but by *faith*, if he dreamed of the future of music would also have to have dreamed of a redemption from the music of the north, and in his ears he would have the prelude of a deeper, more powerful, perhaps more evil and mysterious music, a supra-German music that does not fade, yellow, and pale at the sight of the blue voluptuous sea and the Mediterranean brilliance of the sky, as all German music does, a supra-European music, that is justified even before the brown sunsets of the desert, whose soul is related to palm trees and knows how to be at home and to roam among big, beautiful, solitary predators . . . . . I could imagine a music whose rarest magic consisted in its no longer knowing anything of good and evil, only perhaps here and there some sailor's longing, some golden shadows and delicate weaknesses would pass over it: an art that would see fleeing toward it from a great distance the colors of a setting *moral* world that had become almost incomprehensible, and would be hospitable and profound enough to receive such late refugees.—

256[55]

Thanks to the pathological alienation that the insanity of nationality has thrown down between the peoples of Europe and is still throwing down, thanks likewise to the politicians of shortsightedness and the hasty hand, who are riding high today with the help of this insanity and do not suspect at all how much the dissolution politics they practice can of necessity only be an entr'acte politics — thanks to all this and to some things that are completely unmentionable today, people are now overlooking or arbitrarily and mendaciously reinterpreting the most unequivocal signs expressing the view that *Europe wants to become one.*[56] In all the deeper and more comprehensive human beings of this century it was the real overall direction in the mysterious workings of their soul to prepare the way for this new *synthesis* and to experimentally anticipate the European of the future: only in their foregrounds or in weaker hours, perhaps in old age, did they belong to the "fatherlands" — they were only resting from themselves when they became "patriots." I am thinking of people like Napoleon, Goethe, Beethoven, Stendhal, Heinrich Heine, Schopenhauer: and do not hold it against me that I include Richard Wagner here too, for we should not allow ourselves to be led astray by his own misunderstandings — geniuses of his kind rarely have the right to understand themselves. Even less so should we be led astray by the loutish clamor with which Richard Wagner is now being blocked out and locked out in France: — the fact remains nonetheless that the *French late romanticism* of the forties and Richard Wagner belong together most closely and intimately. They are related in all the highs and lows of their needs, fundamentally related: it is Europe, the one Europe, whose soul surges and longs outward and upward from their multifarious and tempestuous art — where to? to a new light? to a new sun? But who could express accurately what all these masters of innovative linguistic methods did not know how to express clearly? What is certain is that the same storm and stress tormented them, that they *searched* in the same way, these last great seekers! All of them dominated up to their eyes and ears by literature — the first artists educated in world literature — most of them even themselves writers, poets, mediators and mixers of the arts and the senses (Wagner as a musician belongs among the painters, as poet among the

musicians, as an artist generally among the actors); all of them
were fanatics of *expression* "at any cost" — I emphasize Dela-
croix, Wagner's closest kin — all of them great discoverers in
the realm of the sublime, also of the hideous and the horrific,
even greater discoverers in the realm of effects, in exhibition,
in the art of window displays, all of them talents far beyond
their genius — virtuosos through and through, with uncanny
passages to everything that seduces, lures, compels, over-
throws, born enemies of logic and straight lines, greedy for the
foreign, the exotic, the monstrous, the crooked, and the self-
contradictory; as human beings Tantaluses[57] of the will, plebeians who rose above, who in their lives and creativity knew
themselves incapable of a noble tempo, a *lento*[58] — think for
instance of Balzac — unbridled workers, nearly self-destroyers
through work; antinomians and agitators toward customs,
ambitious and insatiable without balance and enjoyment; all
of them finally breaking down and sinking to their knees
before the Christian cross (and this rightly so: for who among
them would have been profound and original enough for a
philosophy of the *Antichrist*? —) on the whole an audaciously
daring, magnificently violent, high-flying and uplifting kind
of higher[59] human being who first had to teach their century — and it is the century of the *masses*! — the concept of
"higher human being"[60] . . . . . Let the friends of Wagner deliberate amongst themselves as to whether there is something
absolutely German in Wagnerian music, or whether perhaps
its distinction is not precisely that it derives from *supra-
German* sources and impulses: here it should not be underestimated how Paris in particular was indispensable for the development of his type, how at the most decisive moment the
depth of his instinct made him crave to be there, and finally
how his entire manner of appearance and his self-apostolate
could only perfect itself in the face of the French socialist
model. Upon closer comparison, we will perhaps find, to the
honor of the German nature of Richard Wagner, that he did
everything in a stronger, more daring, harder, higher way than

a Frenchman of the nineteenth century could do—thanks to the circumstance that we Germans are still closer to barbarism than the French—; perhaps the most remarkable thing Richard Wagner created is inaccessible, incapable of being felt, and inimitable forever for the whole Latin race which is so mature, not just for today: it is the figure of Siegfried, that *very free* human being who may indeed be far too free, hard, cheerful, healthy, too *anti-Catholic* for the taste of old and decaying cultures. He may have even been a sin against romanticism, this anti-Romanic Siegfried: well now, Wagner abundantly discharged this sin in his old gloomy days when—anticipating a taste that has since become politics—he started to preach *the way to Rome*, if not to walk it, with his characteristic religious vehemence.[61]—So that these final words of mine are not misunderstood, I want to enlist the aid of a few energetic rhymes that will reveal even to less subtle ears what I want—what I have *against* the "late Wagner" and his *Parsifal*-music.

—Is this even German?—

> From German hearts such steamy lamentation?
> From German bodies this self-flagellation?
> German these priestly outstretched arms,
> These incense-reeking sensuous charms?
> German this halting, plunging, reeling,
> This inexplicit ding-dong-pealing?
> This nunnish ogling midst *Ave*-tinkling knells,
> This heaven over-heavened by phony rapture spells?
> —Is this even German?—
> Stop and think! You are still at the gate:—
> For what you hear is *Rome,—without the words*[62] *Rome's faith*!

Part Nine

What Is Noble?

257[1]

Every enhancement so far in the type "human being" was the work of an aristocratic society—and it will be this way again and again: a society that believes in a long ladder of rank order and value-difference between one person and another and in some sense requires slavery. Without the *pathos of distance* as it grows out of the ingrained difference between classes, out of the constant looking out and looking down of the ruling caste on subordinates and instruments, and out of its likewise constant exercise of obeying and commanding, of keeping down and keeping apart, neither could that other more mysterious pathos grow at all, that craving in the soul for ever new expansion of distance, the development of ever higher, rarer, more remote, more widespread and comprehensive states, in brief, the enhancement of the type "human being," the ongoing "self-overcoming of humanity," to use a moral formula in a supra-moral sense. Of course: we must not succumb to any humanitarian illusions about the history of the origins of an aristocratic society (hence of the prerequisite of that enhancement of the type "human being" —): the truth is harsh. Let us admit to ourselves unsparingly how so far every higher culture on earth has *begun*! Human beings with a still natural nature, barbarians in every terrible sense of the word, predatory men who still possessed unbroken strength of will and lust for power hurled themselves on weaker, more civilized, more peaceful races, perhaps those who were traders, or keepers of livestock, or on old decaying cultures in whom the last signs of vitality were flaring out in brilliant fireworks of spirit and corruption. In the beginning the noble caste was always the barbarian caste: its superiority was not chiefly in physical but in psychical strength—they were *more whole* human beings (which at every stage also amounts to "more whole beasts"—).

258[2]

Corruption as the indication that anarchy is a threat among the instincts, and that the foundation of the affects, what we call "life," is shattered: corruption is something fundamentally different depending on the life-form in which it manifests itself. When for instance an aristocracy like that of France at the beginning of the Revolution throws away its privileges with a sublime disgust and sacrifices itself to an extravagance of its moral feeling, then this is corruption:—it was really only the final act of that centuries-long corruption by virtue of which it relinquished its authority to rule and demoted itself to being a *function* of the monarchy (ultimately even its pomp and showpiece). But what is essential in a good and healthy aristocracy is that it does *not* feel itself to be a function (be it of the monarchy or of the polity), but its *meaning* and highest justification—that it therefore accepts in good conscience the sacrifice of countless people who *for its sake* have to be oppressed and reduced to incomplete human beings, to slaves and instruments. Its fundamental belief must simply be that society *cannot* exist for society's sake, but only as the substructure and framework on which a choice kind of being is able to climb up to its highest task and generally to a higher level of *being*: comparable to those sun-addicted climbing plants on Java—they are called *Sipo Matador*—that wrap their arms around an oak tree for so long and so often that finally, high above it but still leaning on it, they unfold their leafy crown in the open light of day and are able to display their happiness.—

259

To mutually refrain from injury, violence, and exploitation, and to place one's will on an equal footing with someone else's: this can in a certain crude sense become good manners between individuals if the conditions for it exist (namely their actual similarity in amounts of strength and value-standards and their shared membership in a single body). But as soon as anyone tried to take this principle further and possibly even as the *fundamental principle of society*, it would immediately be shown for what it is: the will to *denial* of life, the principle of disintegration and decline. Here we have to thoroughly think to the bottom and resist all sentimental weakness: life itself is *essentially* appropriation, injury, overpowering of what is foreign and weaker, oppression, harshness, imposition of one's own forms, incorporation and at least, at its mildest, exploitation — but why should we always have to use precisely those words on which from time immemorial a slanderous intention has been stamped? Even those bodies within which, as assumed earlier, individuals treat each other as equal — it happens in every healthy aristocracy — must, if it is a living and not a dying body, itself do to other bodies everything that the individuals within it refrain from doing to each other: it will have to be the incarnate will to power, it will grow, spread out, pull things in, try to gain the upper hand — not due to some morality or immorality, but because it *lives*, and because life simply *is* will to power. But in no point is the crude consciousness of Europeans more reluctant to learn than here; today people everywhere are raving, even under scientific pretexts, about future conditions of society from which "the exploitative character" will be removed: — to my ears this sounds as if one were promising to invent a life that would refrain from all organic functions. "Exploitation" does not belong to a spoiled or imperfect and primitive society: it belongs to the *essence* of what lives, as organic basic function, it is a consequence of the actual will to power, which is simply the will of life. — Suppose this is in theory an innovation — as reality it is the *primordial fact* of all history: let us be honest with ourselves to this extent! —

260

While wandering through the many subtler and cruder moralities that have prevailed so far on earth or still prevail, I found certain traits regularly recurring with one another and connected to each other: until finally two basic types revealed themselves to me and a fundamental difference leapt forth. There is *master-morality* and *slave-morality*; — I hasten to add that in all higher and more mixed cultures attempts at mediation of both moralities also appear, even more frequently the intermingling of the two and mutual misunderstanding, indeed on occasion their close coexistence — even in the same human being, within a single soul. Moral value-distinctions have arisen either under a dominating type, that became pleasantly aware of its difference vis-à-vis the dominated — or under the dominated, the slaves and those who are dependent to every degree. In the first case, when the ruling group determines the concept "good," it is the elevated, proud states of the soul that are perceived as distinguishing and determining the rank order. The noble human being sets apart from himself those in whom the opposite of such elevated, proud states expresses itself: he despises them. We note at once that in this first kind of morality the contrast between "good" and "bad" amounts to "noble" and "contemptible": — the contrast between "good" and "*evil*" is of a different origin.[3] Contempt is felt for the cowardly, the anxious, the petty, and the one who thinks about his own narrow utility; likewise the suspicious with their burdened glances, those who debase themselves, the dog-like people who allow themselves to be abused, the begging sycophants, and above all the liars: — it is a basic belief of all aristocrats that the common folk are mendacious. "We truthful ones"[4] — this is what the nobility in ancient Greece called themselves. It is plain to see that moral value-distinctions were first applied everywhere to *human be-ings* and only derivatively and later to *actions*: that is why it is a serious mistake when historians of morality proceed from such questions as "why are compassionate acts praised?" The noble kind of human being feels *itself* to be value-determining, does not need approval, judges "what is harmful to me is harmful in and of itself," knows itself to be that which imparts honor to things in the first place, is *value-creating*. Everything it recognizes in itself it honors: such a morality is self-glorification. In the foreground there is the feeling of fullness, of power that wants to overflow, the happiness of high ten-sion, the consciousness of wealth that would bestow and give of itself: — the noble human being also helps the unfortunate, but not or almost not from compassion, but from an urge pro-duced by an excess of power. The noble human being honors in itself the one who is powerful, also the one who has power over itself, who knows how to speak and to keep silent, who joyfully exercises discipline and harshness over itself and re-spects everything that is severe and harsh. "A hard heart Wotan has put into my breast" reads a line from an old Scan-dinavian saga: this is fitting poetry indeed from the soul of a proud Viking. Such a human being is proud that it is *not* made for compassion, which is why the hero of the saga adds the warning "if someone's heart is not already hard in youth, his heart will never become hard." Noble and courageous hu-man beings who think in this manner are furthest from that morality that sees the distinguishing feature of morality pre-cisely in compassion or in acting on behalf of others or in *désintéressement*;[5] belief in oneself, pride in oneself, a funda-mental hostility and irony toward "selflessness" belong just as surely to noble morality as a mild disdain and caution toward sympathy and a "warm heart." — It is the powerful who *un-derstand* how to honor, it is their art, their realm of invention. Deep reverence for age and for one's background — all law is based on this double reverence — faith and prejudice in favor of one's forefathers and at the expense of future generations are

typical in the morality of the powerful; and conversely when
people of "modern ideas" almost instinctively believe in "progress" and "the future" and increasingly lose their respect for
age, this in itself suffices to expose the ignoble descent of
these "ideas." But most of all a morality of ruling types is
foreign and painful to contemporary taste in the severity of
its principle that one has duties only to one's peers; that toward beings of a lower rank and toward everything alien one
can behave as he pleases or "as the heart desires" and in any
case "beyond good and evil"—: this is where compassion and
so on might belong. The capacity and duty for long gratitude
and long revenge—both only among peers—subtlety in
retaliation, refinement of the concept of friendship, a certain
necessity for having enemies (as it were as safety valves for
the affects of envy, quarrelsomeness, impudence—basically
in order to be a good *friend*): all of these are typical traits of
noble morality which, as indicated above, is not a morality
of "modern ideas" and is therefore difficult to empathize
with today, also difficult to excavate and uncover.—Things
are different with the second type of morality, *slave-morality*.
Suppose the violated, oppressed, suffering, unfree, those who
are unsure of themselves, and the weary were to moralize:
what would their moral valuations have in common? Probably a pessimistic suspicion of the whole condition of humanity will find expression, perhaps a condemnation of humanity along with his condition. The slave's gaze is not favorable
to the virtues of the powerful: he is skeptical and suspicious,
he has a *subtle* mistrust of everything "good" that is honored
there—he wants to convince himself that even their happiness is not genuine. Conversely those qualities are foregrounded and highlighted that serve to alleviate the existence
of sufferers: here compassion, the obliging and helping hand,
a warm heart, patience, industriousness, humility and friend-
liness are held in honor—since here these are the most useful
qualities and practically the only means of enduring the pressure of existence. Slave-morality is essentially the morality of

utility. This is the cradle of the emergence of that famous opposition of "good" and "evil": — power and danger are
sensed to belong to evil, a certain dreadfulness, subtlety and
strength that prohibits the rise of contempt. According to
slave-morality then, "evil" arouses fear; according to master-
morality it is precisely the "good" who arouse and want to arouse
fear, whereas the "bad" are perceived as contemptible. The opposition comes to a head when, following the logic of slave-
morality, ultimately a tinge of disdain is also associated with the
"good" of this morality—it may be mild and benevolent—because the good within the slave's way of thinking has to be the
undangerous human being in any case: he is good-natured, easy to
deceive, maybe a bit stupid, *un bonhomme*.[6] Wherever slave-
morality gains the upper hand, language reveals a tendency to
conflate the words "good" and "stupid." — One last fundamental difference: the longing for *freedom*, the instinct for happiness
and the subtleties of feeling for freedom belong just as necessarily
to slave-morals and slave-morality[7] as the art and fanaticism of
reverence and devotion are regular symptoms of an aristocratic
way of thinking and valuing. — From this we can readily understand why love *as passion*—it is our European specialty—absolutely has to be of noble lineage: as is well known its invention is
traced to the knight-troubadours of Provence, those magnificent, inventive human beings of the "*gai saber*"[8] to whom Europe owes so much and nearly its very self. —

261

Belonging to those things that are perhaps most difficult for
a noble human being to understand is vanity: he is tempted to
deny it even where a different kind of person believes he can
grasp it in his hands. His problem is imagining beings who
seek to inspire a good opinion about themselves that they do
not themselves possess — and thus also do not "deserve" — and
who afterward *believe* in this good opinion themselves. This
seems to him half tasteless and disrespectful of oneself, and
half so baroque and unreasonable that he would prefer to

interpret vanity as an exception and doubts its existence in most cases when it is spoken of. He would say for instance: "I can be mistaken about my value and still demand that my value be acknowledged by others exactly as I define it—but that is not vanity (but conceit or more frequently what is known as 'humility' or even 'modesty')." Or: "I can be pleased for many reasons about the good opinion of others, perhaps because I honor and love them and take pleasure in each of their joys, perhaps because the good opinion of others even in cases where I do not share it still is useful to me or promises to be of use—but all that is not vanity." The noble human being first has to force himself to grasp, with the aid of history, that since time immemorial in all strata of the population that were dependent to any extent, a common person *was* merely what people *considered* him to be:—not at all accustomed to positing values himself, he did not ascribe any other value to himself than what his masters ascribed to him (creating values is the true *right of masters*). We might understand it as the result of a tremendous atavism that the ordinary human being even now still *waits* for an opinion about himself and then instinctively subjects himself to it: but by no means only a "good" opinion, rather even a bad and unfair one (think for example of the majority of self-estimations and self-underestimations that devout women accept from their father confessors, and in general what a devout Christian accepts from his church). In fact now, in accordance with the slowly arising democratic order of things (and its cause, the blood-mixing of masters and slaves),[9] the originally noble and rare urge to attribute a value to oneself on one's own initiative, and to "think well" of oneself, is being increasingly encouraged and propagated: but it is always opposed by an urge that is older, broader and more fundamentally ingrained—and in the phenomenon of "envy" this older urge becomes master over the younger. The vain man is delighted by *every* good opinion he hears about himself (quite apart from all considerations of its utility and likewise indifferent to whether true or false), just as he suffers from every bad opinion: for he subjects himself to both, he *feels* himself subjected to them on account of that oldest instinct of submission that breaks out in him. — It is "the slave" in the blood of the vain man, a residue of the cunning of the slave—and how much residual "slave" remains for example in woman!—who tries to *seduce* people to good opinions about her; it is also the slave who immediately afterward prostrates himself before these opinions as if he had not summoned them. — And to say it again: vanity is an atavism.[10]

262

A *species* emerges, a type becomes fixed and strong under the long struggle with essentially constant *unfavorable* conditions. Conversely we know from the experience of breeders that species that are treated to overabundant nourishment and generally to an excess of protection and care soon tend most strongly toward variation of the type and are rich in oddities and monstrosities (also in monstrous vices). Now look for a moment at an aristocratic community, say an ancient Greek city-state or Venice, as an arrangement, whether voluntary or involuntary, for the purpose of *breeding*: there we have people together and relying on each other who want their species to succeed, most often because they *must* succeed or they run the terrible risk of being exterminated. Lacking here is that benefit, that excess and protection under which variation is favored; the species needs itself as a species, as something that can succeed at all and make itself durable precisely by virtue of its harshness, uniformity and simplicity of form during constant struggle with its neighbors or with oppressed subjects who rebel or threaten rebellion. Experience of the most diverse kind teaches it which qualities it primarily has to thank for the fact that it still exists, despite all gods and human beings, that it still triumphs: these qualities it calls virtues, and it nurtures[11] these virtues alone. It does this with harshness, indeed it wants harshness; every aristocratic morality is intolerant in the education of youth, in disposing over women, in marriage

customs, in relationships between old and young, in its penal code (which focuses only on deviants): — it considers
intolerance itself to be a virtue, under the rubric of "justice."
In this manner a type with few but very strong traits, a kind of
people who are austere, warlike, prudently silent, closed to the
outside and closed-mouthed (and as such possessing the subtlest feeling for the charms and nuances of their society) becomes fixed beyond the changing of generations; the ongoing
struggle with ever-constant *unfavorable* conditions is, as I said,
what causes a type to become fixed and hard. Finally, however, a successful scenario arises and the tremendous tension
eases up; perhaps there are no more enemies among their
neighbors, and the means to life, even to enjoy life are abundantly present. With one stroke the bond and the constraint
of the old discipline are torn: it no longer feels necessary, like a
condition of existence — if it wanted to persist then it could
only do so as a form of *luxury*, as an archaizing *taste*. Suddenly
variation arrives on the scene in the greatest fullness and splendor, whether as deviation (into something higher, finer, rarer)
or as degeneration and monstrosity, and the individual dares
to be individual and to stand out. At these turning points of
history a glorious, multifarious, jungle-like growth spurt and
upward striving, a kind of *tropical* tempo in the competition
for growth and a tremendous destruction and drive to self-
destruction manifest themselves alongside one another and
often interwoven and tangled together, thanks to the egoisms
savagely turned against one another and exploding as it were,
that wrestle each other "for sun and light" and can no longer
extract any limit, any restraint or consideration from the previous morality. It was this very morality that had stockpiled
energy so prodigiously, and bent the bow in such a threatening
manner: — now it is and is being "outlived." The dangerous
and uncanny moment has been reached when the greater,
more diverse, more comprehensive life *lives over and beyond* the
old morality; the "individual" now stands there, compelled to
a legislating of his own, to his own arts and wiles of self-

preservation, self-enhancement, self-redemption. Now there is nothing but new whys, nothing but new hows, no more shared formulas, misunderstanding and disrespect are in league, decline, ruin and the highest cravings are horrifically entangled, the genius of the race is flooding over from all cornucopia of good and bad, a disastrous simultaneity of spring and autumn full of new charms and veils suited to the young and as yet unexhausted, as yet unwearied corruption. Once again danger is there, the mother of morality, great danger, this time displaced into the individual, into neighbors and friends, onto the street, into one's own child, into one's own heart, into all of one's most private and secret places of desire and will: what will the moral philosophers who are emerging around this time have to preach about now?[12] They are discovering, these keen observers and loafers, that everything around them is spoiled and spoils everything else, that nothing will remain standing after tomorrow except for one kind of human being, the incurably *mediocre*. The mediocre alone have the prospect of continuing themselves, of propagating—they are the people of the future, the only survivors; "be like them! become mediocre!" is now the only morality that still has meaning, that still finds listeners. — But it is hard to preach, this morality of mediocrity![13] — since it must never confess what it is and what it wants! it must speak of moderation and dignity and duty and love of one's neighbor—it will have a hard time *concealing the irony!* —

263

There is an *instinct for rank* that more than anything is already the sign of a *high* rank; there is a *delight* in the nuances of respect that allows us to detect noble lineage and habits. The subtlety, goodness and height of a soul are dangerously put to the test when something that is of first rank passes it by but is not yet protected by the awe of authority against obtrusive grabbing and clumsiness: something that goes its way unmarked, undiscovered, tempting, perhaps voluntarily veiled

and disguised, like a living touchstone. Whoever possesses
the task and practice of exploring souls will avail himself of
this very art in many different forms, in order to determine the
ultimate value of a soul, the unshakable, innate rank order to
which it belongs: he will put it to the test regarding its *instinct
of respect. Différence engendre haine*:[14] the crudeness of many
natures suddenly spurts like dirty water when any sacred vessel,
any precious thing from locked shrines, any book with mark-
ings of great destiny is carried past; and on the other hand
there is an involuntary hush, a hesitant glance, a stillness of all
gestures expressing that a soul *feels* the proximity of what is
most venerable. The manner in which respect for the *Bible* has
been maintained on the whole in Europe is perhaps the best
piece of discipline and refinement of custom so far that Europe
owes to Christianity: such books of profundity and ultimate
meaning need an outside tyranny of authority for their protection, in order to gain those millennia of *duration* necessary for
exhausting and deciphering them. Much has been accomplished if in the end the great masses (the shallow and speedy-
boweled of every kind) have bred into them the feeling that
they are not permitted to touch everything; that there are sacred experiences that require them to remove their shoes and
refrain from touching with their dirty hands — such moments
are practically their highest elevation to humanity. Conversely,
perhaps nothing is more disgusting about so-called educated
people, the believers in "modern ideas," as their lack of shame,
the smug impudence in their eyes and hands that they use to
touch, lick, and fondle everything; and it is possible that today
among the common people, the simple folk, particularly among
peasants, we will find more *relative* nobility of taste and tact for
respect than among the newspaper-reading demimonde of the
spirit, the educated.

264

What one's forefathers liked to do most and most often cannot
be expunged from the psyche of a human being: whether they

were perhaps thrifty savers and accessories of a desk and cash box, modest and bourgeois in their desires, modest also in their virtues: or whether they lived accustomed to giving orders from dawn till dusk, fond of rough pleasures and in addition perhaps even rougher duties and responsibilities; or whether finally at some time they sacrificed their old privileges of birth and property in order to live entirely for their faith — their "God" — as the people of an implacable and delicate conscience that blushes at any accommodation. It is not in the least possible that a human being might *not* have the qualities and preferences of his parents and ancestors in his body: whatever appearances may indicate to the contrary. This is the problem of race. Supposing we know something about the parents, an inference about the child is permitted: any repugnant indulgence, any secret envy, a clumsy need to be right — as these three together have constituted the real rabble-type throughout the ages — something of this kind has to transfer to the child as certainly as contaminated blood; and with the help of the best upbringing and education the most that can be achieved is to *deceive* people about such a heredity. — And what else do upbringing and education aim for today! In our very populist, that is to say rabble-like age "upbringing" and "education" *must* essentially be the art of deceiving — about our descent, the inherited rabble in our bodies and souls. An educator who today would preach truthfulness above all and constantly exhorted his students "be true! be natural! be what you are!" — even such a virtuous and true-hearted jackass would learn after a while to reach for that *furca* of Horace,[15] in order *naturam expellere*: but with what success? "Rabble" *usque recurret*.[16] —

265

At the risk of offending innocent ears, I propose: egoism belongs to the essence of a noble soul, I mean that unshakable belief that other beings must by nature be subservient and sacrifice themselves to beings such as "we are." The noble soul accepts this fact of its egoism without any question mark, without even a feeling of harshness, compulsion, or caprice, on the contrary as something that may be grounded in the primordial law of things: — if it were to look for a name for it, then it would say "it is justice itself." It admits under certain circumstances that cause it to hesitate at first that there are others with rights equal to its own; as soon as it has achieved clarity about this question of rank, it moves among these equals and equally entitled modestly and with tender respect, with the same confidence it shows in its behavior toward itself—in accordance with an innate, celestial mechanics familiar to all stars. It is just one *more* piece of its egoism, this subtlety and self-limitation in dealing with its equals—every star is such an egoist—: it honors *itself* in them and in the rights it cedes them, it does not doubt that the exchange of honors and rights, being the *nature* of all interaction, likewise belongs to the natural state of things. The noble soul gives as it takes, drawing on the passionate and irritable[17] instinct of retaliation that lies at its bottom. The concept "mercy" has no meaning and fragrance *inter pares*;[18] there might be a sublime way of letting gifts from above descend as it were upon oneself, and thirstily drinking them up: but for this art and gesture the noble soul has no talent. Its egoism hinders it here: in general it dislikes looking "upward" at all—but either *ahead*, horizontally and slowly, or down: — *it knows itself to be in the heights.* —

266[19]

"One can highly esteem only those who do not *seek* themselves."—Goethe to Councilor Schlosser.[20]

267

There is a proverb among the Chinese that the mothers already teach their children: *siao-sin*—"make your heart *small*!"[21] This is the actual fundamental tendency in late civilizations: I do not doubt that the first thing an ancient Greek would recognize also in us Europeans of today is self-diminution—on that basis alone we would "offend his taste." —

268[22]

What in the end is baseness?[23] — Words are acoustical signs for concepts; but concepts are more or less specific visual signs for frequently recurring sensations that arrive together, for groups of sensations. It does not yet suffice for purposes of understanding one another to merely use the same words: we must also use the same words for the same species of inner experiences, we must ultimately have our experience *in common*. This is why representatives of a single people understand each other better than those who belong to different peoples even when they use the same language; or rather, when human beings have lived for a long time under similar conditions (of climate, soil, danger, needs, work), then something *emerges* that "understands itself," a people. In all souls an equal number of frequently recurring[24] experiences has gained the upper hand over those that come more rarely: people understand one another on the basis of them, quickly and ever more quickly — the history of language is the history of a process of abbreviation —; and on the basis of this quick comprehension people are bound closer and closer together. The greater the danger, the greater the need to agree quickly and easily on what needs to be done; not to misunderstand one another in a time of danger is what people absolutely cannot do without when communicating. Even in every friendship or love affair people test this principle: nothing of the kind can endure as soon as one of them discovers that, despite using the same words, the other feels, thinks, intuits, wishes and fears differently. (Fear of "eternal misunderstanding": this is the benevolent genius that so often deters persons of the opposite sex from entering hasty relationships urged by their senses and their hearts — and *not* some Schopenhauerian "genius of the species" — !) Those groups of sensations within a soul that are aroused most quickly, speak up and give the command, decide the entire rank order of its values, and ultimately determine its table of goods. The valuations of a human being reveal something of the *structure* of his soul, and where it sees its conditions of life, its real need.[25] Supposing now that from the start need has brought together only those people who could signify similar requirements and experiences with similar signs, then what results on the whole is that the easy *communicability* of needs, that is, in the final analysis the experiencing of only average and *common* experiences, must have been the most powerful force of all to have disposed over human beings so far.[26] People who are more similar and more ordinary were and always are at an advantage, while the more select, refined and difficult to understand easily remain alone, succumb to accidents in their isolation and rarely reproduce. Tremendous counter-forces would have to be summoned to cross this natural, all-too-natural *progressus in simile*,[27] this continuing development of human beings toward the similar, ordinary, average, herd-like — toward what is *base*!

269

The more a psychologist — a born, inevitable psychologist and diviner of souls — turns his attention to the more choice cases and human beings, the greater his danger becomes of choking on compassion: he *needs* hardness and cheerfulness more than other people do. For corruption and destruction of the higher human beings, of souls of a stranger type, is the rule: it is a ter-rible thing to constantly have this rule before one's eyes. The manifold torments of the psychologist who discovered this de-struction, who first discovers and then *almost* always rediscovers throughout all history this whole inner "hopelessness" of the higher human being, this eternal "too late!" in every sense — it could possibly lead him someday to turn bitterly against his fate and attempt his own self-destruction — lead him to his own "corruption." With nearly every psychologist we will perceive a telling predisposition and pleasure in associating with ordi-nary and well-adjusted people: this reveals that he always needs a cure, that he needs a kind of escape and forgetting, away from what his insights and incisions, from what his "craft" has placed on his conscience. He is characterized by fear of his memory. He is easily silenced by the judgment of others: he listens with a stony face as others venerate, admire, love and transfigure where he has actually *seen*—or he conceals even his silence by expressly agreeing with some foreground opinion. Perhaps the paradox of his situation grows horrible to the extent that the masses, the educated, and the fanatics develop their own great admiration precisely where he developed great compassion alongside great contempt—their admiration for "great men" and prodigies, for whose sake they bless and honor the fatherland, the earth, the dignity of humanity and themselves, who are held up as models for the education of youth . . . . And who knows whether in all great cases so far it has not been the same: that the masses worshipped a god—and the "god" was only a wretched sacrificial animal! Success has always been the biggest liar—and the "work" itself is a success; the great statesman, the conqueror, the discoverer are disguised in their creations to the point of unrecognizability; the "work" of the artist and of the philosopher only invents the man who created it, who was supposed to have created it; the "great men" as they are venerated are small, paltry fictions after the fact; in the world of historical values counterfeiting is the *rule*. These great poets for instance, your Byron, Musset, Poe, Leopardi, Kleist, Gogol[28]—as they simply are and perhaps must be: human beings of the moment, inspired, sensual, childish, frivolous and precipitous in their mistrust and trust; with souls harboring some breach that needs repairing; often taking revenge in their works for an inner contamination, often trying to find forgetfulness in their high-flying from an all-too-faithful memory, often lost in the mud and in love with it, until they become like the will-o'-the-wisps around the swamps and *pretend* to be like stars—the people will probably call them idealists now—often struggling with a long nausea, with a recurring ghost of lost faith that chills them and forces them to pine for *gloria*[29] and to devour "faith in itself" from the hands of intoxicated sycophants:—what a *torment* these great artists and

higher human beings generally are for someone who has figured them out! It is so understandable that *they* so readily enjoy those eruptions of boundless, most devotional *compassion*
from women—who are clairvoyant in the world of suffering
and unfortunately also addicted to helping and rescuing far
beyond their own powers—eruptions that the masses, especially the admiring masses, do not understand and on which
they pile their curious and self-complacent interpretations.
This compassion routinely deceives itself about its power;
women want to believe that love can do *anything*—it is their
true *faith*.[30] Oh, those who know hearts realize how poor,
stupid,[31] helpless, presumptuous, mistake-prone, more likely
to destroy than to rescue is even the best profoundest love!—It
is possible that beneath the sacred fable and disguise of the life
of Jesus lies hidden one of the most painful cases of martyrdom
of *knowledge about love*:[32] the martyrdom of the most innocent and desiring heart, that could not get enough from any
human love, that *demanded* love, to be loved and nothing else,
with hardness, with madness, with terrible outbursts against
those who denied him love; the story of a poor man unsated
and insatiable in love, who had to invent hell in order to have
a place to send those who did not *want* to love him—and who
finally, after learning the truth about human love, had to
invent a god who is all love, all *capacity* for love—who has
mercy on human love because it is so utterly wretched, so
ignorant![33] Whoever feels this way, whoever *knows* this much
about love—*seeks* death.—But why dwell on such painful
things?[34] Assuming that we do not have to.—

270

The spiritual arrogance and nausea of anyone who has suffered deeply—*how* deeply people can suffer practically determines rank order—his shuddering certainty, completely per-
meating and coloring him, of *knowing more* than the cleverest
and wisest could know by virtue of his suffering, of being familiar with and once having been "at home" in many remote, ap-

palling worlds[35] of which "*you* know nothing!" . . . . . this spiritual, silent arrogance of the sufferer, this pride of the chosen one of knowledge, of the "initiate," of the one who was almost sacrificed finds it necessary to have all forms of disguise in order to protect itself from contact with obtrusive and compassionate hands and generally from everything that is not his peer in matters of pain. Deep suffering makes noble; it separates. One of the most subtle forms of disguise is Epicureanism and a certain openly displayed courageousness of taste that takes suffering lightly and resists everything sad and profound. There are "cheerful people" who use cheerfulness because on its account they are misunderstood: — they *want* to be misunderstood. There are "scientific people" who use science because it provides a cheerful appearance, and because scientific character lets others infer that someone is superficial: — they *want* to seduce others to a false conclusion. There are free impudent spirits who would like to conceal and deny that they are shattered, proud and incurable hearts;[36] and sometimes foolishness itself is the mask for an ill-fated, all-too-certain knowledge. — From which it follows that part of a more refined humanity is having respect "for the mask" and not practicing psychology and curiosity in the wrong place.

271

What separates two people most deeply is a different sense and degree of cleanliness. What good is all decency and mutual advantage, what good is all good will for each other: when in the end what it comes down to is — they "cannot stand the smell of one another!" The highest instinct of cleanliness places the one who is afflicted with it in the oddest and most dangerous isolation, like a saint: for that is exactly what saintliness is — the highest spiritualization of said instinct. Some kind of shared knowledge of an indescribable fullness in the happiness of bathing, some kind of ardor and thirstiness that constantly drives the soul out of the night into the morning, and out of the gloom, of "gloominess" into brightness, brilliance, profundity and subtlety — : just as such a propensity *distinguishes* — it is a noble propensity — it also *separates*. — The compassion of a saint is compassion for the *dirt* in the human, all-too-human. And there are degrees and heights where even compassion is felt by him as something that pollutes, as dirt . . . . .

272

Signs of nobility: never thinking about downgrading our duties to duties for everyone; not wanting to delegate or to share our own responsibility; counting our privileges and their exercise among our *duties*.

273

Someone who strives for greatness regards everyone he meets on his way either as a means or as a delay and obstacle — or as a temporary place to rest. His unique and superior *graciousness* toward fellow human beings is only possible when he is at his height and he rules. Impatience and his consciousness that until such time he is always condemned to comedy — since even war is a comedy and conceals the end like every means — ruins any company for him: this kind of human being knows solitude and what is most poisonous about it.

274

The problem of those who wait. — Strokes of luck are needed and many incalculable things before a higher human being, in whom the solution to a problem lies dormant, is able to act at the right time — "to break out," as we might say. Ordinarily this does *not* happen, and in every corner of the earth sit men who scarcely know to what extent they are waiting, and even less that they are waiting in vain. Sometimes, too, the wake-up call comes too late, the accident that gives "permission" to act — when his best youth and strength to act have already been used up in sitting still; and how many discovered in horror, as they "sprang" to their feet, that their limbs had fallen asleep and their spirit was too heavy! "It's too late"—he says to himself, no longer believing in himself and henceforth forever useless.—In the realm of genius is "Raphael without hands,"[37] the phrase taken in the broadest sense, perhaps not the exception but the rule?—Perhaps genius is not so rare at all: but the five hundred *hands* it needs in order to tyrannize the καιρός, "the right time"—in order to grab chance by the hair!

275[38]

Whoever *wishes* not to see what is lofty in a man looks that much closer at what is low and foreground in him—and thereby reveals himself.

276

In all kinds of injury and loss the lower and cruder soul has it better than the noble: the dangers of the latter must be greater, and the probability that it will have an accident and be destroyed is tremendous, given the multiplicity of its conditions for life.—In lizards a finger grows back when it is lost: not so in human beings.—

277[39]

—Bad enough! The same old story! After we have finished building our house, we notice that in the process, we inadvertently learned something we really *should* have known, before we—started building. The eternal tedious "too late!"—The melancholy of all *finishing!* . . .

278[40]

—Wanderer, who are you? I see you going your way, without scorn, without love, with inscrutable eyes; wet and sad like a plumb line that returns from the depths unsated, back to the light of day—what did it seek down there?—with a breast that does not sigh, with lips that conceal their disgust, with a hand that only slowly grasps: who are you? what did you do? Rest here: this spot is hospitable for everyone—recuperate! And whoever you might be: what would you like now? What would help you recuperate? Just name it: what I have I offer to you!—"To recuperate? To recuperate? Oh how inquisitive you are, and what are you saying! But give me, please——" What? What? just say it!—"Another mask! A second mask!" . . . .

279[41]

People of deep sadness betray themselves when they are happy: they have a way of seizing happiness, as if out of jealousy they wanted to crush or choke it—oh, they know too well that it will run away from them!

280

"Bad! Bad! What? isn't he going—backwards?"—Yes! But you understand him poorly if you complain about that. He is going backward, as does anyone, who wants to make a big leap.——

281

—"Will they believe me? but I demand that they believe me: I have always thought about myself badly, only in quite rare cases, only when forced, always without any joy 'in the matter,' ready to digress away from 'me,' always without faith in the result thanks to an indefatigable mistrust of the *possibility* of self-knowledge, that has led me to the point of perceiving a *contradictio in adjecto*[42] even in the concept of 'immediate knowledge' that the theorists allow themselves:—this whole fact is nearly the most certain thing I know about myself. There must be some kind of aversion in me to *believe* in anything definite about myself.—Is there a riddle in this? Probably; but fortunately none for my own teeth.—Perhaps it reveals the species to which I belong?—But not to me: and I'm happy enough with that.—"

282

"But what happened to you?"—"I don't know," he said, hesitantly; "maybe Harpies flew over my table."—Occasionally it happens these days that a mild-mannered, moderate, reserved person will suddenly start raving, smashing dishes, turn the table over, scream, go berserk, insult everyone—and finally he goes off to the side, embarrassed, furious at himself—where? why? In order to starve in some isolated place? In order to choke on his memory?—Whoever has the desires of a lofty, selective soul and only rarely finds his table set and his food ready will be in great danger at all times: but today it is extraordinary. Thrown into a noisy and rabble-like age, with whom he does not wish to eat from the same bowl, he could easily perish of hunger and thirst or, if he were to "dig in" at last—of sudden nausea.—Perhaps all of us at one time have sat at tables where we did not belong; and precisely the most spiritual among us, those hardest to feed, know that dangerous dyspepsia that stems from a sudden insight and disappointment about our food and our table mates—the *nausea of dessert.*

283[43]

Assuming that anyone wants to give praise in the first place, it is a subtle and at the same time noble self-control that always wants to praise where we do *not* agree:—otherwise we would be praising ourselves, which is offensive to good taste—of course this is a kind of self-mastery that offers a perfect occasion and opportunity for constantly being *misunderstood*. In order to allow ourselves this real luxury of taste and morality we must not live among the oafs of the spirit, but instead among human beings whose misunderstandings and mistakes are still entertaining for their subtlety—or else we will pay dearly for it!—"He praises me: *therefore* he is saying I am right"—this asinine inference spoils half the life of us

hermits, since it brings asses into our neighborhood and
friendship.

284[44]

To live with tremendous and proud composure; always
beyond—. To arbitrarily have and not have our affects, our
pros and cons, to condescend to them for hours; to *sit* on them
as we would on a horse or an ass:—after all, we have to know
how to use their stupidity as well as their fire. To reserve our
three hundred foregrounds, also the dark glasses: because
there are cases where no one is permitted to look into our eyes,
and still less into our "grounds." And to choose as company
that mischievous and cheerful vice, courtesy. And to remain
master of our four virtues: courage, insight, sympathy, solitude.
For solitude is a virtue for us, as a sublime yearning and urge
for cleanliness[45] that realizes how whenever there is person-to-
person contact—"in society"—there is unavoidable soiling.
Community of any kind somehow, somewhere, some way
makes us—"base."[46]

285

The greatest events and thoughts—but the greatest thoughts
are the greatest[47] events—are the last to be comprehended: the
generations that are contemporaneous with them do not *experience* such events—they live past them. Something happens
here that is similar to the realm of the stars. The light of the
most distant stars is the latest to reach human beings; and until
it has arrived we even *deny*—that there are stars out there.
"How many centuries are required for a spirit to be comprehended?"—this too is a standard, with this too we create a rank
order and etiquette that are still needed: for spirit and star.—

286

"Here the view is clear, spirit[48] uplifting."[49]—But there is
an opposite kind of human being who is also on a height and
also has a free prospect—but looks *down*.

287[50]

—What is noble? What does the word "noble" mean to us today? What reveals and how do we recognize a noble human being under this heavily veiled sky of incipient rule by the rabble, which makes everything opaque and leaden? — His actions will not prove him — actions are always ambiguous, always unfathomable—; nor is it his "works." Today we find among artists and scholars plenty whose works reveal that they are motivated by a deep desire for nobility: but precisely this need *for* what is noble is fundamentally different from the needs of the noble soul itself, and it is precisely the eloquent and dangerous mark of its absence. It is not the works, it is *faith* that decides here, that determines the rank order here, to take up once more an old religious formula and use it in a new and deeper sense: some fundamental certainty that a noble soul has about itself, something that cannot be sought, cannot be found and perhaps cannot be lost either. — *The noble soul has respect for itself.* —

288

There are people who have spirit in an inevitable way, no matter how they twist and turn and put their hands up to cover their telltale eyes (— as if their hands did not betray them! —): ultimately it is always revealed that they have something they hide, namely spirit. One of the subtlest means for deceiving people as long as possible and successfully pretending to be more stupid than we are — which in ordinary life is often as desirable as an umbrella — is called *enthusiasm*: including what goes along with it, for example virtue. For as Galiani says, and he must have known — : *vertu est enthousiasme.*[51]

289[52]

In the writings of a hermit we can always hear something of the echo of the wasteland, something of whispered tones and the furtive looking around of solitude; even from his strongest words, from his very shouts there is the sound of a new and more dangerous kind of silence, of keeping silent. If someone has sat year in, year out and day and night alone with his soul in intimate discord and dialogue, if he has sat in his cave — be it a labyrinth or even a gold mine — and turned into a cave bear or treasure hunter or treasure guardian and dragon: then even his concepts in the end take on a peculiar twilight color, an odor of mold just as much as of profundity, something incommunicable and distasteful that blows a chill on anyone who passes by. A hermit does not believe that a philosopher — assuming that a philosopher was always a hermit first — ever expressed his genuine and ultimate opinions in books: do people not write books precisely to conceal what they are keeping to themselves? — indeed, he will doubt whether a philosopher *could* have "ultimate and genuine" opinions at all, whether behind every cave there does not lie, must not lie a still deeper cave — a more comprehensive, stranger, richer world above a surface, an abyss behind every ground, under every giving of "grounds."[53] Every philosophy is a foreground philosophy — this is a hermit judgment: "there is something arbitrary in *his* having stopped here, having looked back, having looked around, that *here* he did not dig any deeper and laid aside the shovel[54] — there is also something suspicious about it." Every philosophy also *conceals* a philosophy; every opinion is also a hiding place, every word also a mask.

290

Every deep thinker fears being understood more than being misunderstood. His vanity might be wounded by the latter; but by the former are wounded his heart and his sympathy, which always say: "Oh, why do *you* want to have it as difficult as I do?"

291

The human being, a manifold, mendacious, artificial and opaque animal, uncanny to other animals more by cunning and cleverness than by strength, invented good conscience in order to just be able to enjoy his soul as *simple*; and the whole of morality is an intrepid, long forgery that enables us to take some kind of pleasure at the sight of the soul. From this standpoint there is perhaps much more to the concept of "art" than we generally believe.

292

A philosopher: that is a human being who constantly experiences, sees, hears, suspects, hopes and dreams extraordinary things; who is struck by his own thoughts as if from outside, from above and below, by *his* kind of events and lightning bolts; who is himself possibly a thunderhead pregnant with new lightning bolts; a fatal human being around whom there is always rumbling and growling, gaping chasms and uncanny activity. A philosopher: oh, a being that often runs away from himself, often is afraid of himself—but is too curious not to "come to himself" again and again . . . . .

293

A man who says: "I like this, I will take this and make it my own and protect it against anyone"; a man who can plead his case, carry out a resolution, keep faith with an idea, hold on to a woman, punish and vanquish the insolent; a man who has his wrath and his sword, and who attracts the weak, the suffering, the distressed and even animals, all of whom belong to him by nature, in short a man who is a *master* by nature—when such a man has compassion, well now! *this* compassion has value! But what good is the compassion of sufferers![55] Or for that matter of the preachers of compassion! Almost everywhere in Europe today there is a pathological sensitivity and irritability to pain, likewise a repulsive lack of restraint in whining, a tenderization that tries to dress itself up as something higher with religion and philosophical odds and ends—there is a veritable cult of suffering. The *unmanliness* of what is christened "compassion" in such circles of fanatics is the first thing that meets the eye, in my opinion. — This latest style of bad taste has to be energetically and thoroughly excommunicated; and finally I wish that people would wear the good amulet "*gai saber*" around their hearts and necks to ward it off, — "joyful science," to put it in plain German.[56]

294[57]

The Olympian vice. — In defiance of that philosopher who as a genuine Englishman tried to give a bad reputation to laughter among all thinking minds — "laughter is a grave illness of human nature, which every thinking mind will strive to overcome" (Hobbes[58]) — I would even allow myself to propose a rank order of philosophers according to the rank of their laughter — all the way up to those who are capable of *golden* laughter. And supposing that gods, too, philosophize, something to which many a conclusion has driven me to believe — then I do not doubt that they also know how to laugh in a superhuman and innovative way — and at the expense of all serious things! Gods are fond of ridicule: it appears they can not refrain from laughing even during sacred rites.

295[59]

The genius of the heart, as possessed by that great hidden one, the tempter-god and born pied piper of consciences whose voice knows how to descend into the underworld of every soul, who does not say a word, does not glance a glance in which there is not a consideration and recess of temptation, whose mastery includes that he knows how to seem — and not what he is but whatever is one *more* compulsion for his followers to press ever closer to him, in order to follow him ever more inwardly and thoroughly: — the genius of the heart, that causes everything loud and self-satisfied to fall silent and teaches it to listen, that smooths rough souls and gives them a taste of a new yearning — to lie still as a mirror so that the deep sky mirrors itself in them — ; the genius of the heart, that teaches the oafish and over-hasty hand to pause and reach out more delicately; that guesses the hidden and forgotten treasure, the drop of kindness and sweet spirituality beneath dull, thick ice and is a divining rod for every grain of gold that has lain buried for a long time in a dungeon of much mud and sand; the genius of the heart, from whose contact everyone walks away richer, not graced and surprised, not as if blessed and oppressed by some external good, but instead richer in himself, newer than before, broken open, blown upon and sounded out by a thawing wind, less certain perhaps, more delicate, more fragile and more broken but full of hopes that still have no name, full of new willing and currents, full of new unwillingness and countercurrents . . . . . but what am I doing, my friends? Of whom am I speaking to you? Have I forgotten myself to the point where I did not even mention his name to you? unless of course you have not already guessed on your own who this questionable spirit and god is, who wants to be *praised* in such a manner. For as happens to everyone who since childhood has always been on the move and in foreign parts, many strange and not undangerous spirits have also crossed my path, but above all the one of whom I just spoke, and him again and again, namely none other than the god *Dionysus*, that great ambiguous one and tempter god to whom, as you know, I once offered my firstborn in all secrecy and reverence—[60] as the last one it seems who offered a *sacrifice* to him: for I have found no one who could have understood what I did back then.[61] Meanwhile I learned much, all-too-much more about the philosophy of this god[62] and, as I said, from mouth to mouth—I, the last disciple and initiate of the god Dionysus: and so surely I should finally start giving you, my friends, a bit of a taste of this philosophy, as far as I am permitted? In undertones, as is only fair: since we are dealing with many secret, new, foreign, odd and uncanny things. Even the fact that Dionysus is a philosopher and that gods therefore also philosophize seems to me a novelty that is not innocuous and will arouse suspicion precisely among philosophers—among you, my friends, it has less against it, unless it arrives too late

and not at the right hour: since these days you do not like to
believe in God and gods, as I've been told. Perhaps, too, I will
have to go further in the frankness of my narrative than is
always endearing to the strict habits of your ears? Certainly
the god in question went further, very much further in dialogues of this kind and was always out ahead of me by several
steps . . . . Indeed, if it were permitted to ascribe beautiful,
solemn names of splendor and virtue to him, in keeping with
human custom, I would have to greatly extol his explorer and
discoverer courage, his daring honesty, truthfulness and love
of wisdom. But such a god does not know what to do with all
this venerable junk and splendor. "Keep this," he would say,
"for yourself and for your kind and whoever else needs it!
I—have no reason to cover my nakedness!"—As one might
guess: this kind of deity and philosopher is perhaps lacking in
shame?—Thus he once said: "under certain circumstances I
love humans"—and with this he was alluding to Ariadne, who
was present—: "the human being to me is a pleasant, brave
and inventive animal without peers on earth, it can find its
way in any labyrinth. I think highly of it: I often think about
how I can advance it and make it stronger, more evil, deeper
than it is."—"Stronger, more evil and deeper?" I asked, star-
tled. "Yes," he said once more, "stronger, more evil and deeper;
also more beautiful"—and at that the tempter god smiled
his halcyon smile, as if he had just uttered a charming compli-
ment. Here we also see: this deity is lacking not only shame—;
and there are good reasons to conjecture that in some matters
all the gods could learn from us human beings. We humans
are—more humane . . .

296[63]

Oh, what are you anyway, my written and painted thoughts!
It was not long ago that you were still so colorful, young and
malicious, so full of thorns and secret spices that you made me
sneeze and laugh—and now? You have already taken off your
novelty and a few of you, I fear, are ready to become truths:

they already look so immortal, so heart-breakingly righteous, so boring! And was it ever any different? Which things do we copy with our writing and painting,[64] we Mandarins with our Chinese brushes, we immortalizers of things that *can* be written, what is it that we alone are capable of painting? Oh, always the same things on the verge of wilting and starting to lose their fragrance! Oh, always the same fleeting and exhausted storms and yellowed, late feelings! Oh, always the same birds that flew themselves weary and flew astray and now can be caught by hand—by *our* hand! We immortalize whatever cannot live and fly much longer, only things that are tired and worn down! And it is only your *afternoon*, my written and painted thoughts, only for it do I have colors, perhaps many colors, many colorful tender strokes and fifty yellows and browns and greens and reds: — but no one will guess from them what you looked like in your morning, you sudden sparks and wonders of my solitude,[65] you my old beloved——*wicked* thoughts![66]

*   *
*

From Lofty Mountains[67]

Aftersong

Oh lifetime's noon! Oh summer festive rite!
    Oh garden at hand!
Restless in my joy, I wait and watch and stand: —
I await my friends, ready day and night,
Where are you friends? Come now! The time is right!

Is it not for you that the glacier's gray
    In crimson dresses?
The brook looks for you, the ardent wind presses,
Clouds strain higher into the blue today,
Watch for you from bird's-eye view far away.

I've set a place for you, the tallest height: —
    Whose neighbors are stars,
Who dwells so near the abysmal chasm's scars?
My realm — whose realm exceeds the reach of sight?
And my honey — who knows its sweet delight? . . . . .[68]

— There you *are*, friends! — What, it's not *me* at all
    Whom you are seeking?
You hesitate, amazed — but you're not speaking!
Me — no longer? Wrong hand, wrong face, too small?
And *what* I am, my friends — you don't recall?

Aus hohen Bergen.

Nachgesang.

Oh Lebens Mittag! Feierliche Zeit!
    Oh Sommergarten!
Unruhig Glück im Stehn und Spähn und Warten: —
Der Freunde harr' ich, Tag und Nacht bereit,
Wo bleibt ihr Freunde? Kommt! 's ist Zeit! 's ist Zeit!

War's nicht für euch, dass sich des Gletschers Grau
    Heut schmückt mit Rosen?
Euch sucht der Bach, sehnsüchtig drängen, stossen
Sich Wind und Wolke höher heut in's Blau,
Nach euch zu spähn aus fernster Vogel-Schau.

Im Höchsten ward für euch mein Tisch gedeckt: —
    Wer wohnt den Sternen
So nahe, wer des Abgrunds grausten Fernen?
Mein Reich — welch Reich hat weiter sich gereckt?
Und meinen Honig — wer hat ihn geschmeckt? . . . . .

— Da *seid* ihr, Freunde! — Weh, doch *ich* bin's nicht,
    Zu dem ihr wolltet?
Ihr zögert, staunt — ach, dass ihr lieber grolltet!
Ich — bin's nicht mehr? Vertauscht Hand, Schritt, Gesicht?
Und *was* ich bin, euch Freunden — bin ich's nicht?

I have become someone else? Strange to me?
        From me unseated?
A wrestler by himself pinned and defeated?
Who strained against himself too forcefully,
Wounded and blocked by his own victory?

I searched where winds blow sharpest cutting air?
        I stayed alive
Where no one lives, polar wastes that bears survive,
Lost to man and God and curse and prayer?
Turned ghost, and glided over glaciers there?

—You old friends! Look! How pale and shocked are you,
        Full of love and fear!
No, leave! Don't be angry! *You* could not—live here:
Between remotest cliffs of icy blue—
Here you must be hunter and chamois too.

A *wicked* hunter am I!—How the wood
        Tenses in my bow!
Only the strongest archer can bend it so——:
Beware! *This* threatens like no other could,
This arrow—leave here now! For your own good! . . . . .[69]

You turn away?—Oh heart, set yourself free,
        Your hope remained strong:
Now open your doors, let *new* friends come along!
Let old ones go! Let go the memory!
Once you were young—now be so fittingly!

What bond we shared, our common hope has passed—
        Who can read the signs
Once inscribed by love, these blurred and pallid lines?
This seems a parchment that my hand won't clasp
For *loathing*—brown and burnt, and fading fast.

Ein Andrer ward ich? Und mir selber fremd?
    Mir selbst entsprungen?
Ein Ringer, der zu oft sich selbst bezwungen?
Zu oft sich gegen eigne Kraft gestemmt,
Durch eignen Sieg verwundet und gehemmt?

Ich suchte, wo der Wind am schärfsten weht?
    Ich lernte wohnen,
Wo Niemand wohnt, in öden Eisbär-Zonen,
Verlernte Mensch und Gott, Fluch und Gebet?
Ward zum Gespenst, das über Gletscher geht?

—Ihr alten Freunde! Seht! Nun blickt ihr bleich,
    Voll Lieb' und Grausen!
Nein, geht! Zürnt nicht! Hier—könntet *ihr* nicht hausen:
Hier zwischen fernstem Eis- und Felsenreich—
Hier muss man Jäger sein und gemsengleich.

Ein *schlimmer* Jäger ward ich!—Seht, wie steil
    Gespannt mein Bogen!
Der Stärkste war's, der solchen Zug gezogen——:
Doch wehe nun! Gefährlich ist *der* Pfeil,
Wie *kein* Pfeil,—fort von hier! Zu eurem Heil! . . . . .

Ihr wendet euch?—Oh Herz, du trugst genung,
    Stark blieb dein Hoffen:
Halt *neuen* Freunden deine Thüren offen!
Die alten lass! Lass die Erinnerung!
Warst einst du jung, jetzt—bist du besser jung!

Was je uns knüpfte, Einer Hoffnung Band,—
    Wer liest die Zeichen,
Die Liebe einst hineinschrieb, noch, die bleichen?
Dem Pergament vergleich ich's, das die Hand
zu fassen *scheut*,—ihm gleich verbräunt, verbrannt.

No longer friends, they are—I know not what?—
    Merely ghosts of friends!
At night they haunt my house and my heart rends,
They speak to me, "we *were* friends, were we not?"—
—Oh withered word, whose roses turned to rot![70]

Youthful longing, you miscalculated!
    Those *I* yearned to see,
Whom I dreamed had transformed to be more like me,
They grew *old,* and age made them outdated:
He who transforms stays to me related.

Oh lifetime's noon! Oh second youth's new rite!
    Summer garden land!
Restless in my joy, I wait and watch and stand!
I await my friends, ready day and night,
Await *new* friends! Come now! The time is right!

         *   *
            *

This song is done—longing's sweet protest flew
    Before I could speak:
A wizard did it, a friend when times were bleak,
The friend of noon—no! do not ask me who—
It was at noon that One turned into Two . . . . .

Now we celebrate, as triumph[71] unites,
    The fest of all fests:
Friend *Zarathustra*[72] came, the guest of all guests![73]
The world laughs now, torn is the shroud of fright,
The wedding came of darkness and of light . . . . .[74]

Nicht Freunde mehr, das sind—wie nenn' ich's doch?—
      Nur Freunds-Gespenster!
Das klopft mir wohl noch Nachts an Herz und Fenster,
Das sieht mich an und spricht: "wir *waren's* doch?"—
—Oh welkes Wort, das einst wie Rosen roch!

Oh Jugend-Sehnen, das sich missverstand!
      Die *ich* ersehnte,
Die ich mir selbst verwandt-verwandelt wähnte,
Dass *alt* sie wurden, hat sie weggebannt:
Nur wer sich wandelt, bleibt mit mir verwandt.

Oh Lebens Mittag! Zweite Jugendzeit!
      Oh Sommergarten!
Unruhig Glück im Stehn und Spähn und Warten!
Der Freunde harr' ich, Tag und Nacht bereit,
Der *neuen* Freunde! Kommt! 's ist Zeit! 's ist Zeit!

*   *
      *

Dies Lied ist aus,—der Sehnsucht süsser Schrei
      Erstarb im Munde:
Ein Zaubrer that's, der Freund zur rechten Stunde,
Der Mittags-Freund—nein! fragt nicht, wer es sei—
Um Mittag war's, da wurde Eins zu Zwei . . . . .

Nun feiern wir, vereinten Siegs gewiss,
      Das Fest der Feste:
Freund *Zarathustra* kam, der Gast der Gäste!
Nun lacht die Welt, der grause Vorhang riss,
Die Hochzeit kam für Licht und Finsterniss . . . . .

On the Genealogy of Morality

A Polemic

Preface

I

We are unknown to ourselves, we knowing ones: and this for a good reason. We have never sought ourselves — how could it happen that we would some day *find* ourselves? Someone rightly said: "wherever your treasure is, there your heart is also";[1] *our* treasure is where the beehives of our knowledge are. We are always on our way to them, as born winged animals and honey-gatherers of the spirit, concerned from the heart about really only one thing — something "to bring home." Whatever else life involves, the so-called "experiences" — who of us even has enough seriousness for them? Or enough time? In such matters, I fear, we were never really "focused on the matter": we just do not have our hearts there — and not even our ears! On the contrary, like someone divinely distracted and immersed in himself, who has just had his ears rung by the full force of the bell's twelve strokes of noon, suddenly wakes up and asks himself "what was that tolling anyway?" so we, too, sometimes rub our ears *afterward* and ask, quite amazed, quite disconcerted, "what did we really experience here?" and moreover: "who *are* we really?" and then we count, afterward as stated, all the trembling twelve bell strokes of our experience, of our life, our *being* — oh! and then we lose count . . . We simply remain strangers to ourselves by necessity, we do not understand ourselves, we *have to* mistake ourselves, for us the proposition "each is furthest from himself"[2] applies for all eternity—for ourselves we are not "knowing ones" . . .

2

—My thoughts on the *descent* of our moral prejudices—for this is the subject of my polemic—found their first thrifty and tentative expression in that collection of aphorisms that bears the title *Human, All Too Human: A Book for Free Spirits*, whose writing had begun in Sorrento during a winter that allowed me to stop as a wanderer stops and to survey the broad and dangerous land through which my spirit had wandered up till then. This happened in winter of 1876–77; the thoughts themselves are older. Mainly they were the same thoughts that I take up again in the treatises at hand:—let us hope that the long interval has done them good, that they have become riper, brighter, stronger, more perfect! But *that* I still hold on to them today, that in the meantime they themselves have held ever more firmly to each other, indeed have grown into and through each other, strengthens me in my joyful assurance that from the start they might have originated in me not in isolation, not arbitrarily and sporadically, but from a common root, from a *fundamental will* of knowledge commanding from the depths, speaking ever more precisely, demanding ever more precision. For this alone is how it should be with a philosopher. We have no right to be *isolated* about anything: we may neither make isolated errors nor hit the truth in isolated instances. On the contrary, our values, our Yeses and Nos and Ifs and Whethers grow out of our thoughts with the necessity of a tree bearing its fruit—all related and connected to each other and testifying to one will, one health, one soil, one sun. — Whether *you* like their taste, these fruits of ours? — But what do the trees care about that![3] What do *we* care, we philosophers! . . .

3[4]

Given qualms peculiar to me that I do not like to admit—since they concern *morality*, everything that has so far been celebrated as morality on earth—qualms that appeared so early in my life, so uninvited, so irresistibly, so in opposition to my environment, age, models, and ancestry that I almost had the right to call them my "a priori"—my curiosity as well as my suspicion had to stop soon enough at the question of *what* is the real *origin* of our good and evil. In fact the problem of evil hounded me already as a thirteen-year-old boy: I devoted my first literary child's play to it, my first philosophical composition exercise at an age when you have "half childish games, half God in your heart"[5]—and as for my "solution" to the problem back then, well, as is only fair I gave the honor to God and made him the *father* of evil. Is *this* precisely what my "a priori" wanted of me? that new, unmoral or at least immoralistic "a priori" and the, alas! so anti-Kantian, so enigmatic "categorical imperative" that spoke from it, to which since then I have listened more and more, and not just listened? . . . Fortunately I learned early on to differentiate between theological and moral prejudice and I no longer looked for the origin of evil *behind* the world. Some historical and philological schooling, along with an innate, discriminating sense with respect to psychological questions generally, soon transformed my problem into the other: under which conditions did humanity invent the value-judgments good and evil? *and what value do they have themselves?* Have they so far promoted or hindered the thriving of human beings? Are they a sign of distress, impoverishment, degeneration of life? Or conversely, do they reveal the fullness, strength, and will to life, its courage, confidence, its future?—To these questions I found and ventured many different answers, I distinguished between ages, peoples, degrees of rank among individuals, I specialized my problem, from the answers emerged new questions, investigations, conjectures and probabilities: until finally I had my own land, my own ground, an entire unmentioned, growing, blossoming world, secret gardens as it were, of which no one could have an inkling . . . Oh how *fortunate* we are, we knowing ones, provided only that we know how to keep silent long enough! . . .

4

My first impetus to announce anything about my hypotheses
on the origin of morality was provided by a clear, tidy and
clever, even precociously clever little book in which I first
encountered an inverse and perverse kind of genealogical
hypothesis, its genuinely *English* kind, and I was attracted to
it — with that power of attraction possessed by everything
contrary, everything antipodal. The title of the little book was
The Origin of Moral Sensations; its author Dr. Paul Rée; its year
of publication 1877. I have probably never read anything to
which I said No to myself to the extent that I did with this
book, proposition by proposition, conclusion by conclusion;
yet entirely without annoyance and impatience. In the volume
I mentioned earlier, on which I was working at the time, I
made a convenient or inconvenient reference or two to the
propositions of that book, not by refuting them — what do I
care about refutations! — but as befits a positive spirit, by replacing something improbable with something more probable,
and in certain circumstances replacing one error with another.
At the time, as I said, I first brought to light those hypotheses
on descent to which these treatises are dedicated, awkwardly,
as I would conceal from myself last of all, still unfreely, still
without my own language for these things and with many a
relapse and vacillation. In particular compare what I say in
Hum{an,} All Too Hum{an} section 45[6] about the dual prehistory of good and evil (namely from the sphere of the nobles
and that of the slaves); likewise section 136 on the value and
origin of ascetic morality; likewise sections 96 and 99 and Vol.
II, section 89 on the "morality of customs," that much older
and more original kind of morality that diverges *toto coelo*[7]
from the altruistic manner of valuation (in which Dr. Rée, like
all English moral genealogists, sees the moral manner of valuation *in itself*); likewise section 92 of *Wanderer*, section 112 of
Da{wn} on the descent of justice as a settlement between
those roughly equal in power (balance as prerequisite of all

contracts, consequently of all law); likewise on the descent of
punishment *Wand{erer}* sections 22 and 33,[8] for which the aim
of terrorizing is neither essential nor the origin (as Dr. Rée
claims: — on the contrary it is only inserted under certain
circumstances, and always as something incidental, as something added).

5

At bottom something much more important was on my mind
at that precise time than my own or anyone else's indulgence
in hypotheses on the origin of morality (or more precisely: the
latter only for the sake of an end to which it was one means
among many). For me it was a matter of the *value* of morality —
and over this I had to come to terms almost exclusively with
my great teacher Schopenhauer, to whom that book and the
passion and secret contradiction of that book are addressed as
if to a contemporary (— for that book was a "polemic" too).
In particular it was a matter of the value of the "unegoistic,"
the instincts of compassion, self-denial and self-sacrifice that
this very Schopenhauer had gilded, deified and projected
into the beyond for so long that in the end they remained
"values in themselves" to him, on the basis of which he *said No*
to life and also to himself. But against precisely *these* instincts an ever more fundamental mistrust, an ever more
deeply delving skepticism expressed itself in me! Precisely here
I saw the *great* danger of humankind,[9] its most sublime en-
ticement and seduction — where to? to nothingness? — right
here I saw the beginning of the end, the stopping, the
backward-looking[10] weariness, the will turned *against* life, the
ultimate sickness announcing itself tenderly and sadly: I understood the increasingly spreading morality of compassion,
that seized and afflicted even the philosophers, as the most
uncanny symptom of our European culture turned uncanny,
as its detour to a new Buddhism? to a European Buddhism,
to — *nihilism?*[11] . . . After all, this modern privileging and
overestimation of compassion by philosophers is something

new: until now the philosophers had been in agreement about precisely the *worthlessness* of compassion. I will name only Plato, Spinoza, La Rochefoucauld and Kant,[12] four minds as different from one another as possible but united in one thing: in their disdain for compassion. —

6

This problem of the *value* of compassion and of the morality of compassion (—I am an opponent of the disgraceful modern softening of feeling[13]) at first seems to be something isolated, a question mark unto itself; but whoever tarries here, and *learns* to question here, will experience what I experienced: — a tremendous new vista opens up for him, a possibility seizes him like a dizzy spell, every kind of mistrust, suspicion, fear leaps forth, faith in morality, in all morality falters — finally a new demand makes itself heard. Let us pronounce it, this *new demand*: we need a *critique* of moral values, *the value of these values must itself first be questioned* and for this what is needed is knowledge of the conditions and circumstances from which they grew and under which they developed and shifted (morality as consequence, as symptom, as mask, as tartuffery, as illness, as misunderstanding; but also morality as cause, as remedy, as stimulus, as obstacle, as poison), such knowledge as has never before existed or even been desired. People took the *value* of these "values" as given, as factual, as beyond all questioning; until now they have not even doubted or hesitated in the least to posit "the good one" as higher in value than "the evil one," higher in value in the sense of promotion, usefulness, beneficiality with respect to *the* human being generally (including the future of human beings). What? if the opposite were true? What? if there were a symptom of regression in the "good" too, likewise a danger, a seduction, a poison, a narcotic through which perhaps the present lived *at the expense of the future*? Perhaps more comfortably, less dangerously, but also in a pettier style, more basely? . . . So that precisely morality would be to blame if the *highest powerfulness and magnificence* of the human type, in itself possible, were never attained? So that precisely morality were the danger of dangers? . . .

7

Suffice it to say that ever since this vista opened up for me, I had reasons to look around for scholarly, bold and industrious comrades (I am still doing it today). The job at hand is to traverse the enormous, distant and so well hidden land of morality—that which has actually existed, actually been lived—with entirely new questions and as it were with new eyes: and does this not mean almost to *discover* this land for the first time? . . . If in doing so I also thought about the above-mentioned Dr. Rée, among others, then it happened because I did not doubt at all that he himself would be pushed to a more correct method of arriving at answers by the very nature of his questions. Did I deceive myself in this? In any case it was my desire to give such a sharp and disinterested eye a better direction, the direction to a real *history of morality* and to warn him in time against such English indulgence in random hypotheses *out of the blue*. It is plain as day which color has to be a hundred times more important than blue for a genealogist of morals, namely *gray*, that is to say, whatever can be documented, what is actually ascertainable, what actually existed, in sum, the whole long, difficult to decipher hieroglyphic text of our human moral past!— *This* was unknown to Dr. Rée; but he had read Darwin:—and so in his hypotheses the Darwinian beast and the extremely modern, unassuming moral sissy who "no longer bites"[14] obligingly join hands, the latter with an expression of a certain good-natured and refined indolence on his face, in which even a grain of pessimism, of weariness is mixed: as if it were not really worthwhile in the least to take all these things—these problems of morality—so seriously. On the contrary it seems to me that there is nothing at all more *worthy* of being taken seriously; and so for instance their reward is that someday we will perhaps be granted permission to take them *cheerfully*. For cheerfulness, or to say it in my language, *the joyful science*—is a reward: a reward for a long, brave, industrious and subterranean seriousness that is of course not for everyone. But on that day when we can say from the fullness of our hearts: "forward! our old morality also belongs *in the comedy!*" we will have discovered a new complication and possibility for the Dionysian drama of the "destiny of the soul"—: and he will put it to good use, he will, that great ancient, eternal comic poet of our existence, this we can bet on! . . .

8

—If this text is incomprehensible to anyone and grates on their ears, then the blame as I see it does not necessarily lie with me. It is clear enough, assuming as I assume that one has first read my earlier writings[15] and done so without sparing considerable effort; these are in fact not easily accessible. For instance as concerns my *Zarathustra*, I will regard no one as its connoisseur who at some time was not deeply wounded and at some time not deeply delighted by its every word: for only then may he enjoy the privilege of reverent participation in the halcyon element out of which this work was born, in its sunny brilliance, distance, breadth and certainty. In other cases the aphoristic form presents a difficulty: this is based on the fact that today this form is *not taken seriously enough*. An aphorism that is properly stamped and poured is not yet "deciphered" just because someone has read it through; on the contrary, its *interpretation* must first begin now, which requires an art of interpretation. In the third treatise of this book I have offered a sample of what I call "interpretation" in such a case:—this treatise is preceded by an aphorism, and the treatise itself is its commentary. Of course one thing above all is necessary in order to practice reading as an *art* to this extent, a skill that today has been unlearned best of all—which is why more time must pass for my writings to be "readable"—something for which it is almost necessary to be a cow and in any case *not* a "modern man": *rumination* . . .

Sils-Maria, UPPER ENGADINE,

IN JULY 1887.

"Good and Evil," "Good and Bad."

I

—These English psychologists whom we also have to thank for the only attempts so far to arrive at a history of the emergence of morality—they themselves pose no small riddle to us; I confess that as riddles in the flesh they even have an essential advantage over their books—*they themselves are interesting!* These English psychologists—what do they really want? We always find them, whether willingly or unwillingly, at work on the same thing, namely on forcing the *partie honteuse*[1] of our inner world into the foreground and seeking what is truly effective, guiding, decisive for our development, precisely where the intellectual pride of humanity would least *wish* to find it (for example in the *vis inertiae*[2] of habit or in forgetfulness or in a blind and random interlocking and mechanism of ideas or in some purely passive, automatic, reflexive, molecular and thoroughly stupid thing)—what really drives these psychologists in *this* particular direction? Is it perhaps a secret, malicious, base instinct to belittle humanity, perhaps impossible to acknowledge to itself? Or possibly a pessimistic suspicion, the mistrust of disappointed, gloomy idealists turned poisonous and green? Or a small subterranean hostility and rancor toward Christianity (and Plato), that perhaps never made it across the threshold to consciousness? Or even a lustful taste for the disconcerting, the painfully paradoxical, the questionable

and absurd aspects of existence? Or finally—some of everything, a bit of the base, a bit of gloom, a bit of anti-Christianity,
a bit of tickle and need for pepper? . . . But I am told they are
simply old, cold, boring frogs that crawl and hop around on
humans, into humans, as if they were so properly in their element there, namely in a *swamp*. I hear this with defiance, even
more, I do not believe it; and if one is allowed to wish where
one cannot know, then I wish from my heart that it were otherwise with them—that these explorers and microscopists of
the soul were at bottom courageous, magnanimous and proud
animals, who know how to keep their passions and their pain
reined in and have trained themselves to sacrifice all desirability
to truth, to *every* truth, even the plain, harsh, ugly, repulsive,
unchristian, immoral truth . . . For such truths do exist.—

2^3

All due respect therefore to the good spirits who may reign
within these historians of morality! But unfortunately it is
certain that they lack the *historical spirit*[4] itself, that they
themselves have been left in the lurch by all good spirits of history! They all think in an *essentially* unhistorical manner, as is
simply the old custom among philosophers; there is no doubt
of this. The bungling of their moral genealogy shows right
from the start, where it is a matter of determining the descent
of the concept and judgment "good." "Originally"—so they
decreed—"unegoistic acts were praised and called good on
the part of those to whom they were done, therefore by those
to whom they were *useful*; later the origin of the praise was
forgotten and the unegoistic acts were simply perceived as good
because they were always *habitually* praised as good—as if
they were something good in themselves." We see at once:
this first derivation already contains all the typical features of
English psychological idiosyncrasy—we have "usefulness,"
"forgetting," "habit" and in the end "error," all as the basis of
a valuation of which the higher human being up till now has
been proud, as if it were a kind of privilege of humanity gener-

ally. This pride *must* be humbled, this valuation devalued: has this been achieved? . . . Now it is plain to me first of all that the real cradle of the concept "good" is sought and situated in the wrong place by this theory: the judgment "good" does *not* stem from those to whom "good things" are rendered! Rather it was "the good" themselves, that is, the noble, powerful, higher ranking and high-minded who perceived and determined themselves and their doings as good, that is, as ranking foremost, as opposed to all who were lowly, low-minded, base and of the rabble. From this *pathos of distance* they first took for themselves the right to create values, to coin names for values: what did they care about usefulness! The viewpoint of utility is as foreign and unsuited as can possibly be, particularly with respect to such a hot outpouring of the highest rank-ordering and rank-distinguishing value-judgments: here feeling has reached the opposite of that lowly degree of warmth presupposed by any calculating prudence, any calculation of utility—and not only once, not only for an hour of exception, but for the long term. The pathos of nobility and distance, as I said, the lasting and dominating overall and basic feeling of a higher ruling order in relation to a lower order, to a "below"—*that* is the origin of the opposition "good" and "bad." (The master's right to give names goes so far as to allow us to conceive of the origin of language itself as an expression of power on the part of the rulers; they say "this *is* thus and such," they seal every thing and occurrence with a sound and thereby take possession of it, so to speak.) It is due to this origin that from the start the word "good" was definitely *not* attached by necessity to "unegoistic" acts: as is the superstition of those moral genealogists. Rather, it is only with a *decline* of aristocratic value-judgments that this whole opposition of "egoistic" and "unegoistic" imposes more and more on the human conscience—to use my language for it, it is *the herd instinct* that finally gets a word in (also *words* plural). And even then it takes a long time for this instinct to become master to the extent that moral valuation actually hangs on and sticks to that opposition (as is the case for instance in present-day Europe: today the prevailing prejudice already takes "moral," "unegoistic," "*désintéressé*" to be concepts of equal value, with the force of a "fixed idea" and sickness of the brain).

3

But in the second place: quite aside from the historical unten-ability of that hypothesis on the descent of the value-judgment "good," it suffers from an inherent psychological absurdity. The utility of an unegoistic action is supposed to be the origin of its praise, and this origin is supposed to have been *forgotten*: — how is this forgetting even *possible*? Did the utility of such actions perhaps cease at some point? The opposite is the case: this utility has instead been the day-to-day experience at all times, thus something that was continuously underscored anew; consequently, instead of disappearing from consciousness, in-stead of becoming forgettable, it had to impress itself on con-sciousness with ever greater clarity. How much more reason-able is that opposing theory advocated for instance by Herbert Spencer[5] (it is not therefore truer—), that posits the concept "good" as essentially identical with the concept "useful," "ex-pedient," so that precisely in the judgments "good" and "bad" humankind has summed up and sanctioned its *unforgotten* and *unforgettable* experiences concerning useful-expedient, concerning harmful-inexpedient. According to this theory good is whatever has proven itself to be useful from time im-memorial: with this it may claim validity as "valuable in the highest degree," as "valuable in itself." This way of explana-tion is also false, as I said, but at least the explanation is in it-self reasonable and psychologically tenable.

4[6]

—I was pointed in the *right* direction by the question of what the terms for "good" really mean in an etymological respect as formulated by the different languages: here I found that they all lead back to the *same conceptual transformation*—that ev-

erywhere in the context of classes "noble," "lordly" is the basic concept from which "good" in the sense of "noble of soul,"
"lordly," of "superior of soul," "privileged of soul" necessarily
develops: a development that always runs parallel with the
other that ultimately causes "common," "rabble-like,"
"lowly" to cross over to the concept "bad." The most eloquent
example of the latter is the German word *"schlecht"*[7] itself:
which is identical with *"schlicht"*[8] — compare *"schlechtweg,"*
"schlechterdings"[9] — and originally referred to the simple, common man still viewed without a suspicious second glance,
simply contrasted with a nobleman. Around the time of the
Thirty Years' War, late enough therefore, the meaning shifted
to that used today. — This seems to me an *essential* insight
with respect to moral genealogy; that it was only discovered
so late is due to the inhibiting influence exerted by the democratic prejudice in the modern world concerning all questions
of descent, and this extends into the seemingly most objective
sphere of natural science and physiology, as can merely be suggested here. But the mischief that this prejudice can cause
especially for morality and history, once it is unleashed to the
point of hatred, is shown by the infamous case of Buckle;[10]
here the *plebeianism* of the modern spirit, which is of English
extraction, burst forth once more from its native soil, violently
like a muddy volcano and with the oversalted, overloud, vulgar eloquence with which all volcanoes so far have spoken. —

5[11]

With respect to *our* problem, that for good reasons can be
called a *quiet* problem and addresses itself only selectively to a
few ears, it is of no small interest to establish that many times
in those words and roots referring to "good" the main nuance
shines through, on the basis of which as human beings
the noble felt themselves to be of a higher rank. Of course in
the most frequent cases they probably named themselves
after their superiority of power (as "the powerful," "the masters," "the commanders") or after the most visible sign of this

superiority, for example as "the rich," "the owners" (this is the meaning of *arya*[12] and corresponding expressions in Iranian and Slavic). But also after a *typical character trait*: and this is the case that concerns us here. For instance, they call themselves "the truthful": led by the Greek nobility whose mouthpiece is the Megarian poet Theognis.[13] The word ἐσθλός[14] coined for this means in its root someone who *is*, who has reality, who is real, who is true; then, with a subjective turn, the true man as the truthful: in this phase of the conceptual transformation it becomes the by- and catchword of the nobility and goes over completely to the sense of "noble," as distinguished from the *lying* common man as Theognis[15] takes and describes him—until finally after the decline of the nobility the word remains as the description of the *noblesse*[16] of the soul and becomes sweet and ripe, so to speak. In the word κακός[17] as in δειλός[18] (the plebeian as opposed to ἀγαθός[19]) cowardice is underscored: perhaps this provides a clue as to which direction we must take to seek the etymological descent of ἀγαθός, which can be interpreted in many ways. In Latin *malus*[20] (which I place beside μέλας[21]) could refer to the common man as dark-colored, above all as black-haired ("*hic niger est*[22]—") as the pre-Aryan inhabitant of Italian soil, who stood out most conspicuously from the blonds who had become rulers, namely the Aryan conqueror-race; in any case Gaelic offered me the exact corresponding case—*fin*[23] (for example in the name Fin-Gal), the distinguishing word of the nobility, ultimately the good, noble, pure man, originally the blond-headed as opposed to the dark, black-haired original inhabitants. The Celts, incidentally, were definitely a blond race; we do them an injustice when we associate those traits of an essentially dark-haired population, that are noticeable on the more careful ethnographic maps of Germany, with any kind of Celtic descent and mixed blood, as is still done by Virchow:[24] rather it is the *pre-Aryan* population of Germany that shows up in these places. (The same is true for nearly all of Europe: essentially the subjugated race in the end regained the upper hand there, in color, shortness of the skull, perhaps even in the intellectual and social instincts: indeed, who is to say whether modern democracy, even more modern anarchism and specifically that penchant for the "commune," for the most primitive form of society that is common to all socialists of Europe today, does not signify a tremendous *retaliation* on the whole—and that the conqueror- and *master-race*, that of the Aryans, has not succumbed physiologically as well? . . .) The Latin *bonus*[25] I believe I may interpret as "the warrior": assuming I am right in tracing *bonus* to an older *duonus*[26] (compare *bellum = duellum = duen-lum*, in which that *duonus* seems to me to be preserved). *Bonus* therefore as man of strife, of division (*duo*), as man of war: one sees what constituted the "goodness" of a man in ancient Rome. Our German "*gut*" itself: is it not supposed to mean "the godly one," the man "of godly race"? And is it not identical with the popular (originally noble) name of the Goths? The reasons for this supposition do not belong here. —

6

For the time being it is not yet an exception to this rule that the political concept of superiority always resolves itself into a concept of the superiority of the soul (even though it provides occasion for exceptions) when the highest caste is at the same time the *priestly* caste and consequently prefers for its collective designation a predicate reminiscent of its priestly function. Here for instance "pure" and "impure" first appear opposite each other as class distinctions: and here too a "good" and "bad" are later developed in a sense no longer based on class. As for the rest, we should be cautious from the start of taking these concepts "pure" and "impure" too seriously, too broadly or even symbolically: rather, all concepts of more ancient humankind were understood initially in a crude, clumsy, superficial, narrow, straightforward and especially *unsymbolic* sense to an extent that is scarcely conceivable to us. The "pure man" from the beginning is merely someone who washes himself,

who forbids himself certain foods that cause skin diseases,
who does not sleep with the dirty women of the lower common people, who has an aversion to blood—nothing more,
not much more! On the other hand of course it becomes clear
from the whole nature of an essentially priestly aristocracy
why precisely here the valuation opposites could soon become
internalized and sharpened in a dangerous manner; and in
fact through them chasms were ultimately ripped open between one human being and another, over which even an
Achilles of free-spiritedness could not leap without shuddering. From the start there has been something *unhealthy* in
such priestly aristocracies and in the habits prevailing there,
that shy away from action and are partly brooding, partly
emotionally explosive, and whose consequence seems to be
an intestinal disease and neurasthenia that almost inevitably
afflicts priests throughout time; but what they themselves
invented as a remedy against this disease—must we not
conclude that ultimately in its aftereffects it has proven itself a
hundred times more dangerous than the disease from which it
was supposed to redeem? Humankind itself is still sickened by
the aftereffects of these naïve priestly cures! Think for example
of certain dietary forms (avoidance of meat), of fasting, of
sexual abstinence, of the flight "into the wilderness" (Weir
Mitchell isolation cure, of course without the ensuing fattening cure and over-feeding, which contain the most effective
antidotes for all the hysteria of the ascetic ideal): added to this
the whole metaphysics of the priests, hostile to the senses,
making them lazy and cunning, their self-hypnotization in
the manner of fakirs and Brahmins—Brahma used as a glass
button and fixed idea—and the final, only too understandable
general sense of being fed up along with its radical cure, *nothingness* (or God:—the longing for an *unio mystica*[27] with God
is the longing of a Buddhist for nothingness, Nirvana—and
nothing more![28]) For with priests *everything* gets more dangerous, not only curatives and healing arts, but also arrogance,
revenge, perspicacity, dissipation, love, lust to rule, virtue,

sickness; — of course with some fairness we could also add that it was only on the soil of this *essentially dangerous* form of human existence, the priestly form, that human beings became *an interesting animal* at all, that only here the human soul acquired *depth* in a higher sense and became *evil*—and these are in fact the two basic forms to date of the superiority of human beings over other creatures! . .

7

— One will have already guessed how easily the priestly manner of valuation can branch off from the knightly-aristocratic and then develop into its opposite; this is given a special impetus every time the priestly caste and the warrior caste go up against one another jealously and cannot agree on a price. The knightly-aristocratic value judgments presuppose a powerful physicality, a blossoming, rich, even overflowing health along with whatever is required for their preservation: war, adventure, hunting, dancing, war games and in general everything that includes strong, free and cheerful activity. The priestly-noble manner of valuation — as we saw — has different prerequisites: all the worse for it if it comes down to war! As is well known, priests are the *most evil enemies* — but why is this so? Because they are the most impotent. From their impotence their hatred grows to tremendous and uncanny proportions, to the most spiritual and poisonous variety. Priests have always been the truly great haters in world history, also the most ingenious haters: — compared with the spirit of priestly revenge all other spirit barely merits consideration. Human history would be a far too stupid matter without the spirit it has acquired on the part of the impotent: — let us immediately take the greatest example. Everything that has been done on earth against "the noble," "the mighty," "the masters," "the power-holders" is not worth mentioning in comparison with what *the Jews* have done against them: the Jews, that priestly people who in the end were only able to achieve satisfaction from their enemies and conquerors through a radical revaluation of their values, hence through an act of the *most spiritual re-venge*. This way alone was suitable for a priestly people, the people of the most deeply repressed priestly vengeful-ness. It was the Jews who countered the aristocratic value equation   (good = noble = powerful = beautiful = happy = be-loved of God) by daring with fear-inspiring consistency to invert it, and held on to it by the teeth of the most abysmal hatred (the hatred of the impotent), namely "only the miser-able are the good, the poor, impotent, lowly alone are the good, the suffering, deprived, sick, ugly are also the only pi-ous ones, the only ones blessed by God, there is blessedness for them only—whereas you, you noble and mighty, you are in all eternity the evil, cruel, lustful, insatiable, godless, you will also eternally be the unblessed, accursed and damned!" . . . We know *who* inherited this Jewish revaluation . . . I will re-mind my readers of the proposition I arrived at on a different occasion (*Beyond Good and Evil* 195) with respect to the tre-mendous initiative, disastrous beyond all measure, that the Jews gave us with this most fundamental of all declarations of war—namely that with the Jews begins *the slave revolt in morality*: that revolt with a two-thousand year history be-hind it, that has only shifted from our focus because it has been—victorious . . .

8

—But you do not understand this? You do not have eyes for something that needed two millennia to achieve victory? . . . There is nothing surprising about this: all *long* things are dif-ficult to view, to survey. *That* however is how it came about: from the trunk of that tree of revenge and hatred, of Jewish hatred—of the deepest and most sublime hatred moreover, capable of creating ideals and re-creating values, whose like never before existed on earth—grew something just as incom-parable, a *new love*, the deepest and most sublime of all kinds of love:—from what other trunk could it have grown? . . . But we should certainly not suppose that it grew somehow as the actual negation of that thirst for revenge, as the opposite of Jewish hatred! No, the reverse is the truth! This love grew out of it as its crown, as the triumphant crown unfolding itself ever more broadly in the brightest daylight and fullness of sunlight, bent on the goals of that hatred, on victory, on prey, on seduction in the realm of light and of the heights with the same urge, as it were, with which the roots of that hatred had sunk themselves ever more thoroughly and greedily into everything that had depth and was evil. This Jesus of Nazareth as the incarnate gospel of love, this "redeemer" who brought blessedness and victory to the poor, sinners, and the sick — was he not precisely seduction in its most uncanny and irresistible form, seduction and a detour to precisely those *Jewish* values and revisions of their ideal? Did Israel not achieve the final goal of its sublime revenge using this very detour of the "redeemer," this apparent adversary and disintegrator[29] of Israel? Is it not part of the secret black art of a truly *grand* politics of revenge, a far-sighted, subterranean, slow-working and pre-calculating revenge that in front of the whole world Israel itself had to repudiate as its mortal enemy and nail to the cross the actual instrument of its revenge, so that the "whole world," namely all opponents of Israel could unhesitatingly bite into this very bait? And for that matter could anyone in the total sophistication of their spirit have thought up a more *dangerous* bait? Anything that might equal that symbol of the "holy cross" in alluring, intoxicating, benumbing, corrupting power, that grisly paradox of a "god on the cross," that mystery of an inconceivable, ultimate, most extreme cruelty and self-crucifixion of God *for the salvation of humanity*? . . . What is certain at least is that *sub hoc signo*[30] Israel with its revenge and revaluation of all values has so far triumphed again and again over all other ideals, over all *more noble* ideals. — —

9

— "But why are you still talking about *more noble* ideals! Let us acquiesce to the facts: the common people have won — or

'the slaves,' or 'the rabble,' or 'the herd' or whatever you prefer
to call it—if this happened through the Jews, so be it! then
never has a people had a more world-historic mission. 'The
masters' have been dismissed; the morality of the common man
has been victorious. One might at the same time take this victory as a blood-poisoning (it has mixed the races together)—I
do not contradict; but without a doubt this intoxication has
succeeded. The 'redemption' of the human race (namely from
'the masters') is well on its way; everything is noticeably becoming jewified or christianized or rabbleized (what do words
matter!). The progress of this poisoning throughout the entire
body of humankind seems unstoppable, its tempo and pace
from now on can be ever slower, more subtle, less audible,
more thoughtful—one has time after all . . . Does the church
today even have a *necessary* task to this end, even a right to exist at all? Or could we do without it? *Quaeritur.*[31] It appears
that it sooner hinders and retards than accelerates that progress? Well, that in itself could be its usefulness . . . Certainly
by now it has become something crude and peasant-like that
repels a more delicate intelligence and a truly modern taste.
Should it not at least refine itself somewhat? . . . It alienates
today more than it seduces . . . Which of us would even be a
freethinker[32] if the church did not exist? The church repels us,
not its poison . . . Apart from the church, we too love the poison . . ."—This as the epilogue of a "freethinker" to my speech,
an honest beast as he has richly demonstrated, moreover a
democrat; he had listened to me up till then and could not
stand to hear me be silent. You see, there is much for me to be
silent about at this point.—

10

The slave revolt in morality begins when *ressentiment*[33] itself
becomes creative and gives birth to values: the *ressentiment* of
those beings who are denied genuine reaction, that of the deed,
who make up for it only through imaginary revenge. Whereas
all noble morality grows out of a triumphant Yes-saying to

oneself, slave morality from the start says No to an "outside," to a "different," to a "non-self": and *this* No is its creative deed. This reversal of the value-positing gaze—this *necessary* direction to the outside instead of back onto oneself—belongs to the very essence of *ressentiment*: in order to arise, slave morality always first needs an opposing and external world; physiologically speaking it needs external stimuli in order to act at all—its action is reaction from the ground up. The reverse is the case with the noble manner of valuation: it acts and grows spontaneously, it only seeks its opposite in order to say Yes to itself more gratefully, more jubilantly—its negative concept "low," "base" and "bad" is only a late-born, pale and contrasting image compared with its positive basic concept, saturated through and through with life and passion: "We noble ones, we good, beautiful, happy ones!" When the noble manner of valuation errs and sins against reality, this happens relative to the sphere that is *not* sufficiently known to it, indeed, against any real knowledge of which it has rigidly defended itself: under certain circumstances it misjudges the sphere it despises, that of the common man, of the lowly people; on the other hand we should consider that in any case the affect of contempt, of looking down on, of the superior gaze, assuming that it *falsifies* the image of what is despised, will fall far short of the falsification with which the repressed hatred, the revenge of the impotent will assault its opponent—in effigy of course—. Indeed, mixed into contempt are too much carelessness, too much taking-lightly, too much looking-away and impatience, even too much personal joyfulness for it to be capable of transforming its object into a genuine caricature and monster. We should not fail to hear the almost benevolent nuances that for example the Greek nobility puts into all the words they use to distinguish themselves from the lowly people; how a constant kind of regret, consideration, and forbearance get mixed and sugared in, to the point that almost all words reserved for the common man ultimately survive as expressions for "unhappy," "pitiful" (compare δειλός, δείλαιος, πονηϱός, μοχθηϱός,[34] the latter

two actually referring to the common man as work slave and
beast of burden)—and how on the other hand "bad," "lowly,"
"unhappy" never again ceased to resonate in the Greek ear in
a single note with a tone color in which "unhappy" predomi-
nates: this as the heirloom of the ancient, more noble aristocratic manner of valuation that does not deny itself even when
despising (—philologists are to be reminded of the sense in
which οἴζυρός, ἄνολβος, τλήμων, δυςτυχεῖν, ξυμφορά[35]
are used). The "well-born" simply *felt* themselves to be the
"happy"; they did not have to first artificially construct their
happiness by looking at their enemies, or in some cases talking
themselves, *lying themselves into it* (as all people of *ressentiment*
are accustomed to doing); and likewise as full human beings
overloaded with power and consequently active *of necessity*
they knew not to separate actions from happiness—being
active is for them by necessity included in happiness (whence
εὖ πράττειν[36] takes its descent)—all of this very much opposed to the "happiness" on the level of the impotent and
oppressed who festered in poisonous and hostile feelings, in
whom it appears essentially as narcotic, anesthetic, calm,
peace, "Sabbath," relaxing of mental tension and stretching of
limbs, in brief, *passively*. Whereas the noble human being
lives with himself confidently and openly (γενναῖος "noble-
born" underscores the nuance "upright" and probably also "naïve"), the human being of *ressentiment* is neither upright nor
naïve, nor honest and straightforward with himself. His soul
squints; his spirit loves hiding places, secret passages and
back doors, everything hidden seems like *his* world to him,
his security, *his* refreshment; he knows the skill of keeping
silent, not forgetting, waiting, temporarily belittling himself,
humbling himself. A race of such human beings of *ressentiment* will in the end be necessarily *more clever* than any noble
race, and it will also honor cleverness to an entirely different
degree: namely as an existential condition of the first order,
whereas cleverness in noble people easily has a subtle after-
taste of luxury and sophistication about it:—here it is by far

less essential than the perfect functional reliability of the regulating *unconscious* instincts or even a certain imprudence,
such as bravely going at it, be it against danger, be it against
an enemy, or that fanatical suddenness of anger, love, respect, gratitude and revenge by which noble souls have recognized one another throughout time. For the *ressentiment* of
the noble human being, when it does appear in him, consum-
mates and exhausts itself in an immediate reaction, and it
therefore does not *poison*: on the other hand it does not appear
at all in countless cases, where it is unavoidable in all who are
weak and impotent. Not being able to take seriously for any
length of time one's enemies, one's accidents, even one's *misdeeds*—that is the sign of strong, full natures in whom there is
an excess of plastic, reconstructive, healing and even forgetting-
inducing power (a good example of this in the modern world is
Mirabeau, who had no memory for insults and churlish deeds
committed against him and was not able to forgive only because he—forgot). Such a human being simply shakes off with
a single shrug all manner of worms that dig deeply into others;
here alone real "*love* of one's enemies" is also possible—assuming that it is possible at all on earth. How much respect for his
enemies has a noble man!—and such respect is already a bridge
to love . . . For he demands his enemy as his distinction, indeed
he tolerates no other enemy than the one in whom there is
nothing to despise and *very much* to honor![37] Now conversely
imagine "the enemy" as the man of *ressentiment* conceives of
him—and precisely here is his deed, his creation: he has conceived of "the evil enemy," "*the evil one*," and this in fact as a
basic concept out of which he then thinks up a "good one" as
an afterimage and counterpart—himself! . . .

II

The exact opposite, therefore, of the noble man who conceives
the basic concept "good" in advance and spontaneously, namely
out of himself, and from there first creates for himself an idea
of "bad." This "bad" of noble origin and that "evil" from the

cauldron of unsatiated hate — the first a by-product, something incidental, a complementary color; the second on the contrary the original, the beginning, the actual *deed* in the conception of a slave morality — how differently these two words "bad" and "evil" stand there, although they are seemingly juxtaposed with the same concept "good"! But it is *not* the same concept "good": instead we should ask ourselves *who* is actually "evil" in the sense of the morality of *ressentiment*. Answered in all strictness: *precisely* the "good one" of the other morality, precisely the noble, the powerful, the ruler, only recolored, only reinterpreted, only reseen through the poisonous eye of *ressentiment*. Here there is one thing we wish least to deny: whoever got to know those "good ones" only as enemies also got to know nothing but *evil enemies*, and those same human beings who are so strictly held in check *inter pares*[38] by custom, veneration, habit, gratitude, even more by mutual guardedness and jealousy, but who on the other hand prove to be so inventive in consideration, self-control, tenderness, loyalty, pride and friendship in their dealings with one another — they are not much better than unleashed predators in their behavior toward the outside world, where what is foreign, where *the*[39] foreign lands begin. There they enjoy freedom from all social constraint; in the wilderness they make up for the tension brought about by long periods of confinement and enclosure within the peace of the community; they step *back* into the innocence of the predator conscience as jubilant monsters who perhaps walk away from a horrific string of murder, arson, rape and torture in high spirits, with equanimity of the soul, as if they had merely pulled some student prank, convinced that the poets once again have something to sing and praise for a long time to come. What constitutes the ground of all these noble races is the predator, the magnificent *blond beast*[40] roaming about lustily after prey and victory; a discharging of this hidden ground is needed from time to time; the animal must emerge once more, must return to the wilderness: — Roman, Arabic, Teutonic, Japanese nobility, Homeric heroes, Scandinavian Vikings — they are all the same in this need. It is the noble races who have left the concept "barbarian" on all tracks wherever they have gone; even from their highest culture an awareness of this betrays itself, and pride in it as well (for example when Pericles says to his Athenians in that famous funeral oration, "to every land and sea our boldness has broken a path, erecting timeless memorials to itself everywhere for things good *and wicked*"[41]). This "boldness" of noble races, insane, absurd, sudden in its expression; the unpredictable and even improbable nature of their undertakings — Pericles[42] emphasizes the ῥαΘυμία[43] of the Athenians with distinction — their indifference and contempt for security, body, life, comfort; their appalling cheerfulness and depth of lust in all destruction, in all the lusty expressions of victory and cruelty — for those who suffered from this everything was summed up in the image of the "barbarian," of the "evil enemy," perhaps of "Goths" and "Vandals." The profound, icy mistrust that a German arouses as soon as he comes to power, again even now — is still an atavism of that inextinguishable horror with which Europe has for centuries watched the raging of the blond Teutonic beast[44] (although there is scarcely a conceptual, let alone a blood relationship between us Germans and the ancient Teutons). I once drew attention[45] to the embarrassment Hesiod experienced when he thought up the succession of the cultural ages and tried to express them as gold, silver and bronze: he knew of no other way to deal with the contradiction posed by the magnificent but likewise so horrific and violent world of Homer than to make two ages out of a single one, which he now placed one after the other — first the age of the heroes and demigods of Troy and Thebes, as that world had survived in the memory of the noble races who had their own ancestors there; then the bronze age, as that same world appeared to the descendants of the oppressed, pillaged, abused, abducted, sold into slavery: an age of bronze, as mentioned earlier; hard, cold, cruel, bereft of feeling and conscience, crushing everything and drenching it with blood. Supposing that what is now believed anyway to be "truth" were actually true, that it is simply the *meaning of all culture* to breed, from the beast of prey "human being," a tame and civilized animal, a *domestic animal*, then undoubtedly we would have to regard all those instincts of reaction and *ressentiment* with whose help the noble races along with their ideals were ultimately wrecked and overwhelmed as the actual *instruments of culture*; this would of course not necessarily mean that their *bearers* simultaneously represented culture themselves. On the contrary the opposite would not only be probable — no! today it is *obvious*! These bearers of oppressing and retaliation-craving instincts, the descendants of all European and non-European slavery, all pre-Aryan population in particular — they represent the *regression* of humankind! These "instruments of culture" are a disgrace to human beings, and rather a suspicion, a counter-argument against "culture" generally! We might be entirely justified in clinging to our fear of the blond beast[46] at the core of all noble races, in being on guard: but who would not rather fear a hundred times more if he could admire at the same time, than *not* fear but then no longer be able to escape the nauseating sight of the deformed, dwarfed, atrophied and poisoned? And is this not *our* doom? What today constitutes *our* aversion to "human beings"? — for we *suffer* from human beings, there is no doubt. — *Not* fear; rather, that we have nothing more to fear from human beings; that the worm "human" is at the forefront and teeming; that the "tame human," the hopelessly mediocre and unpleasant soul has already learned to feel like the goal and pinnacle, the meaning of history, like a "higher human being"; — indeed, that he has a certain right to feel this way, inasmuch as he feels himself distanced from the profusion of deformed, diseased, weary, worn-out people of which Europe is beginning to stink today, like something then that at least is relatively well-formed, at least still viable, at least able to say Yes to life . . .

12

—At this point I cannot suppress a sigh and a final confidence. What is it that I in particular find wholly unbearable? That with which I alone cannot cope, which makes me suffocate and languish? Bad air! Bad air! That anything deformed comes near me; that I have to smell the entrails of a deformed soul! . . . What are we not able to bear in terms of distress, deprivation, nasty weather, infirmity, toil, isolation? Basically we are able to come to grips with everything else, born as we are to a subterranean and fighting existence; we always emerge again and again into the light, we experience again and again the golden hour of victory—and then we stand there, as we were born, unbreakable, tensed, ready for new, more difficult, more distant things like a bow that only gets pulled tauter by any distress.—But from time to time grant me—assuming there are heavenly benefactresses beyond good and evil—a glimpse, grant me only a single glimpse of something perfect, formed to completion, happy, powerful, triumphant in which there is still something to fear! Of a human being who justifies *the* human being, of a complementary and redeeming stroke of luck of a human being, for whose sake we can hold on to our *faith*[47] *in human beings*! . . . For this is the way things are: the diminution and leveling of the European human conceals *our* greatest danger, because this sight makes us weary . . . Today we do not see anything that wishes to be greater, we sense that things are still going downhill, further down into what is thinner, more good-natured, more prudent, more comfortable, more mediocre, more indifferent, more Chinese, more Christian—human beings, there can be no doubt, are getting "better" all the time . . . It is precisely here that Europe's doom lies—along with the fear of humans we also forfeited our love for them, our respect for them, our hope for them, indeed our will to them. The sight of human beings now makes us weary—what is nihilism today if not *that*? . . . We are weary *of human beings* . . .

13

— But let us return: the problem of the *other* origin of "good,"
of the good man as conceived by the man of *ressentiment*, demands its conclusion. — It does not seem strange that lambs
bear a grudge against the great birds of prey: only this is no
reason to hold it against the great birds of prey that they
snatch themselves little lambs.[48] And when the lambs say to
each other "these birds of prey are evil; and whoever is a bird
of prey to the least possible extent, rather even its opposite, a
lamb — does he not have to be good?" then there is nothing
wrong with this construction of an ideal, even if the birds of
prey were to look upon this a bit sarcastically and perhaps say
to themselves: "*we* do not bear a grudge against them, these
good lambs, in fact we love them: nothing is tastier than a
tender lamb." — To demand of strength that it *not* express
itself as strength, that it *not* be a will to overwhelm, a will to
topple, a will to become master, a thirst for enemies and obstacles and triumphs, is just as absurd as demanding of weakness, that it express itself as strength. A quantum of force is
just such a quantum of drive, of will, of effect — moreover it
is nothing but this very driving, willing, effecting, and it can
only appear otherwise under the seduction of language (and
the basic errors of reason petrified in it), which understands
and misunderstands all effecting as conditioned by something
that effects, by a "subject." For instance, just as ordinary people
separate lightning from its flashing and take the latter as its
doing, as the effect of a subject that is called lightning, so too
popular morality separates strength from the expressions of
strength, as if behind the strong one there were an indifferent
substratum *free to* express strength or not to. But there is no
such substratum; there is no "being" behind the doing, effecting, becoming; the "doer" is merely tacked on as a fiction to
the doing — the doing is everything. The people basically
double the doing when they have the lightning flashing; this is
a doing-doing: it posits the same occurrence once as cause and

then once more as its effect. Natural scientists do no better when they say "force moves, force causes" and so on — despite all its coolness, its freedom from affect, our entire science still stands under the seduction of language and has not gotten rid of the false changelings foisted upon it, the "subjects" (the atom for instance is such a changeling, likewise the Kantian "thing in itself"): no wonder that the repressed, secretly glowing affects of revenge and hatred exploit this belief for themselves and basically even uphold no belief more ardently than the one that says *the strong is free* to be weak, and the bird of prey to be a lamb: — this way after all they gain the right to make the bird of prey *accountable* for being a bird of prey . . . When from the vengeful cunning of their impotence the oppressed, the downtrodden, and the violated encourage one another, saying: "Let's be different than the evil ones, namely good! And good is whoever does not violate, injures no one, whoever does not attack, does not retaliate, leaves revenge to God, whoever like us keeps himself hidden, steers clear of all evil and generally demands little of life, like us patient, humble, righteous souls" — then this really means, heard dispassionately and without prejudice, nothing more than: "we weak ones simply happen to be weak; it is good that we do nothing *that we are not strong enough to do*" — but this harsh matter of fact, this prudence of the lowest sort possessed even by insects (who presumably play dead when in grave danger in order not to do "too much"), has disguised itself in the pomp of resigning, quiet and patient virtue thanks to that counterfeiting and self-deception of impotence, just as if the very weakness of the weak — that is of course his *essence*, his effect, his entire singular, unavoidable, inseparable reality — were a voluntary achievement, something willed, chosen, a *deed*, a *merit*. This kind of human being *needs* the belief in an indifferent elective "subject" due to his instinct of self-preservation and self-affirmation, in which every lie tends to sanctify itself. The subject (or, to speak in more popular terms, the *soul*) is perhaps the best article of faith on earth so far, because it enabled the majority of mortals, the weak and oppressed of every kind, to interpret weakness itself as freedom, and their being thus-and-such as a *merit*.

14

— Does anyone want to go down and take a little peek into the secret of how *ideals are fabricated* on earth? Who has the courage to do this? . . . Well then! Here we have an open view into this dark workshop. Wait just another minute, Mr. Nosey and Daredevil: Your eyes need first to get used to this falsely shimmering light . . . So! Enough! Speak up now! What's going on down there? Tell us what you see, man of the most dangerous curiosity — now *I* am the one who's listening. —

— "I don't see anything, but I hear all the more. There's a cautious, malicious, soft rumoring and whispering coming from all the corners and nooks. It seems to me people are lying; a sugary smoothness clings to every sound. Weakness is in the process of being lied into a *merit*, there is no doubt — it's just as you said it was." —

— Go on!

— "and impotence that does not retaliate into 'kindness'; anxious baseness into 'humility'; subjugation to those whom they hate into 'obedience' (namely to the one they say commands this subjugation — they call him God). The inoffensiveness of the weak man, cowardice itself, of which he has a wealth; his standing-at-the-door, his unavoidable having-to-wait assume a good name here, as 'patience,' it is even called *the* virtue; not being able to avenge oneself is called not wanting to avenge oneself, perhaps even forgiveness ('for *they* know not what they do[49] — we alone know what *they* do!'). They're also talking about 'love of their enemies'[50] — and sweating[51] at the same time."

— Go on!

— "They're miserable, no doubt about it, all these whisperers and nook-dwelling counterfeiters, even though they're crouching together warmly — but they tell me their misery is an election and selection by God, that people beat the dogs they love most; maybe this misery is also a preparation, a test, a schooling, maybe it's even more — something that will one day be compensated for and paid out with tremendous interest in gold, no! in happiness. They call it 'blessedness.'"

— Go on!

— "Now they're letting me know that they're not only better than the mighty, the rulers of the earth whose spittle they have to lick (*not* out of fear, not in the least out of fear! but because God commands that all the authorities be honored[52]) — that they are not only better, but even 'have it better,' or in any case will have it better someday. But enough! enough! I can't take it anymore. Bad air! Bad air! This work-shop where they *fabricate ideals* — it seems to me it stinks of nothing but lies."

— No! Wait a minute! You haven't said anything yet about the masterpiece of these black magic artists who produce white, milk and innocence from every black: — haven't you noticed what is their ultimate in refinement, their boldest, subtlest, most ingenious, most mendacious artistic stroke? Pay attention! These cellar animals full of vengeance and hatred — what exactly do they make out of vengeance and hatred? Did you ever hear these words? If you trusted only their words, would you suspect you were among people of *ressentiment*? . . .

— "I understand, I'll open my ears again (oh! oh! oh! and *close* my nose). Now I am hearing again what they have so often said before: 'We good — *we are the just*' — what they demand they do not call retaliation, but 'the triumph of *justice*'; what they hate is not their enemy, no! they hate '*injustice*,' 'godlessness'; what they believe and hope is not the hope for revenge, the drunkenness of sweet revenge (— 'sweeter than honey' Homer[53] already called it), but the victory of God, of the *just* God over the godless; what remains for them to love on earth are not their brothers in hate, but their 'brothers in love,'[54] as they say, all the good and just of the earth."

— And what do they call that which serves as their comfort against all the sufferings of life — their phantasmagoria of anticipated future blessedness?

— "What? Did I hear right? They call it "the last judgment," the coming of *their* kingdom, the 'kingdom of God' — *meanwhile* however they live 'in faith,' 'in love,' 'in hope.'"[55]

— Enough! Enough!

15

In faith in what? In love of what? In hope of what? — These weak ones — for *they* too want to be the strong ones someday, there is no doubt, someday *their* "kingdom" too shall come — "the kingdom of God" as they simply call it, as I mentioned earlier: they are so humble in all things after all! Even to experience *that*, people will need to live a long time, beyond death — indeed, they need eternal life so that in the "kingdom of God" they can recoup their losses from that earthly life "in faith, in love, in hope." Recoup their losses for what? Recoup their losses through what? . . . It seems to me Dante committed a gross blunder when, with terror-instilling ingenuousness, he placed the inscription "eternal love also created me"[56] over the gate to his hell: — in any case, over the gate of Christian paradise and its "eternal blessedness" a more justified inscription would be "eternal *hatred* also created me" — assuming a truth can be displayed over the gate to a lie! For *what* is the blessedness of that paradise anyway? . . . We would probably guess it on our own; but it is better to have it expressly confirmed by Thomas Aquinas,[57] the great teacher and saint, an authority not to be underestimated in such matters: "*Beati in regno coelesti*," he says, gently as a lamb, "*videbunt poenas damnatorum, ut beatitudo illis magis complaceat.*"[58] Or if one wishes to hear it in a stronger key, say from the mouth of a triumphing church father who counseled his Christians against the cruel delights of the public spectacles — and why? "Faith offers us much more indeed," — he says, *De Spec-taculis* chs. 29f. — "*something much stronger*; thanks to salvation there are entirely different joys at our disposal; instead of athletes we have our martyrs; if we want blood, well, then we have the blood of Christ . . . But what awaits us only on the day of his return, of his triumph!" — and now he continues, the rapturous visionary:[59] "*At enim supersunt alia spectacula, ille ultimus et perpetuus judicii dies, ille nationibus insperatus, ille derisus, cum tanta saeculi vetustas et tot ejus nativitates uno igne haurientur. Quae tunc spectaculi latitudo!* **Quid admirer! Quid rideam! Ubi gaudeam! Ubi exultem**, spectans tot et tantos **reges**, qui in coelum recepti nuntiabantur, cum ipso Jove et ipsis suis testibus in imis tenebris congemescentes! Item praesi-des* (the provincial governors) *persecutores dominici nominis saevioribus quam ipsi flammis saevierunt insultantibus contra Christianos liquescentes! Quos praeterea sapientes illos philoso-phos coram discipulis suis una conflagrantibus erubescentes, qui-bus nihil ad deum pertinere suadebant, quibus animas aut nullas aut non in pristina corpora redituras affirmabant! Etiam poëtàs non ad Rhadamanti nec ad Minois, sed ad inopinati Christi tri-bunal palpitantes! Tunc magis tragoedi audiendi, magis scilicet vocales* (in better voice, even worse screamers) *in sua propria calamitate; tunc histriones cognoscendi, solutiores multo per ig-nem; tunc spectandus auriga in flammea rota totus rubens, tunc xystici contemplandi non in gymnasiis, sed in igne jaculati, nisi quod ne tunc quidem illos velim vivos,*[60] *ut qui malim ad eos potius conspectum **insatiabilem** conferre, qui in dominum de-saevierunt. 'Hic est ille, dicam, fabri aut quaestuariae filius* (as everything that follows shows, and likewise this well-known term from the Talmud for the mother of Jesus, Tertullian from here on means the Jews), *sabbati destructor, Samarites et daemonium habens. Hic est, quem a Juda redemistis, hic est ille arundine et colaphis diverberatus, sputamentis dedecoratus, felle et aceto potatus. Hic est, quem clam discentes subripuerunt, ut resurrexisse dicatur vel hortulanus detraxit, ne lactucae suae frequentia commeantium laederentur.' Ut talia spectes, **ut talibus** *exultes*, *quis tibi praetor aut consul aut quaestor aut sacerdos de sua liberalitate praestabit? Et tamen haec jam habemus quodammodo **per fidem** spiritu imaginante repraesentata. Ceterum qualia illa sunt, quae nec oculus vidit nec auris audivit nec in cor hominis ascenderunt?* (1 Cor. 2:9) *Credo circo et utraque cavea* (first and fourth rank or, according to others, the comic and tragic stage) *et omni stadio gratiora.*" — **Per fidem**:[61] thus it is written.

16

Let us conclude. The two *opposing* values "good and bad," "good and evil" have waged a terrible, millennia-long struggle on earth; and just as certainly as the second value has long been preponderant, even now there is no shortage of places where the struggle continues undecided. One could even say that in the meantime it has been carried ever higher and therefore has become ever deeper, ever more spiritual: so that today perhaps no mark of the "*higher nature*," of the more spiritual nature is more decisive than being split in this sense and still a real battleground for those opposites. The symbol of this struggle, written in a script that has remained legible across all of human history to date, is called "Rome against Judea, Judea against Rome":— so far there has been no greater event than *this* struggle, *this* formulation of the question, *this* deadly contradiction. Rome sensed in the Jew something like anti-nature itself, its antipodal monstrosity, so to speak; in Rome the Jew was considered to be "*convicted* of hatred against the whole human race":[62] rightly so, insofar as we have a right to link the salvation and future of the human race to the unconditional rule of aristocratic values, of Roman values. What, on the other hand, did the Jews feel toward Rome? This can be guessed from a thousand signs; but it suffices to recall once more the Apocalypse of John, that most wanton of all written outbursts that revenge has on its conscience. (We should not underestimate, by the way, the profound consistency of the Christian

instinct when it titled precisely this book of hatred with the
name of the disciple of love, the same one to whom it attributed that enamored-fanatical gospel —: therein lies a piece of
truth, no matter how much literary counterfeiting may have
been necessary for this purpose.) The Romans were indeed the
strong and noble, such that stronger and nobler have never
existed since on earth, and have never even been dreamed of;
every vestige of them, every inscription thrills us, supposing
that one can guess *what* is doing the writing there. The Jews
conversely were the priestly people of *ressentiment* par excellence, endowed with a popular-moral genius without peer:
just compare the similarly talented peoples with the Jews, for
instance the Chinese[63] or the Germans, to really understand
what is first and what is fifth rank. Which of them has *triumphed* in the meantime, Rome or Judea? But there is simply
no doubt: just consider before whom people bow today in
Rome itself as if bowing before the epitome of all the highest
values — and not only in Rome, but over almost half the earth,
wherever human beings have become tame or want to become tame — before *three Jews*, as is well-known, and *one
Jewess* (before Jesus of Nazareth, the fisherman Peter, the
carpet-weaver Paul and the mother of the aforementioned
Jesus, called Mary). This is quite remarkable: Rome has succumbed beyond all doubt. Of course in the Renaissance there
was a brilliant-uncanny revival of the classical ideal, of the
noble manner of valuation of all things: Rome itself moved
like someone awakened from apparent death, under the pressure of the new Judaized Rome built on top of it, which gave
the appearance of an ecumenical synagogue and was called
"church": but Judea triumphed again immediately, thanks to
that thoroughly rabble-like (German and English) *ressentiment*-
movement we call the Reformation, along with what had to
result from it, the restoration of the church — the restoration
as well of the ancient sepulchral slumber of classical Rome. In
an even more decisive and profound sense than before, Judea

once again achieved victory over the classical ideal with the French Revolution: the last political nobleness that existed in Europe, that of the seventeenth and eighteenth *French* centuries, collapsed under the popular instincts of *ressentiment*—never on earth had a greater jubilation, a noisier enthusiasm been heard! To be sure, in the midst of all this the most tremendous, the most unexpected thing happened: the ideal of antiquity itself stepped *bodily* and with unheard-of splendor before the eyes and conscience of humankind—and once again, but stronger, simpler, more penetratingly than ever, the terrible and delightful counter-slogan of the *privilege of the few* rang out against *ressentiment*'s old lying slogan of the *privilege of the many*, against the will to lowering, to debasement, to leveling, to the movement downward and evening-ward of humankind! Like a final sign pointing to the *other* way Napoleon appeared, the most singular and late-born human being there ever was, and in him the incarnate problem of the *noble ideal in itself*—and consider well just *what* kind of problem it is: Napoleon, this synthesis of an *inhuman* and a *superhuman* . . .

17

—Was that the end of it? Was the greatest of all oppositions of ideals thus placed *ad acta*[64] for all time? Or only postponed, postponed for a long time? . . . Should there not someday have to be an even more terrible flaring up of the old fire, one much longer in the making? Still more: would precisely *that* not be something to desire with all our might? even to will? even to promote? . . . Whoever starts to reflect at this point, like my readers, and to think about it further will be hard put to come to the end of it soon—reason enough for me to come to the end, providing that I have long since clarified sufficiently what I *want*, what I want precisely with that dangerous slogan worn so well by my last book: "*Beyond Good and Evil*" . . . This at least does *not* mean "Beyond Good and Bad."——

Note. I take the opportunity provided by this treatise to publicly and formally express a wish that up till now I have only expressed in occasional conversations with scholars: namely that some philosophy faculty might perform an extraordinary service by launching a series of academic prize essays devoted to the promotion of *moral-historical* studies: — perhaps this book will serve to give a strong impetus in just such a direction. Regarding a possibility of this kind allow me to suggest the following question: it merits the attention of philologists and historians just as much as that of actual philosophy scholars by profession:

"*What clues are provided by linguistics, in particular etymological research, to the history of the development of moral concepts?*"

— On the other hand it is of course just as necessary to win the participation of physiologists and physicians for these problems (of the *value* of estimations so far): for which it can be left to the professional philosophers to act as advocates and mediators in this particular case as well, after they have succeeded on the whole in restructuring the originally so dismissive, so mistrustful relationship between philosophy, physiology and medicine into the most cordial and fruitful exchange. In fact all tablets of good, all "thou shalts" of which history or ethnological research is aware, first of all require *physiological* illumination and interpretation, in any case before the psychological kind; likewise all of them await a critique on the part of medical science. The question: what is this or that tablet of good and "morality" *worth*? needs to be posed from the most diverse perspectives, for the question of "value *for what*?" cannot be analyzed too minutely. For instance, something that had obvious value with respect to the greatest possible longevity of a race (or to increasing its adaptive powers to a certain climate or to the preservation of the greatest number) would absolutely not have the same value if it were instead a matter of developing a stronger type. The welfare of the majority and the welfare of the few are opposing value viewpoints: holding the former to be of higher value *in itself* is something we will have to leave to the naïveté of English biologists . . . *All* the sciences from now on must work in advance on this task understood to be that the philosopher has to solve the *problem of values*, that he has to determine the *rank order of values*. —

"Guilt," "Bad Conscience," and Related Matters.

I

To breed an animal that *is allowed to promise* — is this not precisely the paradoxical task that nature has set for itself with respect to human beings? is it not the genuine problem *of* human beings? . . . That this problem has been solved to a high degree must seem all the more amazing to someone who fully appreciates the force that works in opposition here, that of *forgetfulness*. Forgetfulness is not merely a *vis inertiae*,[1] as the shallow believe, rather it is an active, positive faculty of repression in the strictest sense, which is accountable for the fact that whatever we experience, learn, or take in while we are in our digestive state (it could just as well be called "ensouling"[2]) is able to enter our consciousness just as little as the whole thousand-fold process with which our physical nourishment takes place, so-called embodying. Temporarily closing the doors and windows of consciousness; remaining undisturbed by the noise and struggle with which our underworld of service organs works for and against each other; a bit of quiet, a bit of *tabula rasa*[3] of consciousness, so that there is room again for new things, above all for the nobler functions and functionaries, for ruling, anticipating, predetermining (since our organism is oligarchically organized) — this is the use of the active forgetfulness referred to above, a doorkeeper so to speak, an upholder of psychic order, of rest, of etiquette: from which it can be immediately deduced that no happiness, no cheerfulness, no hope, no pride, no *present* could exist without forgetfulness. The person in whom this repression apparatus is damaged and ceases to function can be compared to a dyspeptic (and not merely compared—) he cannot "finish" anything . . . Precisely this necessarily forgetful animal in whom forgetting represents a force, a form of *strong* health, has now bred in itself a counter-faculty, a memory with whose help forgetfulness is exempted for certain cases—namely for those cases where promises are to be made; thus it is by no means a merely passive incapacity to let go of an impression that has been carved, not merely the indigestion of a once-pledged word with which someone is unable to finish, but an active process of not *wanting* to get rid of something, a willing on and on of something once willed, an actual *memory of the will*: so that between the original "I will," "I will do" and the actual discharge of the will, its *act*, a world of new foreign things and circumstances, even acts of will can be unhesitatingly placed in between, without breaking this long chain of willing. But how many different things this presupposes! How humanity must have first learned to separate necessary from accidental occurrences in order to control the future in advance, to think causally, to see and anticipate what is remote as if present, to posit with certainty what is the end, what is the means for this, in general to reckon and be able to calculate—how humanity itself must have first become *calculable, regular, necessary*, even to itself for its own image, in order finally to be able to vouch for itself *as future* to the extent that someone who promises does!

2

Precisely that is the long history of the descent of *responsibility*. As we have already grasped, that task of breeding an animal that is allowed to promise includes as a condition and preparation the closer task of first *making* the human being necessary, uniform, like among like, regular and consequently predictable to a certain degree. The tremendous labor of what I have called the "morality of custom" (cf. *Dawn*, 9, 14, 16[4])—the actual labor of human beings on themselves in the longest period of time of the human race, its entire *prehistoric* labor has its meaning in this, its great justification, regardless of how much harshness, tyranny, obtuseness and idiocy are also inherent in it: human beings were really *made* predictable with the help of the morality of custom and the social strait-jacket. Conversely, if we place ourselves at the end of this tre-mendous process, where the tree finally bears its fruit, where society and its morality of custom finally brings about that *for which* it was only the means: then we find as the ripest fruit on its tree the *sovereign individual,* like only unto himself, the autonomous, supermoral individual who has liberated himself from the morality of custom (for "autonomous" and "moral" are mutually exclusive), in brief, a human being of his own independent, long will who *is allowed to promise*—and in him a proud consciousness twitching in every muscle of *what* has been achieved and has become flesh in him, an actual con-sciousness of power and freedom, a feeling of completion of the human being generally. This individual who has become free, who is really *allowed* to promise, this master of the *free* will, this sovereign—how could he not know what superiority he has here over all who cannot promise and vouch for them-selves, how much trust, how much fear, how much respect he arouses—he *"earns"* all three—and how with this mastery over himself he has necessarily also been handed mastery over circumstances, over nature and all shorter-willed and less reli-able creatures? The "free" human being, the owner of a long, unbreakable will, also has his *standard of value* in this pos-session: gazing out from himself upon others, he either hon-ors or despises; and just as necessarily as he is honored by his peers, the strong and the reliable (those who are *allowed* to promise)—hence everyone who speaks like a sovereign, sol-emnly, rarely, slowly, who is stingy with his trust, whose trust is *distinguishing,* who gives his word as something that can be trusted because he knows himself to be strong enough to keep it even against accidents, even "against fate"—: just as necessarily he will have a kick ready for the feeble reprobates who make promises without being allowed, and his corrective rod for the liar who breaks his word just as soon as it leaves his mouth. The proud knowledge of the extraordinary privilege of *responsibility*, the consciousness of this rare freedom, of this power over himself and fate has settled in him to his uttermost depths and has become instinct, the dominating instinct:—what will he call it, this dominating instinct, supposing that he even needs a word for it? But there is no doubt: this sovereign human being calls it his *conscience* . . .

3

His conscience? . . . It can be sensed in advance that the concept "conscience" that we encounter here in its highest, almost alarming form already has a long history and form-conversion behind it. To be allowed to vouch for oneself and with pride, hence also to be *allowed to say Yes* to oneself—that is a ripe fruit, as I said before, but also a *late* fruit:—how long this fruit had to hang bitter and sour on the tree! And for an even much longer period of time there was nothing at all to be seen of such fruit—no one could have promised it, however certainly everything on this tree was prepared and growing with only it in mind!—"How does one make a capacity for memory in the human animal? How does one impress upon this partly dull, partly distracted momentary understanding, this forgetfulness incarnate, in such a way that it remains present?" . . . This ancient problem was not solved with tender answers and means, as one can well imagine; in fact, perhaps nothing is more terrible and uncanny about the whole prehistory of humans than their *mnemo-technique*. "Something has to be burned in so that it stays in the memory: only whatever does not cease *to hurt* stays in the memory"—that is a main principle from the oldest psychology on earth (unfortunately also the longest). One might even say that wherever solemnity, seriousness, secrecy, gloomy colors still exist today in the lives of people and peoples there is something of

an *aftereffect* of the terror with which earlier times promised,
pledged and vowed: the past, the longest, deepest, harshest
past breathes on us and wells up in us when we become "serious." It never got done without blood, torture, sacrifice when
humanity considered it necessary to make a memory for itself;
the most horrific sacrifices and pledges (which include the
sacrifice of the firstborn), the most repulsive mutilations (for
example castrations), the cruelest ritual forms of all religious
cults (and all religions at their deepest foundations are systems
of cruelty) — all of this has its origin in that instinct that intuited pain to be the most powerful mnemonic aid. In a certain
sense all asceticism belongs here: a couple of ideas are supposed to be made indelible, omnipresent, unforgettable,
"fixed" for the purpose of hypnotizing the whole nervous
and intellectual system through these "fixed ideas" — and the
ascetic procedures and forms of life are a means to free those
ideas from competition with all other ideas in order to make
them "unforgettable." The worse humankind was "at memory," the more terrible was the appearance of its practices; the
harshness of penal laws in particular provides a benchmark for
how much effort it took for these slaves of momentary affect
and desire to be victorious over forgetfulness and to keep *present* a few primitive demands of social coexistence. We Germans certainly do not consider ourselves an especially cruel
and hard-hearted people, less still as especially frivolous and
living for the day; but just look at our old penal code in order
to discover what it took in terms of effort to breed a "people of
thinkers" on this earth (that is to say: *the* people of Europe,
among whom today we can still find a maximum of trust, seriousness, tastelessness and matter-of-factness, qualities with
which it has a right to breed every kind of Europe's mandarin).
These Germans have used terrible means to make a memory for
themselves, in order to become master over their rabble-like
instincts and their attending brutal clumsiness: think of the
old German punishments, for example stoning (— even leg-
end has the millstone falling on the head of the guilty one),

breaking on the wheel (the most characteristic invention and specialty of German genius in the realm of punishment!), throwing stakes, tearing or trampling by horses ("quartering"), boiling the criminal in oil or wine (still used in the fourteenth and fifteenth centuries), the popular flaying alive ("cutting strips"), carving flesh from the chest; and surely also smearing the evildoer with honey and leaving him to the flies under the burning sun.[5] With the help of such images and procedures people finally retained five, six "I will nots" in their memory, with respect to which they gave their *promise* in order to share in the advantages of society—and really! with the help of this kind of memory they finally came "to reason"!—Ah, reason, seriousness, mastery over the affects, this whole gloomy business we call reflection, all these prerogatives and showpieces of the human being: how dearly they have been bought! how much blood and horror are at the bottom of all "good things"! . . .

4

But how then did that other "gloomy thing," the consciousness of guilt, the whole "bad conscience" come into the world?—And with this we return to our genealogists of morality. To say it again—or have I not yet said it at all?—they are worthless. Merely their own "modern" experience, five spans long; no knowledge, no will to knowledge of the past; even less a historical instinct, a "second sight" necessary here above all—and yet they do history of morality: in all fairness this must culminate in results that stand in a relation to truth that is more than just coy. Have these previous genealogists of morality allowed themselves even just to dream from a distance that, for example, the major moral concept "guilt" has its origin[6] in the very material concept "debt"[7]? Or that punishment as *retribution* developed completely apart from any presupposition over freedom or non-freedom of the will?—and this to the extent moreover that there must always first be a *high* level of humanization before the animal "human being" begins to make those much more primitive distinctions such as "deliberate," "negligent," "accidental," "accountable" and their opposites and brings them to bear in meting out punishment. That now so cheap and so apparently natural, unavoidable thought that clearly had to serve as an explanation in the first place for how the feeling of justice came into being on earth, "a criminal deserves punishment *because* he could have acted differently," is in fact a form of human judgment and inference that was achieved extremely late and is quite refined; whoever places it in the beginnings fumbles with crude fingers around the psychology of more ancient humankind. For the longest period of human history punishment was definitely *not* meted out *because* the perpetrator was held responsible for his deed, therefore *not* under the presupposition that only the guilty one was to be punished: — rather, just as parents today still punish their children, from anger over injury suffered, that vents itself against the offender — but this anger is held in check and modified by the idea that every injury has its *equivalent* somewhere and can actually be paid off, even if only through the *pain* of the offender. Where did this ancient, deep-rooted and perhaps now no longer eradicable idea get its power, this idea of an equivalence of injury and pain? I already revealed the answer: in the contractual relationship between *creditor* and *debtor*, which is as old as the existence of "legal subjects" and for its part points back to the basic forms of buying, selling, trading, commerce and traffic.

5

Of course calling to mind these contractual relationships arouses all kinds of suspicion and resistance against the older humankind that created or permitted them, as one would expect from the start given what was noted earlier. Precisely here *promising* takes place; precisely here what matters is *making* a memory for the one who promises; precisely here, we may suspect, there will be a trove of harsh, cruel, painful things. The debtor, in order to inspire trust for his promise of repayment, in order to give a guarantee for the seriousness and the sacredness of his promise, in order to convince his own conscience that repayment is a duty, an obligation, pledges something by virtue of a contract to the creditor in the event he does not pay, something that he otherwise "owns" or over which he otherwise still has power, for example his body or his wife or his freedom or even his life (or, under certain religious presuppositions, even his blessedness, the salvation of his soul, ultimately even peace in the grave: as in Egypt, where the corpse of the debtor had no peace from the creditor even in the grave — and of course this peace truly meant something to the Egyptians in particular).[8] For example, the creditor could subject the body of the debtor to all kinds of indignity and torture, such as cutting off as much of it as seemed appropriate for the size of the debt: — and early on and everywhere assessments were made on this basis, assessments in part horrific for their attention to minute detail, assessments *in law* of individual limbs and body parts. I regard it as progress, as evidence of a freer, more grandly calculating, more *Roman* conception of justice that Rome's Twelve Tables[9] legislation decreed it was a matter of indifference as to how much or how little the creditors carved away in such a case, "*si plus minusve secuerunt, ne fraude esto.*"[10] Let us make the logic of this whole form of compensation clear to ourselves: it is foreign enough. The equivalence is provided by the fact that in place of an advantage that pays directly for the injury (thus in place of compensation in money, land or possession of any kind) the creditor is granted a kind of *pleasure* as repayment and compensation — the pleasure of being allowed to vent his power uninhibitedly on someone powerless, the thrill "*de faire le mal pour le plaisir de le faire*,"[11] the enjoyment of violating: which enjoyment is valued all the higher the deeper and lower the creditor stands in the social order, and which can easily seem to him a delectable morsel, indeed a foretaste of a higher rank. By means of "punishment" of the debtor the creditor partakes of a *master's right*: finally he too arrives for once at the elevating feeling of being allowed to despise and abuse a creature as something "beneath

him"—or at least, in case the actual punishing authority, the
execution of punishment has already transferred to "the authorities," he is able to *see* the creature despised and abused.
The compensation therefore consists in a court order and right
to practice cruelty.—

6

In *this* sphere, hence in legal obligations, the moral conceptual world of "guilt," "conscience," "duty," "sacredness of duty"
has its cradle—its beginning, like the beginning of everything
great on earth, was thoroughly drenched, and for a long time,
in blood. And might we not add that this world at bottom has
never quite lost its odor of blood and torture? (not even in old
Kant: the categorical imperative smells of cruelty . . .) Here
likewise that uncanny and perhaps now inextricable inter-
weaving of the ideas "guilt and suffering" was first knitted. To
ask it again: to what extent can suffering be a compensation
for "debts"? Insofar as *making* someone suffer felt good in the
highest degree, insofar as the injured one traded an extraordinary counter-pleasure for the loss, including the displeasure
over the loss: *making* someone suffer—a real *festival*, something that, as mentioned, was priced more highly the more it
contradicted the rank and the social standing of the creditor.
This said as conjecture: for it is difficult to see to the bottom of
such subterranean things, not to mention embarrassing; and
whoever at this point clumsily throws in the concept of "revenge" veils and obscures his insight more than he facilitates
it (—revenge itself only leads us back to the same problem:
"how can making someone suffer be a compensation?").[12] It
seems to me that the delicacy and even more the tartuffery of
tame domestic animals (that is modern human beings, that is
us) resists imagining with all its power the degree to which
precisely *cruelty* constitutes the great festival joy of more ancient humankind, indeed accompanies almost all of their joys
as an ingredient; how naïvely, on the other hand, and how in-
nocently its need for cruelty emerges, how absolutely it posits

its "disinterested malice" (or, to use Spinoza's words, its *sym-pathia malevolens*[13]) as a *normal* human trait—: thus as some-thing to which the conscience heartily says *Yes*! For a more profound eye, even now there would perhaps be enough to perceive of this oldest and most thorough festival joy of hu-man beings; in *Beyond Good and Evil* 229[14] (even earlier in *Dawn* 18, 77, 113) I cautiously pointed to the ever increasing spiritualization and "deification" of cruelty that runs through the entire history of higher culture (and, taken in a significant sense, even constitutes it). In any case it was not all that long ago that people could not imagine royal weddings and folk festivals on a grand scale without executions, torturings or perhaps an auto-da-fé, and likewise no noble household was without beings on whom one could uninhibitedly vent one's malice and cruel teasing (—think for example of Don Qui-xote at the court of the Duchess: today we read the whole *Don Quixote* with a bitter taste in our mouths, almost with a feel-ing of torment, and in this we would seem very strange, very inscrutable to its author and his contemporaries—but they read it with the best possible conscience as the most cheerful of books, they nearly laughed themselves to death over it).[15] Seeing suffering feels good, making someone suffer even more so—it is a harsh proposition, but an ancient, powerful human, all-too-human principle that, by the way, even the apes would probably endorse: for it is said that in thinking up bizarre cru-elties they richly foreshadow and as it were play "prelude" to humans. Without cruelty, no festival: thus the most ancient, longest period of human history teaches—and also in pun-ishment there is so much that is *festive*!—

7

—With these thoughts, by the way, I am absolutely not will-ing to concede new grist to our pessimists for their discordant and creaking mills of life-weariness; on the contrary, I ex-plicitly intend to demonstrate that back when humankind was not yet ashamed of its cruelty, life on earth was more cheerful than now, where we have pessimists. The darkening of the sky above humanity has always increased in proportion to how humans' shame *at humans* has grown. The weary pessimistic gaze, the mistrust of the enigma of life, the icy No of disgust at life—these are not the indicators of the *most evil* ages of the human race: rather they first come to light as the swamp plants they are, when the swamp to which they belong itself appears,—I mean the pathological tenderization and moralization by virtue of which the creature "human being" ultimately learns to be ashamed of all its instincts. On their path to becoming "angels" (not to use a harsher word here) humans have bred themselves that ruined stomach and that coated tongue through which not only the joy and innocence of the animal have become repugnant to them, but even life itself has become distasteful:—so that sometimes they stand there holding their noses in each other's company, along with Pope Innocent the Third disapprovingly drawing up a catalogue of their repulsive traits ("impure begetting, disgusting nourishment in the womb, vileness of the material from which humans develop, hideous stench, excretion of saliva, urine and feces"[16]). Today, when suffering must always be paraded as the first of arguments *against* existence, as its worst question mark, we do well to remember the times when people judged oppositely, because *making* suffer was indispensable and they saw in it an enchantment of the first order, a genuine seductive lure *to* life. Perhaps back then—and I say this to console the sissies—pain did not yet hurt as much as today; in any case a physician could draw this conclusion if he treated Negroes (these taken as representatives of prehistoric people—) for severe internal infections that would drive even the best-constituted European nearly to despair;—in Negroes they do *not* do this. (In fact the curve of human capacity for pain seems to drop extraordinarily and almost abruptly as soon as we leave behind the upper ten thousand or ten million of the super-cultured; and for my part I do not doubt that the suffering of all animals taken together that have so far been required to answer scientific questions at the point of a scalpel simply does not merit consideration compared with a single painful night in the life of one little hysterical educated woman.) Perhaps it is even permitted to entertain the possibility that the delight in cruelty really need not have died out: in relation to how pain hurts more today, it merely needed a certain sublimation and subtilization, that is, it had to be translated into the imaginative and psychical and adorned with such completely innocuous names that even the tenderest hypocritical conscience would not suspect them ("tragic compassion" is such a name; another is "*les nostalgies de la croix*"[17]). What causes indignation against suffering is not suffering in itself, but the meaninglessness of suffering: yet neither for the Christian who has interpreted an entire secret salvation machinery into his suffering, nor for the naïve human being of earlier times who knew how to interpret all suffering in terms of spectators or agents of suffering, was there ever any such *meaningless* suffering. In order for the world to be rid of hidden, undiscovered, unwitnessed suffering and to honestly negate it, people back then were practically forced to invent gods and intermediate beings of all heights and depths, in short, things that also roam around in secret, that also see in the dark and do not easily allow an interesting, painful spectacle to elude them. Now with the help of such inventions life at that time knew how to perform the trick that it has always known how to perform, to justify itself, to justify its "evil"; for this it would probably need other auxiliary inventions (for instance life as riddle, life as epistemological problem). "Every evil is justified, if the sight of it uplifts a god": thus rang the prehistoric logic of feeling—and really was it only the prehistoric? The gods conceived as friends of *cruel* spectacles—oh how far this ancient idea projects even into our European humanization! on this we might consult Calvin or Luther. It is certain in any case that the *Greeks* still knew of no more pleasant side dish for the happiness of their gods than the joys of cruelty. With what eyes then do you think Homer[18] had his gods look down on the destinies of human beings? What at bottom was the ultimate meaning of Trojan wars and similar tragic horrors? It cannot be doubted in the least: they were intended as *festival games* for the gods: and insofar as the poet is of a more "godlike" disposition in these matters than other people, probably also as festival games for the poets . . . Later the moral philosophers of Greece thought no differently with respect to the eyes of a god looking down on the moral struggle, the heroism and self-torment of the virtuous: the "Heracles of duty" was on a stage, he knew himself to be on it too; virtue without witnesses was completely inconceivable for this thespian people. Was not that so audacious, so fateful invention of the philosophers, which was first made at the time for Europe, that of "free will," of the absolute spontaneity of human beings in good and evil, not made above all in order to create a right to the idea that the gods' interest in humans, in human virtue *could never exhaust itself*? On this earthly stage there was never supposed to be a shortage of really new, of really unheard-of tensions, complications, catastrophes: a completely deterministically conceived world would have been predictable for gods and consequently also tiresome after a brief while — reason enough for these *friends of the gods*, the philosophers, not to ascribe such a deterministic world to their gods! The whole humankind of antiquity is full of delicate consideration for "the spectator," as an essentially public, essentially visible world that could not imagine happiness without spectacles and festivals. — And, as stated previously, even in great *punishment* there is so much that is festive! . . .

8

The feeling of guilt, of personal responsibility, to return again to the course of our investigation, has its origin as we saw in the oldest and most primitive personal relationship of all, in the relationship between buyer and seller, creditor and debtor: here for the first time person confronted person, here a person first *measured himself* against another person. Up till now no level of civilization, regardless how low, has been discovered in which something of this relationship did not already show. Setting prices, measuring values, thinking up equivalents, exchanging—this preoccupied the very first thinking of human beings to such an extent that in a certain sense it is *the* thinking per se: here the oldest kind of shrewdness was bred, and likewise here we could suspect the first stirrings of human pride, their feeling of superiority with respect to other animals. Perhaps our word "human" (*manas*[19]) still expresses precisely something of *this* self-esteem: man[20] described himself as the being that measures values, values and measures, as the "valuating animal in itself." Purchase and sale, along with their psychological apparatus, are older than even the beginnings of any kind of social organizational forms and associations: from the most rudimentary form of personal legal rights the budding feeling of exchange, contract, guilt, right, obligation, compensation first *transferred* into the crudest and most nascent complexes (in their relationship to similar complexes), along with the custom of comparing, measuring and calculating power against power. The eye was simply adjusted to this perspective: and with that clumsy consistency unique to older humankind, ponderous at first but then inexorably proceeding in the same direction, they soon arrived at the great generalization "each thing has its price; *everything* can be paid for"—the oldest and most naïve moral canon of *justice*, the beginning of all "good-naturedness," all "fairness," all "good will," all "objectivity" on earth. Justice at this first level is the good will among those who are roughly equal in power to come to terms with one another, to reach an "understanding" again through a settlement—and with respect to those who are less powerful, to *force* them to settle among themselves. —

9

Measured always by the standard of prehistory (which prehistory by the way is present at all times or is possible again): so too the community stands to its members in that important basic relationship of the creditor to his debtors. People live in a community, they enjoy the advantages of a community (oh what advantages! we sometimes underestimate this today), they live protected, cared for, in peace and trust, carefree with respect to certain injuries and hostilities to which the man *outside*, the "outlaw" is exposed—a German understands what "Elend," *êlend* originally meant[21]—as people pledged and obligated themselves to the community with respect to precisely these injuries and hostilities. What will happen *otherwise*? The community, the deceived creditor, will get whatever repayment it can, we can count on this. What is least at stake here is the direct injury caused by the offender: aside from this, the lawbreaker is above all a "breaker," a breaker of his contract and word *to the whole*, with respect to all the goods and conveniences of communal life in which he had shared up till now. The lawbreaker is a debtor who not only does not repay the advantages and advances granted him, but who even attacks his creditor: therefore from now on, as is fair, not only does he lose all these goods and advantages—rather, he is now reminded of *what these goods are worth*. The anger of the injured creditor, of the community restores him to the wild and outlaw condition from which he was previously protected: it pushes him away—and now every manner of hostility may be vented on him. At this level of civilization "punishment" is merely the copy, the *mimus*[22] of normal behavior toward the hated, disarmed, defeated enemy who has lost not only every right and protection, but also every mercy; thus the law of war and the victory celebration of the *vae victis!*[23] in all their mercilessness and cruelty:—which explains why war itself (including the warlike cult of sacrifice) has produced all the *forms* in which punishment has appeared throughout history.

10

As its power increases, a community no longer takes so seriously the transgressions of the individual, because they can no longer be regarded as dangerous and destabilizing for the existence of the whole to the same degree as earlier: the evildoer is no longer "declared an outlaw" and banished, the general anger is no longer allowed to vent itself on him unbridled as before — rather, from now on the whole will carefully defend and protect the evildoer against this anger, especially that of the directly injured party. Compromise with the anger of those chiefly affected by the misdeed; efforts to localize the case and to prevent a further or even general participation and unrest; attempts to find equivalents and to settle the whole matter (the *compositio*[24]); above all the ever more clearly emerging will to take every transgression as *dischargeable* in some manner, therefore at least to a certain extent *isolating*[25] the criminal and his deed from each other — these traits are imprinted with increasing clarity on the further development of penal law. If the power and self-confidence of a community grow, then its penal law always becomes milder; every weakening and deeper endangerment of the former again brings to light the harsher forms of the latter. The "creditor" has always become more humane to the degree that he has become richer; ultimately how much impairment he can endure without suffering from it even determines the *measure* of his wealth. A *consciousness of power* in society could be imagined according to which society would afford itself the noblest luxury available to it — that of letting its offender *go unpunished*. "What do I care about my parasites?" it might say then. "May they live and prosper: I am still strong enough for that!" . . . The justice that began with "everything is dischargeable, everything must be discharged" ends by looking the other way and allowing the one who is incapable of paying to go free — it ends like every good thing on earth, by *sublating itself*. This self-sublation of justice: we know by what beautiful name it calls itself — *mercy*; it remains, as is self-evident, the prerogative of the most powerful, or better yet, his beyond-the-law.[26]

11

— Here a repudiating word against recent attempts to seek the origin of justice on quite different ground — namely on that of *ressentiment*. Let me whisper something first to the psychologists, supposing they have any desire to personally study *ressentiment* up close: this plant now blossoms most beautifully among anarchists and anti-Semites, in secret, by the way, as it always has, like the violet but with a different fragrance. And just as like must necessarily issue from like, it will not surprise us to see attempts emanating again from such circles as they have often in the past — compare section 14 above — to sanctify *revenge* under the name of *justice* — as if justice were at bottom only a further development of the feeling of being injured — and with revenge to retroactively restore the honor of the *reactive* affects generally and collectively. I would be least offended by the latter: it would even appear to me to be a *merit* with respect to the whole biological problem (in relation to which the value of those affects so far has been underestimated). All I am pointing out is the circumstance that it is the spirit of *ressentiment* itself from which this new nuance of scientific fairness grows (in favor of hatred, envy, ill will, suspicion, rancor, revenge). For this "scientific fairness" ceases at once and makes room for accents of lethal hostility and prejudice as soon as it is a matter of a different group of affects that, it seems to me, are of a still far higher biological value than those reactive ones, and consequently really deserve to be *scientifically* appraised and esteemed: namely the genuinely *active* affects like lust to rule, greed and so on. (E. Dühring, *Value of Life*; *Course in Philosophy*; and basically throughout.[27]) So much in opposition to this tendency in general: but as concerns the specific proposition of Dühring that the homeland of justice must be sought on the soil of reactive feelings, for the sake of truth this has to be sharply rebutted with a counterproposition: the *last* soil conquered by the spirit of justice is the soil of reactive feeling! If it really happens that the just human being remains just even toward his offender (and not only cold, moderate, distant, indifferent: being just is always a *positive* behavior); if even under the onslaught of personal injury, scorn and accusation the lofty, clear objectivity of the just, the *judging* eye, whose gaze is as deep as it is mild, does not grow dim, well then, this is a piece of perfection and supreme mastery on earth — indeed something that prudently is not expected here, something in any case that should certainly not be easily *believed*. It is certain that on average even with the most just persons a small dose of attack, malice and insinuation suffices to pump the blood into their eyes and the fairness *out* of their eyes. The active, attacking, infringing individual is always a hundred paces closer to justice than the reactive; it is simply not necessary at all for him to appraise his object falsely and with prejudice in the way the reactive person does, and must do. Therefore in all ages the aggressive human being, as the stronger, braver, nobler, has in fact also had the *freer* eye, the *better* conscience on his side: conversely it is easy to guess who has the invention of "bad conscience" on their conscience in the first place — the human of *ressentiment*! Finally, just look around in history: in which sphere so far has the whole administration of law, and also the real need for law been at home? In the sphere of reactive human beings perhaps? Not in the least: rather in the sphere of the active, strong, spontaneous, aggressive. Viewed historically law on earth represents — to the dismay of the aforementioned agitator, let it be said (who himself once confessed: "the doctrine of revenge is the red thread of justice running through all my works and efforts"[28]) — precisely the struggle *against* reactive feelings, the war against them on the part of active and aggressive powers, who spent part of their strength in putting an end to and imposing moderation on the excesses of reactive pathos and to forcing a settlement. Wherever justice is practiced and upheld we see a stronger power in relation to weaker ones subordinate to it (whether groups or individuals) seeking a means to make an end of the senseless raging of *ressentiment* among them, partly by removing the object of *ressentiment* from the hands of revenge, partly by substituting for revenge the struggle against the enemies of peace and order, partly by finding, suggesting or under certain circumstances imposing settlements, partly by raising certain equivalents of injuries to serve as norms with which *ressentiment* must henceforth comply once and for all. But the most decisive thing that supreme power does and enforces against the predominance of counter- and after-feelings—it does it all the time as soon as it is strong enough for this—is the establishment of *law*, the imperative declaration generally of what in its eyes will count as permissible, as just, as forbidden and unjust; insofar as after the establishment of law it treats infringements and wanton acts of individuals or whole groups as violations of the law, as rejection of the supreme power itself, it channels the emotion of its subjects away from the direct injuries inflicted by such violations, thereby achieving for the long term the opposite of what all revenge wants, which only sees and only grants legitimacy to the viewpoint of the injured party—: from now on the eye will be practiced for an increasingly *impersonal* appraisal of the deed, even the eye of the injured party himself (although this last of all, as mentioned earlier). —Accordingly "justice" and "injustice" exist only once law is established (and *not*, as Dühring wants, beginning with the injurious act). To speak of justice and injustice *in themselves* is devoid of all meaning, *in itself* of course an injury, violation, annihilation cannot be "unjust," insofar as life functions *essentially* in an injurious, violating, exploitative, annihilating manner specifically in its basic functions, and cannot be thought of at all without this character. We even have to admit to ourselves something more disturbing: that from the highest biological standpoint, legal circumstances can always be only *exceptional circumstances*, as partial restrictions of the actual will to life that aims at power, and they are subordinate as individual means to that will's overall goal: namely as a means to create *greater* units of power. A legal system conceived as sovereign and universal, not as a means in the struggle of power complexes but as a means *against* all struggle generally, perhaps in accordance with Dühring's communist cliché that every will has to consider every other will as equal, would be a principle *hostile to life*, an annihilator and dissolver of humanity, an assassination attempt on humanity's future, a sign of weariness, a secret path to nothingness.[29] —

12

Here another word about the origin and purpose of punishment—two problems that are separate, or should be separate:[30] though unfortunately they are often conflated. How do the previous genealogists of morality go about it in this case? Naïvely, as they have always done—: they discover some "purpose" in punishment, for instance revenge or deterrence, then they blithely place this purpose at the beginning, as *causa fiendi*[31] of punishment, and—they're finished. But the "purpose of law" should be used as the very last resort for the history of the emergence of law: on the contrary, for every kind of history no proposition is more important than that derived with such effort but which also *should be* derived—namely that the cause of the emergence of a thing and its ultimate utility, its actual application and integration into a system of purposes lie apart *toto coelo*;[32] that something already existing, something that has somehow come into being is always interpreted for new views, newly appropriated, transformed and reorganized for a new purpose by a superior power; that all occurrences in the organic world are an *overpowering*, a becoming-master and that in turn all overpowering and becoming-master are a new interpreting, a contriving in which the previous "meaning" and "purpose" must necessarily be obscured or entirely extinguished. However well we may have grasped the *utility* of some physiological organ (or also of a legal institution, or a social custom, a political practice, a form in the arts or in religious cults), still we have understood nothing with respect to its emergence: as uncomfortable and unpleasant as it may sound to older ears—since it has been believed from time immemorial that understanding the demonstrable purpose, the utility of a thing, a form or an institution also meant understanding the reason for its emergence, the eye as made for seeing, the hand as made for grasping. So too we imagined punishment as invented for punishing. But all purposes, all utilities are only *signs* that a will to power has become master over something less powerful and has impressed its own functional meaning onto it; and the entire history of a "thing," an organ, a practice can thus be a continuous sign-chain of ever new interpretations and contrivances whose causes do not have to be related even among themselves, but on the contrary at times merely follow and replace one another accidentally. The "evolution" of a thing, a practice, an organ is accordingly least of all its *progressus* toward a goal, even less a logical and shortest *progressus* achieved with the least expenditure of energy and cost—instead, it is the succession of more or less profound, more or less mutually independent processes of overpowering playing themselves out in it, along with the resistances applied to them each time, the attempted transformations for the purpose of defense and reaction, also the results of successful counter-actions.[33] The form is fluid, but the "meaning" is even more so . . . Even within each individual organism things are no different: with every substantial growth of the whole the "meaning" of the individual organs also shifts—sometimes their partial destruction, their decline in number (for example through annihilation of the intermediary members) can be a sign of growing strength and perfection. I meant to say: even the partial *loss of utility*, atrophying and degenerating, loss of meaning and purposiveness, in short, death belong to the conditions of actual *progressus*: which always appears in the form of a will and way to *greater power* and is always asserted at the expense of numerous smaller powers. The magnitude of "progress" is indeed *measured* by the mass of whatever had to be sacrificed for it; humankind as a mass sacrificed for the flourishing of a single *stronger* species of human—that *would* be progress . . . —I emphasize this major viewpoint of historical method all the more because basically it opposes the now prevailing instincts and taste of the age that would sooner reconcile itself with the absolute randomness, indeed mechanistic absurdity of all events, than with the theory of a *power-will* playing itself out in all events. The democratic idiosyncrasy against everything that rules and wants to rule, the modern *misarchism* (to coin a bad word for a bad thing) has gradually transposed and disguised itself into the spiritual, the most spiritual of things to such an extent that today it penetrates into the most rigorous, seemingly most objective sciences, and is *allowed* to; indeed to me it seems to have already become master over the whole of physiology and the doctrine of life, to its detriment as is self-evident, since it has conjured away one of its basic concepts, that of actual *activity*. In place of it, under the pressure of that idiosyncrasy, "adaptation" is placed in the foreground, that is, a second-class activity, a mere reactivity, indeed life itself has been defined as an increasingly purposive inner adaptation to external circumstances (Herbert Spencer). But in doing so the essence of life, its *will to power* goes unheeded; in so doing we overlook the principal superiority of the spontaneous, attacking, infringing, reinterpreting, reordering and shaping powers, upon whose effect "adaptation" first follows; in so doing the mastering role of the highest functionaries is denied in the organism itself, in which the will to life appears active and form-giving. We recall what Huxley[34] accused Spencer of—his "administrative nihilism": but there is *more* at stake here than "administering" . . .

13

—To return now to the subject, that is to *punishment*, two things in it must be distinguished: first what is relatively *lasting* in it, the practice, the act, the "drama," a certain strict sequence of procedures, and on the other hand what is *fluid* in it, the meaning, the purpose, the expectation associated with

the execution of such procedures. For this it is assumed without fanfare, *per analogiam*,[35] according to the major viewpoint
of historical method just developed, that the procedure itself
will be something older, earlier than its use for punishment,
that the latter is only *inserted into* and interpreted into the
procedure (which had long existed but was used in a different
sense), in brief, that matters do *not* stand as our naïve genealogists of morality and law so far assumed, all of whom thought
of the procedure as *invented* for the purpose of punishment,
just as earlier the hand was thought of as invented for the
purpose of grasping. Now as concerns that other element in
punishment, the fluid, its "meaning," the concept "punishment" in a very late stage of culture (for example in today's
Europe) in fact no longer represents one meaning at all, but a
whole synthesis of "meanings": the previous history of punishment generally, the history of its exploitation for the most diverse purposes, ultimately crystallizes into a kind of unity that
is difficult to sort out, difficult to analyze and, it must be emphasized, entirely *undefinable*. (Today it is impossible to say
with certainty *why* people punish: all concepts in which an
entire process summarizes itself semiotically elude definition;
only that which has no history is definable.) On the other
hand, in an earlier stage that synthesis of "meanings" seems
more capable of being sorted out, also more shiftable; we can
still perceive how for each individual case the elements of
synthesis change their valence and accordingly rearrange
themselves, so that now this, now that element steps forth
and dominates at the expenses of the others, indeed at times a
single element (say the purpose of deterrence) seems to cancel
out all the rest of the elements. In order at least to give an idea
of how uncertain, how subsequent, how accidental is "the
meaning" of punishment and how one and the same procedure can be used, interpreted and contrived for fundamentally different purposes: let me offer here the scheme I came
up with on the basis of a relatively small and random sample
of material. Punishment as rendering harmless, as prevention

of further injury. Punishment as repayment to the injured party for injury in some form (also in that of affect-compensation). Punishment as isolation of a disturbance of equilibrium in order to prevent the spread of the disturbance. Punishment as instilling fear of those who determine and carry out punishment. Punishment as a kind of compensation for the benefits that the criminal has enjoyed up to that point (for instance when he is made useful as a slave in the mines). Punishment as the eliminating of a degenerating element (at times of an entire branch, as according to Chinese law:[36] thus as a means of preserving the purity of the race or maintaining a social type). Punishment as festival, namely as violation and mockery of a finally conquered enemy. Punishment as making a memory, whether for the one who experiences the punishment — so-called "improvement," or for the witnesses of the execution. Punishment as payment of an honorarium, stipulated on the part of the power that protects the evildoer from the excesses of revenge. Punishment as a compromise with the natural state of revenge, insofar as the latter is still upheld and claimed as a privilege by powerful clans. Punishment as a declaration of war and as war-measures against an enemy of the peace, of law, of order and of the authorities, who is opposed as dangerous for the community, as a breaker of contracts relating to its preconditions, as a rebel, traitor and breaker of the peace, using the means presented by war. —

14

This list is certainly not complete; obviously punishment is overloaded with utilities of all kinds. All the more reason to deduct from it an *alleged* utility that of course is regarded as its most essential one in the popular consciousness — today faith in punishment that is teetering for many reasons finds its strongest support precisely in it. Punishment is alleged to have the value of awakening the *feeling of guilt* in the guilty party, in it is sought the actual *instrumentum* of that psychical reaction called "bad conscience," and "sting of conscience." But in doing so we desecrate reality and psychology even for today: and how much more so for the longest part of human history, its prehistory! The genuine sting of conscience is something extremely rare precisely among criminals and prisoners; the jails and prisons are *not* breeding grounds where this species of gnawing worm prefers to thrive: — on this all conscientious observers agree, who in many cases abandon such a judgment reluctantly enough and against their deepest inclinations. All in all, punishment makes people hard and cold; it concentrates, it sharpens the feeling of alienation; it strengthens the power of resistance. If it should happen that it breaks one's energy and brings about a pitiful prostration and self-abasement, then such a result is certainly even less enjoyable than the average effect of punishment: characterized by a dry, gloomy seriousness. But if we think instead of those millennia *before* human history, then we can judge unhesitatingly that precisely through punishment the development of the feeling of guilt has been most strongly *hindered* — at least with respect to the victims on whom the punishing force vented itself. For we should not underestimate the extent to which the criminal himself is hindered by the very sight of judicial and executive procedures from perceiving his deed, the nature of his deed, as reprehensible *in itself*: after all, he sees the exact same kind of deeds practiced in the service of justice and then approved, and practiced with good conscience: thus spying, deception, bribery, setting traps, the whole sneaky and underhanded art of police and prosecutors, then the robbing, overpowering, slandering, taking prisoner, torturing, murdering as they unfold in the different kinds of punishment, on principle and lacking even the excuse of emotion — all of them by no means actions *in themselves* repudiated and condemned by his judges, but only in a certain respect and practical application. "Bad conscience," this most uncanny and interesting plant of our earthly vegetation, did *not* grow from this soil — in fact for the longest time in the consciousness of the judging and the punishing themselves *nothing* indicated that they were dealing with a "guilty" party. But instead with a perpetrator of injury, with an irresponsible piece of fate. And that very one upon whom punishment later fell, again like a piece of fate, had no other "inner anguish" during all this than that caused by the sudden appearance of something unforeseen, a terrible natural event, a plummeting, crushing boulder against which there can be no more fighting.

15

Spinoza once became conscious of this in an insidious manner (to the annoyance of his interpreters who truly *labor* to misunderstand him on this point, for example Kuno Fischer[37]), when one afternoon, chafing at who knows what kind of recollection, he dwelled on the question of what really remained for him of the famous *morsus conscientiae*[38] — he, who had banished good and evil to the realm of human illusions and had seethingly defended the honor of his "free" God against those blasphemers whose assertion implied that God works everything *sub ratione boni*[39] ("but that would subject God to fate and would truly be the greatest of all absurdities"[40] —). For Spinoza the world had reverted to that innocence in which it lay before the invention of bad conscience: now what had become of the *morsus conscientiae*? "The opposite of *gaudium*,"[41] he said to himself, finally, — "a sadness accompanied by the notion of a bygone matter that turned out counter to all expectations." *Eth. III propos. XVIII schol. I. II.* For thousands of years instigators of evil overtaken by punishment have felt *no differently than Spinoza* with respect to their "transgression": "here something unexpectedly went wrong," *not*: "I shouldn't have done that" — they submitted to punishment the way someone submits to a sickness or a misfortune or death, with that resolute fatalism without revolt that even today gives the Russians, for example, an advantage over us westerners in dealing with life. If there was a critique of the deed back then, it was prudence that exercised this critique of the deed: without question we must seek the actual *effect* of punishment

above all in a sharpening of prudence, in an extension of
memory, in a will henceforth to work more cautiously, more
mistrustfully, more secretively, in the realization once and for
all that people are too weak for many things, in a kind of
improvement in self-assessment. What can be achieved by
punishment on the whole, with humans and animals, is an
increase of fear, a sharpening of prudence, a mastery of one's
desires: this is how punishment *tames* a human being, but it
does not make him "better"—we could with greater justice
claim the very opposite. ("Injury makes you prudent," say the
common folk: insofar as it makes prudent, it also makes bad.
Fortunately it often enough makes stupid.)

16

At this point there is no getting around helping my own
hypothesis on the origin of "bad conscience" to its first preliminary expression: it is not easy to voice and it needs to be
thought out, watched over and slept on for a long time. I regard bad conscience as the deep sickness to which humans
had to succumb under the pressure of that most fundamental
of all changes they could ever experience—that change of
finding themselves locked once and for all under the spell
of society and peace. No differently than it must have been
for aquatic animals when they were forced either to become
land animals or to perish, so too it must have been with these
semi-animals who had adapted so successfully to the wilderness, warfare, roaming around and adventure—all at once all
of their instincts were devalued and "disconnected." From
now on they would have to go on foot and "carry themselves," when earlier they were carried by the water: a horrific
gravity lay upon them. They felt awkward doing the simplest
chores, they no longer had their old guide for this new unknown world, the regulating drives that unconsciously guided
them safely—they were reduced to thinking, inferring, calculating, combining causes and effects, these wretches, reduced
to their "consciousness," to their most feeble and most mistake-

prone organ! I believe that never on earth had such a feeling of misery, such a leaden uneasiness, existed — and what's more those old instincts had not all of a sudden ceased to make their demands! Only it was difficult and rarely possible to comply with them: for the most part they had to seek out new and as it were subterranean gratifications. All instincts that do not discharge themselves externally now *turn inward*— this is what I call the *internalization* of human beings: now for the first time human beings grow what later is called the "soul." The whole inner world, originally thin as if stretched between two membranes, spread out and opened up, gained depth, breadth and height to the same extent that the external discharging of human beings became *obstructed*. Those terrible bulwarks with which the state apparatus protected itself against the old instincts of freedom — punishments above all belong to these bulwarks — managed to turn all those instincts of the wild, free, roaming human beings backward *against human beings themselves*. Enmity, cruelty, lust in persecution, in assault, in change, in destruction — all of that turning against the possessors of such instincts: *that* is the origin of "bad conscience." The human being who for lack of external enemies and obstacles impatiently tore at himself, persecuted, gnawed on, stirred up and mistreated himself, jammed into an oppressive narrowness and routine of customs, this animal that hurled itself raw against the bars of its cage, that others want to "tame"; this deprived creature eaten up by homesickness for the desert, who had to make himself into an adventure, a torture chamber, an unsafe wilderness — this fool, this yearning and desperate prisoner became the inventor of "bad conscience." But along with him the greatest and uncanniest sickness was introduced, from which humankind has not recovered to this day, the suffering of humans *from humans*, from *themselves*: this as the result of a violent separation from his animal past, of a leap and plunge as it were into new situations and conditions of existence, of a declaration of war against the old instincts upon which till then his

strength, joy and terribleness had rested. Let us immediately
add, on the other hand, that the existence of an animal psyche
turning against itself, taking sides against itself, brought about
on earth something so new, profound, unheard of, enigmatic,
contradictory *and full of future* that the aspect of the earth
changed essentially as a result. Indeed, it required divine spectators to appreciate the spectacle that began here and whose end is
by no means foreseeable—a spectacle too subtle, too wonderful,
too paradoxical for it to play out senselessly and unnoticed on
some ridiculous planet! Since then humanity *too* has counted
among the most unexpected and exciting lucky throws played by
the "great child" of Heraclitus,[42] whether we call it Zeus or
chance—he has been stimulating interest in himself, an antici-
pation, a hope, almost a certainty, as if something new were
announcing and preparing itself in him, as if humanity
were not a goal, but only a way, an episode, a bridge, a great
promise . . .

17

This hypothesis on the origin of bad conscience presupposes,
firstly, that this change was not a gradual, not a voluntary one
and did not manifest itself as an organic growing into the new
conditions, but as a break, a leap, a compulsion, an unavoidable disaster against which there was no struggle and not even
ressentiment. But secondly, that the shaping of a previously
unrestricted and unformed population into a fixed form, inasmuch as its beginning was an act of force, was only brought
to completion by sheer acts of force—that the oldest "state"
accordingly emerged and continued to function as a terrible
tyranny, as an oppressive and ruthless machinery until finally
such a raw material of people and semi-animal was not only
thoroughly kneaded and pliable, but also *formed*. I used the
word "state": it should be self-evident who is meant by
this—some pack of blond beasts of prey, a conqueror- and
master-race that, organized in a warlike manner and with the
strength to organize, does not hesitate to lay its terrible paws

on a perhaps tremendously superior population in terms of numbers, but one that is still shapeless, still roaming about. That is indeed how the "state" begins on earth: I think we have gotten beyond that wishful fantasy that has it beginning with a "contract." Whoever can command, whoever is by nature "master," whoever behaves violently in deed and gesture—what does he care about contracts! Such beings are not reckoned with, they come like fate, without grounds, reason, consideration, pretext; they are there as the lightning is there, too terrible, too sudden, too convincing, too "different" even to be hated. Their work is an instinctive creating of form, impressing of form; they are the most involuntary, unconscious artists in existence:—in a short time something new stands where they appeared, a ruling structure that *lives*, in which parts and functions are delimited and coordinated, in which nothing at all can find a place unless a "meaning" in relation to the whole has first been implanted in it. They do not know what guilt, what responsibility, what consideration are, these born organizers; in them reigns that terrible artist-egoism that gazes like bronze and knows itself justified for all eternity in its "work," like the mother in her child. *They* are not the ones in whom "bad conscience" grew, so much is clear from the outset—but *without them* it would not have grown, this ugly plant, it would be missing if a tremendous quantum of freedom had not been banished from the world, at least from sight, and rendered *latent* as it were under the pressure of their hammer blows, their artist's violence. This *instinct of freedom* violently rendered latent—as we have already grasped—this instinct for freedom repressed, pushed back, imprisoned deep within and ultimately discharging and venting itself only on itself: this, and only this is *bad conscience* in its beginnings.

18

We should beware of thinking contemptuously of this whole phenomenon just because from the outset it is ugly and painful. At bottom it is in fact the same active, state-building force[43]

at work on a grander scale in those violence-artists and organizers that here, internally, on a smaller, pettier scale, in a
backward direction and in the "labyrinth of the breast"[44] as
Goethe called it, creates for itself the bad conscience and negative ideals, precisely that *instinct of freedom* (in my language:
the will to power): only the material on which the formative
and violating nature of this force vents itself is precisely humanity itself, its entire animal ancient self—and *not*, as in
that greater and more obvious phenomenon, the *other* human
being, *other* human beings. This secretive self-violation, this
artist's cruelty, this joy in giving a form to oneself as heavy,
resisting, suffering matter, in branding oneself with a will, a
critique, a contradiction, a contempt, a No, this uncanny
and appallingly enjoyable labor of a soul voluntarily split in
itself, making itself suffer out of delight in making itself suffer, this whole *active* "bad conscience" as the genuine womb
of all ideal and imaginative events has ultimately—as we
already guessed—also brought to light a plenitude of strange
new beauty and affirmation, perhaps even beauty *itself*. . .
For what would "beautiful" be if contradiction had not first
risen to consciousness of itself, if the ugly had not first said to
itself: "I am ugly"? . . . At least after this hint there will be less
riddle to the enigma of how an ideal, a beauty can be implied
by contradictory concepts such as *selflessness, self-denial, self-
sacrifice*; and one thing we know henceforth, I have no doubt
of it—namely what kind of *joy* it is that the selfless, the self-
denying, the self-sacrificing person feels from the beginning:
this joy belongs in the realm of cruelty.—So much for the
time being on the descent of the "unegoistic" as a *moral* value
and for staking out the ground from which this value has
grown: only bad conscience, only the will to self-mistreatment
provides the prerequisite for the *value* of the unegoistic.—

19

It is a sickness, bad conscience, this is not subject to doubt,
but a sickness as pregnancy is a sickness. Let us seek out the

conditions under which this sickness has reached its most terrible and most sublime pinnacle: — we will then see what really made its first appearance in the world. For this we will need to take a deep breath — and first of all we must return once again to an earlier viewpoint. The civil-law relationship of the debtor to his creditor, of which we already spoke at length, was once again interpreted into a relationship, moreover in a way that historically is exceedingly remarkable and disturbing, in which it is probably most incomprehensible for us modern human beings: namely into the relationship of the *present generation* and their *ancestors*. Within the original tribal community — we are speaking of primeval times — the living generation each time acknowledges a juridical obligation to the earlier and in particular to the earliest, tribe-founding generation (and by no means a mere sentimental liability: there are grounds on which the latter could even be denied altogether for the longest period of human existence). Here the conviction prevails that the tribe absolutely *exists* only through the sacrifice and achievements of the ancestors — and that they have to *repay* them through sacrifice and achievements: thus a *debt* is acknowledged that constantly grows inasmuch as these forebears do not cease in their continued existence as powerful spirits to grant the tribe new advantages and advances drawing on their strength. For nothing perhaps? But there is no "for nothing" in these brutal and "soul-impoverished" ages. What can they give back to them? Sacrifices (initially only nourishment in the crudest sense), festivals, shrines, tributes, and above all obedience — for all customs, as works of ancestors, are also their statutes and commands — : are they ever given enough? This suspicion remains and grows: from time to time it forces a great pay-off in one fell swoop, some kind of tremendous counter-payment to the "creditors" (the notorious sacrifice of the first-born, for instance, blood, human blood in any case). The *fear* of the ancestor and his power, the awareness of debts to him necessarily increases according to this kind of logic in exactly the same

measure as the power of the tribe itself increases, since the
tribe itself emerges ever more victorious, independent, revered
and feared. By no means the other way around! Every step toward the atrophying of a tribe, all miserable chance occurrences, all signs of degeneration, of approaching dissolution
on the contrary always *diminish* the fear of the spirit of the
founder and provide an ever smaller notion of his cleverness,
foresightedness and presence of power. This crude kind of
logic should be thought to its conclusion: ultimately the ancestors of the *mightiest* tribes must have grown to prodigious
proportions through the imagination of growing fear, and
they must have been pushed back into the darkness of a divine
uncanniness and inconceivability: — in the end the ancestor is
necessarily transfigured into a *god*. Perhaps here we have even
the origin of the gods, hence an origin from *fear*! . . . And
whoever finds it necessary to add: "but also from piety!" would
scarcely be right for that longest period of the human race, for
its prehistory. All the more, to be sure, for the *middle* period in
which the noble tribes develop: — who in fact returned with
interest to their progenitors, their ancestors (heroes, gods) all
the qualities that meanwhile had become obvious in themselves, the *noble* qualities. Later we will take a look at the
aristocratizing and ennoblement of the gods (which of course
is absolutely not their "hallowing"): for now let us just trace
this whole development of the consciousness of guilt to its
conclusion.

20

The consciousness of having debts to the deity, as history
teaches, has by no means come to an end after the decline of
the "community" organized according to blood relationships;
in the same way it inherited the concepts "good and bad" from
the tribal nobility (along with its basic psychological tendency
to establish rank orders), with the inheritance of tribal and
family deities humankind also received the pressure of yet

unpaid debts and of the longing to discharge them. (The transition is made by those broad slave and serf populations that adapted to the cults of their masters' gods, whether through force or through submissiveness and mimicry: from them this inheritance then overflows in all directions.) The feeling of debt to the deity did not cease to grow for several millennia, and in fact it continued always in the same proportion as the concept of God and the feeling for God grew on earth and was carried to the heights. (The whole history of ethnic fighting, triumphing, reconciling, merging, everything that precedes the final rank order of all ethnic elements in every great racial synthesis,[45] is reflected in the genealogical confusion of their gods; the advance toward universal empires is always also the advance toward universal deities; despotism with its overpowering of the independent nobility also always paves the way for some kind of monotheism.) The rise of the Christian God as the maximal god achieved to date therefore also brought to the fore a maximum of guilt feeling on earth. Assuming we have set out in virtually the *opposite* direction, then with no small probability we can infer from the inexorable decline of faith in the Christian God that now we also have a considerable decline in the human consciousness of guilt; indeed the prospect cannot be dismissed that the perfect and ultimate victory of atheism could redeem humankind from this entire feeling of having debts to its beginnings, to its *causa prima*.[46] Atheism and a kind of *second innocence* belong together. —

21

This for the time being, briefly and crudely, on the relationship of the concepts "guilt" and "duty" to religious presuppositions: I have deliberately left aside the actual moralization of these concepts (how they are pushed back into the conscience, or more specifically, the conflation of *bad* conscience with the concept of God) up till now, and at the conclusion of the previous section I even spoke as if this moralization did not exist, consequently as if those concepts necessarily came to an end once their prerequisite fell through, namely faith in our "creditor," in God. But the facts contradict this in a terrible way. With the moralization of the concepts guilt and duty, with their being pushed back into *bad* conscience we actually have the attempt to *reverse* the direction of the development just described, or at least to put a stop to its movement: now precisely the prospect of an ultimate discharge once and for all *is supposed to* be pessimistically closed, now the gaze *is supposed to* disconsolately ricochet and recoil off a brazen impossibility, now those concepts "guilt" and "duty" *are supposed to* turn themselves backward — but against *whom*? There can be no doubt: first against the "debtor," in whom bad conscience now firmly takes hold, eating into him, spreading out and growing like a polyp in all directions, until along with the impossibility of discharging debt, the thought of the impossibility of discharging penance is also conceived, the notion that it cannot be discharged (of *"eternal* punishment") — ; but in the end even against the "creditor," think here of the *causa prima* of humankind, of the beginning of the human race, of its progenitor who is now afflicted with a curse ("Adam," "Original Sin," "unfreedom of the will") or of nature, from whose womb humans arise and into which the evil principle is now placed ("demonizing of nature") or of existence in general, remaining only as *worthlessness in itself* (nihilistic turning away from it, a longing for oblivion or longing for its "opposite," for a different being, Buddhism and the like) — until all of a sudden we stand before the paradoxical and horrifying way out in which tortured humankind found a temporary relief, that stroke of genius of *Christianity*: God sacrificing himself for the guilt of humanity, God himself making payment to himself, God as the only one who can redeem from humans what for humans has become irredeemable — the creditor sacrificing himself for his debtor, out of *love* (can you believe it? —) out of love for his debtor! . . .

22

One will have already guessed *what* really happened with all of this and *under* it all: that will to self-torment, that suppressed cruelty of the human animal who had been made inward and scared back into himself, of the creature imprisoned in the "state" for the purpose of taming, who invented bad conscience in order to hurt himself after the *more natural* outlet for this desire to hurt was obstructed—this human of bad conscience has taken over the presupposition of religion in order to drive his self-torture to its most gruesome harshness and sharpness. Guilt before *God*: this thought becomes an instrument of torture for him. He captures in "God" the ultimate antitheses he is able to find for his actual and inescapable animal instincts, he even reinterprets these animal instincts as guilt against God (as hostility, rebellion, insurrection against the "master," the "father," the primal ancestor and beginning of the world), he stretches himself between the contradiction "God" and "devil," every kind of No he says to himself, nature, naturalness, to the actuality of his being he inverts and throws out as a Yes, as existing, corporeal, actual, as God, as the holiness of God, as God's judging, as God's executing, as Beyond, as eternity, as torment without end, as hell, as immeasurability of punishment and guilt. This is a kind of madness of the will in psychic cruelty that has absolutely no equal: the *will* of a human being to find himself guilty and reprehensible to the point of unatonability, his *will* to imagine himself punished without the possibility of the punishment ever being equivalent to the guilt, his *will* to infect and poison the deepest ground of things with the problem of punishment and guilt in order to cut himself off once and for all from a way out of this labyrinth of "fixed ideas," his *will* to erect an ideal—that of the "holy God"—in order to be palpably certain of his absolute unworthiness in the face of this ideal. Oh this insane sad beast human being! What ideas occur to it, what anti-nature, what paroxysms of nonsense, what *bestiality of idea* immediately breaks out as soon as it is prevented a bit from being the *beast of deed*! . . . All of this is interesting to the point of excess, but it is also of such black, gloomy, unnerving sadness that we have to forcibly forbid ourselves from looking too long into these abysses. Here is *sickness*, there is no doubt of it, the most terrible sickness that ever raged in humans: — and whoever can still hear (but today people no longer have the ears for it! —) how in this night of torment and absurdity the cry of *love* rang out, the cry of the most longing delight, of redemption in *love*, he will turn away, seized by an invincible horror . . . There is so much of the horrific in humans! . . . The earth has been a madhouse for too long! . . .

23

Let this suffice once and for all regarding the descent of this "holy God." — That *in itself* the conception of gods must not necessarily lead to this degradation of the imagination whose calling to mind we could not forgo for a moment, that there are *nobler* ways of using the creation of gods than for this self-crucifixion and self-defilement of humanity, in which the last millennia of Europe have had their mastery — that fortunately can be read from every glance we cast at the *Greek gods*, these reflections of noble and autocratic human beings in whom the *animal* in humans felt itself deified and did *not* tear itself apart, did *not* rage against itself! These Greeks used their gods for the longest time precisely to keep "bad conscience" at a distance, in order to remain cheerful about their freedom of soul: and so in the opposite sense of Christianity's use of its God. They went *very far* in this, these magnificent and lion-hearted foolish children; and no less an authority than Homer's Zeus himself lets it be understood here and there that they make it too easy for themselves. "A wonder!" he says once — it concerns the case of Aegisthus, a *very* serious case —

> "A wonder how much the mortals complain against the
> gods!

> *Only from us evil comes,* they think; but they themselves
> Create through lack of understanding, even counter to
> fate, misery for themselves."[47]

Yet at the same time we hear and see here that even this Olympian spectator and judge is far from holding a grudge against them for this, and thinking evil of them: "how *foolish* they are!" is how he thinks of the misdeeds of mortals—and "folly," "lack of understanding," a bit of "disturbance in the head," this much even the Greeks of the strongest, bravest age *allowed* themselves as the reason for much that was bad and disastrous:—folly, *not* sin! do you understand this? . . . But even this disturbance in the head was a problem—"yes, how is it even possible? where could it have come from really, with minds such as *ours*, we human beings of noble descent, of fortune, of good breeding, of the best society, of nobility, of virtue?"—for centuries the noble Greek asked himself such questions in the face of every incomprehensible atrocity and sacrilege with which one of his peers had sullied himself. "Certainly a *god* must have beguiled him," he said finally, shaking his head . . . This way out is *typical* for Greeks . . . In this manner the gods back then served to some extent to justify humans even in bad things, they served as causes of evil—in those days they did not take the punishment upon themselves, but, as is *nobler*, the guilt . . .

24

—I am concluding with three question marks, as is plain to see. "Is an ideal being erected here or is one being broken down?" one might ask . . . But have you ever asked yourselves sufficiently how dearly the erecting of *every* ideal on earth had to be purchased? How much reality always had to be slandered and denied, how much lying sanctified, how much conscience disturbed, how much "God" sacrificed each time? In order for a temple to be erected *a temple must be destroyed*: that is the law—show me the case where this is not fulfilled! . . .

We modern human beings, we are the heirs of thousands of years of conscience-vivisection and self-animal-cruelty: in this we have our longest practice, perhaps our artistry, in any case our subtlety, our pampered taste. Humans have all-too-long regarded their natural inclinations with an "evil eye," so that in them they have finally become wedded to "bad conscience." A reverse attempt would be possible *in itself*—but who is strong enough for it?—namely to wed to bad conscience the *unnatural* inclinations, all those aspirations to the Beyond, to what is counter to the senses, instincts, nature, animal, in short, the previous ideals, all of which are ideals hostile to life, ideals that slander the world. To whom should we turn today with *such* hopes and demands? . . . For this we would have precisely the *good* people against us; additionally, as is only fair, the comfortable, the reconciled, the vain, the fanatical, the weary . . . What offends more deeply, what distinguishes as thoroughly as letting show something of the rigor and loftiness with which we treat ourselves? And in turn — how accommodating, how kindly everyone behaves toward us as soon as we do things like everyone else and "let ourselves go" like everyone else! . . . For that goal a *different* kind of spirit would be needed than is probable in this age of ours: spirits strengthened by wars and victories, for whom conquest, adventure, danger and pain have even become a need; for this, people would need to be acclimatized to sharp, high air, to winter journeys, to ice and mountains in every sense of the word; what would be needed for this is a kind of sublime malice itself, a final superlatively self-confident mischief of knowledge that belongs to great health, in brief, and bad enough, precisely this *great health* would be needed! . . . Is such health even possible today? . . . But someday, in a stronger time than this decaying, self-doubting present, he really must come to us, the *redeeming* human being of great love and contempt, the creative spirit who time and again is driven away from any aloofness or Beyond by his surging strength, whose solitude is misunderstood by the common people as if it were a flight *from* reality—: whereas it is merely his immersion, burial, absorption *in* reality, so that someday when he again comes to light he can bring home with him the *redemption* of this reality: its redemption from the curse placed on it by the previous ideal. This human of the future who will redeem us from the previous ideal as much as from *what had to grow out of it*, from the great nausea, from the will to nothingness, from nihilism; this bell-chime of noon and of the great decision, that makes the will free, that gives back to the earth its goal and to humanity its hope; this anti-Christian and anti-nihilist; this conqueror of God and of nothingness—*someday he must come . . .* [48]

25

—But what am I saying here? Enough! Enough! At this point only one thing befits me, to be silent: otherwise I would profane what only a younger man is at liberty to do, a "more future one," a stronger one than I am—what *Zarathustra* alone is at liberty to do, *Zarathustra the godless . . .*

What Do Ascetic Ideals Mean?

Heedless, mocking, violent — that's how
wisdom wants *us*: she is a woman and only
ever loves a warrior.

Thus Spoke Zarathustra.

I[1]

What do ascetic ideals mean? — In artists, nothing or too
many things; in philosophers and scholars, something like a keen
nose and instinct for the favorable preconditions of high spirituality; in women, in the best case, one *more* charming trait of
seduction, a bit of *morbidezza*[2] on lovely flesh, the angelical appearance of a pretty, plump animal; in the physiological failures
and the depressed (in the *majority* of mortals), an attempt to appear to themselves as "too good" for this world, a holy form of
excess, their major weapon in the battle against slow pain and
boredom; in priests, the genuine priest's faith, their best instrument of power, also the "supreme" permission to power; in saints,
finally, a pretext for hibernation, their *novissima gloriae cupido*,[3]
their repose in nothingness ("God"), their form of insanity. But
that the ascetic ideal has meant so much to humanity generally is
the expression of the basic fact of the human will, its *horror va-
cui*:[4] *it needs a goal* — and it would sooner will *nothingness* than
not will. — Am I understood? . . . Have I been understood? . . .
"Absolutely not! Sir!" — Then let us start at the beginning.

2

What do ascetic ideals mean? — Or, to take a specific case with
respect to which I have often enough been asked for advice,

what does it mean for instance when an artist like Richard
Wagner in his old age pays homage to chastity? In a certain
sense, of course, he always did this; but only at the very end in
an ascetic sense. What does this change of "sense" mean, this
radical reversal of sense? — for that is what it was; here Wagner suddenly switched over into his opposite. What does it
mean when an artist switches over into his opposite? . . . Here
we are reminded at once, assuming that we wish to pause for a
while at this question, of perhaps the best, strongest, most
cheerful, *most courageous* time ever in Wagner's life: it was
back when the thought of Luther's wedding[5] occupied him
intensely and deeply. Who knows what chance circumstances
really determined that today we have the *Meistersinger*[6] instead of this wedding music? And how much of the latter still
echoes perhaps in the former? But there is no doubt that even
this "Luther's Wedding" would have dealt with a praise of
chastity. Of course also with a praise of sensuality: — and that
to me is precisely how it would have seemed in order, and that
is also precisely how it would have been "Wagnerian." For
there is no necessary opposition between chastity and sensuality; every good marriage, every genuine affair of the heart
transcends this opposition. It seems to me that Wagner would
have done well once again to call to mind this *pleasant* fact to
his Germans, with the help of a lovely and bold Luther comedy, for there are and were among Germans always many slanderers of sensuality; and Luther's service is perhaps nowhere
greater than in having had the courage of his *sensuality*— (back
then it was called, delicately enough, the "Protestant freedom" . . .) But even where there really is that opposition
between chastity and sensuality, fortunately it need not by any
means be a tragic opposition. This should at least apply for all
better-constituted, better-tempered mortals who are far from
blithely counting their labile equilibrium between "animal
and angel" among the arguments against existence — the subtlest and brightest, like Goethe, like Hafiz,[7] have even seen in
it one *more* stimulus to life. Just such "contradictions" seduce

us to existence . . . On the other hand it is only too clear
that once swinish failures get to the point of worshipping
chastity—and there are such swine!—they will only see
and worship in it their opposite, the opposite of swinish
failures—and oh with what tragic grunting and zeal! we can
imagine it—that embarrassing and superfluous opposition
that Richard Wagner indisputably still wanted to set to music
and to stage at the end of his life. *But why*? as is only fair to
ask. For what did he, what do we care about swine?—

3

Here, of course, we cannot ignore that other question, namely:
what did he care anyway about that manly (alas, so unmanly)
"country bumpkin," that poor devil and nature boy Parsifal,
whom he finally made over into a Catholic using his so insidious methods—what? was this Parsifal in any way meant *seriously*? For one could be tempted to conjecture the opposite,
even to wish it—that Wagner's *Parsifal* was meant as a joke,
as an epilogue and satyr play with which the tragedian Wagner wanted to take leave from us, also from himself, and above
all *from tragedy* in a manner precisely suited to and worthy of
himself, namely with an excess of the highest and most mischievous parody of tragedy itself, of the whole horrific earthly
seriousness and earthly misery of former times, of the *crudest
form* in the anti-nature of the ascetic ideal, now finally overcome. That, as noted, would have been worthy of precisely a
great tragedian: who, like any artist, only comes to the
pinnacle of his greatness when he knows how to see himself
and his art *beneath* him—when he knows how to *laugh* at
himself. Is Wagner's *Parsifal* his secret laugh of superiority at
himself, the triumph of his ultimate, highest artist's freedom,
artist's transcendence? We would like to think so, as noted, for
what would a *seriously meant* Parsifal be? Do we really have to
see in him (as someone expressed it to me) "the spawn of an
insane hatred of knowledge, spirit and sensuality"? A curse
on the senses and the spirit in a single hatred and breath? An

apostasy and return to Christian-pathological and obscurantist ideals? And in the end even this self-denial and self-effacement on the part of an artist who up till then had aimed with all the power of his will for the opposite, namely for the *highest spiritualization and sensualization* of his art? And not only his art: his life, too. Recall how enthusiastically Wagner followed in the footsteps of the philosopher Feuerbach back in his day: Feuerbach's words about "healthy sensuality"[8] — in the thirties and forties that sounded to Wagner as to many Germans (— they called themselves the *"young* Germans"[9]) like the watchword of salvation. Did he *learn otherwise* in the end? Because at least it appears that in the end he had the will to *teach otherwise* . . . And not only from the stage with his *Parsifal* trombones: — in the murky writings of his last years, as unfree as they are clueless, there are a hundred passages betraying a secret desire and will, a despondent, uncertain, unacknowledged will quite literally to preach reversal, conversion, negation, Christianity, medievalism and to tell his disciples "it's no good! Seek salvation somewhere else!" Even the "blood of the Redeemer"[10] is invoked at one point . . .

4

To state my opinion in such a case, which has much that is embarrassing — and it is a *typical* case — one certainly does best to separate an artist from his work, to the extent that he is not taken as seriously as his work. Ultimately he is only the precondition of his work, the womb, the soil and sometimes the fertilizer and manure on and from which it grows — hence in most cases something that we have to forget if we want to enjoy the work itself. Insight into the *descent* of a work concerns the physiologists and vivisectionists of the spirit: never ever the aesthetic people, the artists! The poet and shaper of *Parsifal* was no more spared a deep, thorough, even frightening living immersion and descent into medieval contrasts of the soul, a hostile departure from all height, rigor[11] and discipline of the spirit, a kind of intellectual *perversity* (if I may be

pardoned for saying so) than a pregnant woman is spared the
repulsive and bizarre aspects of pregnancy: which, as noted,
have to be *forgotten* in order to enjoy the child. We have to be
on guard against the confusion that only too easily befalls an
artist himself, out of psychological contiguity,[12] as the English
say: as if he himself *were* that which he can represent, think up
and express. In fact, as matters stand, *if* he were that, he would
absolutely not represent, think up or express it; a Homer would
not have created an Achilles, nor a Goethe a Faust, if Homer
had been an Achilles and Goethe a Faust.[13] A perfect and
complete artist is for all eternity separate from the "real," from
the actual; on the other hand it is understandable how he
sometimes grows weary to the point of despair of this eternal
"unreality" and falseness of his innermost existence — and
that he then may well attempt for once to infringe on what is
most forbidden precisely to him, to infringe on reality, on
being real. With what success? One can guess . . . It is *the
typical velleity* of the artist: the same velleity to which the
aged Wagner succumbed and for which he had to pay so
dearly, so fatefully (— because of it he lost the valuable portion of his friends). Finally, however, and still quite apart from
this velleity, who does not wish for Wagner's own sake that he
had taken leave of us and his art *differently*, not with a Parsifal,
but more victorious, more self-confident, more Wagnerian — less
deceiving, less ambiguous with respect to all that he willed,
less Schopenhauerian, less nihilistic? . . .

5

— What then do ascetic ideals mean? In the case of an artist,
as we now understand: *nothing at all*! . . . Or so many things
that it is as good as nothing at all! . . . Let us first of all eliminate the artists: they[14] do not stand nearly independently
enough in the world and *against* the world for their valuations
and their changes to them to merit interest *in themselves*! During all ages they have been valets of a morality or philosophy
or religion; quite apart from the fact that unfortunately they

have often enough been the all-too-pliant courtiers of their
followers and patrons, and keen-nosed sycophants of old or
newly rising powers. In any case they always need protection,
backing, a previously established authority: artists never stand
on their own, and standing alone is counter to their deepest
instincts. So for example "when the time came," Richard
Wagner took the philosopher Schopenhauer as his front man,
as his protection: — who would even consider it imaginable
that he would have had the *courage* for an ascetic ideal without
the backing granted him by Schopenhauer's philosophy, without the authority of Schopenhauer that in the seventies was
becoming *predominant* in Europe? (and this without even taking into account whether in the *new* Germany an artist could
have existed at all without the milk of a pious, imperially pious way of thinking). — And with this we have arrived at the
more serious question: what does it mean when a real *philosopher* pays homage to the ascetic ideal, a spirit genuinely standing on his own like Schopenhauer, a man and knight with a
steely gaze who has the courage to be himself, who knows how
to stand alone and does not first wait for the front men and
nods from above?[15] — Here let us immediately consider the
remarkable and, for many kinds of people, even fascinating
position taken by Schopenhauer on *art*: since obviously it was
for its sake that Richard Wagner *initially* went over to Schopenhauer (persuaded to do so by a poet, as is well known, by
Herwegh[16]), and this to the extent that a complete theoretical
contradiction opened up between his early and his later aesthetic beliefs — the former expressed for example in *Opera and
Drama*, the latter in the writings he published from 1870 on.
In particular from that time on, perhaps most disconcertingly,
Wagner ruthlessly revised his judgment concerning the value
and standing of *music* itself: what did it matter to him that previously he had made of it a means, a medium, a "woman" that
absolutely needed a purpose, a man in order to thrive — namely
drama! Suddenly he grasped that with Schopenhauer's theory
and innovation there was *more* to be made *in majorem musicae*

gloriam[17] — namely with the *sovereignty* of music as Schopenhauer understood it: music set apart against all other arts, the independent art in itself, *not* offering copies of phenomenality like the others, but rather speaking the language *of the* will itself, directly from the "abyss" as its most authentic, most original, least derivative revelation. With this extraordinary rise in the value of music as it seemed to grow from Schopenhauerian philosophy, all at once the value of *the musician* himself also rose in price in a manner unheard of: from now on he became an oracle, a priest, indeed more than a priest, a mouthpiece of the "in-itself" of things, a telephone of the Beyond — henceforth he spoke not only music, this ventriloquist of God — he spoke metaphysics: is it any wonder that finally one day he spoke *ascetic ideals?* . . .

6[18]

Schopenhauer made use of the Kantian version of the aesthetic problem — although he quite certainly did not view it with Kantian eyes. Kant intended to honor art when among the predicates of beauty he gave preference to and foregrounded those constituting the honor of knowledge: impersonality and universality. This is not the place to discuss whether on the whole this was not a mistake; all I want to underscore is that Kant, like all philosophers, instead of envisaging the aesthetic problem from the experiences of the artist (of the creator) only reflected on art and the beautiful from the standpoint of the "spectator" and thereby without noticing managed to get the "spectator" himself into the concept "beautiful." Now if only this "spectator" had been sufficiently familiar to the philosophers of the beautiful! — namely as a great *personal* fact and experience, as a bounty of the most authentic, strongest experiences, desires, surprises, delights in the realm of the beautiful! But I fear the opposite was always the case: and so from the start what we get from them are definitions in which, as in that famous definition of the beautiful already given by

Kant, the lack of more refined personal experience ends up taking the shape of a thick worm of basic error. "The beautiful," Kant said, "is what pleases *without interest*."[19] Without interest! Compare this definition with another made by a real "spectator" and artist—Stendhal, who once called the beautiful *une promesse de bonheur*.[20] Here in any case what is *rejected* and crossed out is precisely the one thing Kant emphasizes in the aesthetic condition: *le désintéressement*.[21] Who is right, Kant or Stendhal?—Of course if our aestheticians never tire of throwing into the balance in Kant's favor that under the charm of beauty *even* undressed female statues can be viewed "without interest," surely we can laugh a bit at their expense:—the experiences of the *artists* concerning this tricky point are "more interesting," and in any case Pygmalion was *not* necessarily an "unaesthetic human being." Let us think all the more kindly of the innocence of our aestheticians as reflected in such arguments; let us for instance honor Kant for what he was able to teach us, with the naïveté of a country preacher, about the unique properties of the sense of touch!—And here we return to Schopenhauer, who stood closer to the arts by a considerable measure than Kant and yet did not find his way out of the spell of the Kantian definition: how did that happen? The circumstance is odd enough: he interpreted the words "without interest" in the most personal way possible, on the basis of an experience that must have been among his most routine. Schopenhauer speaks about few things as certainly as he does about the effect of aesthetic contemplation: of it he says that it counteracts precisely *sexual* "interestedness," and is thus similar to lupulin and camphor; he never tired of glorifying *this* breaking-free of the "will" as the great merit and benefit of the aesthetic condition. Indeed we might be tempted to ask whether his basic conception of "will and representation," the thought that a redemption from the "will" is only possible through "representation," did not have its origin as a generalization of that sexual experi-

ence. (In all questions concerning Schopenhauerian philosophy, by the way, attention should always be paid to the fact
that it is the conception of a twenty-six year-old youth; so that
it partakes not only of the specific qualities of Schopenhauer,
but also of the specific qualities of that season of his life.) Let
us listen, for instance, to one of the most expressive passages
among the countless he wrote in praise of the aesthetic condition (*World as Will and Representation*, I, § 38); listen to the
tone, the suffering, the happiness, gratitude with which such
words were spoken. "This is the painless condition praised by
Epicurus as the highest good and the condition of the gods;
for a moment we are freed from the vile pressure of the will,
we celebrate the Sabbath of the penal servitude of willing,
the wheel of Ixion stands still." . . . What vehemence of
words! What images of torture and protracted loathing!
What almost pathological temporal juxtaposing of "that moment" and the usual "wheel of Ixion," of "penal servitude of
willing," of "vile pressure of the will"! — But supposing
Schopenhauer had been right a hundred times for himself,
what would this have accomplished for insight into the nature of the beautiful? Schopenhauer described one effect of the
beautiful, the will-calming one — is it even a regular one?
Stendhal, as noted, a no less sensual nature than Schopenhauer but one that turned out more happily, stresses a different effect of the beautiful: "the beautiful *promises* happiness,"
to him precisely the *stimulating of the will* ("of interest") by
beauty seems to be the fact of the matter. And finally could
we not object that Schopenhauer himself in this matter is
very wrong to consider himself a Kantian, that he did not in
the least understand the Kantian definition of the beautiful in
a Kantian sense — that he too likes the beautiful out of "interest," even out of the strongest and most personal interest of all:
that of the tortured man who breaks free of his torture? . . .
And, returning to our first question, "what does it *mean* when
a philosopher pays homage to the ascetic ideal?" — here at
least we get a first hint: he wants *to break free of a torture.* —

7

Let us beware of making gloomy faces right away at the mention of the word "torture": in this particular case there is enough to offset it, enough to deduct — there is even something left to laugh about. For let us not underestimate that Schopenhauer, who in fact treated sexuality as a personal enemy (including its tool, woman, this "*instrumentum diaboli*"[22]), *needed* enemies in order to remain in good spirits; that he loved grim, galling, black-green words; that he grew angry for the sake of being angry, out of passion; that he would have become ill, would have become a *pessimist* (— for he was not one, as much as he desired to be) without enemies, without Hegel, woman, sensuality and the whole will to existence, to continued existence. Schopenhauer would otherwise *not* have continued existing, we can bet on it, he would have run away: his enemies held on to him, his enemies seduced him again and again into existence, his anger, just like that of the ancient Cynics, was his balm, his refreshment, his reward, his *remedium*[23] against nausea, his *happiness*. So much with respect to what is most personal in the case of Schopenhauer; on the other hand there is also something typical about him — and only here do we again come to our problem. It is indisputable that as long as there have been philosophers on earth and wherever there have been philosophers (from India to England, to take the most antithetical poles of philosophical talent) a genuine philosophers' irritability and rancor has existed against sensuality — Schopenhauer is only its most eloquent and, if one has the ear for it, also most captivating and enchanting outbreak —; by the same token there exists a genuine philosophers' prejudice and cordiality with respect to the entire ascetic ideal, and we should not fool ourselves about or against this. Both belong, as noted, to the type; if both are lacking in a philosopher then he is — of this we can be sure — always only a "so-called" philosopher. What does that *mean?* For this fact first has to be interpreted: *in himself* he stands there

stupidly for all eternity, like every "thing in itself." Every animal, and thus also *la bête philosophe*,[24] strives instinctively for
an optimum of favorable conditions under which it can completely let out its power and reach its maximum of feeling of
power; just as instinctively and with a keenness of scent that
"passeth all understanding,"[25] every animal abhors any kind
of troublemaker and obstacle that lays or could lay itself across
its path to the optimum (— it is *not* its path to "happiness" of
which I speak, but its path to power, to deeds, to the mightiest
activity and in most cases in fact its path to unhappiness). In
this manner the philosopher abhors *marriage* along with whatever might persuade him to it — marriage as obstacle and disaster on his path to the optimum. What great philosopher so
far has been married? Heraclitus, Plato, Descartes, Spinoza,
Leibniz, Kant, Schopenhauer — they were not; even more, we
can not even *imagine* them as married. A married philosopher
belongs *in comedy*, that is my proposition: and that exception
Socrates, the malicious Socrates, it seems, married out of
irony, just to demonstrate *this* proposition. Every philosopher
would speak as Buddha once spoke when the birth of a son
was announced to him: "Râhula has been born to me, a fetter has been forged for me"[26] (Râhula here means "a little
demon"); every "free spirit" would have to be faced with a
thoughtful hour, assuming that he previously had a thoughtless one, as it once came to the same Buddha — "narrowly
constrained," he thought to himself, "is life in the house, a
place of impurity; freedom is in leaving the house": "as he
was thinking thus, he left the house."[27] In the ascetic ideal so
many bridges to *independence* are indicated that a philosopher
has to jubilate inwardly and clap his hands when he hears the
story of all those resolute men who one day said No to every
kind of unfreedom and went into some *desert*: even supposing
that they were merely strong asses and quite the opposite of a
strong spirit. What accordingly does the ascetic ideal mean in
a philosopher? My answer is — as you will have guessed long
ago: the philosopher smiles at the sight of it, seeing it as an

optimum of the conditions of highest and boldest spirituality—
he does *not* deny "existence" this way, on the contrary in doing this he affirms *his* existence and *only* his existence, and
this perhaps to the point that he is not far from the sacrile-
gious wish: *pereat mundus, fiat philosophia, fiat philosophus,
fiam*! . . . [28]

8

As we can see, these philosophers are not exactly unimpeach-
able witnesses and judges of the *value* of the ascetic ideal! They
think of *themselves*—what do they care about "the saint"! What
they are thinking about here is what is most indispensable precisely to *them*: freedom from compulsion, disturbance, noise,
from business, duties, worries; clarity of mind; dance, leap
and flight of ideas; good air, thin, clear, free, dry like the air of
the heights in which all animal being becomes more spiritual
and grows wings; calm in all underground places; all dogs
nicely on a chain; no barking of hostility and shaggy rancor;
no gnawing worms of thwarted ambition; meek and submis-
sive intestines, busy as millworks but far away; a heart that is
foreign, beyond, future, posthumous—on the whole they
think of the ascetic ideal as the cheerful asceticism of an animal deified and fully fledged, soaring above life more than
resting. We know the three great slogans of the ascetic ideal:
poverty, humility, chastity: and now take a close look at the
lives of all great, terrible, inventive spirits—you will always
find all three in them to a certain degree. Definitely *not*, as is
self-evident, as if perhaps these were their "virtues"—what
does this kind of human being have to do with virtues!—but
as the most authentic and natural conditions of their *best* existence, their *most beautiful* fruitfulness. For this it is entirely
possible that their dominating spirituality first had to pull in
the reins on an unruly and irritable pride or a willful sensuality, or that perhaps they sustained their will to the "desert" only
with difficulty in the face of a tendency for luxury and the most
exquisite things, likewise in the face of wasteful liberality of

heart and hand. But it did so, precisely as the *dominating* instinct that asserted its demands against all other instincts — it is still doing it; if it did not, then it would not
dominate. So there is nothing of "virtue" in all this. The *desert*,
incidentally, of which I just spoke and to which the strong,
independently inclined spirits retreat and grow lonely — oh
how different it looks from the desert imagined by educated
people! — sometimes they themselves are the desert, these educated ones. And what is certain is that all actors of the spirit
would simply not survive in it — for them it is not nearly romantic and Syrian enough, not nearly enough theater-desert!
Of course even in it there is no lack of camels: but the similarity ends here. Perhaps a voluntary obscurity; avoiding oneself;
an aversion to noise, veneration, newspapers, influence; a minor position, a routine, something that conceals as opposed
to bringing to light; an occasional association with harmless,
cheerful beasts and fowl who are refreshing to look at; mountains for company, but not dead ones, ones with *eyes* (that is,
with lakes); at times even a room in a full, ordinary inn where
one is sure to go unrecognized and can talk with impunity to
everyone — that is "desert" here: oh it is lonely enough, believe
me! When Heraclitus retreated to the courtyards and colon-
nades of the magnificent temple of Artemis, this "desert" was
more worthy, I admit: why do we *lack* such temples? (— perhaps they are *not* lacking: just now I am recalling my most
beautiful study, the Piazzo di San Marco, assuming it is spring
and likewise forenoon, the time between 10 and 12.) But what
Heraclitus shunned is still the same thing that *we* now avoid:
the noise and the democratic babble of Ephesians, their politics, their news from the "empire" (Persia, you understand),
their market junk of "today" — for we philosophers first need
rest from one thing: above all from "today." We honor the quiet,
the cold, the noble, the distant, the past, everything generally
whose aspect does not require the soul to defend and wrap itself shut — something with which we can speak without speaking *out loud*. Just listen to the sound a spirit makes when it

speaks: every spirit has its sound, loves its sound. That over there for instance has to be an agitator, that is to say, a hollow head, a hollow pot: whatever goes into it comes out dull and thick, burdened by the echo of a great vacuum. That one there rarely speaks other than hoarsely: did he perhaps *think* himself hoarse? That would be possible — just ask the physiologists — but whoever thinks in *words* thinks as an orator and not as a thinker (it reveals that at bottom he does not think facts, does not think factually but only with respect to facts; that he really thinks *himself* and his listeners). This third one here speaks obtrusively, he gets too close to us physically, we feel his breath on us — involuntarily we close our mouths, even though it is a book through which he speaks to us: the sound of his style tells us the reason why — because he has no time, because he does not really believe in himself, because he will either get his word in today or never. But a spirit that is sure of itself speaks softly; it seeks seclusion, it keeps people waiting. A philosopher is recognized on the basis of three glittering and loud things he avoids, fame, princes and women: which is not to say they would not come to him. He shies away from all-too-bright light: therefore he shies away from his time and its "day." In this he is like a shadow: the more his sun goes down, the bigger he becomes. As for his "humility," just as he endures the dark he also endures a certain dependence and eclipse: even more, he is fearful of being disrupted by lightning, he recoils at the unprotectedness of an all-too-isolated and exposed tree on which every bad weather vents its mood, every mood its bad weather. His "maternal" instinct, his secret love for what grows in him, directs him to situations where others relieve him of the burden of thinking *of himself*; in the same sense as the instinct of the *mother* in woman has heretofore preserved the dependent situation of women generally. In the end they demand little enough, these philosophers, their motto is "whoever possesses becomes possessed" —: *not*, as I must say again and again, out of a virtue, out of a meritorious will to contentedness and simplicity, but because their supreme master *thus* demands it of them, prudently and relentlessly demands it; this master has a mind for one thing only, and he gathers and saves everything exclusively for it, time, strength, love, interest. This kind of person does not love to be disturbed by enmities, nor by friendships: he easily forgets or despises. He considers it bad taste to play the martyr; "to *suffer* for the truth"—he leaves that to the ambitious and the stage heroes of the spirit and whoever else has enough time for it (—they themselves, the philosophers, have something to *do* for the truth). They make sparing use of big words; it is said that even the word "truth" repulses them: it sounds boastful . . . Finally as concerns the "chastity" of the philosophers, obviously this kind of spirit has its fruitfulness elsewhere than in children; perhaps elsewhere, too, the continued existence of its name, its little immortality (among philosophers in ancient India one expressed oneself even more immodestly "who needs progeny if his soul is the world?"). In this there is nothing of chastity out of some ascetic scruple and hatred of the senses, no more so than it is chastity when an athlete or jockey abstains from women: rather, this is how their dominating instinct would have it, at least for times of great pregnancy. Every artist knows how harmful is the effect of sexual intercourse in conditions of great spiritual tension and preparation; the most powerful and those with the surest instincts do not first need to experience it, to experience it negatively—instead, it is their "maternal" instinct here that ruthlessly disposes of all other stores and allowances of energy, of the vigor of animal vitality, for the benefit of the work in progress: the greater energy then *consumes* the lesser.—Incidentally we should piece together the aforementioned case of Schopenhauer in line with this interpretation: the sight of the beautiful obviously acted in him as a triggering stimulus on the *main force* of his nature (the force of concentration and of the engrossed gaze); so that the latter then exploded and all at once became master of his consciousness. Here the possibility should not be precluded in the least that the peculiar sweetness and fullness unique to the aesthetic condition could take its descent precisely from the ingredient "sensuality" (just as that "idealism" of pubescent girls stems from the same source) — therefore that sensuality is not suspended at the onset of the aesthetic condition, as Schopenhauer believed, but only transfigures itself and no longer enters consciousness as sexual stimulus. (I will return to this viewpoint another time, in connection with the still more delicate problem of the heretofore so untouched, so unexplored *physiology of aesthetics*.)

9

A certain asceticism, as we saw, a hard and cheerful renunciation with the best of intentions belongs to the most favorable conditions of highest spirituality, likewise also to its most natural consequences: so from the outset it is no wonder that the ascetic ideal has never been treated without a bit of favoritism by philosophers in particular. Upon serious historical examination it is revealed that the bond between ascetic ideal and philosophy is even much closer and stricter still. One could say that only on the *apron strings* of this ideal did philosophy learn to take its first steps and baby steps on earth at all — alas still so clumsily, alas with so much pouting, alas so ready to fall down and lie on its belly, this timid little toddler and sissy with crooked legs! In the beginning it was with philosophy as with all good things — for a long time they lacked the courage to be themselves, they always looked around to see if there was not someone to come to their aid, and worse still, they were frightened of all who looked at them. Just tally the individual drives and virtues of the philosopher one after the other — his doubting drive, his negating drive, his wait-and-see ("ephectic") drive, his analytic drive, his exploring, seeking, venturing drive, his comparing, balancing drive, his will to neutrality and objectivity, his will to every "*sine ira et studio*"[29] — : have we already grasped that for the longest time all of these went counter to the first demands of morality and conscience? (not to mention of *reason* generally, which Luther

loved to call Lady Shrewdness,[30] the clever whore). That a philosopher, if he *were* to become conscious of himself, would have
had to feel himself to be precisely the incarnation of "*nitimur in
vetitum*"[31]—and consequently *guarded against* "feeling himself" at all, against becoming conscious of himself? . . . As I
said earlier, it is no different with all good things of which we
are proud today; even when measured against the standard of
the ancient Greeks our whole modern being, insofar as it is
not weakness but power and consciousness of power, smacks
of pure hubris and godlessness: after all, for the longest time
the very opposite of what we honor today had conscience on
its side and God as its guardian. Hubris today is our whole
stance on nature, our violation of nature with the help of
machines and the so thoughtless ingenuity of technicians and
engineers; hubris today is our stance on God, that is to say, on
some alleged spider of purpose and morality behind the great
snare-web of causality—we could say along with Carl the
Bold in his struggle with Ludwig XI "*je combats l'universelle
araignée*"[32]—; hubris today is our stance on *ourselves*—for we
experiment with ourselves as we would not permit with any
animals, gleefully and curiously slitting open our souls while
our bodies are still alive: what do we care anymore about the
"salvation" of the soul! Afterward we heal ourselves: being sick
is instructive, we have no doubt, more instructive still than
being healthy—*those who make us ill* today seem more necessary even than any medicine men and "saviors." Now we violate ourselves, there is no doubt of it, we nutcrackers of the
soul, we questioners and questionable ones, as if life were
nothing but nutcracking; and for this very reason we must
necessarily become ever more questionable each day, *worthier*
of questioning, and perhaps therewith also worthier—of
living?[33] . . . All good things were once bad things; every original sin has become an original virtue. Marriage for instance
long seemed a sin against the rights of the community; at one
time people paid a penalty for being so immodest as to presume
a wife for themselves (to this belongs, for instance, the *jus*

primae noctis,[34] still today the privilege of priests in Cambodia, these guardians of "ancient good customs"). The gentle, benevolent, yielding, compassionate feelings — by now so high in value that they are almost "the values in themselves" — were opposed for the longest time by nothing short of self-contempt: people were ashamed of their leniency as today they are ashamed of their harshness (cf. *Beyond Good and Evil* sec. 260). Submission to the *law*: — oh with what resistance of conscience have the noble tribes everywhere on earth renounced vendettas and allowed the law to exercise power over them! "Law" for a long time was a *vetitum*,[35] an outrage, an innovation; it appeared with force, *as* force to which one only conformed by feeling ashamed of oneself. Formerly every smallest step on earth was hard fought with spiritual and physical torments: this whole viewpoint, "that not only stepping forward, no! any stepping, movement, change has needed its countless martyrs," sounds strange to us precisely today — I shed light on it in *Dawn* sec. 18.[36] "Nothing has been purchased more dearly," it says there, "than the little bit of human reason and sense of freedom that make up the sum total of our pride today. It is, however, precisely this pride that makes it virtually impossible today for us to have a feeling for those vast expanses of time that comprise the 'morality of mores' and that precede 'world history' as the actual and decisive main history that has determined the character of humankind: back when it came into currency that suffering was a virtue, cruelty a virtue, dissimulation a virtue, revenge a virtue, denial of reason a virtue, whereas well-being was a danger, thirst for knowledge a danger, peace a danger, pity a danger, being pitied an insult, work an insult, madness godliness, and *change* the thing most immoral and pregnant with destruction!" —

10

In the same book sec. 42 I explained under what valuation, under what *pressure* of valuation the oldest race of contemplative human beings had to live — despised to the very same

extent that they were not feared! Contemplation first appeared
on earth in a disguised form, with a dubious appearance, with
an evil heart and often with an anxious mind: of this there is
no doubt. For a long time the inactive, brooding, unwarlike
aspects of the instincts of contemplative humans spread a deep
mistrust around them: to counter this no other means existed
than to decisively arouse *fear* of themselves. And this for instance is something the ancient Brahmins understood! The
oldest philosophers knew how to give their existence and
presence a meaning, a support and background upon which
people learned to *fear* them: on closer examination, they did
this from an even more fundamental need, namely in order to
win their own fear and respect. For within themselves they
found all value-judgments turned *against* them, they had to
fight down every kind of suspicion and resistance against "the
philosopher in themselves." As people of a terrible age, they
did this with terrible methods: cruelty against themselves,
ingenious self-castigation—this was the principal means of
these power-hungry hermits and innovators of ideas who
first needed to violate the gods and traditions in themselves,
in order to even *believe* in their own innovation. I recall the
famous story of King Vishvamitra, who from thousands of
years of self-torment gained such a feeling of power and self-
confidence that he undertook to build a *new heaven*:[37] the
uncanny symbol of the earliest and latest history of philosophers on earth—everyone who ever built a "new heaven" only
found the power to do so in his *own hell* . . . Let us compress
the whole state of affairs into brief formulas: at first the philosophical spirit always had to disguise and mask itself in the
previously established types of the contemplative human being,
as priest, magician, soothsayer, as religious person generally,
just to *be possible* to any extent: *the ascetic ideal* long served the
philosopher as a form of appearance, as a precondition of existence—he had to *represent* it in order to be a philosopher, and
he had to *believe* in it to represent it. The peculiar aloof stance
of philosophers, world-denying, hostile to life, not believing

the senses, de-sensualized, which has been maintained into most recent times and therefore has emerged as practically the *philosophical attitude in itself*—it is above all a consequence of the distressed conditions under which philosophy arose and survived at all: since philosophy would *not have been possible at all* for the longest time without an ascetic wrap and cloak, without an ascetic self-misunderstanding. Graphically and vividly expressed: until the most recent times, the *ascetic priest* has given us the repulsive and gloomy caterpillar form in which alone philosophy was allowed to live and crawl around . . . Has this really *changed*? Has the colorful and dangerous winged creature, that "spirit" concealed in this caterpillar, really been unfrocked at last and released into the light thanks to a sunnier, warmer, brighter world? Is sufficient pride, daring, courage, self-confidence, will of the spirit, will to responsibility, *freedom of will* available today, so that from now on "the philosopher" on earth is really—*possible*? . . .

II

Only now, after we have caught sight of the *ascetic priest*, do we seriously come to grips with our problem: what does the ascetic ideal mean? — only now does it get "serious": now the actual *representative of seriousness* stands facing us. "What does all seriousness mean?" — perhaps this even more fundamental question is already on our lips here: a question for physiologists, as is only fair, but one we will sidestep for the time being. The ascetic priest has not only his faith in that ideal, but also his will, his power, his interest. His *right* to existence stands and falls with that ideal: no wonder we are up against a terrible opponent here, supposing of course that we were the opponents of that ideal? someone who fights for his existence against the deniers of that ideal? . . . On the other hand it is improbable from the start that such an interested stance toward our problem will be particularly useful to it; the ascetic priest himself will hardly represent the most successful defender of his ideal, for the same reason that a woman tends to fail when she wants to defend "woman as such" — and even less will he be the most objective assessor and judge of the controversy stirred up here. Therefore we would sooner have to help him — this much is already quite plain — defend himself well against us, than we need fear being too effectively refuted by him . . . The idea we are fighting about here is the *valuation* of our life on the part of the ascetic priests: this life (along with that to which it belongs, "nature," "world," the whole sphere of becoming and of transitoriness) is connected by them to a completely different existence that it opposes and excludes, *unless* perhaps it were to turn against itself, *deny itself*: in this case, the case of an ascetic life, life is considered to be a bridge for that other existence. The ascetic treats life as a wrong path that has to be traced back finally to its starting point; or like an error that is refuted by a deed — *should* be refuted: for he *demands* that others go along with him, he forces *his* valuation of existence where he can. What does this mean? Such a monstrous manner of valuation is not inscribed into the history of humankind as an exception and curiosity: it is one of the broadest and longest facts there is. Read from a distant star perhaps the majuscule script of our earthly existence would lead to the conclusion that the earth was the genuine *ascetic planet*, a pocket of discontented, arrogant and repulsive creatures absolutely incapable of ridding themselves of a deep displeasure with themselves, with the earth, with all of life, and who harm themselves as much as possible out of pleasure in doing harm: — probably their only pleasure. Let us consider after all how regularly, how universally, how in almost all times the ascetic priest emerges; he does not belong to a single race; he flourishes everywhere; he grows from all social classes. Not that he cultivates and propagates his manner of valuation through heredity: the reverse is the case — instead a deep instinct forbids him by and large from reproducing. There must be a necessity of the first order that makes this *life-inimical* species grow and prosper time after time — it must surely be an *interest of life itself* that such a type of self-contradiction does not die out. For an ascetic life is a self-contradiction: here reigns a *ressentiment* without equal, that of an insatiable instinct and power-will that wants to be master not over something relating to life, but over life itself, over its deepest, strongest, most primitive conditions; here an attempt is made to use energy to stop up the sources of energy; here the gaze rests green and malicious on physiological flourishing itself, especially on its expression through beauty and joy; whereas pleasure is felt and *sought* in deformity, atrophy, pain, accidents, the ugly, in voluntary deprivation, unselfing, self-flagellation, self-immolation. All of this is paradoxical to the highest degree: we stand here before a conflict that *wants* itself to be conflicted, that *enjoys* itself in this suffering and even becomes increasingly self-confident and triumphant to the extent that its own precondition, its physiological capacity for life, *decreases*. "Triumph precisely in the ultimate agony": under this superlative sign the ascetic ideal has fought since time immemorial; in this enigma of seduction, in this image of delight and torture it has recognized its brightest light, its salvation, its final victory. *Crux, nux, lux*[38] — it is all the same to the ascetic ideal. —

12

Supposing that such an incarnate will to contradiction and anti-nature could be prevailed upon to *philosophize*: on what would it vent its innermost capriciousness? On what is most certainly perceived as true, as real: it will look for *error* precisely where the actual life-instinct most unconditionally posits truth. For instance, like the ascetics of the Vedanta philosophy, it will disparage physicality as an illusion, likewise pain, multiplicity, the whole conceptual opposition "subject" and "object" — errors, nothing but errors! To renounce faith in its ego, to deny itself its own "reality" — what a triumph! — and not merely over the senses, over appearance, but a much higher kind of triumph, a violation and cruelty against *reason*: a lustful delight that reaches its pinnacle when ascetic self-contempt and self-mockery decree: "there *is* a realm of truth and of being, but precisely reason is *excluded* from it!" . . . (Incidentally: there is something of a residue of this lustful ascetic conflict even in the Kantian concept "intelligible character of things," which loves to turn reason against reason: that is, "intelligible character" in Kant means a kind of constitution of things whereby the intellect comprehends just enough to know that for the intellect — it is *utterly incomprehensible*.) — In the end, particularly as knowing ones, let us not be ungrateful toward such resolute reversals of the familiar perspectives and valuations with which the spirit has all too long raged against itself, blasphemously and futilely as it seems: for once to see things differently like this, to *want* to see differently is no small training and preparation of the intellect for its future "objectivity" — the latter not understood as "disinterested contemplation" (which is a non-concept and absurdity), but as the capacity to *have control over* one's pro and con and to deploy them: so that we know precisely how to make the *diversity* of perspectives and affective interpretations useful for knowledge. That is to say, gentlemen philosophers, let us be better from now on in guarding against the dangerous old conceptual mythmaking that posits a "pure, will-less, painless, timeless subject of knowledge," let us guard against the tentacles of such contradictory concepts as "pure reason," "absolute spirituality," "knowledge in itself": — here it is always demanded that we think an eye that cannot be thought at all, an eye that is supposed to have absolutely no direction, in which the active and interpreting forces through which seeing first becomes seeing-something are supposed to be shut down, supposed to be missing; so what is demanded of the eye here is always an absurdity and a non-concept. There is *only* a perspectival seeing, *only* a perspectival "knowing"; and *the more* affects we allow to express themselves on a given thing, *the more* eyes, different eyes we know how to engage for the same thing, the more perfect will be our "concept" of this thing, our "objectivity." But to eliminate the will altogether, to suspend each and every affect, supposing that we even could: what? would this not amount to *castrating*[39] the intellect? . . .

13

But let us return to the problem. A self-contradiction such as the one that seems to manifest itself in the ascetic, "life *against* life," is—this much is plain as day—simply nonsense when considered physiologically and no longer psychologically. It can only be *apparent*; it has to be a kind of provisional expression, an interpretation, formula, contrivance, a psychological misunderstanding of something whose actual nature was for a long time not understood, for a long time could not be described *in itself*—a mere word jammed into an old *gap* in human knowledge. Allow me to briefly counter with the real state of affairs: *the ascetic ideal arises from the protective and healing instinct of a degenerating life*, which tries to preserve itself using all means and fights for its existence; it points to a partial physiological obstruction and exhaustion, against which the deepest instincts of life, remaining intact, incessantly fight with new means and inventions. The ascetic ideal is such a means: things therefore stand exactly opposite to what the admirers of this ideal believe—life wrestles in and through it with death and *against* death, the ascetic ideal is an artifice for the *preservation* of life. That it could rule and become powerful over humanity to the extent that history demonstrates, especially wherever the civilization and taming of humans was carried out, is indicative of a great fact: the *sickliness* of the previous type of human, at least of the human made tame, the physiological struggle of humans with death (more precisely: with weariness of life, with exhaustion, with the desire for the "end"). The ascetic priest is the incarnate desire for a different mode of being, for being in a different place, and moreover he is the highest degree of this desire, its genuine ardor and passion: but the very *power* of his desire is the fetter that binds him here, it is the very thing that makes him a tool that must work on creating more favorable

conditions for being-here and being-human—with this very
power he binds to existence the entire herd of people who are
deformed, depressed, underprivileged, failures, and those of
every kind who suffer from themselves, by instinctively walk-
ing ahead of them as shepherd. I should be understood by
now: this ascetic priest, this seeming enemy of life, this *negating one*—precisely he belongs to the very great *conserving*
and *Yes-creating* forces of life . . . Where does it come from,
this sickliness? For humankind is sicker, more uncertain,
more changing, more indeterminate than any other animal,
there is no doubt of this—he is *the* sick animal: why is that?
Certainly he has also dared, innovated, thwarted, and challenged fate more than all the other animals put together: he,
the great experimenter with himself, the dissatisfied and insatiable one who struggles with animal, nature and gods for
ultimate mastery—he, the one who is still unconquered, the
eternally future one who no longer finds rest from his own
pressing energy, so that his future digs unrelentingly like a
spur into the flesh of every present:—how should such a brave
and rich animal not also be the most endangered, the one
sickest for the longest time and the most seriously ill of all
sick animals? . . . Humankind gets fed up, often enough,
there are entire epidemics of this being fed up (—say around
1348, at the time of the Dance of Death): but even this nausea, this exhaustion, this being weary of himself—it all
erupts from him so powerfully that it immediately becomes a
new fetter. The No he says to life magically brings to light an
abundance of tender Yeses; indeed when he *wounds* himself,
this master of destruction and self-destruction—afterward it
is the wound itself that compels him *to live* . . .

14[40]

The more normal the sickliness in a human being—and we
cannot deny this normality—the higher we should honor the
rare cases of power of soul and body in humans, the human
lucky strokes, and all the more strictly protect from the worst

air, the air of the sickroom, those who turned out well. Is this
what we do? . . . The sick are the biggest danger to the healthy;
not from the strongest does harm come to the strong, but from
the weakest. Is this what we know? . . . By and large it is absolutely not fear of human beings that we should be seeking to
diminish: for this fear compels the strong to be strong, and
sometimes even terrible — it *maintains* the type of human that
turned out well. What is to be feared, what has a disastrous
effect like no other disaster, would not be great fear, but great
disgust for humans, likewise great *compassion* for humans.
Supposing these two were to marry someday, then immediately something most uncanny would inevitably come into
the world, the "last will" of humanity, its will to nothingness,
nihilism. And in fact: much has already been prepared for
this. Whoever has not only his nose for smelling, but also his
eyes and ears, senses almost everywhere he might go today
something like the air of an insane asylum or a hospital — I
am speaking, as is only fair, of humanity's cultural zones, of
every kind of "Europe" there is these days on earth. The *sickly*
are humanity's great danger; *not* the evil, *not* the "predators."
Those who from the start are failures, the downcast, the
broken — it is they, it is the *weakest* who most undermine life
among humans, who call into question and most dangerously
poison our trust in life, in humans, in ourselves. Where could
we hope to escape that veiled gaze from which we turn away
with a profound sadness, that backward-turned gaze of those
deformed from the outset, which betrays how such a human
speaks to himself — that gaze that is a sigh. "If only I could be
someone else!" thus sighs this gaze: "but there is no hope. I am
who I am: how could I get free of myself? And yet — *I am so
sick of myself*!" . . . In such ground of self-contempt, a virtual
swamp ground, every kind of weed, every poisonous plant
grows, and everything so small, so hidden, so dishonest, so
cloying. Here teem the worms of vengeful and rancorous feeling; here the air stinks of secrets and unadmitted things; here
the web of the most malicious conspiracy is constantly being

spun—the conspiracy of the suffering against those who turned out well and are victorious; here the sight of the winner is *hated*. And what mendacity not to admit this hate is hatred! What expenditure of big words and attitudes, what an art of "righteous" slander! These deformed ones: what noble eloquence streams from their lips! How much sugary, slimy, humble devotion wells in their eyes! What do they really want? To at least *represent* justice, love, wisdom, superiority—that is the ambition of these "undermost" types, these sick ones! And how skilled this ambition makes them! Admire for instance the counterfeiter-skill with which the stamp of virtue, even the jingle-jangle, the gold-clinking of virtue, is copied. They have the lease on virtue all to themselves, these weaklings and incurably diseased ones, there's no doubting it: "we alone are the good, the just," they say, "we alone are the *homines bonae voluntatis*."[41] They stroll among us as incarnate reproaches, as warnings to us—as if health, turning out well, strength, pride, feeling of power were depraved things in themselves, for which we will have to atone someday, bitterly atone: oh how at bottom they themselves are ready to *make* people atone, how they thirst to be *executioners*! Among them there are plenty of vengeful types disguised as judges, who constantly carry the word "justice" around in their mouths like a poisonous spittle, lips always pursed, always ready to spit on everyone who does not look dissatisfied and cheerfully goes his way. Among them not even that most disgusting species of the vain is lacking, the mendacious freaks who are bent on portraying "beautiful souls" and who bring their botched sensuality, wrapped in verses and other diapers, to market as "purity of the heart": the species of moral onanists and "self-gratifiers." The will of the sick to represent *any* form of superiority, their instinct for secret paths that lead to a tyranny over the healthy—where is it not found, this will to power of precisely the weakest! The sick woman in particular: no one excels her in the subtleties of ruling, pressuring, tyrannizing. For this the sick woman spares nothing that lives, nothing that is dead, she digs up the most buried of things (the Bogos say: "woman is a hyena"[42]). Just look at the background of every family, every corporation, every community: everywhere the battle of the sick against the healthy—a quiet battle fought mostly with little poisonous powders, with needle pricks, with sly martyred facial expressions, but occasionally also with that invalid's pharisaism of *loud* gestures that loves best to play "the noble indignation." It wants to make itself heard as far as the hallowed halls of science, this hoarse indignant barking of the sickly dogs, this biting rabid mendacity of such "noble" Pharisees (—I once again remind my readers who have ears of that Berliner apostle of revenge, Eugen Dühring, who is making the most indecent and repulsive use of moral boom-boom in contemporary Germany: Dühring, the foremost moralistic bigmouth there is today, even among his kind, the anti-Semites). Those are all humans of *ressentiment*, these physiological failures and worm-eaten ones, an entire trembling earth of underground revenge, inexhaustible, insatiable in outbursts against the happy and likewise in masquerades of revenge, in pretexts for revenge: when would they actually arrive at their ultimate, finest, most sublime triumph of revenge? Undoubtedly when they succeeded in *shoving into the conscience* of the happy their own misery, all misery generally: so that someday they would have to begin to be ashamed of their happiness and perhaps say to one another: "it is a disgrace to be happy! *there is too much misery!*" . . . But there could be no greater and more disastrous misunderstanding than if the happy, those who turned out well, the powerful in body and soul began to doubt their *right to happiness* in this manner. Away with this "inverted world"! Away with this disgraceful tenderizing of feeling! That the sick should *not* make the healthy sick—and this would be such a tenderization—that should of course be the supreme viewpoint on earth:—but this would require above all things that the healthy remain *separated* from the sick, protected against even the sight of the sick, and that they not confuse themselves with the sick. Or would it be their task to be nurses or physicians? . . . But they could not possibly mistake and deny *their* task worse—the higher *must* not debase itself to serve as tool of the lower, the pathos of distance *must* also keep the tasks separate for all eternity! Their right to exist, the privilege of the bell with a full sound against that of a discordant, cracked one, is certainly a thousand-fold greater: they alone are the *guarantors* of the future, they alone are *responsible* for the human future. What *they* can do, what *they* should do is something that the sick can never and should never be able to do: but *in order* to be able to do what only *they* should do, how could they be free to play the role of physician, consoler, "savior" of the sick? . . . And therefore fresh air! fresh air! And in any case away from the proximity of all insane asylums and hospitals of culture! And therefore good company, *our* company! Or solitude, if it must be! But in any case away from the evil fumes of internal rot and the secret worm-food of the sick! . . . So that we may defend ourselves, my friends, at least for a while yet, against the two worst epidemics that may have been reserved just for us—against the *great disgust with human beings*! against the *great compassion for human beings*! . . .

15

If we have grasped in all its depth—and I demand that right here we *reach deeply*, grasp deeply—the extent to which it absolutely *cannot* be the task of the healthy to nurse the sick, to make the sick healthy, then one more necessity has also been grasped—the necessity of physicians and nurses *who themselves are sick*: and now we have and hold in both hands the meaning of the ascetic priest. We have to consider the ascetic priest to be the foreordained savior, shepherd and advocate of the sick herd: only then do we understand his tremendous historical mission. His realm is *dominion over the suffering*, his instincts point him to them, in this he has his most characteristic art, his mastery, his kind of happiness. He himself must be sick, he must be related from the ground up to the sick and the underprivileged in order to understand them—in order to get along with them; but he must also be strong, master of himself even more than over others, unscathed especially in his will to power so that he has the trust and fear of the sick, so that he can be their support, resistance, prop, compulsion, disciplinarian, tyrant, god. He has to defend them, his herd—against whom? Against the healthy, no doubt, also against envying the healthy; he must be the natural antagonist *and despiser* of all brutal, stormy, unbridled, harsh, violently predatory health and powerfulness. The priest is the first form of the *more delicate* animal that sooner despises than hates. He will not be spared from waging war with the predators, a war of cunning (of the "spirit") more than of force, as goes without saying—and for this sometimes he will need to develop in himself almost a new type of predator, or at least *signify* one—a new animal terribleness in which the polar bear, the supple cold patient tiger cat, and not least the fox seem to be bound together in a unity that is just as attractive as fear-inspiring. Supposing that necessity compels him, he then steps forth among the other kinds of predator with bearish seriousness, honorable, clever, cold, feigning superiority as the herald and mouthpiece of secret forces, determined to sow misery, conflict, self-contradiction wherever he can in this soil and, only too certain of his art, always to be the master of those who *suffer*. He brings along salves and balms, to be sure; but he first needs to wound in order to be the physician; when he then stills the pain made by the wound, *he simultaneously poisons the wound*—for that above all is what he knows how to do, this magician and tamer of beasts of prey in whose vicinity everything healthy necessarily becomes sick and everything sick necessarily becomes tame. Indeed he protects his sick herd well enough, this odd shepherd—he defends it against itself as well, against the badness, spite, maliciousness that smolders in the herd itself, and against whatever else is characteristic of all addicts and sick people, he fights cleverly, hard and secretly against anarchy and the omnipresent disintegration within the herd, in which that most dangerous blasting and explosive material, *ressentiment*, piles up higher and higher. To discharge this explosive in such a way that it does not blow up the herd or the shepherd is his genuine feat, and also his supreme utility; if we wanted to summarize the value of priestly existence in the shortest possible formulation, then we would have to say: the priest is the *direction-changer* of *ressentiment*. For every sufferer instinctively looks for a cause of his suffering; more accurately, a perpetrator, more specifically, a *guilty* perpetrator who is receptive to suffering—in brief, some kind of living thing upon which he can discharge his affects in deeds or in effigy based on some pretext: for the discharging of affects is the greatest attempt at relief, namely *anesthetization*, of the sufferer, his involuntarily craved narcotic against torture of any kind. In this alone, I suspect, the real physiological causality of *ressentiment*, revenge and the like are to be found; that is, in a craving for *anesthetization of pain through affect*:—this same causality has commonly been sought, quite erroneously as it seems to me, in the defensive counterblow, a mere protective measure of reaction, a "reflexive movement" in case of some sudden injury and endangerment, of the kind demonstrated by a headless frog in order to rid itself of a corrosive acid. But the difference is fundamental: in the one case we want to prevent being damaged further,[43] in the other case, using a more vehement emotion of some kind, we want to *anesthetize* and at least for the moment eliminate from consciousness a torturous secret pain that threatens to become unbearable—for this one needs an affect, as wild an affect as possible, and for its stimulation, the first best pretext. "Someone or another must be to blame for my feeling bad"—this way of concluding is characteristic of all sickly people, and the more so the more the true cause of their feeling bad, the physiological one, remains hidden (—it can lie for instance in a sickening of the *nervus sympathicus*[44] or in an excessive secretion of bile, or in a deficiency of potassium sulfate and phosphate[45] in the blood, or in pressure spots in the abdomen that impede blood circulation, or in degeneration of the ovaries and so on). All sufferers are of a horrifying readiness and inventiveness in pretexts for painful affects; they even enjoy their suspicion, their brooding over bad deeds and imaginary slights; they dig through the bowels of their past and present for dark questionable stories, where they are free to revel in torturous suspicion and to intoxicate themselves with the poisons of their own malice — they tear open the oldest wounds, they hemorrhage from scars long since healed, they make evildoers out of friends, wife, child and anyone else who is closest to them. "I suffer: someone must be to blame for this" — thus thinks every diseased sheep. But its shepherd, the ascetic priest, says to it: "Right you are, my sheep! someone must be to blame for it: but you yourself are this someone, you alone are to blame — *you alone are to blame for yourself*!" . . . That is bold enough, false enough: but at least one thing is achieved with it, like I said, the direction of *ressentiment* is — *changed*.

16

Now one can guess what, according to my conception, the healing artistic instinct of life has *attempted* through the ascetic priest and why a temporary tyranny of such paradoxical and paralogical concepts as "guilt," "sin," "sinfulness," "corruption," "damnation" has had to serve him: to make the sick *harmless* to a certain extent, to destroy the incurable through themselves, to strictly direct the less seriously afflicted back to themselves, to give a direction back to their *ressentiment* ("one thing is needful"[46] —) and to thus *exploit* the bad instincts of all suffering people for the purpose of self-discipline, self-surveillance, self-overcoming. It is self-evident that with a "medication" of this kind, a mere affect-medication, we absolutely cannot be dealing with a real *healing* of the sick in the physiological sense; we could not even claim that here the instinct of life somehow took healing into consideration and intended it. A kind of crowding together and organizing of the sick on the one hand (— the word "church" is the most popular name for it), a kind of temporary securing of those who turned out healthier, of the more fully-cast on the other hand, resulting in the tearing open of a *chasm* between healthy and sick—for a long time that was it! And it was a lot! It was *very much*! . . . [In this treatise, as one sees, I proceed from the presupposition that I do not first need to justify, given readers as I need them: that "sinfulness" in humans is not a fact, rather only the interpretation of a fact, namely of a physiological depression—the latter seen from a moral-religious perspective that is no longer binding on us.—Saying that someone *feels* "guilty," "sinful," does not yet prove in the least that he justifiably feels this way; no more so than someone is healthy merely because he feels himself to be healthy. Recall the famous witch trials: back then the most perspicacious and philanthropic judges did not doubt that guilt was present here; the "witches" *themselves did not doubt it*—and yet guilt[47] was lacking.—To express that presupposition in an expanded form: I do not at all recognize the "psychological pain" itself as a fact, rather only as an interpretation (causal interpretation) of facts hitherto incapable of accurate formulation: thus as something that is still completely up in the air and is scientifically nonbinding—really a fat word standing in for a very spindly question mark. When someone cannot have done with a "psychological pain," then it is *not*, putting it crudely, due to his "psyche"; more probably due to his belly (crudely put, as stated; which by no means indicates my desire also to be crudely heard and crudely understood . . .). A strong and well-constituted human being digests his experiences (deeds, misdeeds included) as he digests his meals, even when he has to swallow bitter pills. If he cannot "have done" with an experience, then this kind of indigestion is just as physiological as the other kind—and many times in fact only one of the consequences of that other kind.—With such a conception, speaking among ourselves, one can still be the strictest opponent of all materialism . . .]

17

But is he really a *physician*, this ascetic priest? — We already grasped how it is scarcely permissible to call him a physician, however much he likes to feel himself to be a "savior," and allows himself to be revered as a "savior." Only suffering itself, the malaise of the sufferer is fought by him, *not* their cause, *not* the actual sickly state — this has to serve as our fundamental objection against priestly medication. But if for once we adopt the perspective that only the priest knows and has, then there is no end to our admiration of all the things that have been seen, sought and found under it. The *alleviation* of suffering, "consolation" of every kind — this proves to be his very genius: how inventively he has understood his task as consoler, how unhesitatingly and boldly he has chosen his methods for it! Christianity in particular could be called a great treasure house of spiritual means of consolation, so much that is invigorating, alleviating, narcotizing is stored in it, so much of what is most dangerous and audacious has been ventured for this purpose, so subtly, so sophisticatedly, so sophisticatedly in southerly terms in particular has it intuited what stimulant-affects it can use to overcome, at least for a time, deep depression, leaden exhaustion, the black melancholy of the physiologically inhibited. For generally speaking: with all great religions it has mainly been a matter of combating a certain weariness and heaviness that have become epidemic. From the start we can posit as probable that from time to time in certain places on earth a *physiological feeling of inhibition* must almost necessarily become master over large swathes of the population, but for lack of physiological knowledge it does not enter as such into consciousness, so that its "cause," its remedy can only be sought and attempted psychologically and morally (— this in fact is my most general formula for that which is commonly called "*religion*"). Such a feeling of inhibition can be of the most various lineages: perhaps as the result of crossing races that are too dissimilar (or classes — classes too always express difference of lineage and race: European "*Weltschmerz*,"[48] the "pessimism" of the nineteenth century are essentially the result of a senselessly precipitous mixing of classes); or conditioned by a flawed emigration — a race landed in a climate for which its power to adapt does not suffice (the case of the Indians in India); or the aftereffect of age and exhaustion of the race (Parisian pessimism from 1850 on); or the wrong diet (alcoholism of the Middle Ages; the nonsense of vegetarians[49] who of course have on their side the authority of Sir Andrew[50] in Shakespeare[51]); or from corruption of the blood, malaria, syphilis and the like (German depression after the Thirty Years' War, which infected half of Germany with vile diseases and thus prepared the soil for German servility and German faintheartedness). What is attempted on a grand scale every time in such a case is a *battle with the feeling of apathy*; let us inform ourselves briefly about its most important practices and forms. (As is only fair I leave out entirely here the actual *philosophers'* battle against the feeling of apathy, which always tends to be contemporaneous — it is interesting enough, but too absurd, too indifferent in practical terms, too spidery and loaferish, as for instance when pain is supposed to be proven an error under the naïve presupposition that the pain *must* disappear if only the error in it is recognized — but behold! it refuses to disappear . . .) That dominant apathy is *first* combated by means that reduce the feeling of life generally to its lowest point. If possible no willing, no more desire; avoid everything that stirs up affect and the "blood" (eat no salt: hygiene of the fakir); do not love; do not hate; indifference; do not avenge; do not get rich; do not work; beg; if possible no woman, or as little woman as possible: in the spiritual sense Pascal's principle "*il faut s'abêtir.*"[52] The result, psychologically-morally speaking: "un-selfing," "sanctification"; physiologically speaking: hypnotization — the attempt to achieve in humans something approaching the *winter sleep* of some animal species, and *summer sleep*[53] in many plants of the hot climates, a minimum of consumption and metabolism

during which life just barely persists without really entering
into consciousness anymore. An amazing amount of human
energy has been expended on this goal—perhaps in
vain?[54] . . . We cannot doubt in the least that such sports-
men[55] of "sanctity" who are plentiful in all times in almost all
peoples have in fact found a real redemption from what they
fought with such rigorous training[56]—in countless cases they
actually got *rid* of that deep physiological depression with the
help of their system of hypnotics: which is why their method-
ology counts as one of the most universal ethnological facts.
Likewise we have no basis on which to attribute to madness
such an intention to starve the body and the desires as such
(as a clumsy kind of roastbeef-devouring "freethinker" and
Sir Andrew tends to do). It is all the more certain that it
functions and can function as the *way* to all kinds of mental
disturbances, to "inner lights," for instance, as among the
Hesychasts of Mount Athos,[57] to hallucinations of sounds
and figures, to lascivious outpourings and ecstasies of sensuality (the story of Saint Theresa). The interpretation of such
conditions given by those afflicted with them has always been
as fanatically false as possible, it goes without saying: only let
us not fail to hear the tone of ultra-convinced gratitude that
resonates already in the *will* to such a manner of interpretation. The highest state, *redemption* itself, that finally attained
total hypnotization and stillness, is always regarded by them
as the mystery in itself for whose expression even the highest
symbols do not suffice, as a turning inward and returning
home to the ground of things, as becoming free of all delusion, as "knowledge," as "truth," as "being," as a breaking free
of every goal, every desire, every deed, as a Beyond even of
good and evil. "Good and evil," says the Buddhist—"both
are fetters: over both the Perfect One became master"; "what is
done and what is left undone," says the believer in the Vedanta,
"causes him no pain; the good and the evil he shakes off like a
wise man; his realm no longer suffers from any deed; he went
beyond good and evil, beyond both":[58]—a pan-Indian concept

therefore, just as Brahmanistic as Buddhist. (Neither in the Indian nor the Christian way of thinking is that "redemption" supposed to be *attainable* through virtue, through moral improvement, however highly they may posit the hypnotization value of virtue: this we must remember—and moreover it simply corresponds to the facts. To have remained *true* on this issue may perhaps be regarded as the best piece of realism in the three greatest religions, which are otherwise so thoroughly over-moralized.[59] "For the knowing one there is no duty" . . . "redemption does not come about through the *adding on* of virtues, for it consists of being one with Brahma, who is incapable of additional perfection; and just as little through *ridding oneself* of faults: for Brahma is eternally pure, and what constitutes redemption is being one with him"— these passages from the commentary of Shankara, quoted by the first real *expert* of Indian philosophy in Europe, my friend Paul Deussen.[60]) Thus we want to honor "redemption" in the great religions; on the other hand it is a bit difficult for us to remain serious about how *deep sleep* is esteemed by these life-weary types who are too weary even for dreaming—deep sleep, that is, that is already supposed to be an entering into Brahma, an *achieved unio mystica* with God. "Therefore when he has fallen completely asleep"—so it is written in the most ancient venerable "Scripture"—"and is perfectly at rest so that he no longer sees any dream images, then, oh precious one, he is united with Being, he has gone into himself—embraced by the knowledge-like self, he no longer has consciousness of what is outside or inside. This bridge is not crossed by day and night, not by age, not by death, not by suffering, not by good work nor evil work."[61] "In deep sleep," likewise say the believers of this profoundest of the three great religions, "the soul raises itself out of this body, enters into the highest light and thereby appears in its own form: there it is the highest spirit itself that walks about joking and playing and enjoying itself, whether with women or with carriages or with friends; there it no longer thinks back on this appendage of a body, to which the *prâna* (the life-breath) is harnessed as a draught animal to its cart."[62] Nevertheless here, too, as in the case of "redemption," we want to keep in mind that basically what is expressed here is only the same esteem, albeit in the splendor of oriental exaggeration, found in the clear, cool, Hellenically cool but suffering Epicurus: the hypnotic feeling of nothingness, the repose of deepest sleep, in brief, *absence of suffering*— to the suffering and the thoroughly depressed this must already count as the highest good, as the value of values, that *must* be appraised by them as positive, felt as *the* positive itself. (According to the same logic of feeling, in all pessimistic religion nothingness is called *God.*)

18

What is used much more frequently than such a hypnotic overall suppression of sensitivity, of capacity for pain, that presupposes even rarer forces, above all courage, contempt for opinion, and "intellectual stoicism," is a different training against states of depression, which is easier in any case: *mechanical activity*. It is beyond all doubt that with it a suffering existence is alleviated to a not inconsiderable degree: today this fact is called, somewhat dishonestly, "the blessings of work." The alleviation consists in this, that the interest of the suffering is fundamentally diverted from suffering— that constantly one and only one activity enters consciousness and consequently very little room remains there for suffering: for it is *narrow*, this chamber of human consciousness! Mechanical activity and whatever belongs to it— such as absolute regularity, punctual unconscious obedience, a mode of life fixed once and for all, the filling up of time, a certain permission, indeed training for "impersonality," for forgetting oneself, for "*incuria sui*"[63]—: how thoroughly, how subtly the ascetic priest has known how to use them in the battle with pain! Especially when he has had to deal with sufferers of the lower classes, with slave laborers or prisoners (or with women: who of course are both for the most part, slave laborers and prisoners), he needed little more than a small art of name-changing and re-christening in order to make them see from now on a benefit, a relative happiness in despised things: — the dissatisfaction of the slave with his fate was in any case *not* invented by the priests. —An even more treasured means in the struggle with depression is the prescription of a *small joy* that is easily accessible and can be made into a routine; this medication is frequently used in connection with the one discussed above. The most common form in which joy is thus prescribed as a curative is the joy of *giving* joy (as good deeds, gift giving, relieving, helping, encouraging, consoling, praising, rewarding); by prescribing "love of one's neighbor," the ascetic priest at bottom is prescribing a stimulation of the strongest, most life-affirming drive, even if in the most cautious dosage — of the *will to power*. The happiness of the "smallest superiority," as brought about by all good deeds, being useful, helping, rewarding is the most abundant means of consolation that the physiologically inhibited tend to use, if they are well advised: otherwise they hurt each other, naturally by obeying the same basic instinct. When we look for the beginning of Christianity in the Roman world, we find sprouting from the undermost soil of society at that time associations for mutual support, associations for the poor, the sick and for burial, in which that major remedy against depression, the small joy, that of mutual benevolence was consciously practiced — perhaps this was something new back then, a genuine discovery? The "will to mutuality" summoned in this manner, the will to the formation of a herd, to "community" and to "cenacle," must now in turn come to a new and much fuller outburst in that will to power it has triggered, even if on a smaller scale: the *formation of a herd* is an essential step and victory in the battle with depression. In the growth of the community a new interest also gains strength in the individual, which often enough elevates him beyond the most personal aspects of his sullenness, his aversion to *himself* (the "*despectio sui*"[64] of Geulincx[65]). All sick and sickly people strive instinctively for herd organization, out of a longing to shake off their dull malaise and feeling of weakness: the ascetic priest intuits this instinct and promotes it; wherever there are herds it is the instinct of weakness that willed the herd, and the cleverness of the priest that organized it. For this should not be overlooked: the strong strive to *separate* just as naturally and necessarily as the weak strive to *congregate*; when the former unite, this happens only with a view to an aggressive joint action and joint satisfaction of their will to power, with great resistance from the individual conscience; the latter, on the other hand, band together with *pleasure* in this banding together—their instinct here is just as satisfied as the instinct of the born "master" (that is, of the solitary predator species of human being) at bottom is aggravated and unsettled by organization. Beneath every oligarchy—the whole of history teaches this—the *tyrannical* lust always lies concealed; every oligarchy trembles constantly from the tension that each individual in it requires to maintain mastery over this lust. (So it was for example in the *Greeks*: Plato demonstrates it in a hundred passages, Plato who knew his kind—*and* himself . . .)

19

The means of the ascetic priest that we have learned about so far—the overall muting of the feeling of life, mechanical activity, the small joy, above all that of "love of one's neighbor," herd organization, arousal of the community's feeling of power whereby the individual's annoyance with himself is deadened by his pleasure in the prospering of the community—these are, measured by modern standards, his *innocent* means in the battle with malaise: let us now turn to the more interesting ones, the "guilty" ones. In all of them it is really a matter of one thing: some kind of *excess of feeling*—this used against dull, crippling, prolonged painfulness as the most effective means of anesthetizing; which is why priestly sensitivity in thinking through this single question has been nothing short of inexhaustible: "*by what means* does one achieve an excess of feeling?" . . . That sounds harsh: it is plain as day that it would sound lovelier and perhaps be softer on the ears if I were to say perhaps "the ascetic priest has at all times made use of the *enthusiasm* that lies in all strong affects." But why continue to stroke the effeminate ears of our modern sissies? Why should *we* budge even a single step for their tartuffery of words? For us psychologists that would already constitute a tartuffery *of deeds*; apart from the fact that it would make us nauseous. For this is where a psychologist today has his *good taste*, if he has any at all(—others might say: his integrity), namely that he resists shamefully *over-moralized* discourse, which these days covers in slime all modern judging of humans and things. For let us not deceive ourselves here: what constitutes the most characteristic feature of modern souls and modern books is not the lie, but their ingrained *innocence* in moralistic mendacity. To have to discover this "innocence" everywhere again and again—this represents perhaps the most repulsive piece of work among all the questionable chores to which a psychologist must subject himself today; it is a piece of *our* great danger—it is a path that perhaps leads precisely *us* to great nausea . . . I do not doubt what sole *purpose* modern books (assuming they have longevity, which is of course not to be feared, and likewise assuming that there will someday be a posterity with stricter, harsher, *healthier* taste)—what purpose *all* modern things generally would serve for this posterity, could serve for them: as emetics—and this by virtue of its moral sugar-coating and falseness, its innermost feminism, that likes to call itself "idealism" and in any case believes itself to be idealism. Our educated people of today, our "good" people do not lie—this is true; but this does *not* accrue to their honor! The authentic lie, the genuine, resolute "honest" lie (concerning whose value one should listen to Plato[66]) would for them be something far too rigorous, too strong; it would demand what *must* not be demanded of them, that they open their eyes to themselves, that they know how to distinguish between "true" and "false" in themselves. The *dishonest lie* alone suits them; everyone who today feels himself to be a "good human being" is completely incapable of approaching any issues without *dishonest mendacity*, abysmal mendacity, but innocent mendacity, loyal mendacity, naïve mendacity, virtuous mendacity. These "good human beings" — all of them are now over-moralized, thoroughly ruined and botched for all eternity with respect to honesty: who among them could endure even a single *truth* "about humanity"! . . . Or, more graphically phrased: who among them could bear a *true* biography! . . . A couple of indicators: Lord Byron wrote down some highly personal things about himself, but Thomas Moore was "too good" for that: he burned the papers of his friend. Dr. Gwinner, the executor of Schopenhauer's will, is supposed to have done the same thing: since Schopenhauer too had written down some things about himself and even against himself ("εἰς ἑαυτόν").[67] The capable American Thayer, Beethoven's biographer, suddenly stopped his work: having reached a certain point in this honorable and naïve life, he could no longer tolerate it . . . Moral: what prudent man today would still write one honest word about himself? — he would have to belong to the Order of Holy Recklessness. We have been promised an autobiography of Richard Wagner:[68] who doubts that it will be a *prudent* autobiography? . . . Let us recall the comical horror aroused by the Catholic priest Janssen[69] with his impossibly simplistic and innocuous image of the German Reformation movement; what would they bring up if someone told us this movement *differently*, if a real psychologist told us a real Luther, no longer with the moralistic simplicity of a country cleric, no longer with the saccharine and discreet bashfulness of a Protestant historian, but say with a *Taine*-like intrepidness, from a *strength of soul* and not from a prudent indulgence toward strength? (The Germans, by the way, have nicely enough produced the classical type of the latter, in the end — they may already count him as theirs, count him in their favor: namely in their Leopold Ranke, this born classical *advocatus* of every *causa fortior*,[70] this most prudent of all prudent "men of facts.")

20

But I will have been understood already: — all in all reason enough, don't you think, that we psychologists nowadays cannot get rid of a certain mistrust *of ourselves*? . . . Probably we too are still "too good" for our handiwork, probably we too are still victims, prey, the sick of this over-moralized taste of the times, as much as we also feel ourselves to be its despisers — probably it infects *us* too. What did that diplomat[71] warn against when he spoke to his peers? "Gentlemen let us mistrust above all our first impulses!" he said, *"they are almost always good"* . . . This is also how every psychologist today should speak to his peers . . . And with that we come back to our problem, which in fact demands considerable rigor of us, especially considerable mistrust of "first impulses." *The ascetic ideal serving an intent to produce emotional excess*: — whoever recalls the previous treatise will anticipate, compressed into these ten words, the essential content of what will now be demonstrated. To put the human soul for once completely out of joint,[72] to immerse it in terrors, frosts, embers and ecstasies until it is freed of all the smallness and pettiness of malaise, dullness, depression as if by a stroke of lightning: which paths lead to *this* goal? And which of them most surely? . . . At bottom all great affects have the capacity to do so, providing they discharge themselves suddenly; anger, fear, lustfulness, revenge, hope, triumph, despair, cruelty; and indeed the ascetic priest has unscrupulously taken into his service the *whole* pack of wild dogs in humanity and unleashed first this one, then that one, always for the same purpose of waking humanity out of its slow melancholy, of chasing away for a time its dull pain, its lingering misery, and always under a religious interpretation and "justification."

Every excess of this kind has to be *paid for* later on, it goes without saying—it makes the sick sicker—: and therefore this kind of pain remedy measured by modern standards is a "guilty" kind. Yet all the more we must insist, because fairness demands this, that it has been applied *in good conscience*, that the ascetic priest prescribed it with the deepest faith in its utility, indeed its indispensability—and often enough almost breaking down himself in the face of the anguish he created; likewise that the vehement physiological avengings of such excesses, perhaps even mental disturbances, basically do not really contradict the whole sense of this kind of medication: which, as was already demonstrated, was *not* aimed at healing sicknesses but at combating the malaise of depression, at alleviating and anesthetizing it. This goal was also reached *thus*. The main trick the ascetic priest allowed himself for making the human soul resound with heart-rending, ecstatic music of all kinds—everyone knows this—was his exploitation of the *feeling of guilt*. Its descent was briefly suggested in the previous treatise—as a piece of animal psychology, no more: the feeling of guilt there confronted us in its raw state, as it were. Only in the hands of the priest, this genuine artist in feelings of guilt, did it take shape—oh what a shape! "Sin"—for this is what priestly reinterpretation calls the animal "bad conscience" (cruelty turned backward)—has so far been the greatest event in the history of the sick soul: in it we have the most dangerous and fateful artifice of religious interpretation. The human being, suffering from himself somehow, physiologically in any case, something like an animal that is locked in its cage, unclear as to why, what for? thirsting for reasons—reasons relieve—thirsting also for cures and narcotics, finally holds council with someone who also knows hidden things—and behold! he gets a clue, he gets his *first* clue about the "cause" of his suffering from his magician, the ascetic priest: he should seek it in *himself*, in a *guilt*, in a piece of the past; he should understand his suffering itself as a *state of punishment* . . . He has heard, he has understood, this wretch; now he is like the hen around which a line of chalk has been drawn. He can no longer get out of this circle of lines: out of the sick man "the sinner" has been made . . . And now we will not be rid of the sight of this new invalid, "the sinner," for a couple of thousand years—will we ever be rid of him?—wherever we look, everywhere the hypnotic gaze of the sinner who always moves in a single direction (in the direction of "guilt," as the *only* causality of suffering); everywhere the bad conscience, this "abominable beast," to use Luther's words; everywhere the past regurgitated, the deed distorted, the "green eye" for all action; everywhere *wanting*-to-misunderstand suffering gets made into the content of life, its reinterpretation into feelings of guilt, fear and punishment; everywhere the scourge, the hair shirt, the starving body, remorse; everywhere the sinner breaking himself on the cruel wheel of a restless, pathologically lustful conscience; everywhere mute torment, the most extreme fear, the agony of the tortured heart, the spasms of an unknown happiness, the cry for "redemption." Indeed, with this system of procedures the old depression, heaviness and weariness were thoroughly *conquered*, life itself became *very* interesting again: awake, eternally awake, bleary-eyed, glowing, charred, exhausted and yet not tired—this is what the human being looked like, "the sinner," who was initiated into *these* mysteries. This old great magician in his battle with malaise, the ascetic priest—he had obviously won, *his* kingdom had come: already people protested no more *against* pain, they *craved* pain; "*more* pain! *more* pain!" thus cried the longing of his disciples and initiates for hundreds of years. Every emotional excess that caused pain, everything that smashed, toppled, crushed, entranced, the secret of the torture chambers, the inventiveness of hell itself—everything had now been discovered, intuited, exploited, everything stood at the magician's command, everything from now on served the victory of his ideals, the ascetic ideal . . . "my kingdom is not of *this* world!"[73]—he spoke now as before: did he really still have the right to speak this way? . . . Goethe[74] claimed there were only thirty-six tragic situations: one can guess from this, if it were not already known, that Goethe was no ascetic priest. He—knows more . . .

21

With respect to *this* entire kind of priestly medication, the "guilty" kind, any word of criticism is too much. That such an excess of emotion as the ascetic priest in this case tends to prescribe to his patients (under the holiest names, needless to say, likewise permeated by the holiness of his purpose) was actually *useful* to any patient, who would wish to uphold an assertion of this kind? At least we should be in agreement about the word "useful." If it is intended to express that such a system of treatment *improved* humanity, then I do not contradict: only I must add what "improved" means to me—the same as "tamed," "weakened," "discouraged," "refined," "effeminized," "emasculated" (therefore nearly the same as *damaged* . . .) But when we are dealing mainly with the sick, dejected and depressed, then such a system, assuming that it were to make the invalid "better," invariably makes him *sicker*; just ask the physicians in an insane asylum what always accompanies the methodical application of penitential tortures, remorse, and cramps of redemption. Likewise look to history: wherever the ascetic priest imposed this treatment, sickliness grew in depth and breadth with uncanny speed. What was the "success" every time? A shattered nervous system on top of what was already sick; and this on the largest and smallest scale, in individuals as in masses. In the wake of penitence and redemption training we find tremendous epileptic epidemics, the biggest known to history, such as the St. Vitus's and St. John's dancers of the Middle Ages; we find another form of aftereffect in the terrible paralyses and chronic depressions that sometimes transform the temperament of a people or a city (Geneva, Basel) once and for all into its opposite;—witch hysteria also belongs here, as something related to somnambulism (eight major epidemic outbreaks between 1564 and 1605 alone) — ; in its wake we likewise find those suicidal mass deliria whose appalling cry *"evviva la morte"*[75] rang out across the whole of Europe, interrupted by idiosyncrasies now lustful, now destructively raging: just as the same alternation of affects with the same intermittences and shifts is observed everywhere today as well, in any case wherever the ascetic doctrine of sin once again achieves a great success (religious neurosis *appears* as a form of "evil essence": no doubt. What it is? *Quaeritur.*[76]) On the whole, the ascetic ideal and its sublime-moral cult, this most ingenious, unscrupulous and dangerous systematization of all means of emotional excess under the aegis of holy intentions has inscribed itself in a terrible and unforgettable way on the entire history of humanity; and unfortunately *not only* on its history . . . I would scarcely know what else to hold responsible for so destructively affecting the *health* and racial strength of Europeans in particular, if not this ideal; we can without exaggeration call it *the genuine catastrophe* in the history of the health of European humanity. At best, we could say that its influence would be comparable to the specific Germanic influence: I mean the alcohol poisoning of Europe, which has so far kept strict pace with the political and racial ascendancy of the Germanic peoples (— wherever they inoculated their blood, they also inoculated their vices). — Third in this series would have to be syphilis — *magno sed proxima intervallo.*[77]

22

The ascetic priest has ruined the health of the psyche wherever he has come to power, and consequently he has also ruined *taste in artibus et litteris*[78] — he is still ruining it. "Consequently?" — I hope I can simply be conceded this "consequently"; at any rate I do not want first to prove it. One single pointer: it applies to the basic book of Christian literature, its actual model, its "book in itself." Even in the midst of Greco-Roman magnificence, which was also a magnificence of books, in the face of a not yet atrophied and demolished scripture-world of antiquity, at a time when people could still read a few books for whose possession someone today would trade half of an entire literature, the simplicity and vanity of Christian agitators—they are called Church Fathers—already dared to decree: "*we* too have our classical literature, *we do not need that of the Greeks*"—and with that they pointed proudly to books of legends, apostolic epistles, and little apologetic tracts, roughly speaking as today the English "Salvation Army" fights its battle against Shakespeare and other "heathens" with a similar literature. I do not love the "New Testament," you might have already guessed; it almost upsets me to have to stand so all alone with my taste regarding this most treasured, most over-treasured of written works (the taste of two millennia is *against* me): but what can I do! "Here I stand, I cannot do otherwise,"[79] —I have the courage of my bad taste.[80] The *Old* Testament—now that is another thing entirely: all due respect to the Old Testament! In it I find heroic human beings, a heroic landscape and something of the rarest of all things on earth, the incomparable naïveté of a *strong heart*; even more, I find a people. In the New one, on the other hand, nothing but petty sectarianism, nothing but rococo of the soul, nothing but ornamentation, nooks, and oddities, nothing but conventicler air, not to forget an occasional breath of bucolic sweetness that belongs to the epoch (*and* to the Roman province) and is not so much Jewish as Hellenic. Humility and braggadocio side by side; a loquaciousness of feelings that almost numbs; passionateness, but no passion; embarrassing gesticulation; here obviously all good breeding was lacking. How can anyone make such a fuss about his little bad habits the way these pious little men do! That is something no cock would crow about; let alone God. Finally they even want "the crown of eternal life,"[81] all these little people of the province: but to what end? for what? immodesty could not be pushed any further. An "immortal" Peter: who could stand *him*! They have an ambition that is laughable: *this* type regurgitates their most personal things, their stupidities, sorrows and loafer's worries, as if the very existence of things were bound to do something about it, *this* type never tires of dragging God himself into the tiniest misery in which they are stuck. And this constant use of familiar pronouns with God,[82] "thou" of the worst taste! This Jewish and not merely Jewish muzzle-and-paw impertinence toward God! . . . There are small despised "heathen peoples" in eastern Asia from whom these early Christians could have learned something essential, some *tact* of reverence; they do not allow themselves, as Christian missionaries will testify, even to utter the name of their God. This seems delicate enough to me; what is certain is that it is not only for "early" Christians too delicate: so, for instance, in order to feel the contrast we should recall Luther, the "most eloquent" and immodest peasant Germany ever had, and the Lutheran tone that he liked best precisely in his conversations with God. Luther's resistance to the mediator saints of the Church (especially to "the devil's sow, the pope") was no doubt in the final analysis the resistance of a lout who was annoyed by the *good etiquette* of the Church, that reverential etiquette of hieratic taste that only admits the more initiated and laconic into the Holy of Holies and locks it to the louts. They were not supposed to speak here under any circumstances — but Luther, the peasant, absolutely wanted it otherwise, this way was not *German* enough for him: above all he wanted to speak directly, speak himself, "uninhibitedly" speak with his God . . . Well, he did it. — The ascetic ideal, it is easy to guess, was never and nowhere a school of good taste, even less so of good manners — it was in the best case a school of hieratic manners —: this is because it had something deep down that is the deadly enemy of all good manners — lack of moderation, aversion to moderation; it is itself a "*non plus ultra.*"[83]

23

The ascetic ideal has ruined not only health and taste, it has also ruined a third, fourth, fifth, sixth thing — I will refrain from telling *everything* (when would I finish!). It is not what this ideal has *done* that I want to bring to light here; instead, quite simply what it *means*, what it hints at, what lies hidden behind, beneath and in it for which it is the provisional, unclear expression overloaded with questions marks and misunderstandings. And only with respect to *this* purpose should I not spare my reader a glance at the enormity of its effect, and also its disastrous effects: namely in order to prepare them for the ultimate and most terrible aspect that the question of the meaning of that ideal holds for me. What does the very *power* of this ideal mean, the *enormity* of its power? Why has it been given space to this extent? why was no better resistance offered? The ascetic ideal expresses a will: *where* is the counterwill in which a *counterideal* expresses itself? The ascetic ideal has a *goal*—it is universal enough that measured against it all other interests of human existence appear petty and narrow; it relentlessly interprets ages, peoples, human beings according to this single goal; it allows no other interpretation, no other goal to stand, it rejects, denies, affirms and confirms only in the sense of *its* interpretation (— and was there ever a system of interpretations more thoroughly thought through to the end?); it subjects itself to no power, rather it believes in its privilege over every power, in its unconditional *distance in rank* with respect to every power — it believes that there is no power on earth that does not first have to receive from it a meaning, a right to existence, a value as a tool for *its* work, as a way and means to *its* goal, to one goal . . . Where is the *counterpart* to this closed system of will, goal and interpretation? Why is the counterpart *lacking*? . . . Where is the *other* "one goal"? But they tell me it is *not* lacking, it has not only fought a long, successful battle with that ideal, moreover it has achieved mastery over that ideal in all major respects: our entire modern *science* bears testimony to this — this modern science which, as a genuine philosophy of reality, obviously believes only in itself, obviously possesses the courage and the will to itself and so far has gotten along well enough without God, the Beyond and negating virtues. Nevertheless I am not impressed by such noise and agitator babble: these trumpeters of reality are bad musicians, it is audible enough that their voices do *not* come from the depths, the abyss of the scientific conscience does *not* speak through them—for today the scientific conscience is an abyss—the word "science" in such trumpeter snouts is simply an obscenity, an abuse, a shamelessness. Precisely the opposite of what is asserted here is the truth: science today has absolutely *no* faith in itself, let alone an ideal *above* itself—and wherever it still manages to be passion, love, ardor, *suffering*, it is not the opposite of that ascetic ideal, but rather *its latest and most noble form*. Does this sound strange to you? . . . Of course there are enough sturdy and modest laboring folk among the scholars of today, who like their little nooks and, because they like them, occasionally and a bit immodestly voice the demand that people generally *should* be satisfied these days, especially with the sciences—precisely there so much useful work is to be done. I do not contradict; least of all do I wish to spoil the fun these honest workers have at their trade: for I enjoy their work. But just because people are now working hard in the sciences and there are satisfied workers does *not* by any means prove that science on the whole today has a goal, a will, an ideal, a passion of great faith. The opposite, as I said, is the case: where it is not the latest manifestation of the ascetic ideal—there we are dealing with cases that are too rare, noble and select to warrant overruling the general judgment—science today is a *hiding place* for all manner of ill-humor, disbelief, gnawing worms, *despectio sui*, bad conscience—it is the very *unrest* of the lack of ideals, the suffering from a *lack* of great love, the discontent with an *involuntary* contentedness. Oh what does science not conceal today! how much *should* it at least conceal! The competence of our best scholars, their mindless diligence, their heads smoking day and night, their trade mastery itself—how often does all that have its real meaning in no longer allowing something to be visible to oneself! Science as a means of self-anesthetization: *do you know that?* . . . They can be wounded to the marrow—anyone who associates with scholars has experienced this—sometimes by a harmless word, our scholarly friends become embittered toward us in the moment we mean to honor them, they fly off the handle merely because someone was too coarse to realize with whom he was actually dealing, with *sufferers* who do not want to admit to themselves what they are, with anesthetized and unconscious types who fear only one thing: *returning to consciousness . . .*

24[84]

—And now have a look on the other hand at those rarer cases of which I spoke, the last idealists there are among philosophers and scholars: do we perhaps have in them the sought-after *opponents* of the ascetic ideal, its *counter-idealists*? Indeed, they *believe* themselves to be such, these "unbelievers" (for that is what they all are); precisely that seems to be their last piece of faith, namely in being opponents of this ideal, so serious are they on this point, so passionate at just this point do their words and gestures become:—must it therefore be *true*, what they believe? . . . We "knowing ones" are by now mistrustful of every kind of believer; our mistrust has gradually trained us to infer the very opposite of what was previously inferred: namely to infer a certain weakness of demonstrability, even the *improbability* of what is believed, wherever the strength of a belief shows up too prominently in the foreground. We too do not deny that faith "makes blessed": *but for this very reason* we deny that faith *proves* anything—a strong faith that makes someone blessed is a suspicion against that in which he believes; it does not establish "truth," it establishes a certain probability—of *deception*. Now how does it look in this case?—These negaters and outsiders of today, these people who are unconditional about one thing, their claim to intellectual cleanliness; these harsh, strict, abstinent, heroic spirits who constitute the honor of our age, all these pale atheists, antichristians, immoralists, nihilists, these skeptics, ephectics, *hectics* of the spirit (the latter is what they all are, in some sense), these last idealists of knowledge in whom alone today the intellectual conscience dwells and became incarnate — they believe themselves indeed to be as detached as possible from the ascetic ideal, these "free, *very* free spirits": and yet, to divulge to them what they themselves cannot see — for they stand too close to themselves — this ideal is precisely *their* ideal too, they themselves represent it today and perhaps nobody else, they themselves are its most spiritualized spawn, its most advanced front-line troops and scouting party, its most insidious, delicate, intangible form of seduction: — if I am a guesser of riddles in anything, then I want to be one with *this* proposition! . . . Those are not *free* spirits by a long shot: *for they still believe in truth* . . . When the Christian crusaders in the orient encountered that invincible order of Assassins, that free spirit order par excellence whose lowest ranks lived in an obedience whose like was never achieved by an order of monks, by some means or another they also got a hint about that symbol and watchword reserved for only the highest ranks as their *secretum*:[85] "Nothing is true, everything is permitted" . . . Well then, *that* was *freedom* of the spirit, *with that*, faith in truth itself was *renounced* . . . Has any European, any Christian freethinker ever strayed into this proposition and its labyrinthine *consequences*? does he know the minotaur of this cave *from experience*? . . . I doubt it, and moreover I know otherwise: — nothing is more foreign to these men who are unconditional about one thing, these *so-called* "free spirits" than freedom and being unfettered in that sense; in no respect, in fact, are they more strictly bound; precisely in their faith in truth they are rigid and unconditional like nobody else. I know all this perhaps too much from close up: that venerable philosophers' abstinence to which such a belief obligates; that stoicism of the intellect that ultimately forbids itself a No just as firmly as a Yes; that *wanting* to halt before the factual, the *factum* **brutum**,[86] that fatalism of the "*petits faits*" (*ce petit faitalisme*,[87] as I call it), in which French science now seeks a kind of moral superiority over German, that renunciation of interpretation generally (of violating, forcing together, abbreviating, omitting, padding, inventing, falsifying and whatever else belongs to the *essence* of all interpretation)—on the whole this expresses asceticism of virtue just as much as any denial of sensuality (at bottom it is only a mode of this denial). But what *compels* one to this, to this unconditional will to truth, is the *belief in the ascetic ideal itself,* even if as its unconscious imperative—we must not deceive ourselves about this—this is the belief in a *metaphysical* value, a value *in itself of truth* as it is guaranteed and chartered by that ideal alone (it stands and falls with that ideal). Judging strictly, there is no science "without presuppositions" at all, the thought of such a thing is unthinkable, paralogical: a philosophy, a "belief" must always be there first, so that science can gain a direction, a meaning, a boundary, a method, a *right* to existence from it. (Whoever understands it as the opposite, whoever for example embarks on placing philosophy "on a strictly scientific foundation," will first be required to stand not only philosophy but truth itself *on its head*: the most egregious violation of decency there can be with respect to two such venerable females![88]) Indeed, there is no doubt—and at this point I shall allow my *Joyful Science* to speak; compare its fifth book, sec. 344—"the one who is truthful, in that audacious and ultimate sense that the faith in science presupposes, *thus affirms another world* than that of life, nature and history; and insofar as he affirms this 'other world,' what? must he not precisely in so doing—deny its counterpart, this world, *our* world? . . . It is still a *metaphysical faith* upon which our faith in science rests,—even we knowing ones of today, we godless ones and anti-metaphysicians, we too still take *our* fire from that flame lit by a thousand-year-old faith, that Christian faith that was also Plato's faith, that God is the truth, that the truth is *divine* . . . But what if precisely this is becoming more and more unbelievable, if nothing more turns out to be divine except error, blindness, the lie—if God himself turns out to be our *longest lie*?"[89]——At this point it becomes necessary to pause and

reflect for a long time. Science itself now *requires* a justification (which is not to say that there is one for it). On this question look at the oldest and the latest philosophies: in all of
them a consciousness is lacking for the extent to which the
will to truth itself first requires a justification, here every philosophy has a gap — why is that? Because so far the ascetic
ideal was the *master* of all philosophy, because truth was pos-
ited as Being, as God, as supreme authority itself, but truth
was not *allowed* to be a problem at all. Do you understand this
"allowed"? — From that moment when faith in the God of the
ascetic ideal is denied, *there is also a new problem*: that of the
value of truth. — The will to truth requires a critique — let us
here determine our own task — the value of truth has to be for
once experimentally *called into question* . . . (Whoever finds
this stated too briefly is advised to read up on that section of
Joyful Science bearing the title "In What Way We Too Are Still
Pious" (sec. 344), or better still the entire fifth book of that
work, likewise the preface to *Dawn*.)

25

No! Do not speak to me of science when I am looking for the
natural antagonists of the ascetic ideal, when I ask: "*where* is
the opposing will in which its *opposing ideal* expresses itself?"
For this, science does not nearly stand sufficiently on its own,
it first needs a value-ideal in every respect, a value-creating
power in whose *service* it *may believe* in itself — science itself is
never value-creating. Its relationship to the ascetic ideal is in
itself not yet antagonistic in the least; on the whole it sooner
represents the forward-driving energy of its inner development. More closely examined, its contradiction and struggle
does not at all relate to the ideal, but only to its outworks,
disguise, and masquerade, to its temporary hardening, ligni-
fying, dogmatizing — it again liberates the life in the ideal by
negating its exoteric aspects. Both of these, science and the
ascetic ideal, they do after all stand on the same ground — I
already indicated this —: namely on the same overestimation

of truth (more accurately: on the same belief in the *in*estima-
bility, *un*criticizability of truth), which is why they are *necessarily* allies—so that, supposing they are resisted, they can
only be resisted and called into question together. A value-
estimation of the ascetic ideal unavoidably entails a value-
estimation of science: we must keep our eyes open and our
ears pricked to this while there is still time! (*Art*, let me say for
the moment, since I will return to it in detail later on—art, in
which precisely the *lie* sanctifies itself, in which the *will to
deception* has good conscience on its side, is much more fundamentally opposed to the ascetic ideal than science: this was
sensed by Plato's instinct, this greatest enemy of art ever produced by Europe. Plato *contra* Homer: that is the complete,
the genuine antagonism—there the best-willed "man of the
Beyond," the great slanderer of life, here its involuntary dei-
fier, the *golden* nature. Therefore an artist's subservience in the
service of the ascetic ideal is the truest artist's *corruption* there
can be, and unfortunately one of the most common forms: for
nothing is more corruptible than an artist.) When calculated
physiologically, science also rests on the same soil as the ascetic ideal; a certain *impoverishment of life* is the presupposition here—the affects cooled down, the tempo slowed down,
dialectic in place of instinct, *seriousness* stamped on the faces
and gestures (seriousness, this most unmistakable sign of a
more laborious metabolism, of a struggling, harder-working
life). Look at those ages in the history of a people in which the
scholar comes to the fore: they are ages of exhaustion, often
of evening, of decline—overflowing energy, certainty of life,
certainty of the *future* are gone. The predominance of mandarins never signifies anything good; any more so than the rise of
democracy, of peace-arbitration courts in place of wars, of equal
rights for women, of religion of compassion and whatever other
symptoms there are of declining life. (Science formulated as
a problem; what does science mean?—on this cf. the preface
to *Birth of Tragedy*.)—No! this "modern science"—just open
your eyes to it!—is sometimes the *best* ally of the ascetic ideal,

and precisely because it is the most unconscious, the most involuntary, the most secret and subterranean! Up till now they
have played one game, the "poor in spirit"[90] and the scientific
opponents of that ideal (we should guard against thinking,
by the way, that they are their opposites, say the *rich* in
spirit: — they are *not* that, I called them hectics of the spirit).
These famous *victories* of the latter: without doubt they are
victories — but over what? The ascetic ideal was not at all conquered in them, it sooner became stronger, namely more incomprehensible, spiritual, captious by the fact that again and
again a wall, an outwork that had built itself onto the ideal
and *coarsened* its appearance, was mercilessly dismantled and
broken down by science. Does anyone really believe perhaps
that the defeat of theological astronomy meant a defeat of that
ideal? . . . Have humans perhaps become *less in need* of an oth-
erworldly solution to their riddle of existence now that this
existence looks even more arbitrary, loitering and dispensable
in the *visible* order of things? Has not the self-belittlement of
humankind, its *will* to self-belittlement been on an unstoppable progression since Copernicus? Oh the belief in its dignity,
singularity, irreplaceability in the hierarchy of beings is
gone — it has become *animal*, literally and without qualifica-
tion and reservation an animal, when in its earlier belief
it was nearly God ("child of God," "God-man") . . . Since
Copernicus the human being seems to have gotten onto an
inclined plane — he now rolls away ever faster from the mid-
point — where to? into nothingness? into the *"penetrating*
feeling of his nothingness"? . . . Well then! exactly this would
be the straight path — into the *old* ideal? . . . *All* science (and by
no means only astronomy, about whose humiliating and de-
grading effect Kant made a noteworthy confession, "it annihilates my importance"[91] . . .), all science, the natural as well
as the *unnatural* — this is what I call the self-critique of knowledge — aims today to dissuade humans of their previous respect for themselves, as if this has been nothing but a bizarre
conceit; we could even say it has its own pride, its own austere

form of stoic ataraxy, in upholding this laboriously won *self-contempt* of humanity as its last, most serious claim to respect from itself (justifiably, in fact, since the despiser is always still someone who "has not forgotten how to respect" . . .) Does this actually *work against* the ascetic ideal? Do people still in all seriousness believe (as the theologians for a time imagined) that perhaps Kant's *victory* over theological conceptual dogmatism ("God," "soul," "freedom," "immortality") damaged that ideal? — setting aside for the time being whether Kant himself even had any such intention. What is certain is that all kinds of transcendentalists have been playing a winning game since Kant — they have been emancipated from the theologians: what luck! — he revealed to them that secret path on which from now on they may pursue on their own initiative and with the best scientific decorum "their heart's desires." By the same token: who could now begrudge agnostics if, as votaries of the unknown and the mysterious in itself, they now worship *the question mark itself* as God? (Xaver Doudan speaks at one point of the ravages inflicted by "*l'habitude d'admirer l'inintelligible au lieu de rester tout simplement dans l'inconnu*";[92] he thinks the ancients dispensed with this.) Supposing that everything humans "know" does not satisfy their desires, but rather contradicts them and makes them shudder, what divine escape to be allowed to seek the blame for this not in "desiring" but in "knowing"! . . . "There is no knowing: *consequently* — there is a God": what a novel *elegantia syllogismi!*[93] what a *triumph* of the ascetic ideal! —

26

— Or did perhaps the whole of modern historiography reveal a stance more sure of life, more sure of the ideal? Its noblest claim now is that it aspires to be a *mirror*; it rejects all teleology; it no longer wants to "prove" anything; it scorns playing the judge and has its good taste in this — it affirms as little as it denies, it ascertains, it "describes" . . . All of this is ascetic to a high degree; but to an even higher degree it is *nihilistic* at the

same time, let us not deceive ourselves about that! One sees a
sad, harsh but resolute gaze—an eye that *looks out* as an isolated arctic explorer looks out (perhaps in order not to look
within? in order not to look back? . . .) Here there is snow,
here life has gone silent; the last crows that can be heard here
are called "what for?," "in vain!," and "*nada!*"—here nothing
thrives and grows anymore, at best Petersburg metapolitics
and Tolstoyan "compassion."[94] But as concerns that other
kind of historian, a perhaps more "modern" kind, a hedonistic
and lascivious kind who ogles life just as much as he ogles the
ascetic ideal, who uses the word "artist" like a glove and today
has the complete lease on the praising of contemplation: oh
what thirst these sweet ingenious[95] types arouse even for ascetics and winter landscapes! No! this "contemplative" folk
can go to hell! How much more would I prefer to wander
through the gloomy, gray, cold fog with even those historical
nihilists!—indeed, supposing I had to choose, I would not be
averse to lending my ear even to someone who is truly unhistorical, anti-historical (like that Dühring, whose sounds today
in Germany intoxicate a hitherto still shy and unacknowledged species of "beautiful soul," the species *anarchistica*
within the educated proletariat).[96] A hundred times worse are
the "contemplatives"—: I know of nothing so disgusting as
such an "objective" armchair, such a fragrant hedonist in the
face of history, half preacher, half satyr, perfume by Renan,
who already betrays with the high falsetto of his cheering
what he is lacking, *where* he is lacking, *where* in this case the
Fate wielded her cruel scissors, alas! all too surgically! That offends my taste, my patience too: let those who have nothing to
lose by it keep their patience at the sight of such things—sights
like this infuriate me, such "spectators" embitter me toward
the "spectacle" even more than the spectacle (history itself,
you understand me), it makes me prone to unexpected Ana-
creontic moods. This nature that gave horns to the bull, to the
lion χάσμ' ὀδόντων,[97] why did nature give me a foot? . . . For
kicking, by holy Anacreon! and not only for running away: for

kicking to pieces the rotting armchairs, the cowardly contemplativeness, the lascivious eunuchry of history, the ogling at
ascetic ideals, the justice-tartuffery of impotence! All honor to
the ascetic ideal *insofar as it is honest*! as long as it believes in
itself and does not play tricks on us! But I do not like all these
coquettish bedbugs whose ambition is insatiable for smelling
out the infinite until finally the infinite smells of bedbugs; I
do not like the whited sepulchres[98] that play-act life; I do not
like the weary and used-up, who wrap themselves in wisdom
and look "objective"; I do not like the agitators gussied up to
look like heroes, wearing their magic disappearing-cap of the
ideal on their straw-wisp of a head; I do not like the ambitious
artists who would like to play the ascetic and priest but at bottom are only tragic buffoons; and I do not like them either,
these latest speculators in idealism, the anti-Semites today
who roll their eyes with Christian-Aryan-bourgeois pathos
and try to stir up all the horned cattle elements of the people
using the cheapest agitator method of all, moral posturing,
an abuse that exhausts everyone's patience (— that *no* kind of
swindle spirit fails to succeed in today's Germany is connected
to the virtually undeniable and already palpable *desolation* of
the German spirit, whose cause I seek in an all-too-exclusive
diet of newspapers, politics, beer and Wagnerian music, along
with what provides the prerequisite for this diet: first, national
constriction and vanity, the strong but narrow principle
"Deutschland, Deutschland über Alles,"[99] but then the *paralysis agitans*[100] of "modern ideas").[101] Europe is rich and inventive
above all in means of excitation; it seems there is nothing it
needs more than stimulants and distilled liquor: hence also
the tremendous counterfeiting of ideals, these most distilled
liquors of the spirits, hence also the repulsive, foul-smelling,
mendacious pseudo-alcoholic air everywhere.[102] I would like
to know how many shiploads of imitation idealism, of heroes'
costumes and tin noisemakers of big words, how many barrels
of sugared spirituous sympathy (trade name: *la religion de la
souffrance*[103]), how many stilts of "noble indignation" for the

aid of the spiritually flatfooted, how many *comedians* of the Christian-moral ideal would have to be exported today from Europe so that its air could smell fresh again . . . Obviously given this overproduction a new *trade* opportunity has opened up, obviously there is new "business" to be made of little ideal-idols and their accompanying "idealists"—if anyone out there can take a hint! Who has enough courage for it?—we have it in our *hands* to "idealize" the whole earth! . . . But why am I talking about courage: here one thing is needful,[104] just the hand, an uninhibited, a very uninhibited hand . . .

27

—Enough! Enough! Let us abandon these curiosities and complexities of the modern spirit, which are just as laughable as they are annoying: precisely *our* problem can do without them, the problem of the *meaning* of the ascetic ideal—what does it have to do with yesterday and today! Those things will be treated by me more thoroughly and rigorously in another context (under the title "On the History of European Nihilism"; for this I refer to a work I am preparing:[105] *The Will to Power: Attempt at a Revaluation of All Values*). The only thing I care about having shown here is this: at present the ascetic ideal also in the more spiritual realm has only one kind of real enemy and *injurer*: the comedians of this ideal—for they arouse suspicion. Everywhere else that the spirit is at work to-day rigorously, powerfully and without counterfeiting, it now dispenses with the ideal completely—the popular expression for this abstinence is "atheism"—: *except for its will to truth.* But this will, this *remnant* of ideal, is, if I am to be believed, that ideal itself in its most rigorous, most spiritual formula-tion, esoteric through and through, stripped of all outworks and thus not so much its remnant as its *core*. Unconditional and honest atheism (—and *its* air alone do we breathe, we more spiritual men of this age!) accordingly does *not* stand in contrast to that ideal, as it seems to; rather it is only one of its latest phases of development, one of its final forms and inner logical consistencies—it is the awe-inspiring *catastrophe* of a two-thousand-year training in truth, that in the end forbids itself the *lie of believing in God*. (The same course of development in India, but completely independently and therefore proving something; the same ideal compelling to the same conclusion; the decisive point achieved five centuries before the European reckoning of time, with Buddha, to be more precise: already with the Samkhya philosophy, the latter then popularized by Buddha and made into religion.) *What*, asked in all strictness, actually *triumphed* over the Christian God? The answer is found in my *Joyful Science* sec. 357: "Christian morality itself, the more and more rigorous understanding of the concept of truthfulness, the father-confessor-subtlety of the Christian conscience, translated and sublimated into scientific conscience, into intellectual cleanliness at any price. To look at nature as if it were proof of a god's goodness and guardianship; to interpret history in honor of some divine reason, as constant testimony to a moral world order and moral final intentions; to interpret one's own experiences as pious people have long enough interpreted theirs, as if everything were ordained, everything a sign, everything thought out and sent for the sake of the soul's salvation: that is *over* now, that has conscience *against* it, all finer consciences consider it indecent, dishonest, mendacity, femininism,[106] weakness, cowardice,—by virtue of this severity, if by anything, we are *good Europeans*[107] and heirs to Europe's longest and bravest self-overcoming." . . . All great things perish through themselves, by an act of self-sublation: thus the law of life wills it, the law of *necessary* "self-overcoming" in the nature of life—in the end the legislator himself is always issued the call: "*patere legem, quam ipse tulisti.*"[108] This is how Christianity *as dogma* perished, by its own morality; this is also how Christianity *as morality* must now perish—we are standing at the threshold of *this* event. After Christian truthfulness drew one conclusion after another, in the end it will draw its *strongest conclusion*, its conclusion *against* itself; but this will happen when it asks the question: "*what does all will to truth mean?*" . . . And here again I touch on my problem, on our problem, my *unknown* friends (— for as yet I *know* of no friend): what meaning would *our* entire being have if not this, that in us the will to truth came to consciousness of itself *as a problem*? . . . From this coming-to-consciousness of the will to truth — there is no doubt about this — morality will *perish* from now on: that great spectacle in a hundred acts is reserved for Europe's next two centuries, the most terrible, most questionable and perhaps also most hopeful of all spectacles . . .

28

If one disregards the ascetic ideal: then the human being, the *animal* human being had no meaning so far. His existence on earth contained no goal; "why human beings at all?" — was a question without an answer; the *will* for human beings and earth was lacking; behind every great human destiny resounded a still greater refrain of "in vain!" *That* is precisely what the ascetic ideal means: that something was *lacking*, that a tremendous *void* surrounded humanity — he did not know how to justify, to explain, to affirm himself, he *suffered* from the problem of his meaning. He suffered otherwise too, he was for the most part a *sickly* animal: suffering in itself, however, was *not* his problem, but that he lacked the answer to the cry of his question "*why* suffering?" The human being, the animal that is bravest and most accustomed to suffering, does *not* deny suffering as such: he *wants* it, he even seeks it, supposing that he is shown a *meaning* for it, a *purpose* for suffering. The meaninglessness of suffering, *not* suffering, was the curse that lay spread over humankind up till now — *and the ascetic ideal offered it a meaning*! It was the only meaning so far; any meaning is better than no meaning at all; the ascetic ideal was in every sense the all-time "*faute de mieux*"[109] par excellence. In it suffering was *interpreted*; the tremendous void seemed filled; the door closed to all suicidal nihilism. The interpretation — there is no doubt — brought with it new suffering, deeper, more

inward, more poisonous, more life-gnawing: it brought all
suffering under the perspective of *guilt* . . . But in spite of all
this—humanity was *saved* by it, it had a *meaning*, it was
henceforth no longer like a leaf on the wind, a plaything
of nonsense, of "without-sense," it could now *will* something—no matter at first where, to what end, and with what
it willed: *the will itself was saved*. We simply cannot conceal
from ourselves *what* that entire willing that draws its direction
from the ascetic ideal actually expresses: this hatred of the human, even more of the animal, even more of the material, this
abhorrence of the senses, of reason itself, this fear of happiness
and beauty, this longing to get beyond all appearance, change,
becoming, death, desire, longing itself—all of this means, let
us dare to grasp it, a *will to nothingness*, a counterwill[110] against
life, a rejection of the most fundamental presuppositions of
life, but it is and remains a *will*! . . . And, to say once more at
the end what I said at the beginning: humanity would rather
will *nothingness* than *not* will . . .

Reference Matter

Notes

The following symbols are used throughout the text and notes:

[ ]	Deletion by Nietzsche
| |	Addition by Nietzsche
{ }	Addition by the translator
⟨ ⟩	Addition by the editors (Colli and Montinari)
———	Unfinished or incomplete sentence or thought
Italics	Underlined once by Nietzsche
Bold	Underlined twice or more by Nietzsche
NL	Books in Nietzsche's personal library

Variants and editions of Nietzsche's works are referred to by the following abbreviations:

CW	*The Complete Works of Friedrich Nietzsche*
KGB	*Briefwechsel: Kritische Gesamtausgabe*
KGW	*Werke: Kritische Gesamtausgabe*
KSA	*Werke: Kritische Studienausgabe*
Le	Twenty-volume 1894 Leipzig edition of Nietzsche's works (*Großoktav-Ausgabe*)
Pd	Preliminary draft

Pm	Printer's manuscript (clean final copy of handwritten MS)
Sd	Second draft
Se	Subsequent emendation

Titles of Nietzsche's works are referred to by the following abbreviations:

AC	*The Anti-Christian*
BGE	*Beyond Good and Evil*
BT	*The Birth of Tragedy*
D	*Dawn*
DD	*Dionysus Dithyrambs*
DS	*David Strauss the Confessor and the Writer*
EH	*Ecce Homo*
GM	*On the Genealogy of Morality*
HAH	*Human, All Too Human*
HL	*On the Utility and Liability of History for Life*
JS	*The Joyful Science*
MM	*Mixed Opinions and Maxims*
NCW	*Nietzsche Contra Wagner*
SE	*Schopenhauer as Educator*
TI	*Twilight of the Idols*
UO	*Unfashionable Observations*
WA	*The Wagner Case*
WB	*Richard Wagner in Bayreuth*
WP	*The Will to Power*
WS	*The Wanderer and His Shadow*
Z	*Thus Spoke Zarathustra*

Beyond Good and Evil

In a preface from summer/fall 1886 {cf. *CW* 17, 6[4]} for a second volume of *Beyond Good and Evil* that was never completed (the preface was later used for the preface of *HAH* II), N gives a precise description of the place *Beyond Good and Evil* occupies among his writing: "What forms its basis, thoughts, first jottings and sketches of all sort, belongs to my past: namely to that richly enigmatic time in which '*Thus Spoke Zarathustra*' emerged: given this simultaneity it may well provide useful clues for understanding the just mentioned work which is so *difficult to understand*. In particular too it provides clues to understanding its emergence: there is something of merit here. At that time thoughts such as these served me, whether for rejuvenation, whether as self-interrogation and self-justification, in the midst of an infinitely daring and responsible undertaking: may the book that grew from them serve others to a similar purpose! Or perhaps also as a highly convoluted path, that again and again lures unawares to that dangerous and volcanic ground, out of which arose the previously mentioned Zarathustra-gospel. Just as certainly as this 'Prelude to a Philosophy of the Future' offers no commentary nor should it to the speeches of Zarathustra, so perhaps it nonetheless provides a type of provisional glossarium in which the most important conceptual- and value-innovations of that book—an event without model, example, and likeness in all of literature—appear somewhere and are called by name."

Chronologically the oldest layer of *Beyond Good and Evil* goes back to the period before publication of *The Joyful Science*, for some of the aphorisms were back-filled by N from notebooks M III 1 and M III 4a (spring/autumn 1881). The "Epigrams and Interludes," notebooks Z I 1 and Z I 2, stem from the period just before the origin of *Zarathustra* Part I (autumn 1882 to winter 1882–83), additional aphorisms from M III 4b (spring/summer 1883, shortly before the writing of *Zarathustra* II). Notations from the notebooks of spring to autumn 1884 (W I 1 and W I 2) were also used for *Beyond Good and Evil*. Alongside many projects from the year 1885 (after the publication of *Zarathustra* IV) a planned new edition of *HAH* assumed special significance (Nietzsche wanted to buy back and destroy the remaining copies of this work; letter to Gast 24 January 1886 {*KGB* III:3, 142}). The failure of this attempt provided Nietzsche with the impulse to write a new work, *Beyond Good and Evil*, whose printer's manuscript

(*Pm*) he prepared in winter 1885–86, by using in addition to the earlier notebooks mentioned above also those from the year 1885 (W I 3–7, N VII 1–3), along with loose pages of notes (Mp XVI 1). That *Beyond Good and Evil* does *not* come about from the material of the so-called *Will to Power* is clear from this history of its origin. It was literally a preparation, a "prelude" for something that was still to come and — at least as *Will to Power* — did not come (cf. the explanation at the beginning of the Commentary for *CW* 9). The printing lasted from the end of May until August 1886. The page proofs (lost) were read by Nietzsche and Peter Gast together. *Beyond Good and Evil. Prelude to a Philosophy of the Future*, Leipzig, 1886, printed and published by C. G. Naumann was published by Nietzsche at his own expense. Besides the above-mentioned handwritten documents, also preserved are the printer's manuscript prepared by Nietzsche as well as a personal (author's) copy with his notations in it.

Title

1. Re: title: cf. *CW* 15:25[238, 490, 500]; 26[426]; *CW* 16:34[1]; 35[84]; 36[1, 66]; 40[45, 48]; 41[1].

Preface

1. *inept and indecent]* *ungeschickte und unschickliche*, used for alliteration.

2. *female]* *Frauenzimmer*: an archaic and contemptuous expression for a woman.

3. *cultivated to maturity.]* *grossgezüchtet*

4. *Platonism for the "people."]* *Pm*: rabbleized Platonism.

5. *state of emergency]* *Nothstand*

6. *need]* *Noth*: play on words with *Nothstand*. N's antipopulist stance on reading; cf. *Z* "On Reading and Writing."

7. *But . . . goal . . . . .]* *Pm*: Pascal for instance perceived it as a *need*: from the depths of his terrible tension this most profound human being of modern times invented for himself that murderous form of laughter with which he laughed to death the Jesuits of his day. Maybe he was lacking nothing but health and one

more decade of life — or, morally speaking, a southern sky instead of the cloud cover of Port-Royal — in order to laugh to death even his Christianity. —

Part One

1. *Pd* (variant from August–September 1885, W I 7): The desire for truth that led me along not exactly harmless paths occasionally put into my mouth the same most questionable of all questions: I paused longest before the question of the hidden *causes* of this desire, but ultimately I stood still before the question of the value of that desire. *The problem of truthfulness* appeared before me: would you believe that it seems to me that it had been posed, seen, *ventured* for the first time?

Different *Pd* from August–September 1885, W I 5: *Alea jacta est* {the die is cast; underlined in the original}. — The "will to truth" that will yet seduce me to many a risk — what strange questions it has already laid before me [, what wicked questionable questions! No wonder that I finally turn around suspiciously and learn to ask questions for my part before this sphinx! Who is it really who is asking me here?]! What wicked, wonderful and questionable questions! That is a long story: no wonder that I become suspicious, lose my patience and turn around impatiently! That for my part I *learn* to ask questions before this sphinx? Who is it really who is asking me questions here? What in me really "wants the truth"?

2. *nowhere else!"] Pd*: Nowhere else! Spoken more resolutely: Things and conditions of the highest order cannot originate at all — becoming would be unworthy of them, they alone *are* [that which exists], and only God *is* — they are God."

3. *grounding faith] Grundglaube*: N uses *Grund* far too often to ignore its grounding connotations, and while "basis," "fundamental," and "reason" (grounds) are proper translations, no translator should lose sight of *ground*.

4. *"de omnibus dubitandum."]* "all is to be doubted." Descartes.

5. *the truth . . . the selfless] Pd*: of truth, of truthfulness, of the deed called selfless, of the "calm sea" in artistic intuition

6. *And . . . emerging.*] *Pd*: (1) In the end it would even be possible — and I [also share this belief] subscribe to this myself! — that what is worthy in the first place in those vaunted things is worthy only because basically, and viewed consistently, they are nothing other than precisely those seemingly opposed things [whose reputation so far the metaphysicians have treated so miserably — and whose honor has not yet been "rescued" by anyone] and states. But who has the courage to see these "truths" without their veil? Perhaps too there is a permissible modesty before such problems and possibilities. — (2) it is *my* belief! Maybe [things are even much worse] one needs to take his suspicion one step further — and I've done so — : For it would even be possible that *what* constitutes the value of those good and venerated things is only theirs by virtue of the fact that they themselves are related to those wicked, seemingly opposed things in an insidious manner, closely related, and not only related? (*a*) But who [has the desire] is willing to concern himself about such a "perhaps"! It goes against good taste, above all against virtue, when truth begins to be offensive like this, when truth tears off its veil like this and renounces all proper shame: isn't caution advised in dealing with such a female? {*Frauenzimmer*} (*b*) Perhaps! But who is willing to concern himself about this dangerous "perhaps"! That goes against good taste, you tell me, it also goes against [virtue itself] [modesty] virtue. When truth begins to be offensive, when this thoughtless female begins to throw off her veil like this and renounces all [proper] shame: away, away with this seducer! May she go her own way from now on! "And sooner," you say to me, winking, "would we go for a walk with a modest and bashful error, with a nice little *lie* — — "

7. *niaiserie*] "foolishness"

8. *mankind . . . things" . . . . .*] {Reference to Protagoras's saying: "Man is the measure of all things."}

9. *a certain . . . of things" . . . . .*] *Pd*: by virtue of which the will to power *enforces* a specific kind of being (these beings must above all see in a light, close, certain, calculable manner, hence fundamentally from a *logical perspective* —)

10. *judgment*] *Sd*: concept

11. *falsest] Sd*: falsest namely the oldest

12. *judgments] Sd*: concepts

13. First draft in *Pd*: What made me suspicious of the philosophers is not that I recognized how often and easily they err and stray, but that I did not find enough honesty anywhere in them: they all pretend as though they had discovered and reached something through dialectic, whereas at bottom an anticipated proposition is defended by them through a kind of proof: they are advocates of their own prejudices and not honest enough to admit this and tell us from the outset. The tartuffery of the old Kant as he looked for secret paths to his "categ⟨orical⟩ imperative" makes us smile. Or even the mathematical semblance with which Spinoza ⟨imparted⟩ a fortress-like character to his fervent desires, something that was supposed to intimidate the attacker inescapably.

14. *tartuffery]* from the name Tartuffe, eponymous hero of Moliere's play; here, hypocritical piety.

15. Cf. *CW* 13:3[1] 79; N to Lou von Salomé, possibly 16 September 1882 {*KGB* III:1, 259}. First draft in M III 4: I have accustomed myself to regarding the great philosophies as *involuntary memoirs* of their authors: and moreover the moral portion as the potent seed of the whole philosophy, so that for certain purposes the origin of the most far-fetched metaphysical claims can be traced to the moral sphere. I don't believe in a drive for knowledge, but in drives that knowledge uses as tools. And whoever counts the drives will find that they have all done philosophy and would gladly proclaim themselves the ultimate purpose of existence. — With "scholars" it is different: there, thinking really is often a little machine that works without the participation of the overall system of h⟨uman⟩ drives —: the real *interests* therefore most often lie elsewhere, as is the case with all professionals: perhaps with family or politics etc. or earning money. Chance decides on which scientific location such machines are placed: whether a good philologist or chemist results from this — is *not symptomatic* of anyone. Conversely the philosophies are *not in the least bit something impersonal* and morality in particular is a person, that is, a testimony *of which order of rank* among drives exists in the philosopher.

16. *knowledge (and misjudgment!)]* Erkenntniss *(und der Verkenntnis!)*

17. *Epicurus]* Ed. Arrighetti, fragment 93, 18–19.

18. Cf. *CW* 15:26[466].

19. *adventavit asinus, pulcher et fortissimus.]* Quoted in G. Christian Lichtenberg, *Vermischte Schriften* {Assorted Writings}, Göttingen{: Dieterich,} 1867, V, 327. *NL*. {"the ass arrived / beautiful and most strong." From the medieval Christian Feast of the Ass (*Festum Asinorum*), observed on January 14.}

20. First draft in *N VII 1*: Live "according to nature"? Oh you Stoics, what noble mendacity! Imagine a being that is wasteful, indifferent, without intentions, without pity, fruitful and barren, imagine indifference itself—how *could* you live according to this indifference! Life is this not a wanting to be different than this nature? And live according to life? Then how could you not? Why make a principle of it! As a matter of fact you only form nature in the image of your wise man! And then you wish to form yourselves in the image of your image! This also applies to Goethe, to Taine etc.

21. *causa prima]* "first cause"

22. *no . . . seem.]* *Pm*: for it is a matter of dying and perishing everywhere when someone makes such an extravagance out of his virtue.

23. *reality-philosophaster]* Allusion to Eugen Dühring.

24. *right: their]* *Pm*: right [: all these Kants and Schellings, Hegels and Schopenhauers and whatever sprouted after them]: their

25. Cf. *CW* 15:25[303]; 26[412]; 30[10]; *CW* 16:34[62, 79, 82, 185]; 38[7].

First draft in *N VII 1*: "How are synthet⟨ic⟩ judgments *a priori* possible?"—By means of a faculty, i.e., answer: that they are possible, they exist, we *can* do it. But the question asked after the "How"? Thus Kant establishes a fact "that," but there is no explanation here. Ultimately the "faculty" is a hypothetical force, an exception of the kind like the *vis soporifica* {sleep-inducing effect} in opium. My conception: that all ideas like "causality," the absolute, the soul, being, matter, spirit———the concepts originated in a logically skewed manner, namely as we have come to know from etymology, so that one characteristic served as the sign for similar things. The *similarity* gradually was acknowledged less frequently with the sharpening of the senses and attention, and for the inner characterization of a thing the intellect ran through a series of identification marks of recognition marks; that's how it *grasped* the thing and *comprehended* it; there is a seizing and grasping involved. (Cf. *CW* 16:38[14].)

26. *By virtue of a faculty] Vermöge eines Vermögens*: "by means of a means," or "facilitated by a facility/faculty."

27. *niaiserie allemande]* "German foolishness"

28. *"real-political"] real-politisch*, from *Realpolitik*.

29. *Tübingen seminary]* {Where Hegel, Schelling, and Hölderlin studied, and became friends.}

30. *finding" from "inventing"!] "finden" und "erfinden"* whereby *finden* means only finding, but *erfinden* means to invent.

31. *quia est in eo virtus dormitiva, cujus est natura sensus assoupire.]* "Because there is a dormative faculty in it, whose nature is to put the senses to sleep." Cf. Molière's *The Imaginary Invalid*, act III, third interlude.

32. Cf. *CW* 14:15[21]; *CW* 15:26[302, 410, 432].

33. *Pole, Boscovich]* Ruggiero Giuseppe Boscovich was not a Pole but a Dalmatian; in Basel (1873, cf. *CW* 10), N read his *Philosophiae naturalis theoria redacta ad unicam legem virium in natura existentium* {A theory of natural philosophy reduced to a single law of the actions existing in nature}, Vienna, {1759; *KSA* 14 incorrectly has "1769"}.

34. *inventing . . . finding.—]* {The reverse of Kant and his followers; cf. note 29.}

35. *Plato] Laws* 689 a–b.

36. *Pd*: In order to do physiology you have to believe that the sense organs are not mere appearances: as such they certainly couldn't be causes. Thus: sensualism as a regulative hypothesis: as we have it in life. No human being considers a beefsteak an appearance.

37. *reductio ad absurdum]* "reduction to absurdity"

38. *causa sui]* "cause of itself"

39. *contradictio in adjecto]* "contradiction in terms"

40. *that . . . end]* dass *Erkennen ein zu-Ende-Kennen sei*: N is juxtaposing *Erkennen*, the verbal noun for knowing, with *zu-Ende-Kennen*, the verbal compound noun for knowing something to the end.

41. *but . . . truth?"]* Added in *Pm*.

42. *a . . . wants]* Cf. Schopenhauer, *Parerga 2*, 51{: "But thoughts come not when we want them, but when they want to"}; but also J.-J. Rousseau, *Confessions*, Book 4: "*Les idées viennent quand il leur plaît, non quand il me plaît.*" {Ideas come when they want, not when I want.}

43. Cf. *CW* 14: 4[72], 5[1]24, 12[1]156.

44. *L'effet c'est moi]* "The effect is me." Allusion to the claim "*L'État, c'est moi*" ("The State is me"), attributed to Louis XIV.

45. *as . . . emerges—] Pm*: of a social structure of drives and affects: you will have to forgive my innovation in philosophical terminology, that to this extent even the "will" for me is taken into consideration as a moral phenomenon.

46. *Münchhausen]* {Baron Hieronymus Carl Friedrich von Münchhausen (1720–1797), an adventurer and raconteur, is known in the German tradition for spectacular tall tales. In one tale he frees himself and his horse from a swamp by pulling himself (and the horse on which he sits) up by the hair.}

47. *according . . . effects"] Pm*: not excluding the positivists

48. *almost . . . compulsion] Pm*: a symptom of its own feebleness of the will

49. *"la religion de la souffrance humaine"]* "the religion of human suffering" {These are the final words of Paul Bourget's novel *Un crime d'amour* (1886). Cf. *GM* III 26.}

50. *And indeed . . . taste."] Pm*: — And to say it again: the concept of "responsibility" does not suffice for the in-itself of things — no concept at all can.

51. *"Ni dieu, ni maître"]* "Neither God nor master."

52. *The . . . with] Sd*: The sphere of moral prejudices has grown much deeper and more powerfully into humanity than the psychologists up till now have dared to dream: not to mention at all the naïve types à la Hobbes, who———

53. *sacrifizio dell'intelletto]* "sacrifice of the intellect." One of the tenets of Jesuitism.

Part Two

1. Cf. *CW* 13:15[1].
2. *O sancta simplicitas!]* "O holy simplicity!"
3. that *we have composed and forged into shape] Zurecht gedichteten, zurecht gefälschten*
4. *Knights of the Mournful Countenance]* {Reference to Don Quixote, title character of Cervantes's novel of 1605/15.}
5. *in . . . him] Pm*: an infallible sign of this is that someone has been ruined for philosophy
6. *Pd: On the Overcoming of Nausea.* —The higher human, the exceptional human must, if he is predestined to be a knowing one in the grand sense, devote himself to the study of the rule, I mean of the *average* human being: which of course will not happen without a good deal of nausea. This study is difficult and laborious because the average h⟨uman⟩ wraps himself in illusions and beautiful words; therefore it is a find of the first order when the seeker encounters someone who simply acknowledges the animal, the brutishness, or the rule in himself and thus has a sufficient degree of wit and thrill that compels him to speak cynically of himself and his kind and to wallow in his own filth, so to speak: for cynicism is the only form in which coarse souls touch upon that which constitutes honesty and fairness. Enough, for the higher human every form of crude cynicism is an object from which he can learn and for which he should keep his ears open; indeed, he should wish himself luck when the insincere satyr and the jester begin to speak. There are even cases that will nearly enchant him: such a case is Petronius, likewise the Abbé Galiani from the last century; for here the "spirit," even "genius" is linked to the apes. It happens frequently that a "scien⟨tific⟩ mind" is attached to an ape's body and an exceptional intellect as a rule to a coarse soul: — physicians do not infrequently encounter this combination. And wherever someone speaks without embitterment, but harmlessly of humans as beings who are driven by vanity, sexual desires, nutritional needs and nothing else, there

the higher human should listen very carefully: in sum, wherever cynicism speaks without indignation: — for indignant cynicism and whoever tears apart himself or "the world" or God or society with his own teeth is already of higher and rarer lineage — as an animal that suffers from animality.

7. Cf. *CW* 16:1[182]; 3[18]. *Pd*: it is difficult to understand myself; and I would be a fool [and I have taken it upon myself], if I did not give my friends a good bit of leeway for misunderstanding and ⟨were⟩ not already thankful for the good will to some freedom of interpretation

8. *gangasrotogati]* Sanskrit for "as the current of the Ganges moves," i.e., very fast.

9. *kurmagati]* Sanskrit for "as the tortoise moves."

10. Cf. *CW* 16:34[102].

11. *tempo]* N uses Italian *tempo* here, indicating a musical term as well as velocity, weather, the times.

12. *presto]* "very fast tempo"

13. *buffo]* "comic actor in Italian opera"

14. *in moribus et artibus.]* "in morals and arts"

15. *allegrissimo]* "brisk, lively tempo (superlative)"

16. *petit fait]* "small fact"

17. *how . . . conscience.]* *Pm*: and whether no one knows how he becomes derailed, degenerate, split apart, broken — — —

18. *supposing . . . return]* *Pm*: he himself sees it and cannot yet dispense with being seen as no longer able to return to the compassion of others

19. Cf. *CW* 16:40[66]. *Pd* first version: Our highest insights must — and should — sound like crimes when heard without permission by those who are not cut out and predestined for them. The "exoteric" and the "esoteric," a distinction formerly used by philosophers, among Indians as among Greeks and Muslims, in sum wherever people believed in an order of rank for people and not in "equality before God" — : that was distinguished not only in terms of a "viewed-from-without" and a "viewed-from-within," but instead as "viewed-from-below" or — *viewed from above*! What serves the higher type as nourishment, or refreshment, has to nearly be poison to a very different and lower type.

Conversely the virtues of a common man would be vices and blemishes in a philosopher; and if he should once become ill and therefore lose himself, then he surely notices how in his sickly value-estimations he *approximates* the little people and their virtues. There are also books that are ambivalent for souls and health, according to whether a lower soul, a lower health or a higher one makes use of them. What is evangelical, bracing, and the best consolation of the soul for little people cannot possibly function the same way for those who have a higher meaning. The most famous books, the odor of little people clings to them. Wherever "the people" worship, it stinks. You should not go into churches if you want to breathe *clean* air: but not everyone has the right to "clean air."

20. *common people] das Volk*

21. *clings . . . air.] Pd*: the most tenacious of all odors clings to them. Where the people eat and drink, even where they worship, it stinks: and this is no objection either to their means of nourishment ⟨nor⟩ their worship. For instance you should not go into churches if you want to breathe *clean* air: but there are few who have a right to "clean air": who would not perish from clean air. This to deter the suspicion that I want to invite the "freethinkers" into my garden

22. Cf. *CW* 16:41[2]1.

23. Title in *Sd*: *Morality as Prejudice*

Pd in pencil at the end: the *post-moral* epoch

Pd first version: Throughout the longest period of human history the value of an action was measured according to its consequences: thus it was only added on, more or less as today a distinction or disgrace encountered by a Chinese has a retroactive force for his parents. Of course in recent centuries across several great expanses of the earth, people settled on assessing the value or lack of value—according to the intention. Today—should we not be on the threshold of a complete reversal of this judgment? We feel that the value or lack of value of an action lies precisely in that which is *un*intentional: the intention belongs to the surface, to the skin of the "inner human being"—it signifies nothing because it can signify *too many things*——Of course: we would no longer so casually give someone the right to measure value or lack of value according to this new standard: and it is now more than ever high time to reckon moral denunciation or glorification among the signs of bad taste and rabble-like manners.

24. *origin]* Throughout this section, "origin" is translating *Herkunft*, which elsewhere in the *CW* is usually translated as "descent."

25. *advocatus dei]* "advocate of God" (vs. of the devil)

26. *valeurs]* "values"

27. *faith?—] Pd*: faith? Let's assume for once that we, as belonging to the world, if this world is something deceitful—would ourselves be allowed to deceive somewhat? [perhaps] indeed would *have to* deceive?

28. *Pd*: "*il ne cherche le vrai que pour faire le bien*" {"he seeks truth only to do good"} Voltaire—and consequently did not find it—

29. *Humanity]* *Humanität*

30. "*il ne cherche le vrai que pour faire le bien"]* "he seeks truth only to do good"

31. Cf. *CW* 16:38[12].

32. Cf. *CW* 16:1[110].

33. *Pd*: The French Revolution, a horrific and moreover superfluous farce, viewed up close: but the spectators from afar have *interpreted into it* all their decent perceptions and indignations.—A noble posterity could someday *misunderstand* the whole past this way and thereby make the sight of *it* bearable.

34. *Pour . . . est."]* Cf. *CW* 15:26[294, 396]; quoted from P{rosper} Mérimée in "*Notes et souvenirs*" {"Notes and Memories"} on Stendhal, *Correspondance inédite* {"Unpublished Correspondence"}, Paris{: Michel Lévy Frères,}1855. *NL*. {"To be a good philosopher you have to be dry, clear, and without illusion. A banker who has made a fortune has part of the character required to make discoveries in philosophy, that is, to see clearly into what is."} {The source of this quote is misidentified in *KSA* 14; it is not cited in Mérimée's introduction but appears in Stendhal's *Correspondance inédite, Deuxième Série* (Paris: Michel Lévy Frères, 1855), 87.}

35. *Someone . . . gives.* —] *Sd*: person eventually comes to know, not without chills and amazement, the *mask* that he is as he wanders about in the minds and hearts of his friends: but how much secret bitterness does he yet have to drink before he also comes to know the art and the good will of no longer "disappointing" his friends either: that is, to always first translate his plight and his happiness into superficiality, into the "mask," in order to be able to—*communicate* something of himself to them. *Pm* crossed out at the end: Of course it is horrifying when one discovers for the first time the mask that one appears to be:———

36. Cf. *CW* 13:3[146].

37. *every person*] N uses the noun *eine Person* here, instead of the generic *Mensch*. Latin *persona* means "theatrical mask."

38. *Pd*: A new species of philosopher is emerging: I dare to christen them with a name that is not without its dangers. As I know them, as I know myself—for I belong to these coming ones—these philosophers of the future will be satisfied for many reasons, also for many unspeakable reasons, to be characterized as *tempters*. This name itself is ultimately only an attempt and, if you will, a temptation.

39. *Tempters.*] {See *BGE* 295. *Versucher* in the context of the new philosopher based on the tempter-god Dionysus means one who tempts: it also means one who experiments, and as a noun, *Versuch* or *Versuchung*, means experiment (attempt) or temptation. It makes little sense to speak of Dionysus as an "experimenter-god," since what he does is tempt, lure people into uncomfortable places. Of course N knows that a modern-day Dionysian philosopher would be both tempter and experimenter, i.e., both tempter and attempter of new things.}

40. *Pd* first version: We are no dogmatists; it offends our pride that our truth should even be a truth for everyone: which is the ulterior motive of all dogmatic endeavors. We love to look with all kinds of eyes into the world, even with the eyes of the sphinx; it is included in the beautiful shudders for which it is worthwhile to be a philosopher that a thing seen from around the corner looks quite different than we should have even suspected, as long as we seek it with straight looks and on straight

paths. Moreover it seems that the solemn earnestness, the clumsy obtrusiveness with which so far all dogmatists have approached truth, were not the most skillful means to win over this female: what is certain is this, that she has not allowed herself to be won over — and every manner of dogmatism stands there today sulking and discouraged. If it stands at all! Cf. *BGE* preface.

41. *awe] Schauder*, awe or shuddering while in awe of something. See Goethe's *Faust II*, lines 6270–74, where "Awe is the finest portion of mankind."

42. Cf. *CW* 16:34[146].

43. *which . . . head!] Pm*: in which I recognize the *niaiserie moderne par excellence* {modern silliness par excellence}

44. *The plant "human being"]* based on Vittorio Alfieri's proposition: "*la pianta uomo nasce più robusta qui che altrove*" {"the plant human being grows more robustly here than elsewhere"} quoted in Stendhal, *Rome, Naples et Florence*, Paris{: Michel Lévy Frères,} 1854, 383; *NL*, the passage underlined by N.

45. *art of seduction] Versucherkunst*, cf. note 39 above.

46. *"libres penseurs," "liberi pensatori," "Freidenker"]* French, Italian, and German expressions for freethinker.

Part Three

1. *science and conscience] Wissen und Gewissen*, "knowing (science) and conscience (co-knowing)."

2. *homines religiosi]* "religious people"

3. *The . . . would] Pd*: When I was younger I imagined that I was lacking several hundred scholars whom I could drive into the bushes like bloodhounds — I mean into the history of the human soul, into its past and future, in order to hunt my game there. In the meantime I learned, not without much resistance, that for the things that stimulated my curiosity, aids, especially dogs were hard to find. The drawback we have in sending out scholars into hunting grounds where freedom, subtlety and unscrupulousness in every sense are needed, lies in the fact that precisely there they have no eyes and noses for where the danger begins, where the good hunt begins. For guessing and determining, for instance,

what kind of history so far the problem of knowing {*Wissen*} and conscience {*Gewissen*}

4. *imperium Romanum]* "Roman empire"

5. *absurdissimum]* "most absurd thing / pinnacle of absurdity"

6. *Pd* first version: Solitude, fasting and sexual solitude—typical form from which religious neurosis emerges. Alternating extremes of lustfulness and piousness. Foreign-like observation against *themselves*: as if they were glass or 2 persons.

7. *Kundry]* {In Wagner's last opera, *Parsifal*, a wild woman first sent to seduce Parsifal, but later reformed and redeemed by him.}

8. *type vécu]* "a type that has lived"

9. *north.] Sd* crossed out after this: The French free-spiritedness and the whole French war of enlightenment has something of the smolder of a religious movement to it. I am again surprised by the dark colors

10. *"disons . . . mieux? . . . ."]* "Then let us affirm that religion is a product of the normal man, that man is closest to the truth when he is most religious and most assured of an eternal destiny . . . . It is when he is good that he wants virtue to correspond to an eternal order, and when he is contemplating things in a disinterested manner that he finds death revolting and absurd. How is one not to suppose that it is in these moments that man sees best?" . . . .

11. *niaiserie religieuse par excellence]* "religious silliness par excellence"

12. *delicatezza]* "delicate touch"

13. *way of being beside oneself] Aussersichsein*

14. *unio mystica et physica]* "mystical and physical union"

15. Title in *Pd*: *Circulus vitiosus deus* {"God as a vicious circle"}

16. *da capo]* "from the top (play it again)"

17. *circulus vitiosus deus]* "God as a vicious circle"

18. *disgraces] Sd* crossed out after this: In German nobility therefore we still find a good portion of piousness, likewise among the women of those classes that {consider} their women their nobler half with leisure

19. *homines religiosi]* "religious people"

20. *that . . . enough]* Pd: that God can be refuted but not the devil: cf. *CW* 16:1[110].

21. *Pd* first version: That the *meaning* of a religion is ambiguous: for the strong and the independent it is a means to rule or to create calm for oneself from the toil of ruling (like the Brahmins): for the stronger types of h⟨uman being⟩ coming along it gives opportunities to strengthen the will and to learn stoicism: or even adaptability (like Jesuits): for ord⟨inary⟩ h⟨uman beings⟩ it provides *secure* horizons, consolation, community of happiness and suffering and a certain beautification of the common life through a meaningfulness of all events.

22. *Pd* first version: To console the suffering, to give the oppressed, the weak courage, to lead those who are dependent, to bring the immoderate to insight and discipline— *but also to smash the strong* (or at the very least make them insecure), to sicken great hopes, to render suspect great happiness and beauty, self-confidence, the manlier and prouder more domineering instincts: this so far has been the task of Christianity.

Part Four

1. Cf. *CW* 14:3 [1]150; *CW* 15:31[52]; 32[9].

2. Cf. *CW* 14:3[1]133.

3. Cf. *CW* 14:3[1]132; *CW* 15:31[52]; 32[8].

4. {In the original edition of 1886, N mistakenly used the numbers 65 and 73 twice; subsequent standard editions have added the letter "a" to these numbers.}

5. Cf. *CW* 14:3[1]118.

6. Cf. *CW* 14:1[40]; 3[1]226.

7. Cf. *CW* 14:3[1]214.

8. Cf. *CW* 14:3[1]240.

9. Cf. *CW* 14:3[1]229; *CW* 15:31[53]; 32[9].

10. Cf. *CW* 14:3[1]258.

11. Cf. *CW* 14:3[1]256.

12. Cf. *CW* 14:3[1]252.

13. Cf. *CW* 14:3[1]264.

14. Cf. *CW* 14:3[1]270; 12[1]98.

15. Cf. *CW* 14:3[1]265.

16. Cf. *CW* 14:3[1]275.

17. Cf. *CW* 14:3[1]290.

18. Cf. *CW* 14:3[1]276.

19. Cf. *CW* 14:3[1]281.

20. Cf. *CW* 14:2[47]; 3[1]64, 72; 22[3]; *BGE* 163.

21. Cf. *CW* 14:3[1]45; 22[3]; *CW* 15:31[39]; 32[8]; *Z* IV "The Shadow."

22. *"Know thyself!"]* {Used by Plato in *Phaedrus* and other dialogues; Socrates was famous for claiming that he knew only that he knew nothing, and for championing the view that one must first know oneself. The maxim "know thyself" was inscribed in the temple of Apollo at Delphi, and invoked by several Greek sages before and after Socrates.}

23. Cf. *CW* 14:5[11]; 12[1]138; 13[8].

24. Cf. *CW* 14:3[1]44; 12[1]117; 22[3].

25. Cf. *CW* 14:11[11].

26. Cf. *CW* 14:1[50, 111]; 3[1]23; 22[3].

27. Cf. *CW* 14:1[7]; 3[1]20.

28. Cf. *CW* 14:3[1]393; 12[1]109.

29. Cf. *CW* 14:3[1]59; 22[3].

30. Cf. *CW* 14:3[1]41; 22[3]; *CW* 15:30[9]; 31[39].

31. Cf. *CW* 14:3[1]11, 445.

32. Cf. *CW* 14:2[44]; 3[1]61.

33. Cf. *CW* 14:3[1]429; 22[3].

34. Cf. *CW* 14:3[1]313.

35. Cf. *CW* 14:3[1]299.

36. Cf. *CW* 14:3[1]327.

37. *Nausicaa]* {Cf. *The Odyssey*, Bk. VI, where Odysseus is welcomed among the Phaeacians by Nausicaa, daughter of King Alcineus. Although Athena has kindled love for Odysseus in the heart of Nausicaa, they do not marry but become friends.}

38. Cf. *CW* 14:3[1]360, 405.

39. Cf. *CW* 14:3[1]138, 335; 12[1]107; 13[8].

40. Cf. *CW* 14:3[1]243; 12[1]101; 13[16]; 16[7]; 23[5]; *CW* 15:31[35, 36]; 32[10].

41. Cf. *CW* 14:3[1]205.

42. Cf. *CW* 14:3[1]249; 12[1]100; *CW* 15:31[54]; 32[8, 9].

43. Cf. *CW* 14:3[1]244.

44. Cf. *CW* 14:2[9]; 3[1]307.

45. Cf. *CW* 14:3[1]355.

46. Cf. *CW* 14:3[1]378.

47. *pia fraus]* "pious fraud"

48. *impia fraus]* "impious fraud"

49. Cf. *CW* 14:3[1]369.

50. Cf. *CW* 14:3[1]370.

51. Cf. *CW* 14:3[1]374.

52. Cf. *CW* 14:3[1]375; *Z* I "On the Pale Criminal."

53. Cf. *CW* 14:3[1]395.

54. Cf. *CW* 14:3[1]394.

55. Cf. *CW* 14:3[1]382.

56. Cf. *CW* 14:1[87]; 1[108]4; 5[1]62; 12[1]194.

57. Cf. *CW* 14:4[26]; 5[1]56.

58. Cf. *CW* 14:5[1]58.

59. Cf. *CW* 14:5[1]112; 12[1]196.

60. Cf. *CW* 14:4[37]; 5[1]86.

61. Cf. *CW* 14:3[1]423.

62. Cf. *CW* 14:3[1]445.

63. Cf. *CW* 14:3[1]421.

64. Cf. *CW* 14:3[1]416.

65. Cf. *CW* 14:3[1]428.

66. Cf. *CW* 14:3[1]433.

67. Cf. *CW* 14:1[45, 109]; 5[1]50.

68. Cf. *CW* 14:1[70]; 3[1]50; 22[3]; *CW* 15:31[38, 46].

69. Cf. *CW* 14:1[93]; 3[1]3; 12[1]121; 22[1].

70. Cf. *CW* 14:3[1]25; 4[31]; 16[88]; 18[24]; 22[1]; *CW* 15:29[56]; 31[35]; *Z* I "On the Flies of the Marketplace."

71. Cf. *CW* 14:1[70]; 3[1]49; 22[3].

72. Cf. *CW* 14:3[1]31; 4[26]; *Z* III "On Old and New Tablets."

73. Cf. *CW* 14:1[57]; 3[1]48.

74. *Pd* first version: In dealing with scholars and artists we miscalculate in the opposite direction: we expect to find the remarkable human being behind a great scholar—and are disappointed;

and we expect a mediocre human being behind a mediocre artist—and are again disappointed.

75. Cf. *CW* 14:3[1]24; 22[3].

76. *Pm* crossed out title: Return to Nature.— Cf. *CW* 14:3[1]24; 22[3].

77. *in love] in der Liebe*, in (matters of) love, vs. the state of being in love.

78. Cf. *CW* 14:1[97]; 3[1]51; 12[1]72.

79. *Counsel as conundrum] Rath als Räthsel*, wordplay from *Rat, raten* (noun and verb) and *Räthsel*, riddle, conundrum.

80. Cf. *CW* 14:12[1]116.

81. *The lower body] Der Unterleib*, abdomen, lower organs, genitalia.

82. *"Dans le véritable amour c'est l'âme, qui enveloppe le corps."]* "In true love it is the soul that envelops the body."

83. Cf. *CW* 14:3[1]19; 4[43].

84. Cf. *CW* 15:26[337].

85. *buona femmina e mala femmina vuol bastone.]* "both the good and bad woman want a big stick."

86. *Sacchetti, Nov. 86.]* {Franco Sacchetti (1335?–1400?) was an Italian poet and writer of some three hundred *novelle*, or short stories.}

87. Cf. *CW* 14:1[50, 111]; 3[1]16.

88. Cf. *CW* 13:3[66]; *CW* 14:3[1]76.

89. Cf. *CW* 14:3[1]94; 12[1]192.

90. Cf. *CW* 14:3[1]146; 5[1]167.

91. Cf. *CW* 14:3[1]134.

92. Cf. *CW* 14:3[1]143; 5[25]; *CW* 15:31[53, 64]; 33[1]; *Z* IV "On Superior Humans."

93. Cf. *CW* 14:3[1]140.

94. Cf. *CW* 14:3[1]159.

95. Cf. *CW* 14:3[1]174.

96. Cf. *CW* 14:3[1]176.

97. Cf. *CW* 14:3[1]185.

98. Cf. *CW* 14:2[26]; 3[1]191, 194; *CW* 15:31[5].

99. Cf. *CW* 14:2[27]; 3[1]193; *CW* 15:31[5].

100. Cf. *CW* 14:3[1]202; 12[1]204.

101. *Our fellow-man]* Unser Nächster, fellow-man, or neighbor in the biblical sense; wordplay with *Nachbar*, modern word for neighbor, based on *nah*, near.

102. Cf. *CW* 14:2[47]; 3[1]64, 72; 22[3]; *BGE* 79.

103. Cf. *CW* 14:3[1]68; 4[42].

104. Cf. *CW* 14:3[1]71; 22[3].

105. Cf. *CW* 14:3[1]422; 12[1]88; 22[3].

106. Cf. *CW* 14:3[1]418.

107. Cf. *CW* 14:3[1]417.

108. Cf. *CW* 14:3[1]349; 12[1]90; 13[16]; 16[7]; *CW* 15:31[36].

109. Cf. *CW* 14:3[1]141; 12[1]108; *CW* 15:31[53]; 32[9]; *Z* I "On the Flies of the Marketplace."

110. Cf. *CW* 14:3[1]410; 17[13]; 22[3].

111. Cf. *CW* 14:3[1]324.

112. Cf. *CW* 14:3[1]318.

113. Cf. *CW* 14:3[1]109; 4[59]; 12[1]132; *CW* 15:31[52]; 32[10].

114. Cf. *CW* 14:3[1]105.

115. Cf. *CW* 14:3[1]104.

116. Cf. *CW* 14:3[1]139; 12[1]109; 31[53]; 32[9].

117. Cf. *CW* 14:3[1]86; 12[1]113.

118. Cf. *CW* 14:3[1]82; 22[3].

119. Cf. *CW* 14:3[1]272; 4[104]; *Z* I "On the Viper's Bite."

120. {Cf. Luke 6:18: "Bless those who curse you."}

121. Cf. *CW* 14:3[1]339.

122. Cf. *CW* 14:3[1]347; 5[33, 35]; 12[1]142.

123. Cf. *CW* 14:3[1]195; 5[1]127.

124. Cf. *CW* 14:3[1]361.

Part Five

1. *facta]* "facts"

2. *morals]* the Frauenstädt edition used by N (actually p. 137).

3. *neminen laede, imo omnes, quantum potes, juva]* "Harm no one; rather help everyone to the extent that you can." {Although N writes "*immo*," Schopenhauer uses "*imo*" in his text.}

4. Arthur Schopenhauer, *The Two Fundamental Problems of Ethics*, trans. and ed. Christopher Janaway (Cambridge: Cambridge University Press, 2009), 139–40 (N's emphasis).

5. *laisser aller]* "letting go"

6. *the anarchists]* like Eugen Dühring; cf. *BGE* 204.

7. *discipline and cultivation] "Zucht und Züchtung"*

8. *amour-passion]* according to Stendhal, *De l'amour*, book 1, chap. 1.

9. *Pd* first version: *Antiquity's Silliness of Morality.*—No one wants to harm himself and *consequently all evil is involuntary.*—For the evil one inflicts *harm* on *himself,* but believes the *oppo-site.*—Presupposition: the good: what is *of use* to us

10. *really . . . exists] Sd*: I would like to call the Socratic silliness par excellence: for it really does not belong to Plato, but exists in his philosophy

11. πρόσΘε . . . Χίμαιρα] "Plato in front, Plato in back, Chimaera in the middle." Paraphrase of *The Iliad*, VI, 181, where the chimaera is described as "lion-fronted and snake behind, a goat in the middle."

12. *Pd* (autumn 1881): How things happen in the history of the sciences sheds light on the historical events of knowledge. Here too hypotheses, fictions, hasty faith are the *original.* A true "per-ception of the senses," e.g., of the eye, is something very late. It is much **easier** in response to a given stimulus to *re*-produce an image which has already been *frequently* produced (imagination builds using old, practiced mechanisms and its building itself occurs preferably in the accustomed manner). It is awkward and laborious to see and to hear something *new*: for the most part we immediately arrange the sounds we hear in a foreign language according to the only words we know, e.g., "Armbrust" is what the Germans heard in "Arcubalista." We are bad at listening to foreign music. What is novel finds us hostile and reluctant. Our *sensual processes* are made with love hate fear etc.—here already the affects rule: also laziness etc.—Between a movement and a sensation there is *not cause and effect*, but the latter is a *discharg-ing* of our own energy, and the former provides an *impetus* for it—not a measurable relationship. The history of knowledge begins with the history of *fictionalizing.* It would be possible that processes now playing ⟨themselves⟩ out in our senses transpose fictionalizations into nature (colors? harmonies?) These whole

beings, these peasants e.g., are quickly imagined and not *accurately* seen: no more so than a page is accurately read: most of the meaning is *guessed* and most of that probably *falsely guessed* (during rapid reading) Only a rare few are able to *say* **what** *has happened to them* or indeed transpires in them. ⟨*Above the entire page also the word*: Or? —

13. *Armbrust . . . arcubalista]* Literally "arm-breast" in German; both mean "crossbow."

14. *Quidquid luce fuit, tenebris agit]* "What happened in the light, goes on in the dark"

15. *Supposing . . . "flying."] Pm*: Thus in my dreams I have often flown, and as soon as I dream I am aware of the power to fly as if it were a privilege, also as if it were my own enviable happiness. To be able to realize with the slightest impulse every manner of curve and angle, to be a flying geometry with the feeling of divine levity, this "upward" without tension and force, this "downward" without condescension and degradation—without *gravity*!—how should this genre of experiences not ultimately color and differently define the word "happiness" as it applies also to my waking day—how could I not *differently*—long for happiness? than—others? "Soaring inspiration" as this is described by the poets is too muscular, too violent, even too "heavy" compared to that "flying." Cf. *CW* 13:7[37]; *CW* 6:15[60].

16. *Pd* (autumn 1881): The difference of human beings refers to the goods worthy of striving for and to what they regard to be their actual *possessions*. E.g., with respect to a woman this man already considers his sexual pleasure with her as "possessing"; another wants to be loved in such a way that she leaves everything for his sake (thus she is "had" ἔχεται {"had," "was possessed"}); a third, however, wants her not to give up everything for a phantom of him, but that the prerequisite of her love to him should be a *full knowing*—she is only then entirely in his possession when she does not deceive herself about him and nevertheless belongs to him. These are three degrees.—That one wants to possess a people and all means of deception are fine with him. Still another wants this too, but he does not want a phantom of him to rest in the minds of the masses—that is not "he himself," his thirst for

possession is subtler, he does not want to deceive, he himself wants to possess: thus he must above all know himself |and let himself be known|.—As long as I deceive myself about something, I do not possess it—says the poet to himself: and the honest man says: I cannot control myself until I know *what* I am.—To give in to a stirring for others acquires its value according to whether I really know the other or am satisfied with a shadow image of him. Helpful p⟨eople⟩ usually remake {*zurechtmachen*} the one they want to help (as deeply in need of their help, deeply grateful, submissive, as property) Where p⟨eople⟩ see someone *suffering*, they immediately seek to *acquire* a *possession* for themselves there (and are jealous of anyone who gets there first or crosses them in helping)—parents involuntarily make something similar to themselves out of their children, something subject to their own notions and value judgments; they do not doubt themselves in possession of property (Romans—the children slaves) The teacher, the priest, the ruler see in p⟨eople⟩ opportunity for *possessions*.

17. *Cagliostro and Catiline*] {Count Alessandro di Cagliostro, alias of Giuseppe Balsamo (2 June 1743–26 August 1795) occultist, healer, clairvoyant, Freemason, swindler, and medical reformer dedicated to the poor; Catiline, Lucius Sergius Catilina (108–62 BCE) conspired to overthrow Rome using the help of its poor and indigent, to whom he promised debt relief. Here N uses both as examples of demagogues.}

18. *Pd* first version: The *prophets* as tribunes of the people: they have fused "rich" "godless" "evil," "violent," into one.—Here lies the significance of the *Jewish people*: it is the slave revolt in morality. (The Jew and Syrian as born to slavery according to Tacitus) "Luxury as Crime" The name (Ebion) "poor" becomes synonymous with "holy" and "friend of God"; {cf. *CW* 18:11[405] (Renan) and the note to it.}

19. *Tacitus*] *Histories* V, 8.

20. *those . . . see.*] *Pm*: as the astronomers know.

21. *and*] *Pm*: and in truth

22. *with . . . unsaid.*] *Pm*: which precisely he requires

23. *Aristotelianism*] *Pm*: Socratism

24. *Hafiz and Goethe]* {Goethe's last book of poems, *West-östlicher Divan* (*West-Eastern Divan*) (1819), was inspired by the Persian poet Hafiz and written in his spirit. N obviously appreciated Goethe's free-spirited existence as well as his efforts to draw on Eastern sources of art, religion, and philosophy.}

25. *licentia morum]* "moral license"

26. *what . . . moments!] Pd*: despite everything the appearance of an unconditional commander was for the herd-animals, the impression made by Napoleon served as the last great example. In a more refined sense there is a similar need on the part of all knowers and researchers of lower rank for unconditionally commanding philosophers: such types sometimes establish the value-tablets of knowledge for entire millennia, for instance as Plato has done—for Christianity is only a rabbleized Platonism—and how even today half of Asia follows a Sankya-system popularized by Buddha; cf. variant to *BGE*, Preface, note 4, p. 356 above.

27. *origins,] Herkunft,*

28. *magically . . . causes.] Pd*: domineering natures like Caesar and Napoleon. Therefore the *strongest* h⟨umans⟩ appear in ages of the greatest mixing of races and classes, i.e. at times of the greatest longing for *happiness of the herd*, e.g., in the Athens of Pericles, in Rome at the time of Caesar, in Europe at the time of N⟨apoleon⟩. The latter period is still in its beginning; for more distant times a much higher kind of human being is still to be expected, where the great race-mixings will appear, while at the same time the spiritual and material means of power have become enormous

29. *res publica]* "commonwealth"

30. *Let . . . judgments] Pd* first version: I have made a discovery, but it is not bracing: it offends our pride. For however free we may regard ourselves to be, we free spirits—for we are free "among ourselves"—there is also a feeling in us that becomes offended when someone openly counts human beings among the animals: it is almost a crime {*Schuld*}, and it requires an apology {*Entschuldigung*} that I—in referring to us must constantly speak of "herds," "herd instincts" and the like. But here lies my discovery; for I found that in all *moral judgments*

31. *is . . . movement.] Pm*: is the continuation of Christianity.

32. *philosophasters]* the Latin suffix *aster* denotes someone who is inferior or phony; cf. Schopenhauer's frequent use of "philosophaster" to refer to Fichte and Hegel; cf. also "poetaster" for a pseudo-poet.

33. *ni dieu ni maître]* "Neither God nor master."

34. *united . . . Buddhism.] Pm*: gloom of conscience that [touches on] extends to Buddhism (because one cannot [is unable to] rid oneself of suffering! because one intuits that it is [unremovable] even knotted together and entangled with life!

35. *morality in itself,]* the only morality,

36. *absolution . . . past] Pm*: absolution of the entire past

37. *movement . . . "themselves."] Pd*: is the continuation of the Christian: but that even with it the desires and dreams of the same instinct are not fully satisfied is proved by the speeches and the dreams of the future of all socialists: let people just open their ears.

Pd: is the continuation of the Christian. But that even with it the desires and hopes of said instinct are not fully satisfied is proved by the wailing of all socialists. Only socialism is the herd morality thought to its end: namely the principle "equal rights for all" carried out to the consequences "equal demands of all" therefore "one herd and no shepherd" therefore "sheep equals sheep," therefore "peace on earth," therefore "goodwill toward men." Cf. Luke 2:14 and *WS* 350.

38. *Pd* first version: *For the preface*—To push human beings to new resolutions that have dominion over the entire future of humanity: for this, leaders are needed, humans with a way of thinking such as no one perhaps has ever had. The image of such leaders is what constantly hovers before me: the means by which they are to be created, the thoughts by virtue of which they endure carrying the terrible weight of such a task—these are my concerns.—There is perhaps no pain more acute than seeing an extraordinary h⟨uman⟩ go off track and degenerate: but whoever has presented his soul with the monstrous fortuity {*Zufälligkeit*} that has reigned so far on the whole in the destinies of peoples, their relationships and their separations, suffers from a pain for which there is no

comparison: the inspiring happiness over what would be possible with such an accumulation of forces and energies, and what kind of pitiful things suddenly smash promising developments of the highest order———

39. *of the human being] des Menschen*; N uses the singular and plural forms of *Mensch* seventeen times in this section; capturing its nuance requires multiple expressions in English.

40. *culture and cultivation] "Zucht und Züchtung"*: culture (as in agriculture) and cultivation (same etymology).

Part Six

1. *montrer ses plaies]* "showing one's wounds"

2. *Schopenhauer's . . . a] Pm*: Schopenhauer's influence:—with his foolishness regarding Hegel he deprived the entire latest generation of a connection with the latest and most authentic highpoint of the German mind—the

3. *who . . . Hartmann] Pm*: just as today they are precisely as done up as they are "done in"—Herbert Spencer for instance in England, Eduard von Hartmann and Eugen Dühring in Germany

4. *pity] Mitleiden*

5. *type: he] Pm*: type (which, as is self-evident, can therefore still be a type that is just as estimable as indispensable [—notation for asses!] he

6. *ipsissimosity]* "very ownness": N's coinage from Latin *ipsissimus* ("very own").

7. *caput mortuum]* "worthless remains": Alchemical term for "residue."

8. *un tour de force]* literally, in French, "a feat" or "trick"; "*tour de force*" would not have had for N the connotation of an exceptional achievement that it has in contemporary English usage.

9. *Je ne méprise presque rien]* "I despise almost nothing" Later in the section, *presque*="almost" and *presque rien*="almost nothing."

10. Cf. *CW* 16:34[67]. *Pd* first version: Our nineteenth century shows itself in its highs and lows as a skeptical century,

that is as an extended, thinned-out eighteenth century. Almost all subtler scholars and artists today are skeptics, even if they do not want to admit it to themselves and to others. Of course pessimism as a way of thinking that says No, constitutes an exception: it can be traced back to a tendency for comfortable convenience that is part of every democratic age. When the skeptic degenerates, that is becomes lazy, he becomes a pessimist. A sharp mind however, who knows how to preserve some degree of freedom of knowing and conscience today, does not say "No" but "I do not trust myself here." Or, "here the door is open, why enter right away? Why these hasty hypotheses? why absolutely make something round that is crooked? why plug a hole with any old kind of putty? let's just wait a while longer: the uncertain still has its charms; the Sphinx too is a Circe." Thus a skeptic consoles himself—and it is true that he needs a good bit of consolation. Skepticism, after all, is the expression of a certain complex physiological condition as it develops during a great and sudden crossing of races and classes. The inherited value-estimations of different backgrounds are at war with each other, they mutually disrupt one another in growth and becoming strong, the body and the soul lack balance, lack center of gravity, lack perpendicular stability. What unravels and becomes weak in most such mixing-experiments of nature is the will; the old independence and originality of resolve is gone. No one can vouch for themselves anymore. Hence a general ghostly fear of great and small responsibility, hence a passionate tendency to bury one's head and conscience in some kind of majority. But whoever today has inherited a strong commanding and audacious will—chance allows for such exceptions—he also has greater hopes than ever for becoming a ruler. The insecure manner of most people demands and cries out for those who command unconditionally.

11. *nihilin]* {N's coinage, based on "nihilist"; perhaps, like his coinage in *AC* 2 of "*moralin*," indicating a drug-like compound, modeled on the newly isolated (1828) "*Nicotin*," "nicotine."}

12. *bonae voluntatis]* "of goodwill"

13. *l'art pour l'art]* "art for art's sake"

14. Cf. *CW* 16:34[157, 221].

15. *cet esprit fataliste, ironique, méphistophélique]* "that fatalistic, ironic, Mephistophelian spirit."

16. *Michelet]* Source not identified.

17. *"dogmatic slumber,"]* {Kant in *Prolegomena to Any Future Metaphysics* claimed that Hume had awakened him from such slumber.}

18. *woman]* {Germaine de Staël, also Madame de Staël (1766–1817), Swiss writer whose *De l'Allemagne* (*On Germany*, 1810) introduced Germans to Europe primarily through German literature. Her salon in Coppet on Lake Geneva was the hub of European Romanticism. She was a critic of Napoleon, hence N's remarks here and in *BGE* 232.}

19. *Finally . . . German!"—]* Cf. *CW* 16:34[97]; Goethe, discussion with Napoleon, 1808, sketch (2 October 1808): "After he had looked at me attentively, he said: '*Vous êtes un homme.*' {You are a man.} I bow." *Annals or Journals and Yearbooks from 1749 to end of 1822*; cf. also *SE* 3 {*CW* 2, 185}.

20. *deceived . . . German!"]* Sd first version: he deceived himself, his prejudice about skepticism deceived him: he did not know, as a man of peasant-like (or corporal-like) limitation that there are two opposing kinds of skepticism, the skepticism of weakness—*and the skepticism of courage and exuberance* {des Muths und Übermuths}. He thought of the former when he found his son devoted to French atheism, to *esprit* and to aesthetic indulgence:—perhaps the danger of a conversion to this side was not inconsiderable. But it was the *second* kind of skepticism, closely related to the genius for war and conquest, that first entered Germany here, a new kind of audacious *manliness* that ultimately meant much more than brawny limbs, tallness and everything that is supposed to be manly in a grenadier. To this *courageous* skepticism belongs the best of what Germany has since then produced in spiritual leaders and adventurers; and the predominant influence that Germany owes to its critics, philologists and historians in Europe depends on that not undangerous element of *courageous* skepticism and a certain spiritual "militarism" and "Frederickianism." The beautiful daring race of Lessing, Herder, Kant, Friedrich August Wolf, Niebuhr

and whatever all these brave ones are called belong to the features of an awakening German manliness and valor for whom the soldiers of Frederick the Great represent the physiological prelude: indeed they are features of a new race that is coming about slowly and will be strong. Meanwhile the weakened and atrophied type of the older German also maintained itself [— it survives even today], indeed it dominated again from time to time (namely as German Romanticism and German music); and foreigners often stood there doubting and did not know which standard to use for measuring "the Germans" (— contemporary Germany has this doubting and hesitating to thank [perhaps] for a major part of its sudden success.). For centuries, what people abroad imagined when they thought of a German scholar or "poet" for example — and with the best possible justification — was demonstrated by that remarkably astonished comment of Napoleon, made when he caught sight of Goethe — it is never taken profoundly enough: *"Voilà un homme"* — that is to say: "now that is a *man*! a real man! And I had only {expected} a German poet

21. *Pd*: To describe ourselves as a new crowd of critics and analysts who avail themselves of *experiments* in the broadest sense — that would perhaps be a permitted tartuffery to which many things could persuade us. As one of the prerequisites of such beings as we are, we value the possession of qualities that perhaps in themselves make for strong critics: a [spirited] witty courage, an ability to stand alone and answer to oneself, a delight in saying No and dissecting, sureness of the hand that wields the knife "even if the heart bleeds." Along with the critic we have in common a disgust that is always ready: for all that is fanatical, idealistic, feministic, hermaphroditic; and whoever knew how to follow us into the chambers of our heart would surely not find there an intention to reconcile Christian feeling with the taste of antiquity and perhaps even with modern parliamentarism (and whatever sort of conciliatoriness might be possible in our very insecure, and thus very conciliatory century among so-called philosophers). Critical discipline is [as I said something we hold to as if to] cleanliness and rigor in matters of the spirit — among ourselves we speak very differently and with harsh words about

this——: nevertheless we would think we were inflicting no small disgrace on philosophy if we were to say: "Philosophy is science and criticism and nothing more." Of course this value-estimation stands in full bloom precisely today, in all positivists, philosophers of reality and "scientific philosophers" in Germany and France; and maybe it has already flattered the heart and taste of Kant. These advocates of criticism and science are simply critics and scientific people, but not philosophers themselves: even the great Chinese of Königsberg was only a great critic.

22. *Königsberg]* {Baltic (Prussian) seaport where Kant lived; after World War II it became Kaliningrad.}

23. *art] Pm* crossed out after this: (where also history belongs—)

24. *And . . . possible?]* Missing in *Pm*, but replaced with the following crossed-out sentences: the Proteus of a new eye, the diver of life who dives safely into ever deeper depths of life. And to ask once more: [is precisely the philosopher possible today?] is such a greatness still possible today?———But to say it once more: how is something like this possible today?

25. *Pd* first version: There is an aristocracy of problems that excludes many people. This is because these problems are connected with lofty and extraordinary circumstances that few people possess. It is quite inconsequential whether nimble but ordinary minds (like Eduard von Hartmann) or clumsy sturdy empiricists (like Eugen Dühring) occupy themselves with such problems. Their nature is not permitted to enter here: the doors remain closed, or—one smiles.

26. *presto]* "quickly"

Part Seven

1. *bêtise bourgeoise]* "bourgeois stupidity"

2. *homo bonae voluntatis]* "man of good will"

3. Cf. *CW* 13:3[69]; 15:25[492].

4. *mad . . . beings] Sd*: mad. My proposition is that every *elevated* spirituality exists only as the last spawn of moral qualities: it unites all those conditions attributed to the moral human being *in order to function at all*

5. *bonhomme]* "good man"

6. *"suffer . . . compassion" . . . . .] Mitleid* (compassion) and *mit leiden* (to show compassion) are both based on *leiden*, "to suffer." Compare *misery* and *commiserate* or *passion* and *compassion* for a rough analogy.

7. *in moribus et artibus]* "in morals and arts"

8. *in puncto]* "with respect to"

9. *Pd* first version: Our *historical sense* is a result of our semi-barbarism: the latter through the *plebeian* character of our educated classes. With it we are able to sympathize with the majority of the past, because things were almost always semi-barbarian then: our highest is Homer and Shakespeare (this Spanish-Moorish-Saxon type) But the most successful works and individuals remain *inaccessible* to us, e.g., Corneille, Racine, Sophocles etc. — the truly *noble* works and individuals, where great strength stands still before everything that lacks measure and there is subtle joy in restraining and trembling in place, like the rider on a steed champing to move on.

10. *Saint-Évremond]* {Charles de Saint-Évremond (1610–1703) studied with the Jesuits, then joined the military campaign of Marshal Bassompierre and fought in the Thirty Years' War. He studied the works of Montaigne and of Spanish and Italian writers. In his "Dissertation sur le mot de Vaste" ("Dissertation on the Word Vast"), Saint-Évremond refers to Homer's *esprit vaste*. See *Oeuvres meslées de Mr. De Saint-Evremond, Seconde Edition Reveüe Corrigée & Augmentée. Tome Seconde* ("Mixed Works of Mr. Saint-Évremond, Second Edition Reviewed, Corrected, and Augmented. Second Volume") (London: Jacob Tonson, 1709), p. 328.}

11. *esprit vaste]* "vast spirit"

12. *we . . . air] Pd*: Shakespeare and Balzac: how much filth and coarseness, how much rabble is always close by! It affects me like strolling on the enchanting Chiaja of Naples. The sewer stench of the rabble neighborhoods is in the air. Cf. *CW* 15:25[123].

13. Cf. *CW* 16:1[168]; 2[185].

14. *Pd* first version: We want to refine our honesty and push it into the heights such that it will remain standing like a golden pinnacle above the whole dull dismal age. And where it becomes

weak and seems to hesitate, we want to come to its aid with our curiosity, our adventurer's courage, our cruelty, our "*nitimur in vetitum*" and all our devilry, our sole and ultimate virtue: let people mistake it with such aid [—], what does it matter!

15. *nitimur in vetitum]* "We strive for the forbidden." Cf. Ovid, *Amores* III, 4, 17.

16. *Helvétius!] Se*: Helvétius, *ce sénateur Pococurante* {this apathetic senator}, to use Galiani's words — Cf. Galiani, *Lettres à Madame d'Epinay*, I, 217. *NL*.

17. *cant,]* N uses the English word "cant," which he underlines, as well as "comfort" and "fashion," not underlined, below.

18. *Sans . . . esprit!]* "Without genius and without spirit!" To this day Germans use the French *génie* for genius, but they do not provide the acute accent.

19. In *Pm* the following strophe crossed out: Germans, *such* Englishmen / Cattle mentalities / You honor as "philosophy"? / To place [Goethe] Spencer next to [Darwin] Hegel — / — Shame on you, Germans! that's offense against / *Majestatem genii* {the sovereignty of genius}. Cf. *CW* 15:28[45, 46].

20. *Sd* first version: Whoever has recognized as a knowing one that in and around all growth the law of perishing rules and that there has to be inexorable disintegration and annihilation for the sake of creativity: he must also learn to add a kind of joy to this sight, in order to *tolerate* it — or henceforth he is no longer capable of knowledge. That is, he must be capable of a refined cruelty and must train himself for it with a resolute heart. If his power in the rank order of powers stands even higher, if he himself is one of the creators and not only a spectator, then it does not suffice that he is capable of cruelty at the sight of much suffering, degenerating, offending: such a human being must be capable himself of causing misery with his own hand and deed and not merely know it with the eyes of the spirit. Virtuous hypocrisy will not want it said that every higher culture rests to a large extent on the development and spiritualization of cruelty, that painful enjoyment of tragedy belongs to cruelty the same as enjoyment of bullfights, burnings at the stake and combat in the arena, and that almost everything that today affects people pleasantly in so-

called tragic pity gets its sweetness from the added ingredient of cruelty. It is a clumsy idea that the enjoyment of cruelty originates only when someone sees another person suffering; on the contrary there is an abundant and superabundant pleasure in one's own suffering, in making oneself suffer, for example in all religions that demand self-mutilations from people, or penitential seizures or asceticisms or remorse of conscience or even only a subtle *sacrificio dell'intelletto* {sacrifice of the intellect} — they persuade him to all this by means of the seductive mysteries and awe of cruelty directed against oneself. In the end we should consider that every knowing one forces his spirit to work against the inclination of his spirit and mostly also against the wishes of his heart, namely to say No where he would like to affirm and adore; that taking something deeply and thoroughly is itself a kind of contradiction and cruelty against the fundamental will of the spirit, that incessantly strives for appearances and the surface, hence that even in spiritual activities the human being rules as the artist of cruelty.

21. *"milk . . . thinking"]* Quoted from Friedrich Schiller's *Wilhelm Tell*, Act IV, Scene 3.

22. *pity] Mitleiden*

23. *sacrifizio dell'intelletto]* "sacrifice of the intellect"

24. *Pd* first version: To translate humankind back into nature, to become master over the many false interpretations and connotations that the vanity of h⟨umans⟩ has scribbled and smeared over and next to the nature-text "human," to ensure that the human being stands before h⟨umanity⟩ as before nature, and shuts his ears to the seductive voices that whisper to him: "you are more! you are higher, you are of a different lineage!" — this is a harsh and almost cruel task. Whoever works on it has himself as well as his fellow human beings as his opponent. And why does he work toward this end? Especially since he should not even produce the beautiful words "love of truth," "honesty," "sacrifice for knowledge" and the like, after he has shown that all of this is junk and pomp of vanity, in sum, that he is too vain to allow himself such meager satisfactions of his vanity: — why? Such a human being is a problem.

25. *homo natura]* "natural man"

26. Title in *Sd*: *"Woman in itself."*

27. *fatum]* "fate"

28. *"woman in itself"]* *"das Weib an sich"* {with *an sich* used as Kant used *"das Ding an sich,"* i.e., the thing in itself}.

29. *Sd* first version: One cannot think highly enough of women, but this is no reason for anyone to think wrongly of them: here we must be thoroughly on our guard. That they themselves would be in a position to enlighten men about the "Eternal Feminine" is hardly probable: it seems they are too close to themselves for this—and moreover enlightening itself, at least up till now, has been a man's concern, a man's talent. In the end we should reserve a good suspicion of everything that women write about woman: namely as to whether a woman who writes does not quite inadvertently do that which works counter to the desired "enlightenment"—and *puts on her finery?* Does not dressing up belong to the most certain content of the Eternal Feminine? And has anyone ever conceded *profundity* to a female mind? Or to a female heart—justice? Without profundity and justice—what's the use when women judge about woman? Is it not almost a disavowal of female instinct, a *degeneration?* Is the will to "enlightenment" about woman not almost the will to disappointment, to disenchantment, to devaluation of woman for a man? Many women might have a good reason why men should not approach them with praise and love: all told it seems to me that "woman" so far has been held *in contempt* mostly *by women*—and absolutely not by men! Out of concern for women the church decreed: *mulier taceat in ecclesia!* {woman should be silent in church!} For the good of women Napoleon decreed: *mulier taceat de politicis* {woman should be silent about politics}—and for the *rescue of any female charm* I advise: *mulier taceat de muliere!* {woman should be silent about woman!}

30. *eternally-boring in woman"]* {Allusion to Goethe's "Ewig-Weibliche," the Eternal Feminine, which appears at the conclusion of *Faust II,* and which N parodies in *Z* II, "On Poets," and in the *JS* poem "To Goethe."}

31. *mulier taceat in ecclesia!]* "woman should be silent in church!"

32. *mulier taceat in politicis]* "woman should be silent about politics"

33. *women] Frauen*; all previous references to women in this section used the less respectful term *Weib*.

34. *mulier taceat de muliere]* "woman should be silent about woman"

35. Cf. *CW* 15:25[422].

36. *Pd*: Stupidity in the *kitchen*: has a university ever worried about the good *nutrition* of its students? About a healthy sex life? ⟨inserted after "*kitchen*"⟩: one cannot think lower of female intelligence when one considers how thoughtlessly until now the family's and the head of household's *nutritional needs* have been met everywhere by women. Woman does not understand what food *means*: and yet wants to be the cook! If woman were a thinking creature, then as cook for millennia she would surely have to have discovered the greatest physiological facts! Through bad cooks, i.e., *through woman* the development of humans has so far been delayed most!

37. *Madame de Lambert]* {Madame de Lambert, Marquise de Saint-Bris, 1647–1733, French writer and *salonnière*. This remark is quoted in Astolphe de Custine, *Mémoires et voyages ou Lettres écrites à diverses époques, pendant des courses en Suisse, en Calabre, en Angleterre et en Écosse*, 2 vols. (Paris: Alex. Vezard, 1830), I, 187. *NL*.}

38. *"Mon . . . plaisir.]* "My friend, permit yourself only those follies that give you great pleasure."

39. *ella . . . lei]* Cf. *Divina Commedia, Paradiso II, 22*: "*Beatrice in suso, ed io in lei guardava*" {Beatrice looked upward, and I at her.}

40. *the . . . high.] Faust II*, lines 12110f.

41. N's seven rhymes are:

Wie die längste Weile fleucht, kommt ein Mann zu uns gekreucht!

Alter, ach! und Wissenschaft giebt auch schwacher Tugend Kraft.

Schwarz Gewand und Schweigsamkeit kleidet jeglich
   Weib—gescheidt.
Wem im Glück ich dankbar bin? Gott!—und meiner
   Schneiderin.
Jung: beblümtes Höhlenhaus. Alt: ein Drache fährt heraus.
Edler Name, hübsches Bein, Mann dazu: oh wär' er mein!
Kurze Rede, langer Sinn—Glatteis für die Eselin!

42. *man . . . my]* *Pm*: beware, little golden bird!

43. {This aphorism, like the one that precedes it, is also numbered 237 in *KSA*, without explanation, hence 237a.}

44. *who]* *Pd*: who in the manner of St{uart} Mill or Eugen
Dühring

45. *Pd*: As concerns German women: I am far from "cultivating" them even more. First they should not play the piano:
that ruins their nerves (and, as a female kind of finery and co-
quettishness, it enrages every hearty friend of music) and makes
her incapable of bearing strong children. They should be raised
piously: a woman without piety is completely ridiculous in the
eyes of every profound and godless man—indeed it outrages
him when good plants are deprived of the building and protection that alone enables them to blossom into any kind of grace;
and it is a terrible thing, that, to which domineering powers
and a self-improvement least belong, and to see this expected of
women, who immediately fashion it into a "headdress" or a
"chit-chat" for themselves.

46. *emancipation]* In French in the original.

47. {An allusion to Zeus's seduction of Europa in the form of
a white bull. See also the myth of Pasiphaë, wife of King Minos,
who mated with a bull and gave birth to the Minotaur. Ariadne
is the daughter of Minos and Pasiphaë, sister to the Minotaur;
Ariadne is also the companion of Dionysus once she is abandoned by Theseus.}

Part Eight

1. *Sd* first version: I heard the overture of the *Meistersinger*:
this is a magnificent, ornate, heavy and late art that has the pride

of presupposing two centuries of music as *still living* in order to be understood: — it does honor to the Germans that such pride did not miscalculate! What kind of metals are not mixed here! It first strikes us as old-fashioned, then dawning, scholarly, *imprevu* {[*sic*] — unexpected} and moody, then pompous, good-naturedly rough and manly — it has innocence and corruption, all the seasons at once, every kind of budding happiness and likewise every kind of worm infestation and late autumn. There are also moments of inexplicable hesitation, like the gaps springing up between cause and effect, not even a slight nightmarish pressure is lacking, and the kind of things we have encountered in dreams: — but already the old stream of contentment spreads itself wide once more, including the happiness of the artist at the mastery of his methods, which he does not wish to conceal; all in all no beauty, no south, nothing of the southern refined brightness of the sky and heart, no dance, not even logic, instead a certain clumsiness that is underscored as if the artist wanted to say to us: "that is part of my intention"; a clumsy costume, a flurry of scholarly treasures.

2. *flushes]* *Pd*: flushes. At bottom this is a courtesy we show to our forefathers.

3. *in politicis]* "for politics"

4. *'great politics']* Although "*grosse Politik*" is usually translated as "grand politics," (cf. §208), here I use "great" to indicate the resonance with the other appearances of *gross, grosse, Grösse*.

5. *peoples]* *Sd* crossed out after this: — who have their eyes and worries *everywhere* and are not "at home" with themselves, in themselves, nor allowed to be —

6. *I . . . another. —]* *Pm*: and I, in my happiness and corner, weighed to what extent it would be [a happiness] wise in [a] all such personal questions not to be seduced to a Yes or No, about which only a distant, indifferently positioned future could come to an agreement.

7. Cf. *CW* 16:2[13].

8. *"civilization"]* *Pm*: culture

9. *storm and stress]* "*Sturm und Drang*" {A socially aware literary movement in Germany in the 1770s and 1780s, whose name derives from the title of a drama by F. M. Klinger (1777). Feeling

and sensibility were elevated, utilitarianism and reason were re-jected. *Sturm und Drang* writers were generally in their twenties and influenced by Rousseau; their ranks included Goethe, Schil-ler, Klinger, Lenz, Bürger, Herder, Hamann, and Heinse. Argu-ably the most famous *Sturm und Drang* work was Goethe's novel *The Sufferings of Young Werther* (1774).}

10. *storm and stress] Pm*: atavism

11. Cf. *CW* 16:34[114]; 34[97]. *Pd*: People call the Germans *profound*: let us interpret the facts of this less flatteringly and pro-vide an explanation for it if possible. The German soul is mani-fold, of different origins, more pieced together and piled on than actually built. A German who wished to assert "two souls, alas, are dwelling in my breast," would seriously violate the truth. As a people of the most monstrous mixing and blending of races, perhaps even with a preponderance of the pre-Aryan element, as "people of the middle" according to their position in Europe, in every sense of the word the Germans are more incomprehensible, comprehensive, contradictory, unknown, unpredictable, surpris-ing, even more horrifying than other peoples are to themselves: what characterizes the Germans is that the question "what is German?" never dies out for them. The German contains passages and semi-passages, there are caves, hideouts and dungeons in him; his soul is disorderly, he knows the secret paths to chaos. And just as every thing loves its likeness, so too Germans love the clouds and all that is unclear, becoming, twilit, damp and overcast. Foreigners stand amazed before the "reflective" naïveté of the German; the union of genius and *"niaiserie allemande* {German foolishness}" as it is possessed by our greatest poets is disquieting to them [cf. *CW* 16:26[420]: *Mérimée*]. Goethe him-self once defined the famous "German *Gemüt*" as if from abroad, with impatient rejection of that which he himself most lacked: as "indulgence toward the weaknesses of others and oneself." Good-natured and devious—such a pairing would be nonsen-sical applied to any other people: but just live for a time among Swabians! The exterior ponderousness of the German, his social boorishness—just quickly imagine a Bavarian, who is more dan-gerous, bolder, more daring, more secretive, more insidious, more

monstrous, more devious (and consequently "more frank" —) than other Europeans can even imagine. Goethe could have pulled not only Mephistopheles from the *German* soul, but still much more dangerous and also surely more interesting "devils." I mean, Frederick the Second of Prussia was already a more interesting Mephistopheles than that moderately evil comrade of the melancholy university professor Faust: not to mention at all that other and greater Frederick the Second, the mysterious Hohenstaufen. {N here refers to the Hohenstaufen Holy Roman Emperor Frederick II, in contrast to the earlier mentioned Frederick II of Prussia, also known as Frederick the Great.} — All *deep* Germans so far, physically or mentally, climbed over the Alps: they believe in their entitlement to the "south" — they cannot feel themselves to be otherwise than masters of Europe.

12. *"Two . . . breast."]* Goethe's *Faust I*, line 1112.

13. {August Friedrich Wilhelm von Kotzebue (1761–1819) was a prolific writer whose career was filled with controversy. He was assassinated by Karl Ludwig Sand (1795–1820), a theology student, an event used by the conservative Metternich regime to impose strict sanctions on writers and on freedom of speech in central Europe in the form of the Carlsbad Decrees (1819).}

14. *Jean Paul]* in his review of Fichte's *Addresses to the German Nation*, in *Heidelberger Jahrbücher* 1810.

15. *Goethe] Pm*: the German youth

16. {Johann Paul Friedrich Richter (1763–1825) used the pen name Jean Paul. He was a leading figure of the Romantic movement in Germany, widely admired for his style and wit, and one of only a few romantics who earned praise from Schopenhauer. Johann Gottlieb Fichte (1761–1814) was a founder of German Idealism who rose to prominence with his *Science of Knowledge* (1794), which strongly influenced early Romantic writers but was abhorred by Goethe. Fichte's *Addresses to the German Nation* (1810), written during the Napoleonic occupation, forms the basis of modern German nationalism and contains the seeds of German superiority and exclusivity based on language, race, and religion.}

17. *even . . . Fichte]* Source not identified.

18. *angrily . . . Germans?] Pm*: came out raging against Fichte's shameless and mendacious flatteries (indeed one would have to descend to late Wagner and his *Bayreuther Blätter* {newsletter then journal of the Wagnerians from 1878 to 1938} to encounter a morasse of presumptuousness, obscurity and Germanifications {*Deutschthümelei*} resembling Fichte's *Addresses to the German Nation*). What did Goethe think about the Germans?

19. *Gemüt]* {Modernized spelling of N's *Gemüth*. Mind, soul, disposition, attitude, spirit, style, or way; *gemütlich* and *Gemütlichkeit* celebrate good feeling, conviviality, and sentimentality; archaic *Gemüt* usually refers to mind or soul.}

20. *Indulgence . . . themselves]* Cf. Goethe, *Maximen und Reflexionen*, {no. 165 in *Goethes Werke. Hamburger Ausgabe in 14 Bänden*, ed. Erich Trunz and Hans Joachim Schrimpf (Hamburg: Christian Wegner, 1953), vol. 12, 386. N's citation is inaccurate: Goethe's text reads "Nachsicht mit Schwächen, eignen und fremden." ("Indulgence with weaknesses, their own and others.") N's slight miswording has been preserved in the translation.}

21. *ad oculos]* "for the eyes"

22. *go far"!]* Following Goethe's *Faust I*, line 573.

23. *"tiusche . . . Täusche-folk . . .]* {From *tiusch*, Middle High German for *deutsch* ("German"); N is trying to derive *tiusch*, German, from *täuschen* to deceive.}

24. {Carl Maria Friedrich Ernst von Weber (1786–1826) was a leading Romantic composer of operas, conductor, and music critic, who influenced later Romantic composers such as Marschner and Wagner, as well as major composers of the early twentieth century. *Der Freischütz* (1821) and *Oberon* (1826) were two of his operas.}

25. {Heinrich August Marschner (1795–1861) was the leading Romantic composer of operas and *Lieder* between Weber and Wagner.}

26. *girl . . . tangere] Pm*: loafer and sissy; Cf. John 20:17 {do not touch me}.

27. *staccato and rubato]* Musical terms denoting short, crisp playing or singing, and a fluctuation of tempo within a musical phrase.

28. Cf. *CW* 16:34[102].

29. *cannot]* Pm: may not {*darf*}

30. *Jews]* Sd crossed out after this: It was a feeling of Jewish descent that lay spread over the depths of Schopenhauerian thought, it was a thoroughly Jewish curse that he once hurled against us immoralists——Schopenhauer was wrong about this: but we are grateful to him for it

31. Cf. *CW* 16:41[13].

32. {Heinrich von Sybel (1817–95) was a German historian and politician who in his late years was appointed director of the Prussian archives by Bismarck. He was the leading authority on the history of the founding years of the Second Reich.}

33. {Heinrich Gotthard von Treitschke [*sic*] (1834–96) was a German historian and politician known for his strong nationalism and hatred of Britain.}

34. *race]* Rasse; N, like most Germans of his time, uses this term to refer to peoples and ethnic groupings as well as races; cf. §§241, 242, 244, 248, 252.

35. *res . . . picta—]* "something made; something born; something fictitious and unreal—"

36. *aere perennius]* "more enduring than bronze" Quotation from Horace, *Odes*, III, 30.

37. *more . . . does.]* Sd: And *not* perhaps "with open arms"! *Not*, in the manner of fanatics, "drink to brotherhood today" and tomorrow already scratch each other bloody!

38. *Mark]* {The Brandenburg Mark, or Brandenburg March, originally a principality of the Holy Roman Empire of the German Nation, became a province of Prussia in 1806 when Napoleon dissolved the First Empire (Reich). Today Brandenburg is a state of Germany, surrounding but not including Berlin.}

39. *it would be . . . both.]* Sd: and I am pleased in this respect to be in agreement with a famous expert on horses {Bismarck}

about a recipe to be recommended here ("Christian stallions, Jewish mares").

40. *Pd* first version: The English, gloomier, more sensual, stronger-willed and "cruder" than the Germans—and consequently more pious! They *need* Christianity more. All their Christianity even in its literary aftereffect Carlyle, smells somewhat of spleen and alcoholic dissipation: with good reason as antidote to both

41. *"je méprise Locke"]* "I despise Locke" {Actually it is Schiller who attributes this phrase to Schelling in a letter to Goethe, 30 November 1803.}

42. *Just . . . much . . . . .]* Sd first version: tactlessness in this sense:—in this today England's best writers and parliamentary speakers are the same. The above-mentioned Carlyle for instance, one of their richest when speaking of wealth of the soul, moves like a peasant and dolt, even when he is enthused and speaking from the bottom of his heart—leaving aside here the completely unmusical or tin souls like J. St. Mill or H. Spencer, who indeed move like tin figures. In the end watch how the most beautiful Englishwomen *walk*: I will not ask, in order not to ask too much, that we listen to them sing.

43. *Pd* first version: There are truths that can only be known by mediocre minds; we are now e.g., under the influence of English mediocrity (Darwin, Mill, Spencer) and do not want to question the utility of such spirits ruling occasionally. It would be an error to regard precisely the highest natures as particularly skilled in discovering truths: they have to be and to represent something, calculated against which every truth does not even come into consideration. It is the tremendous **gap** between *doing* and *knowing* {Können *und* Wissen} ——! That is, now the scientific discoverers must in a certain sense be poor and one-sided spirits.

44. *âme française]* "French soul"

45. *Hugo]* {Hugo's funeral took place in Paris on June 1, 1885. The procession traveled from the Arc de Triomphe to the Pantheon, and was witnessed by more than two million people, the largest crowd ever assembled in France for the funeral of a public figure.}

46. *âme moderne]* "modern soul"

47. *l'art pour l'art]* "art for art's sake"

48. *The . . . Europe—.] Pd*: the aesthetic passions and devotion to lit⟨erary⟩ form, which for three centuries have continuously built up parties of taste and followings, have also made possible at all times a kind of chamber music of literature through the jealousy of the "small number," which up to now has been missing in Germany: — just consider how big are the ears of German scholars—if they even have ears! [people have e.g., made the accusation, that I] for I am told they did not have time to have ears and it would be demanding too much of them anyway to {concern themselves} with sounds and rhythmic phrases———

49. *romanciers]* "novelists"

50. *boulevardiers de Paris]* "people on the boulevards of Paris"

51. *in voluptate psychologica]* "in the enjoyment of psychology"

52. *Henri Beyle]* {Nineteenth-century French writer better known by his pen name Stendhal.}

53. *protects . . . anemia] Pd*: that over the long term does not tolerate that horrific German gray on gray, the sunless conceptual spookiness and anemia: as powerfully as the Nordic gloom and "twilight of the gods" of Germans has reached and continues to reach across the Rhine even in this century

54. *blood and iron]* "Blut und Eisen" {famous phrase used by Bismarck}.

55. Cf. *CW* 15:25[184].

56. *become one.] Pm*: is, down to the depths and up to the heights of its needs.

57. *Tantaluses]* {In Greek mythology Tantalus is doomed in Hades to stand in water up to his chin, beneath boughs laden with fruit, only to have them recede each time he tries to drink or eat. Cf. *tantalize* in modern English.}

58. *lento]* "slowly" {musical term}

59. *all . . . higher] Pm*: a magnificent, witty-pathological, high-flying violent kind of

60. *"higher human being"] Pm*: "artist"

61. *anticipating . . . vehemence] Pm*: with his *Parsifal* in a saccharine and ambiguous manner

62. *without the words]* ⟨after Mendelssohn's *Songs without Words?*⟩

Part Nine

1. Cf. *CW* 16:1[7, 10]; 2[13]. Crossed out continuation of the aphorism in *Pm*: The "humanization" of barbarians — in part an involuntary process that sets in automatically after an approximate determination of the power ratios — is essentially a process of weakening and alleviating and takes place precisely at the expense of those drives to which it owes its victory and property; and while they master the "human" virtues in this way, perhaps even with a splendid impetuosity and in accordance with their "lust for prey" even in spiritual matters, as conquerors of ancient cultures, arts, and religions — a reverse process unfolds gradually on the part of the oppressed and enslaved. To the extent that they are kept milder and more humane and consequently thrive more richly physically, the *barbarian* develops in them, the strengthened human, the semi-animal with its cravings of the wild: — the barbarian who one day senses himself to be strong enough to resist his humanized, that is weakened masters. The game begins anew: the beginnings of a *higher* culture are once again in place. I mean to say: each time under the pressure of ruling noble castes and cultures a slow counter-pressure has formed from below, a tremendous [instinctive] unplanned overall conspiracy in favor of the preservation and elevation of all who are controlled, exploited, deprived, mediocre, semi-misfits {*Halb-Mißrathenen*}, as a prolonged slave-discontent and slave-revolt that is at first secretive, then increasingly self-aware, as an instinct against every kind of master, in the end even against the concept "master," as a war to the death on every morality from whose loins and consciousness a higher domineering kind of human arises, the kind that *needs* slavery in some form or another and by some name or another as its foundation and condition. All of this always only up to that point in time where such a slave race has become powerful enough — "barbarian" enough! — to make itself the master: immediately then the *reverse* principles and moralities are there. For being master has its instinct, just as

being slave: "nature" is in both—and "morality" too is a piece of nature. —

2. *Pd*: *Corruption* in a ruling caste means something different from in a serving and servile one. E.g., effusive mildness and decrease in energy of the will is corruption in the former. In the latter the increase of independence is corruption, e.g., Eugen Dühring. The privileged of the French Revolution are an example of corruption.

3. *origin]* Herkunft

4. *"We truthful ones"]* Cf. *GM* I, 5.

5. *désintéressement]* "disinterestedness"

6. *un bonhomme]* "a good man"

7. Heretofore in this section, N has used *Herren-Moral* and *Sklaven-Moral*, translated as "master-morality" and "slave-morality." Here, however, he writes "*Sklaven-Moral und -Moralität*."

8. *gai saber]* "gay science"

9. *slaves]* Pm crossed out after this: — and so often in history something similar has happened, —

10. *feels . . . atavism]* Pd: tries to seduce to good opinions of itself in order later to seduce itself to belief in them: — thus the ignoble type wants it.

11. *nurtures]* züchtet sie gross (from the separable prefix verb *grosszüchten*) vs. *züchten* on its own, which means "to breed" or "to cultivate."

12. *now?]* Pm crossed out after this: — it is the time for Socrates and Socratic

13. *mediocrity!]* Pm crossed out after this: (whatever Schopenhauer may say, who was not subtle in these things)

14. *différence engendre haine]* "difference engenders hatred"

15. *Horace]* Epistles, I, 10, 24 : "*naturam expellas furca, tamen usque recurret*" = "Try to expel nature with a pitchfork, it always returns."

16. *with . . . recurret]* Pm: but which is the formula for modern education

17. *irritable]* reizbar, i.e., in the biological sense capable of feeling stimuli.

18. *inter pares]* "among equals"

19. Cf. *CW* 15:26[245]; source not identified.

20. {Johann Friedrich Heinrich Schlosser (1780–1851), befriended Goethe in Jena while studying for his juris doctor degree. He converted from Protestantism to Catholicism in 1814 and devoted himself to Catholic causes. As a member of Frankfurt's city council, he participated in the Congress of Vienna (1814–15). Schlosser collaborated with Goethe on his early-life biography *Poetry and Truth* (1811–33).}

21. {Cf. Évariste Régis Huc, *L'empire chinois*, vol. 1 (Paris: L'Imprimerie impériale, 1854), 243: "Au milieu des embarras et des difficultés, les Chinois disent toujours *siao-sin*, c'est-à-dire rapetisse ton coeur." ("In the midst of embarrassments and difficulties, the Chinese always say *siao-sin*, that is to say, shrink your heart.") This line is quoted by Hippolyte Taine in *Les origines de la France contemporaine: La Révolution. Tome III: Le Gouvernement révolutionnaire* (Paris: Hachette, 1885), 128, which N may very well have read in German translation (the first two volumes remained in his personal library after his death).}

22. Cf. *CW* 16:34[86].

23. *baseness] Gemeinheit*, literally "commonness" but also a pejorative meaning vulgarity, crudeness, meanness, baseness. Inasmuch as N is an animator of the tensions of opposites, baseness in this sense is the obverse of nobleness, as in the title of this chapter "What Is Noble?"

24. *recurring] wiederkehrender*

25. *needs.] Pm* crossed out after this: Need {*Die Noth*}, that by which life is conditioned and founded, each time

26. *force . . . far] Pm*: a selecting and cultivating force has

27. *progressus in simile]* "progression of the same"

28. *Gogol]* Added in *Se*: I do not dare to name much greater names, but I mean them

29. *gloria]* "fame"

30. *faith.] Se*: superstition

31. *stupid]* Crossed out in *Se*.

32. *Knowledge about love] Pm*: higher human beings

33. *love . . . ignorant!] Pm*: love is and also knows him to be loving, whom no one on earth has loved

34. *things?]* *Pm*: possibilities; ⟨N's changes in *Se* were made with an eye toward *NCW*, "The Psychologist Speaks"⟩

35. *worlds]* *Pm* crossed out after this: of suffering and consequently of living

36. *hearts]* *Se* added: (the cynicism of Hamlet—the case of Galiani); cf. *NCW*, "The Psychologist Speaks"

37. *hands"]* Cf. Lessing, *Emilia Galotti*, I, 4; cf. *CW* 16:1[172].

38. Cf. *Z* II "On the Virtuous"; *CW* 14:1[92]; 3[1]4; 12[1]120.

39. *Pd*: When one has built a house he has usually learned something that he should have known before he started building.

40. *Pd* first version: Going his way without scorn and without love, but as a tempter and psychologist, with mute questions for all questionable ones, with slow eyes for everything that is admired, with a plumb line that returns to the light unsated from every depth———Wanderer, who are you? I see you going your way, without scorn, without love, tempting. Your gaze is inscrutable, your questions mute. Question:———I do not know. Perhaps Oedipus. Perhaps the sphinx. Let me go

41. *Pd*: Seize happiness and throttle, choke, suffocate it with his embrace: the melancholy of such experience—it would otherwise flee and slip away?

42. *contradictio in adjecto]* "contradiction in terms"

43. *Pd*: A perfect opportunity and occasion to be misunderstood: I have accustomed myself to give praise only where I do not agree. For in the other case—it seems to me—it would amount to praising myself: something, as is only fair, that we {expect} only among———

44. *Pd*: To live with a tremendous and proud composure: the affect arbitrary, at the right time, a useful foreground, dark glasses so that no one can look into our eyes.

45. *a . . . cleanliness]* *Pm*: a sublime kind of chastity

46. *"base."]* N uses *Gemeinschaft*, community, to underscore that its stem is the word *gemein*, meaning base, common, crude, vulgar, mean. Cf. note 23 above.

47. *the . . . greatest]* *Pm*: thoughts are

48. *spirit]* *Pm*: gaze

49. *Here . . . uplifting."*] *Faust II*, lines 11989–90; cf. *TI* "For-ays," 46. {A reference to the Eternal Feminine, which "lifts us up," but of which N was highly critical. See his poem "To Goethe" in *JS*, and the chapter "On Poets" in *Z* II.}

50. Cf. *CW* 16:35[76]; N's letter to Peter Gast, 23 July 1885 {*KGB* III:3, 68}.

51. *vertu est enthousiasme]* "Virtue is enthusiasm," from Galiani, *Lettres à Madame d'Epinay*, 2, 276.

52. *Pd*: How could anyone even believe that a philosopher ever expressed his genuine opinions in *books*? We write books in order to conceal what ⟨we⟩ — keep to ourselves.

53. *an . . . "grounds."*] *ein Abgrund hinter jedem Grunde, unter jeder "Begründung."*

54. *his . . . shovel]* *Pm*: I stop here and look around, that *here* I dig no deeper and lay aside my shovel

55. *But . . . sufferers!]* *Aber was liegt am Mitleiden Derer, welche leiden! Mitleiden*, to show compassion, to pity, vs. *leiden*, to suffer.

56. *to . . . German.]* *um es den Deutschen zu verdeutlichen.*

57. *Sd* first version: There are so many kinds of laughter: This is dedicated to all those who have the golden laughter.

58. *Hobbes]* {Cf. Thomas Hobbes, *Leviathan*, Part I, Chapter 6, Paragraph 42.}

59. Cf. *CW* 14:24[232]; *CW* 16:34[181].

60. *reverence:* —] *Sd*: reverence — a true smoke and fire sacrifice of youth, and even more smoke than fire!

61. {N is referring to *The Birth of Tragedy*, his first book pub-lication, which offers modernity's most sustained and original analysis of the role of Dionysus in pre-Socratic Greece.}

62. *god] Sd*: god [— and to be sure, as mentioned, from mouth to mouth — :] and perhaps for me too there will come a day of so much stillness and halcyon happiness that [I] my mouth will suddenly have to overflow from everything [I heard] I know — [in sum] that I will tell you, my friends, the ph⟨ilosophy⟩ of D⟨ionysus⟩

63. Title in *Sd*: *Mandarin Wisdom*: A Handful of [Wicked] Thoughts. *Preface and monologue*. *Pd*: Things I know too well and

too long, nothing but departing and exhausted thunderstorms, feelings that wilt and lose their scent: — thoughts [—butterflies lizards] I pinned down because they no longer pricked and plagued me anymore, something that even wanted to become "truth," I mean immortal and lethally boring at the same time ——— something still wondrous and colorful that began to take off its newness ——— cemeteries, where little wreaths stones and mounds, sheer death is supposed to remind us of what once lived

64. *copy . . . painting] abmalen, abschreiben*: the prefix *ab* changes the verbs to connote copying or transcribing from something.

65. *you . . . solitude] Sd*: as I for the first time conceived and experienced you, you sparks and lightning bolts of life!

66. *you . . . thoughts!] Sd*: You my invented and experienced *thoughts*!

67. Originated in autumn 1884 under the title "Hermit's Longing," sent at the end of November 1884 to Heinrich von Stein as "a reminder of Sils-Maria," where Stein had visited N from 26–28 August 1884; cf. "Chronicle" in *CW* 19. The two last strophes were added by N later (in spring 1886). The variants from the first version are designated as *HL* (= Hermit's Longing]. Cf. *CW* 15:28[26, 31]. Cf. also Karl Pestalozzi's interpretation in *Die Entstehung des lyrischen Ich* (Berlin{: de Gruyter,} 1970): 198–246.

68. *Is . . . delight? . . . . .] HL*: I've set a place for you, the tallest height: / Who lives so close / To stars, to light's abysmal distances? / *My* kingdom—I discovered it for me up here—/ And all this mine—was it not discovered for you? // Now even glacier's gray loves and lures you / With young roses, / The brook looks for you, the ardent wind presses, / Clouds strain higher into the blue today / Watch for you from bird's-eye view far away ———

69. *— You . . . good! . . . . .] HL*: A wicked *hunter* am I: — how the wood / Tenses in my bow! / Only the strongest archer can bend it so ——: / Beware! This arrow now, a mere child could / insert it: leave here now! For your own good! — // You *old* friends! Look! How pale and shocked are you, / Full of love and

fear! / No, leave! Don't be angry! You could not — live here! / Between remotest cliffs of icy blue — / Here you must be hunter and chamois too.

70. *What bond . . . to rot!]* *HL*: No longer friends — they are I know not what? / Merely ghosts of friends! / At night they haunt my house and my heart rends, // They speak to me, "we were friends, were we not?" / — Oh withered word, whose roses turned to rot! // And what bond we shared, young wishes' bond has passed — / Who can read the signs, / Once inscribed by love, these blurred and pallid lines? / This seems a parchment that my hand won't clasp / For *loathing* — brown and burnt, and fading fast!

71. *triumph]* *Pm*: happiness

72. *Zarathustra]* Zarathustra {without emphasis}

73. *guests!]* guests {without exclamation point}

74. *This . . . light . . . . .]* *missing in HL*; the drafts and final version of the last two strophes are included in notebook W I 8 (autumn 1885 to autumn 1886), *CW* 16:2. The drafts {which do not, in fact, appear in *KSA* 12/*CW* 16 but only in this note from *KSA* 14} are reproduced here in their entirety in verse form to give a better overview:

> The day [runs away] dies out, already happiness and light are fading
> Noon is far away
> [Recently I sat waiting here — *now* I wait no more]
> [So be it] [Already] Soon comes the cool night, the lightning of the stars
> [The hasty wind, who will break you from the tree]
> Like fruit broken from the tree by a hand
>
> What [I] recently wished, would I [now] like to have it today?
> What I awaited recently, alas [it] why did it not come?
> What do I wait and wait for still? I do not know —

Cf. also the poem fragment *CW* 16:45[7], as *Pd* of this strophe later not included:

> This song is done [; the]. Longing's sweet cry
> [Died on] Faded on my lips

[The true friend came] A wizard did it at the right time:
It was at noon, then One turned into Two
And—*Zarathustra* passed me by.

[Friend Zarath. came]
[Then came the friend—no!] ask not, who it was
There he stood before me—
A wizard [did it] came, the friend at the same right hour
The noon-friend—no! ask not, who it was
It was at noon, then One turned into two

Therewith the entirety of the first of the two concluding strophes
has been drafted; N harked back to the poem fragment in *CW*
14: 3[3] "Portofino" (cf. "Sils-Maria" in *JS* "Songs of Prince Free-
as-a-Bird," 1887); now he harks back in part to the motifs from
notebook W I 8:

Here I sat waiting, waiting—yet for nothing
You Zarathustra, you do not abandon me,
Friend Zarathustra

What was taken from me
You remain to me [friend and higher conscience] true to my
    higher conscience
You were my happiness and autumn

Friend Z. stay, do not leave me!
|What was taken from me, you [—] let me know|
[You remain true to me, my higher conscience!]
And if you did not stay how could I bear burden and duty?
[Friend Zarathustra stay, do not leave me]
Already the day nods, already happiness and light fade . . .
|Now I hang still and ripe in autumn light|
[Now I hang still in autumn sunlight]
Like fruit that a breath breaks from the tree

Nothing was taken from this draft; approaches to the final version are found on the page immediately following:

What I lost, that I will freely let go:
Now I want to know

[Yet you remain to me] You only remain to me, my higher
   conscience,
Friend Zarathustra [you do not leave me] — yes you do not
   leave me!

———————————————————————————————

What do I offer you, Zarathustra? Certainly,
[To the friend] You deserve the best!
A spectacle first, most pampered of guests!
And already it begins — look there! The curtain tore:
It is the marriage of light and darkness

On the following page finally the last version of the two concluding strophes, which scarcely deviate from the published
text.

On the Genealogy of Morality

The handwritten record of *Genealogy of Morality* is very fragmentary. It can be stated that — with the exception of a few pages
and fragmentary notes and their print manuscript in Nietzsche's
handwriting — all the drafts of this "polemic" have been lost. N
wrote them between 10 and 30 July 1887. The printing, as with
Beyond Good and Evil at N's own expense, lasted from the beginning of August until the end of October. The proofs (not preserved) were read by N and Peter Gast. From 21 September on, N
was also in Venice, where Peter Gast was staying; as Gast re-
ported, the five and a half remaining printer's sheets were finished by 19 October. On 12 November 1887 N received the first
copies from Leipzig: *On the Genealogy of Morality: A Polemic*,
(Leipzig: C. G. Naumann).

On the title page as motto in *Pm*: *Tout comprendre c'est
tout* — mépriser? . . . {"To understand all is to — *despise all*?" Cf.
tout comprendre c'est tout pardonner (to understand all is to forgive
all), used by N in *CW* 17:7[10] to criticize romantics and *l'art
pour l'art*. Cf. the note to *CW* 16:1[42] for N's possible source in
Germaine de Staël.} On the reverse side of the title page in the first
printing: Provided as a supplement and clarification of my recently published "*Beyond Good and Evil*"

Preface

1. *wherever . . . also]* Matthew 6:21.

2. *"each . . . himself"]* reversal of Terence, *Andria* IV, 1, 12: *Optimus sum egomet mihi* {I am closest to myself}.

3. *But . . . that!]* perhaps a variation of a quote from Heine, *Die Bäder von Lucca* {*The Baths of Lucca*}, chap. IV: "Mutter, was gehn Ihnen die jrine Beeme an?" {Berlin dialect: "Mother, what do you care about the green trees?"}

4. Cf. *CW* 12:28[7]; *CW* 15:25[525]; 26[390]; *CW* 16:38[19]; Goethe writes something similar about himself in *Fiction and Truth* VIII (at the end).

5. *half . . . heart]* *Faust I*, lines 3781–82 {spoken by the Evil Spirit to Margarete}.

6. {Here and in subsequent references, N refers to pages in the first editions of his works. We have replaced these page references with references to the section in the appropriate work.}

7. *toto coelo]* by the whole heavens, "diametrically"

8. *In . . . 33]* Cf. *HAH* 45, 92, 96, 100, 136; *MM* 89; *WS* 22, 26, 33; *D* 112.

9. *humankind]* Menschheit. In *GM*, I preserve the distinction between *Mensch* ("human") and *Menschheit* ("humankind"); I have also used "humanity" for *Menschen*.

10. *backward-looking]* Pm: nihilistic

11. *our . . . nihilism]* Pm: a European culture turned uncanny, as its detour—to nihilism? . . . To a new Buddhism, a Buddhism of the future

12. {Cf. Plato, *Republic* 606b; Spinoza, *Ethics* IIIp22s, IVp50c (in Definitions of the Emotions XVIII, Spinoza notes that there is no difference between pity [*commiseratio*] and compassion [*misericordia*]); La Rochefoucauld, *Réflexions ou sentences et maximes morales*, §264; Kant, *Metaphysics of Morals, Akademie* edition 6:456–57, and *Critique of Practical Reason, Akademie* edition 5:118.}

13. *I . . . feeling]* Pm: in all my writings, especially in the *Da⟨wn⟩* and the *Joy⟨ful⟩ Sci⟨ence⟩* heavily underlined

14. *unassuming . . . bites"]* Pm: petit bourgeois wimp and cultural philistine; ⟨corrected in unknown handwriting to:⟩ petit

bourgeois voluptuary and house-mouse 〈〈presumably in accordance with N's instructions to the publisher〉〉. 〈On 5 October 1887 {*KGB* III:5, 163} N wrote to his publisher, C. G. Naumann from Venice:〉 To be inserted as the *eighth* section of the *preface*: so that the last section now gets 9 as its number. / 8. / Finally, to at least point with a word to a tremendous and still completely undiscovered state of affairs that has slowly, slowly dawned on me: up till now there were no problems *more fundamental* than moral ones, it was their driving force from which all great conceptions in the realm of values so far have taken their origin (— thus everything that is commonly called "philosophy"; and this down to its final epistemological presupposition) *But there are problems still more fundamental than moral ones*: these are first glimpsed when moral prejudice is left *behind*, when one knows how to look into the world, into life as an *immoralist* . . . 〈Yet on the same day, 5 October 1887, N took these instructions back in the following postcard {*KGB* III:5, 163}〉: Most Esteemed Publisher, the manuscript revision I sent this morning (supplement to the preface) should **not** be used; we will therefore stay with the original arrangement, according to which the preface has 8 sections.

   15. *writings]* Crossed out after this in *Pm*: line for line

First Treatise

   1. *partie honteuse]* "shameful or private parts"
   2. *vis inertiae]* "force of inertia"
   3. Cf. *CW* 16:1[7, 10].
   4. *spirit]* *Pm*: sense
   5. *Herbert Spencer]* in *The Data of Ethics*; cf. *CW* 13:1[11].
   6. Cf. *CW* 13:3[134]; *D* 231.
   7. *"schlecht"]* "bad"
   8. *"schlicht"]* "plain"
   9. *"schlechtweg," "schlechterdings"]* "plainly, simply"
   10. *the . . . Buckle;]* Cf. N to Peter Gast, Chur, 20 May 1887 {*KGB* III:5, 79}: The library in Chur, ca. 20,000 volumes, provides me with a variety of edifying things. For the first time I saw the much celebrated book by Buckle, *Geschichte der Civilisation*

in England {2 vols. Trans. from the English by Arnold Ruge (Leipzig and Heidelberg: Winter, 1860, 1861). Henry Thomas Buckle, *History of Civilization in England* {London: John W. Parker and Son, 1857, 1861}"—and how odd! It turns out B⟨uckle⟩ is one of my strongest antagonists.

11. Cf. *CW* 15:25[472].

12. *Arya*] Sanskrit: "noble"

13. *Theognis*] ed. Diehl: I, 57, 71, 95, 189, 429, 441; cf. also *BGE* 260.

14. ἐσθλός] "good," "brave," "noble"

15. *Theognis*] ed. Diehl: I, 66–68, 607–10.

16. *noblesse*] "nobility"

17. κακός] "bad," "ugly"

18. δειλός] "cowardly," "worthless"

19. ἀγαθός] "good," "well-born," "noble"

20. *malus*] "bad," "evil"

21. μέλας] "black," "dark"

22. *hic niger est*] "he is black." Horace, *Satires*, I, 4, 85.

23. *fin*] Gaelic: "white"

24. *Virchow*] Source not identified.

25. *bonus*] "good"

26. *duonus*] older form of *bonus*

27. *unio mystica*] "mystical union"

28. *only . . . more!*] *Pm*: general sense of being fed up and longing for an *unio mystica*—be it with God, be it with nothingness—it is *one* longing——— {This translation does not usually italicize words N capitalizes for emphasis; here N's capitalization of *Ein* (*one*) warrants an exception.}

29. *"redeemer . . . disintegrator*] {*Erlöser* = redeemer, *Auflöser* (same stem verb) = dissolver, disintegrator.}

30. *sub hoc signo*] "under this sign"

31. *Quaeritur.*] "That is the question."

32. {*Freigeist*; as opposed to *der freie Geist* (the free spirit); cf. *BGE* 44.}

33. *ressentiment*] "resentment," here emphasized by N. Throughout *GM*, N uses the French spelling, though always with an initial capital, suggesting a partially germanicized loan word.

Though the word *Ressentiment* can today be found in German dictionaries, it was not included in Grimm's dictionary, and N's usage, taken from Dühring's *Der Werth des Lebens* (1865), seems to have introduced the term into German. German *Groll* is close, but neither *Groll* nor English *resentment* capture the nuance N brings to the term: when otherwise passive resentment becomes active and creates its own value system in order to compensate for its sense of inferiority, we have *Ressentiment*. For a useful explanation of how N's *Ressentiment* differs from Kierkegaard's "envy," which English translators have erroneously translated as *Ressentiment*, see Walter Kaufmann's introduction in Søren Kierkegaard, *The Present Age*, trans. Alexander Dru (New York: Harper & Row, 1962).

34. δειλός, δείλαιος, πονηρός, μοχΘηρός,] *deilos*: cowardly, worthless, vile; *deilaios*: wretched, paltry; *poneros*: wretched, oppressed by toils; *mochtheros*: suffering hardship, knavish

35. οϊζυρός, ἄνολβος, τλήμων, δυςτυχεῖν, ξυμφορά] *oizyros*: woeful, luckless; *anolbos*: wretched, unblessed; *tlemon*: wretched, miserable, enduring; *dystychein*: to be unlucky, unhappy; *xymphora*: misfortune

36. εὖ πράττειν] "to do well"

37. *he . . . honor!*] Cf. *Z* I "On War and Warriors."

38. *inter pares*] "among equals"

39. *the*] N emphasizes the definite article *die* here to point up a distinction between the definite article *das* in the preceding clause, which italicizing "the" would not get across.

40. *blond beast*] *Pm*: "blond beast" {within quotation marks}; cf. Detlef Brennecke, "Die blonde Bestie. Vom Mißverständnis eines Schlagworts," *Nietzsche-Studien* 5 (1976): 113–45.

41. *to . . . bad"]* Thucydides II, 41.

42. *Pericles]* Cf. Thucydides II, 39.

43. ῥαΘυμία] "carelessness," "indifference. {Thucydides, II, 39.}

44. *blond Teutonic beast]* *Pm*: "blond Teutonic beast" {within quatation marks}

45. *I . . . attention]* Cf. *D* 189; Hesiod, *Works and Days* 143–73.

46. *blond beast]* *Pm*: "blond beast" {within quotation marks}

47. *faith]* Crossed out after this in *Pm*: the will to a future

48. *that . . . lambs.]* Cf. *Z* IV "The Song of Melancholy" 3; *DD* "Just a Fool! Just a Poet!"

49. *They . . . do]* Luke 23:24.

50. *love . . . enemies]* Matthew 5:44.

51. *and sweating]* Cf. *Z* II "On Scholars."

52. *God . . . honored]* Cf. Romans 13:1.

53. *Homer]* Iliad 18, 109.

54. *brothers in love]* 1 Thessalonians 3:12.

55. *in . . . hope]* Cf. 1 Thessalonians 1:3. {Cf. also 1 Corinthians 13:13.}

56. *eternal . . . me]* Divine Comedy, Inferno III, 5–6.

57. *Thomas Aquinas]* Commentary on the Sentences IV, L 2, 4, 4.

58. {"The blessed in the kingdom of heaven will see the punishments of the damned *in order that their bliss be more delightful to them." Summa Theologica* III, *Supplementum* Q. 94, Art. 1.}

59. Tertullian, *De Spectaculis*, ch. 30. English translation by Rev. S. Thewell in *Ante-Nicene Christian Library: Translation of the Writings of the Fathers, Down to AD 325.* Vol. 11: The Writings of Tertullian. Vol. 1, ed. Rev. Alexander Roberts and James Donaldson (Edinburgh: T. & T. Clark, 1869), 34–35: "Yes, and there are other sights: that last day of judgment, with its everlasting issues; that day unlooked for by the nations, the theme of their derision, when the world, hoary with age, and all its many products, shall be consumed in one great flame! How vast a spectacle then bursts upon the eye! *What there excites my admiration? what my derision? Which sight gives me joy? which rouses me to exultation?*—as I see so many illustrious *monarchs*, whose reception into the heavens was publicly announced, groaning now in the lowest darkness with great Jove himself, and those, too, who bore witness of their exaltation; governors of provinces, too, who persecuted the Christian name, in fires more fierce than those with which in the days of their pride they raged against the followers of Christ! What world's wise men besides, the very philosophers, in fact, who taught their followers that God had no concern in ought that is sublunary, and were wont to assure them that either they had no souls, or that they would never return to the bodies which at death they had left, now covered

with shame before the poor deluded ones, as one fire consumes them! Poets also, trembling not before the judgment-seat of Rhadamanthus or Minos, but of the unexpected Christ! I shall have a better opportunity then of hearing the tragedians, louder-voiced in their own calamity; of viewing the play-actors, much more 'dissolute' in the dissolving flame; of looking upon the charioteer, all glowing in his chariot of fire; of witnessing the wrestlers, not in their gymnasia, but tossing in the fiery billows; unless even then I shall not care to attend to such ministers of sin, in my eager wish rather to fix a gaze *insatiable* on those whose fury vented itself against the Lord. 'This,' I shall say, 'this is that carpenter's or harlot's son, that Sabbath-breaker, that Samaritan and devil-possessed! This is He whom you purchased from Judas! This is He whom you struck with reed and fist, whom you contemptuously spat upon, to whom you gave gall and vinegar to drink! This is He whom His disciples secretly stole away, that it might be said He had risen again, or the gardener abstracted, that his lettuces might come to no harm from the crowds of visitants!' What quæstor or priest in his munificence will bestow on you the favor of seeing and *exulting in such things as these*? And yet even now we in a measure have them by *faith* in the picturings of imagination. But what are the things which eye has not seen, and ear has not heard, and which have not so much as dimly dawned upon the human heart? Whatever they are, they are nobler, I believe, than circus, and both theatres, and every race-course."

60. *vivos]* erratum for *visos*, as already noted by Maurice de Gandillac in his commentary: cf. Nietzsche, *Œuvres philosophiques complètes* (French translation of *KGW*), *Par-delà bien et mal. La généalogie de la morale*, Paris{: Gallimard,} 1971, 392f. The transcription by Overbeck, who sent this passage to N in Sils-Maria in July 1887, has not been preserved.

61. *Per fidem]* "by [my] faith"

62. *convicted . . . race"]* Cf. Tacitus, *Annals* XV, 44.

63. *Chinese] Pm*: Indians

64. *ad acta]* "to the files (shelved)"

Second Treatise

1. *vis inertiae]* "force of inertia"

2. *"ensouling"] Einverseelung* (stem noun: soul, psyche, or anima) coined to correspond with *Einverleibung* (stem noun: body; thus embodiment).

3. *tabula rasa]* "blank slate"

4. {When N refers to his earlier works, he does so by page numbers in the first edition; here and elsewhere, we have replaced his page numbers with section numbers.}

5. {Cf. Albert Hermann Post, *Bausteine für eine allgemeine Rechtswissenschaft auf vergleichend-ethnologischer Basis* ("Building Blocks for a General Jurisprudence on a Comparative-Ethnological Basis"), 2 vols. (Oldenburg: Schulze, 1880–81), I: 191–98, where Post chronicles various sorts of punishments, including those N mentions here. *NL.*}

6. *origin] Herkunft*

7. *"guilt" . . . "debt"?] Schuld* (guilt) here juxtaposed with *Schulden* (debts); cf. the verb *schulden*, meaning "to owe."

8. {Cf. Josef Kohler, *Das Recht als Kulturerscheinung. Einleitung in die vergleichende Rechtswissenschaft* ("Law as a Cultural Phenomenon: Introduction to Comparative Jurisprudence") (Würzburg: Stahel, 1885), 18–19. *NL.*}

9. *Twelve Tables]* {Responding to demands by the plebeians, Rome's patricians made public those laws based on custom that had previously been known only to them. The laws were posted in the Forum on twelve tablets, and represent the earliest European efforts to provide a legal code.}

10. *"si plus minusve secuerunt, ne fraude esto."]* "if more or less is secured, let it be no crime."

11. *de . . . faire.]* {"doing evil for the pleasure of doing it"} Cf. P{rosper} Mérimée, *Lettres à une inconnue* {"Letters to an Unknown Woman"}, Paris{: Michel Lévy Frères}, 1874, I, 8; same quotation in *HAH* 50. *NL.*

12. *itself . . . compensation?]* is only a spice, an ingredient in this respect, it is not what is essential in that pleasure

13. *sympathia malevolens]* "malevolent sympathy" {Cf. Harald Höffding: *Psychologie in Umrissen auf Grundlage der Erfahrung*

("Psychology in Outline on the Basis of Experience"), trans. from the Danish by F. Bendixen (Leipzig: Fues [R. Reisland], 1887), 319, where Höffding cites Spinoza's *Ethics*, III, 32 schol. *NL*.}

14. {N refers to pages 117ff., which would bring us to the middle of section 194; *KSA* 14 points us to sections 197ff. Both of these have little to do with the spiritualization of cruelty. Walter Kaufmann suggests that "117ff." was a misprint for "177ff.," i.e., section 229, which does indeed focus on cruelty.}

15. *think . . . death]* Cf. *CW* 12:23[140].

16. *"impure . . . feces."]* {*De Miseria Condicionis Humane* ("On the Misery of the Human Condition"), 1195.}

17. *"les nostalgies de la croix"]* "the nostalgias of the cross"

18. *Homer]* Cf. *MM* 189.

19. *manas]* Sanskrit: "mind"

20. *man]* der Mensch, which I translate here as "man" only to preserve the linkage with "man is the measure of all things."

21. {"misery", but in Old High German, "exiled" or "banished."}

22. *mimus]* {Emphasized by N.}

23. *vae victis!]* "Woe to the conquered!" Livy, *Ab Urbe Condita*, V, 48, 9.

24. *compositio]* "legal settlement"

25. *therefore . . . isolating]* Pm: and this also as much as possible with respect to the direct damages

26. *beyond-the-law]* Jenseits des Rechts. N is playing *Vorrecht* ("prerogative") off of *Jenseits des Rechts*.

27. {Eugen Dühring: *Der Werth des Lebens. Eine philosophische Betrachtung* ("The Value of Life. A Philosophical Reflection") (Breslau: Eduard Trewendt, 1865); *Cursus der Philosophie* [*Cursus der Philosophie als streng wissenschaftlicher Weltanschauung und Lebensgestaltung*] (Leipzig: Erich Koschny, 1875). *NL*.}

28. *"the . . . efforts."]* E. Dühring, *Sache, Leben und Feinde* {"Cause, Life and Enemies"}, Karlsruhe and Leipzig{: H. Reuther}, 1882, 283. *NL*.

29. *sign . . . nothingness]* Pm: a secret path to nihilism

30. *Here . . . separately]* Pm first version: In every kind of history eventually a viewpoint is produced that in itself is extremely

offensive to intellectual justice:—it is perhaps our greatest triumph over the *vis inertiae* of the human intellect

31. *causa fiendi]* "cause of the origin"

32. *toto coelo]* "by the whole heavens," "diametrically"

33. *counter-actions]* Pm crossed out after this: of spontaneous attacks, interferences, efforts on the part of the thing that is developing. The thing, as a quantum of organized force, must for its part move from the inside to the outside, as weak as it may be, in order to animate and enrich itself on this "outside," in order to take it into itself and to impress *its* law, *its* meaning on it. Even———

34. *Huxley]* {Thomas Henry Huxley, *More Criticism on Darwin, and Administrative Nihilism* (New York: Appleton, 1872); cf. also "Administrative Nihilism [1871]" in *Collected Essays I: Method and Results* (London: Macmillan, 1893), 251–89.}

35. *per analogiam]* "by analogy"

36. *according to Chinese law]* Cf. J. Kohler, *Das chinesische Strafrecht. Ein Beitrag zur Universalgeschichte des Strafrechts* ("Chinese Criminal Law: A Contribution to the Universal History of Criminal Law"), Würzburg{: Stahel}, 1886. *NL.*

37. *Fischer]* N's source on Spinoza; cf. the note to *CW* 13:11[193] {Kuno Fischer, *Geschichte der neuern Philosophie I, 2, Descartes' Schule. Geulinx, Malebranche. Baruch Spinoza.* 2nd ed. (Heidelberg: Friedrich Bassermann, 1865).}

38. *morsus conscientiae]* "sting [literally: bite] of conscience"

39. *sub ratione boni]* "for a good reason"

40. *"but . . . absurdities."]* Spinoza, *Ethics* I, 33, schol. 2.

41. *gaudium]* "joy"

42. *Heraclitus]* fragment 52 (Diels–Kranz).

43. *state-building force]* Pm: , but turned outward

44. *"labyrinth of the breast"]* Cf. Goethe, "To the Moon."

45. *everything . . . synthesis,]* Pm: the entire actuality of the final rank order of all elements of the people in every great synthesis of peoples

46. *causa prima]* "first cause"

47. *Odyssey* I, 32–34.

48. *reality . . . come . . .]* Pm: becomes . . . This human of the future who will redeem us from previous ideals, the conqueror of God *must* come some day ⟨later revised by adding § 25⟩

Third Treatise

1. This section was added later; §2 was the beginning of the Third Treatise in *Pm*.

2. *morbidezza]* "softness," "delicacy"

3. *novissima gloriae cupido]* "newest lust for glory." Tacitus, *Histories*, IV, 6.

4. *horror vacui]* "horror of a vacuum/void"

5. *Luther's wedding]* {N refers here to Wagner's unperformed 1868 sketch *Luthers Hochzeit* ("Luther's Wedding").}

6. *Meistersinger]* {*Die Meistersinger von Nürnberg* (The Mastersingers of Nuremberg), 1868, was Wagner's only comedic opera.}

7. {Cf. note 24 to *BGE* 198.}

8. *Feuerbach's . . . sensuality"]* {Cf. *CW* 17:7[4], where N writes: "*Feuerbach's* 'healthy and fresh sensuality,' / 'Principles of *the* Philosophy of the Future' 1843, / against 'abstract philosophy.'" N takes this comment, and the phrase "healthy and fresh sensuality," from Kuno Fischer, *Geschichte der neuern Philosophie*, vol. I, part 2: *Descartes' Schule: Geulincx, Malebranche, Baruch Spinoza* (Heidelberg: Bassermann, 1865), 561. The Fischer volume is not in *Nietzsches persönliche Bibliothek*, and Thomas Brobjer (*Nietzsche's Philosophical Context* [Urbana: University of Illinois Press, 2008], 80) points out that Overbeck sent him a library copy.}

9. *young Germans]* {*Junges Deutschland* ("Young Germany") was a progressive literary movement of the 1830s and 1840s whose proponents championed liberal causes during the repressive Metternich era; both anticlassical and antiromantic, its writers included, among others, Heinrich Heine, Karl Gutzkow, and Georg Büchner.}

10. *"blood . . . Redeemer"]* {Wagner refers to the "Blood of the Redeemer" in *Religion und Kunst* ("Religion and Art," 1880). See Richard Wagner, *Gesammelte Schriften und Dichtungen* (Leipzig: Fritsch, 1883), vol. 10, 357. *NL*.}

11. *hostile . . . rigor] Pm*: ruthless departure from all brightness and magnificence

12. *contiguity,]* N's English.

13. *a . . . Faust.]* Cf. *HAH* 211.

14. *Let . . . they]* Se: In the end, what does it matter! — The gentlemen artists

15. *And . . . above?]* Crossed out by N in *Se*.

16. *Richard Wagner . . . Herwegh]* Cf. R. Wagner, *Mein Leben*, ed. Martin Gregor-Dellin. Munich{: List,} 1969, 521f. N knew Wagner's autobiography from the private edition in three volumes printed in Basel: Part 1 (1813–1842) 1870; Part 2 (1842–1850) 1872; Part 3 (1850–1862) 1875. Part 4 (1861–1864) was printed in Bayreuth in 1880 and would have remained unknown to him; cf. Martin Gregor-Dellin's afterword to his edition.

17. *in majorem musicae gloriam]* "to the greater glory of music"; a pun on the motto of the Jesuits, "ad majorem Dei gloriam" (to the greater glory of God).

18. Cf. *CW* 15:25[154].

19. {Cf. Kant, *Critique of Judgment*, §59: "[The beautiful] pleases *apart from any interest*."}

20. *Stendhal . . . bonheur]* Cf. Stendhal, *Rome, Naples et Florence*, Paris{: Michel Lévy Frères,} 1854, 30, *NL*: "La beauté n'est jamais, ce me semble, qu'une *promesse de bonheur*." {"Beauty, it seems to me, is only ever *a promise of happiness*."}

21. *le désintéressement.]* "disinterestedness"

22. *"instrumentum diaboli"]* "instrument of the Devil"

23. *remedium]* "medicine"

24. *la bête philosophe]* "the philosophical animal"

25. *"passeth all understanding"]* {Cf. Philippians 4:7.}

26. *Râhula . . . me]* Cf. H{ermann} Oldenberg, *Buddha. Sein Leben, seine Lehre, seine Gemeinde* {"Buddha: His Life, His Teaching, His Community"}, Berlin{: Hertz,} 1881, 122. *NL*.

27. *narrowly . . . house.]* Oldenberg, 124.

28. *pereat mundus, fiat philosophia, fiat philosophus, **fiam**! . . .]* "Let the world perish, let there be philosophy, let there be philosophers, *let there be me*! . . ."

29. *"**sine** ira et studio"]* "*without* anger and partiality"; Tacitus, *Annals*, I, 1.

30. *Lady Shrewdness]* *Fraw Klüglin*

31. *"nitimur in **vetitum**"]* "We strive for *the forbidden*"; Ovid, *Amores*, III, 4, 17.

32. *"je combats l'universelle araignée"]* "I combat the universal spider"

33. *violate . . . living?]* *Pm*: crack around on us today, like nutcrackers of the soul, as if we were nothing but nuts and riddles; what is certain is that *precisely* with this we are daily becoming more enigmatic to ourselves, that we love life itself ever more tenderly for the sake of our riddle-man nature— *learn* to love it!

34. *jus primae noctis]* "right of the first night," i.e., right of rulers to deflower the wives of their subjects on the wedding night.

35. *vetitum]* "something forbidden"

36. {N has changed one word from the passage as it appears in *D* (in the first sentence, *"welches"* becomes *"was"*), and in *D*, "actual . . . humankind" is emphasized, while "change" is not. In this passage cited from *CW* 5, *Sittlichkeit der Sitte* is translated "morality of mores"; elsewhere in this volume, it has been translated "morality of custom."}

37. *I . . . heaven]* Cf. *D* 113.

38. *Crux, nux, lux]* "Cross, nut, light"; cf. *CW* 13:12[231].

39. *what? . . . castrating]* *Pm*: that would mean castrating the intellect— Even worse: it would mean— not thinking!

40. Cf. *CW* 16:1[7, 10].

41. *homines bonae voluntatis]* "men of good will"; cf. Luke 2:14 in the Latin Vulgate translation.

42. *hyena"]* {Cf. Post, *Bausteine für eine allgemeine Rechtswissenschaft auf vergleichend-ethnologischer Basis*, I, 67.}

43. *further]* Crossed out after this in *Pm*: often enough even without awareness of pain even if [———]

44. *nervus sympathicus]* "sympathetic nerve"

45. *deficiency . . . phosphate]* Cf. *CW* 13:11[244]; 12[31].

46. *One thing is needful]* Luke 10:42.

47. *back . . . guilt]* Cf. *JS* 250.

48. {Literally: world pain or grief; in cultural and intellectual history, a romantic suffering from the world; in general emotional terms, sadness at the state of the world. Cf. Goethe's *The Sufferings of Young Werther*.}

49. *vegetarians]* N's English.

50. *Andrew]* Crossed out after this in *Pm*: I am a great eater of beef, I believe [———] {N uses "Squire Christopher" instead

of "Sir Andrew" based on the standard German translation of *Twelfth Night* by August Wilhelm Schlegel.}

51. *Sir . . . Shakespeare]* in *Twelfth Night* I, 3 {where Sir Andrew explains: "I am a / great eater of beef and I believe that does harm to my wit"}.

52. *"il faut s'abêtir."]* "One needs to make oneself stupid."

53. *winter sleep . . . summer sleep]* {The technical terms are "hibernation" (*Winterschlaf*) and "estivation" (*Sommerschlaf*), but more literal translations are preserved here because *der tiefe Schlaf,* deep sleep, is emphasized in the conclusion of this section.}

54. *An . . . vain?]* Pm: The procedures of most of the desert-saints, by the way, are aimed at this sleep—and many of them attained it—at absolute boredom that is no longer perceived as boredom, rather as nothingness, as the feeling of nothingness [———]

55. *sportsmen]* N's English.

56. *training]* N's English.

57. *Mount Athos]* {Mount Athos, or Holy Mountain, in northern Greece, has been the site of Greek and Slavic Orthodox monasteries since 963 CE. The *Hesychasts* were quietist monks.}

58. Cf. Oldenberg, *Buddha*, 50.

59. *over-moralized]* vermoralisirt

60. *Paul Deussen]* N is referring here to *Das System des Vedânta*, Leipzig{: Brockhaus,} 1883, *NL*; *Die Sûtra's des Vedânta aus dem Sanskrit übersetzt von Paul Deussen,* Leipzig{: Brockhaus,} 1887. *NL.*

61. {Cf. Deussen, *Die Sûtra's des Vedânta,* 154, 510, 518.}

62. {Cf. Deussen, *Das System des Vedânta,* 199.}

63. *"incuria sui"]* "neglect of oneself"

64. *"despectio sui"]* "self-contempt" {Cf. Fischer, *Geschichte der neuern Philosophie,* 26.}

65. *the . . . Geulincx]* Cf. *CW* 13:11[194].

66. *Plato] Republic* 414 b–c; 382 c; 389 b; 459 c–d; *Laws* 663 e.

67. εἰς ἑαυτόν] "about or against himself"

68. *Byron . . . Wagner:]* Cf. *Lord Byron's Vermischte Schriften,* trans. E{rnst} Ortlepp, Stuttgart{: Scheible, 1830?} *NL*; W{ilhelm} Gewinner, *Arthur Schopenhauer aus persönlichem Umgange dargestellt*

{"Arthur Schopenhauer Portrayed from Personal Acquaintance"},
Leipzig{: Brockhaus,} 1862; A{lexander} W{heelock} Thayer,
Ludwig van Beethoven's Leben, Berlin{: Ferdinand Schneider,}
1866 ff. For Richard Wagner's autobiography, cf. note 16 above.

69. *Janssen]* J{ohann} Janssen, *Geschichte des deutschen Volks
seit dem Mittelalter* {"History of the German People since the
Middle Ages"}, Freiburg{: Herder,} 1877; N bought this work on
31 December 1878, but it is not among his books in *NL*. Concerning Janssen, cf. N to Peter Gast on 5 October 1879 {*KGB* II:5, 451}.

70. *causa fortior]* "stronger cause"

71. *diplomat]* Talleyrand; cf. *CW* 17, 10[78].

72. *out of joint,]* {N is most likely alluding here to August
Wilhelm Schlegel's German translation of "the time is out of
joint" ("*die Zeit ist aus den Fugen*") from *Hamlet* (1798).}

73. *my . . . world!]* John 18:36.

74. *Goethe]* to Eckermann, 14 February 1830 {Eckermann's
Conversations with Goethe}.

75. *"evviva la morte"]* "long live death"

76. *Quaeritur.]* "That is the question."

77. *magno sed proxima intervallo.]* "next but by a great distance"
{Cf. Vergil, *Aeneid*, 5, 320.}

78. *in artibus et litteris]* "in arts and letters"

79. *"Here . . . otherwise."]* {Luther's famous words at the Diet
of Worms, 1521, where he refused to recant his ideas and teachings as expressed in part in his Ninety-Five Theses.}

80. *I . . . taste.]* like Julien Sorel in Stendhal's *Le Rouge et le
noir*; cf. *CW* 15:25[169].

81. *"the crown of eternal life"]* {Cf. Revelation 2:10.}

82. *God]* In German, God is addressed using the familiar
second-person pronoun *Du*, "thou" in archaic English (as in the
Bible, the Lord's Prayer, etc.). This archaic "thou" is also used in
poetry.

83. *"non plus ultra."]* "highest of its kind."

84. Cf. *CW* 15:25[304, 340]; 26[225].

85. *secretum]* "privileged information"

86. *factum **brutum**]* "mere fact"

87. *"petits faits" (ce petit faitalisme]* "small facts" (that petty factalism {N puns here with "fatalism."}

88. *females]* In German, the words for "philosophy" (*die Philosophie*) and "truth" (*die Wahrheit*) are both grammatically feminine.

89. In *JS* 344, "longest lie" is not italicized and is followed by an em dash.

90. *"poor in spirit"]* {Cf. Matthew 5:3.}

91. {Cf. Immanuel Kant, *Critique of Practical Reason*, in *Practical Philosophy*, ed. Mary J. Gregor (Cambridge: Cambridge University Press, 1996), Conclusion, 269: "The first view of a countless multitude of worlds annihilates, as it were, my importance as an *animal creature*, which after it has been for a short time provided with vital force (one knows not how) must give back to the planet (a mere speck in the universe) the matter from which it came."}

92. *"l'habitude **d'admirer** l'inintelligible au lieu de rester tout simplement dans l'inconnu"]* "the habit of *admiring* the unintelligible instead of remaining quite simply in the unknown" {Cf. Ximénès Doudan, *Lettres* (Paris: Calmann Lévy, 1879), III, 24.}

93. *elegantia syllogismi!]* "elegance of syllogism!"

94. *metapolitics . . . compassion."]* *Pm*: metaphysics and Dostoevsky

95. *sweet ingenious]* *Pm*: sweet cowards

96. *truly . . . proletariat.]* *Pm* first version: listen for once to that poor screaming devil of an agitator (like that [poor communist] Dühring who, by slobbering over the whole of history, wants to persuade us in this manner that he is its "historian" [just as much as its] and "Judgment Day" [likewise that his slobber means justice itself]

97. χάσμ' ὀδόντων] "chasm of teeth" *Anacreontea*, 24.

98. *whited sepulchres]* {Cf. Matthew 23:27.}

99. {German national anthem refrain based on Hoffmann von Fallersleben's poem "Das Lied der Deutschen."}

100. *paralysis agitans]* "shaking palsy"

101. *diet . . . ideas."]* *Pm* second version: ideas, the *paralysis agitans* of modern ideas that calls itself "progress," the democratization to which Germany has now fallen victim along with all of Europe's countries: an incurable disease!

102. *either, . . . everywhere.]* Pm first version: nor the [piously eloquent idealists] speculators in "idealism," who today roll their eyes with a Christian-German-anti-Semitic pathos and [cleverly enough] want to cloak their [bad instincts] [little] worms and private matters, envy, [coarseness, wounded vanity] spasms of vanity and incurable mediocrity through a display of disdainful moral attitudes (— that *no* kind of swindle spirit fails to succeed in today's Germany is connected to the virtually undeniable and already palpable [dumbing down and] *desolation* of the German spirit, whose cause I [may seek] seek in an all-too-exclusive diet of newspapers, politics, beer and Wagnerian music, along with what provides the prerequisite for this diet, the whole national-patriotic [neurosis] hysteria which has now sickened Germany along with all countries in Europe and *above all* Germany. *Cette race douce énergique meditative et passionée* {that gentle energetic meditative passionate race [another quotation from Doudan]} — where has it gone! where have the Germans gone! . . .) The idealistic swindle ruins the air not only in Germany; today it ruins the air throughout Europe — Europe today is in an embarrassing manner terribly in foul-smelling — — —

103. *la religion de la souffrance]* "the religion of suffering" {Cf. *BGE* 21, where N also quotes these final words of Paul Bourget's novel *Un crime d'amour* (1886).}

104. *needful,]* {Cf. note to *GM* III, note 46 above.}

105. *a . . . preparing]* Pm: my main work currently in progress

106. *femininism]* Femininismus. At the time, both "*Feminismus*" and "*Femininismus*" were in use, although the former was more common.

107. {In *JS* 357, "good" is italicized but "Europeans" is not.}

108. *"patere legem, quam ipse tulisti."]* "submit to the law you yourself proposed."

109. *" faute de mieux"]* "for lack of anything better"

110. *counterwill]* Widerwille, aversion or strong reluctance; "counterwill" preserves the stem noun *Wille*.

Afterword to *Beyond Good and Evil* and *On the Genealogy of Morality*

Giorgio Colli

A philosopher who has the feeling that he has not yet fully realized himself—he has spoken about the Greeks, spoken up as a psychologist, moralist, and historian and finally with *Thus Spoke Zarathustra* reached a poetic high point but wants to assert himself also in the theoretical sphere—strives perhaps even with systematic intent to issue laws concerning the principles of existence. This philosopher is Nietzsche in his final period of creativity, as he begins to show himself in *Beyond Good and Evil*. Already the earlier writings, above all those unpublished, had revealed this ambition especially in the sphere of epistemology. Whereas in his theory of morals the polemic against Schopenhauer now sharpens further, it retreats in the sphere of theoretical inquiry, where Nietzsche shelves a few hard-won results, such as the primacy of the intellect over will and feeling. Nevertheless, other anti-Schopenhauerian themes remain, and the significant critique of the concept of "subject" is continued in *Beyond Good and Evil* and in the *Genealogy of Morality*. And yet one notices a renewed convergence with Schopenhauer (not for nothing does Nietzsche write in §5 of the Preface to the *Genealogy of Morality* of his "great teacher Schopenhauer") and even with metaphysics, for the reduction of all reality to the idea of "will to power," through which the *principium individuationis* is governed, this tracing back of all qualities to a single, albeit multiform, root, is a metaphysical position despite Nietzsche's intention to the contrary.

The construction of a "system" of will to power begins precisely at this time, and the first elaboration of this unifying substance—albeit beholden to Nietzsche's unique concrete method of observing the historical world—exists not without difficulty alongside the moral condemnation of metaphysical philosophers who in the third treatise of the *Genealogy of Morality* are accused of having promoted the hegemony of ascetic ideals. The relatedness of the new philosophical principle of the "will to power" with the Schopenhauerian principle of the "will to life" is obvious and indisputable (Nietzsche says so himself); indeed, the former turns out to be a variant of the latter. The core of both conceptions is the same, and Schopenhauer's principle was just as immanent in kind as Nietzsche's: in both cases we are dealing with an irrational substance that is in us (all theology has been overcome) and in which we participate through direct apprehension. The difference lies only in that Schopenhauer rejects this substance and wants to deny it, while Nietzsche, on the other hand, accepts and wants to affirm it. Thus Nietzsche's originality does not lie in the principle itself but in the reaction to the principle, in his stance on it, which for that matter goes back to the time of *Birth of Tragedy*. As he now enters the final phase of his creativity, which initially displays considerable composure with the beginning of *Beyond Good and Evil* (observe the frugal doses of pathos, whose intensity only rises in the final pages), Nietzsche again takes up this theme whose symbolic expression is found in the Greek god of tragedy.

Of course Dionysus is no longer an aesthetic symbol but appears now on an ethical-theoretical level. For Nietzsche resists carrying out a theoretical or even metaphysical investigation using the commensurate concepts. This is attempted only in his unpublished notes from the period after 1884. The elaboration of the philosophical concept "will to power" in *Beyond Good and Evil*, the *Genealogy of Morality*, and even later relies henceforth on his experiences as moralist and psychologist and avails itself, as is only to be expected, of images and concepts created earlier. Dionysus now, in *Beyond Good and Evil*, becomes the one who knows that the nature of the world is will to power ("that Dionysus is a philosopher and that gods therefore also philosophize," *BGE* 295). He accepts this, wills this to be so. The moral stance completes the theoretical sounding of the problem, which therefore cannot remain isolated. In this manner the philosophical investigation also continues to be linked to the sphere of affects. The philosophical principle is veiled by the manner in which the philosopher "perceives" it.

In *Beyond Good and Evil* and the *Genealogy of Morality* the concept of suffering, along with the ideas connected to or deriving from it, becomes a touchstone for the philosophy of "will to power." Here too Schopenhauer determines the interpretation: the emphasis with which this philosopher inserts suffering into the image of life was for Nietzsche a youthful experience (suffering is an essential component of the Dionysian conception of *Birth of Tragedy*) from which he never could free himself. With the rise of the metaphysics of the will to power, suffering, along with everything connected to it, becomes a mediator enabling Nietzsche to transfer the discussion to the sphere of historical becoming. In fact it is difficult to speak of will to power in itself, yet from the viewpoint of suffering, of judging *on suffering*, it becomes possible to observe the moral reaction to the metaphysical impulse.

The will to power is accompanied by suffering—this is the terrible realization that Nietzsche calls "Dionysian." Every morality, every worldview that wants to shut off suffering—and this applies not only for Buddhism and for Schopenhauer but for everything that Nietzsche characterizes with the attribute decadent, including the democratic movement of "modern ideas"—therefore also rejects the will to power, hence life itself. The weakness of modernity, its decadence, lies "in lethal hatred for suffering generally, in [their] almost feminine inability to remain spectators and to *let* suffering be" (*BGE* 202). On the other hand stands the Dionysian position: "You want [. . .] *to abolish suffering*; and we? — it seems as though *we* would prefer to have it even higher and worse than it ever was!" (*BGE* 225). The substance of the world must not be veiled or sanctimoniously concealed; and if there is something terrible in the abyss of life, then the "pathos of truth" requires us to make it known. "[W]hat constitutes the most character-istic feature of modern souls [. . .] is [. . .] their ingrained *innocence* in moralistic mendacity" (*GM* III 19). For worse than those who would deny life in the face of the abyss are those who close their eyes to it and would have you believe that suf-fering does not exist at all deep down and we can steer clear of it. "[T]hey belong to the *levelers*, these wrongly designated 'free spirits' [. . .] only they are quite unfree and ridiculously superficial, especially with their fundamental tendency to more or less see the cause of *all* human misery and failure in the forms of the previous old society [. . .] — and suffering itself is construed by them as something that must be *abol-ished*" (*BGE* 44).

This thematic of suffering also sheds light on the sharp antithesis between master morality and slave morality as it is developed above all in the *Genealogy of Morality*. Here too Nietzsche is driven by his "truthfulness" fanaticism, that is, the impulse to demonstrate the suffering of the world to the last (even if one cannot overlook certain inconsistencies and shrill tones in which the exposing of wounds that would cause shame for civilized human beings switches over to uncon-trolled glorification). The famous thesis of the "blond beast," of aggressive violence on which every master morality bases itself, means that human society is based on terrible crimes, and that it will always be so. Dionysus commands that this truth be spoken without disguise and simultaneously accepted and affirmed. It is the same view of reality that is demon-strated by Thucydides in the dialogue between the Melians and the envoys from Athens. Nietzsche praises violence just as little as Thucydides does. The Athenians who exterminate the inhabitants of Melos with ruthless cruelty are the same ones — that is, Athenians of the same generation — praised by Pericles in his funeral oration as the educators of Greece, as the friends of the beautiful and of wisdom. For Nietzsche, not to want to see this means either to deny life generally or to testify falsely about the principle of life. Herd morality for its part is based on hatred and revenge, whereas its culture, which rejects suffering, embarks on the path of decadence and nihilism. Such a claim may be false if considered only as historical interpretation, but the significance of Nietzsche's theory lies in the "truthful" relationship to the essence of the world and in the Dionysian demand to accept the suffering that can only be suppressed *along* with life — when we interpret it as the kind of life from which Greek tragedy or the philosophy of Dionysus emerges.

The theme of suffering therefore winds through the work like a red thread; perhaps it does not get noticed right away, yet in reality it connects the different themes Nietzsche treats here and illuminates the new course of his thoughts. It is a discursive reflection of that unsettling knowledge that in *Thus Spoke Zarathustra* carries over into the motif of the "eternal recurrence." The modern world's assessment of suffering is used by Nietzsche to deduce his own assessment of this world, which though unhistorical is elemental. For this he dissects the different expressions of suffering and the reactions to it — one can say he runs the entire circuit of suffering. In this manner he returns to the realm of analysis that characterized the works written before *Zarathustra*, and in this investigation he anticipates several important results of his later psychology. This is above all the case in the second and third treatises of the *Genealogy of Morality*, that is, in the thesis of active forgetfulness ("Forgetfulness is not merely a *vis inertiae* [. . .]; rather, it is an active, positive faculty of repression in the strictest sense, which is accountable for the fact that whatever we experience, learn or take in [. . .] is able to enter our consciousness

just as little" (*GM* II 1); of the internalization of instincts ("All
instincts that do not discharge themselves externally now *turn
inward*" (*GM* II 16) and similar themes. But the concept of
suffering, which is the foundation of this ideational development, should be interpreted by the later psychology in the
opposite manner, something Nietzsche almost foresees when
he says: "as for instance when pain is supposed to be proven an
error under the naïve presupposition that the pain *must* disappear if only the error in it is recognized—but behold! it refuses to disappear . . ." (*GM* III 17).

Of course suffering is greatest in the knowing one, in the
one who grasps the will to power in its origin. Philosophy itself, as well as its contradictory opinions, is a mask in order to
endure this suffering. Knowledge is no longer a value in itself
as in the works before *Zarathustra*, and in fact in the last part
of the *Genealogy of Morality* arguments and themes against
science begin to appear. "All that is profound loves a mask; the
very profoundest things even have a hatred for images and
likenesses. Shouldn't the *opposite* be the only proper disguise
to accompany the shame of a god?" (*BGE* 40) This means do
not take me so literally; it can be that what I think is the opposite of what I say. And the "recuperation" that the wanderer
desires turns out to be " 'Another mask! A second mask!' "
(*BGE* 278). "*[H]ow* deeply people can suffer practically determines rank order [. . .]. Deep suffering makes noble [. . .]
and sometimes foolishness itself is the mask for an ill-fated,
all-too-certain knowledge" (*BGE* 270). "A hermit does not
believe that a philosopher [. . .] ever expressed his genuine
and ultimate opinions in books; do people not write books
precisely to conceal what they are keeping to themselves? [. . .]
Every philosophy also *conceals* a philosophy; every opinion is
also a hiding place, every word also a mask" (*BGE* 289).

Up until now we have emphasized those themes that mark
the beginning of Nietzsche's last period of creativity in *Beyond
Good and Evil* and the *Genealogy of Morality*. There is also a
stylistic transition to be seen here, above all in the decrease of

the aphoristic form, used only occasionally in *Beyond Good and Evil* and then totally abandoned in the *Genealogy of Morality*. The style is mature, without distortions and effusions, and pathos is kept under control. One also recognizes in this a certain weariness, almost a satiety. In the *Genealogy of Morality* a development can then be seen toward a systematic attempt with occasionally dogmatic, almost pedantic, stresses or a provocative and even confused paradoxicality.

On the other hand, according to Nietzsche's own testimony, *Beyond Good and Evil* represents the clarification and the conceptual development of several themes that in *Thus Spoke Zarathustra* had been treated symbolically, lyrically, or only in intimations (thus, for example, we confronted earlier the motif of suffering with that of the eternal recurrence). We should also recall that the drafts of many passages of *Beyond Good and Evil* can be traced to earlier years. The two works under consideration here therefore once again raise and further develop central themes from the period of *Human, All Too Human* until the *Joyful Science*, in particular the discussion of the nature and origin of moral concepts. Seen in this manner, *Beyond Good and Evil* above all can be regarded as an end, a conclusion — and in any case that is what it is for the inner experience of its author.

Nietzsche is no longer able to see the subsequent works as detached from himself, as stages along his way; instead he is more and more inescapably drawn into them. Perhaps an indication of this can be found in the observation that during the years of insanity the sole evidence of Nietzsche's writing down anything was his attempt to write into a small notebook, with an uncontrolled hand, the first verses of the poem "From Lofty Mountains," which concludes *Beyond Good and Evil*. Here ended the confused recollections of his past life, and what followed was completely extinguished by the gradually progressing and ultimately final trauma of his existence.

Translator's Afterword

Adrian Del Caro

The titles in this volume were published in 1886 and 1887, respectively, following close on the heels of *Thus Spoke Zarathustra* (four parts, 1883–85), the work Nietzsche regarded as his crowning achievement. *Beyond Good and Evil* and *On the Genealogy of Morality* owe much to *Zarathustra* both in content and motivation, but this is almost counterintuitive when the style of these works is compared—*Zarathustra* is inspired philosophical poetry, written mostly in verse form (cf. the post-Kaufmann translations), intensely metaphorical, and rich in literary ambiguity—while the two works that followed are written in Nietzsche's most elegant, lucid, and persuasive prose. In a draft of a preface for a planned second volume of *Beyond* (the draft was used instead for the preface of *Human, All Too Human II*), Nietzsche explained that its beginnings (ideas, first writings, and drafts of all kinds) were traceable to his "enigmatic" Zarathustra period, that *Beyond* would therefore provide "valuable tips for understanding" *Zarathustra*, and though certainly not intended as a commentary on the speeches of Zarathustra, *Beyond* would indeed serve as "a type of provisional glossarium in which the most important conceptual- and value-innovations of that book" are set forth (cf. Prefatory Note to *BGE*, p. 354). The reverse side of the title page to the first edition of *On the Genealogy of Morality* contains the phrase "provided as a supplement and clarification of my recently published 'Beyond Good and Evil,'" further underscoring the notion that the works of 1886 and 1887 were explanatory and expository in nature and very much devoted to the writing of philosophy in the new manner that would be commensurate with the "unpacking" of *Zarathustra*. Nor can we afford to forget that Nietzsche was tremendously disappointed with the general lack of response to *Zarathustra*, such that the fourth part was only printed in a tiny edition of forty copies and distributed privately. The real philosophical elaboration of the ideas from the Zarathustra period (1882–85), as opposed to their deliberately exoteric and esoteric, and therefore initially unacknowledged, delivery in *Zarathustra* (subtitle: *A Book for All and None*), seems to have motivated Nietzsche to perform some of his most effective philosophical writing. If the word "philosophy" is not to be found in *Zarathustra*, which has few direct references to historical persons and events (Jesus Christ is one, Goethe another), then at least the next two works will make Nietzsche's philosophical aspirations quite clear, as *Beyond* is subtitled "Prelude to a Philosophy of the Future" and opens with the chapter "On the Prejudices of Philosophers."

Beyond Good and Evil and *On the Genealogy of Morality* represent a different strain in Nietzsche's thinking and writing on several levels. I referred earlier to the marked difference in style from *Zarathustra*, which stands out and has its own good reasons, but in addition the sections from these two works can no longer be called "aphorisms" in the sense of the earlier aphoristic writing that began with *Human, All Too Human* and included *Dawn* and *The Joyful Science*. While the aphoristic style was well suited to experimentation and to illustrating the creative values of the free spirit, after *Zarathustra* Nietzsche referred frequently to his philosophical "task" (*Aufgabe*), which required more sustained focus on issues relevant to his "new philosophizing," and treatment more expository and argumentative than that of the aphoristic works. The titles of 1886 and 1887 have chapters with a relatively tight focus, all contributing in an even and balanced way to the coherence of the whole. In contrast, the headings of *Human, All Too Human* reveal an interest in critiquing metaphysics, in the genealogy of morals, religious life, art, culture, the state, and human affairs, but these would have to be regarded as aphoristic forays compared to the treatment of similar issues in *Beyond Good and Evil* and *On the Genealogy of Morality*. Similarly, *Dawn* (1880), unified in theme as indicated by its subtitle "Thoughts on the Presumptions of Morality," is divided into "books" without chapter headings; *The Joyful Science* was originally conceived as a continuation of *Dawn* (Nietzsche had done this with *Human* already), and it too has no chapter headings except for Book Five (more on this below), added in 1887. The point here is not to detract from the excellence of these aphoristic volumes but only to illustrate that they were less focused, more aphoristic in style, and not yet promulgating the task whose essence is signaled by the *Zarathustra* nexus of ideas.

This major difference is clearly signaled by Nietzsche's post-Zarathustra debut as a philosopher. While claiming *Zarathustra* as his greatest book, he still made a point of describing *Beyond Good and Evil* as the "prelude to a philosophy of the future," meaning that his priorities were now to establish a new basis on which philosophizing could be done in a liberated, heretofore unseen, manner. Instead of Zarathustran prophecy issued in the form of speeches, dreams, and riddles, Nietzsche now addresses his audience straightforwardly with chapters beginning with "On the Prejudices of Philosophers," as if to establish a baseline for his new philosophizing. The 296 consecutively numbered sections of *Beyond*, with the notable exception of the "Epigrams and Interludes" (Part Four), consist mainly of detailed treatments in the form of short essays, all related to one another and often two to four pages in length. Occasional aphorisms are mixed in, some as short as two lines, others up to half a page in length, as if to demonstrate his intention to write in a new style commensurate with the needs of the new philosophy. Yet even the shortest aphorisms interspersed among the essays are on theme, and they do not disrupt the narrative so much as they provide variety and multiple perspectives (more on this later, when I discuss problems connected with the translation of Nietzsche's prose, which consists of sentences ranging from crisp, clear statements and assertions to lengthy, compartmentalized, or layered clauses designed to build up effect).

In a very real sense, *Beyond Good and Evil* and *On the Genealogy of Morality* are the two mature works in which Nietzsche elaborates on his philosophical priorities. Giorgio Colli (see his Afterword in this book) makes the point, perhaps a bit too strongly, that these are the last two Nietzsche works in which he was in control, which remained detached or independent of himself, while he is inescapably drawn into the works of 1888. For Colli the 1886 and 1887 titles therefore represent a conclusion or culmination of Nietzsche's thought. Here caution is advised, since it is all too easy to speculate on the works of 1888 in terms of impending madness and mental deterioration. We can well grant that the 1886–87 books were Nietzsche's most coherent and advanced in philosophical terms, but we must not on that account begin to diminish the works of 1888. *Twilight of the Idols*, *The Case of Wagner*, *The Anti-Christian,* and *Ecce Homo* are all very different from one another, and they all contain new material without which we would have only an incomplete picture of Nietzsche as a philosopher. While it is possible that individually these works do not match up well with *Beyond Good and Evil* and *On the Genealogy of Morality*, it is clear at the same time that they represent the sovereign, "fearless" Nietzsche who added a fifth book to *The Joyful Science* in 1887 and called it "We Fearless Ones." Colli praises Nietzsche for his restraint in the works of 1886–87 and obviously misses that restraint in the works of 1888, which were indeed written in the afterglow of Nietzsche's "discovery" by the Danish literary theorist Georg Brandes. Once he knew his writings were admired and of growing influence, and particularly once he knew Brandes was lecturing on him at the University of Copenhagen, Nietzsche in a sense pulled out all the stops and drew the most radical consequences of his philosophy, even announcing to Brandes in his letter of October 20, 1888 (*KGB* III:5, 456–57), that his next work, the soon to be published *Twilight of the Idols*, "is my philosophy *in nuce*—radical to the point of criminality. . . ." It is obviously a buoyant and upbeat Nietzsche who takes up the pen throughout 1888, a new Nietzsche who has suddenly become aware of readers in Europe and North America (and soon even in Germany, the slowest to catch on). In this context, on the heels of a long-awaited breakthrough, restraint gave way to celebration and affirmation—the works of 1888 are vintage Nietzsche, even if they are not his most polished.

Finally, with respect to the place occupied by these two titles in the published works overall, we must recall that the fifth book of *The Joyful Science* was added for a "second edition" in 1887, along with the poems "Songs of Prince Free-as-a-Bird." As he had done with the first edition of his earlier books in 1886, Nietzsche used the remaining unsold copies and in this instance had the new fifth book attached to them, a brilliant early example of recycling but a rather dubious claim to a "second edition." In content, the material from Book Five of *The Joyful Science* closely resembles the thematics of *Beyond Good and Evil*, particularly the chapters on the free spirit, the natural history of morality, scholars, the religious character, peoples and fatherlands, and what is noble. Most of the forty new aphorisms for Book Five, which Nietzsche titled "We Fearless Ones," could have been slotted into the aforementioned chapters of *Beyond*, but for the fact of course that Nietzsche insisted on this "new edition" with new material. A much smaller number of the aphorisms would also have fit well into *On the Genealogy of Morality*, insofar as they treat the priestly type, the origin or morals, morality as an expression of illness, and the extent to which science retains a metaphysical and ascetic character despite its claims to the contrary. In my estimation Nietzsche disrupted the coherence and flow of *The Joyful*

Science by adding the fifth book, for the original four books represented an improvement over the earlier aphoristic works in terms of coherence and balance — it also served perfectly as the threshold to *Thus Spoke Zarathustra*, since it featured the aphorisms on the death of God (125) and the eternal recurrence of the same (341), which form the backbone of Zarathustra's doctrine of life affirmation.

Thus *Beyond Good and Evil* and *On the Genealogy of Morality* are notable for explicating the enigmatic and sometimes hermetic *Thus Spoke Zarathustra* as mature expressions of Nietzsche's most philosophical and sustained treatment of issues he had explored in the aphoristic works beginning with *Human, All Too Human* and as works superior in execution, coherence, and balance to the hastily written and far more radical works of 1888, which do indeed reveal a more strident and self-centered Nietzsche, albeit with hefty doses of self-parody and humor. Nietzsche was engaged in calibrating, deepening, and clarifying his discourse in the works of 1886 and 1887, after the highly emotional experience of writing *Zarathustra* and then hearing virtually no response to that work. The news he received from Brandes late in 1887 set the tone for a flurry of publications in 1888, in which Nietzsche's tone is rather triumphant and celebratory. While careful readers are accustomed to Nietzsche's celebratory observations beginning already with *The Birth of Tragedy* (1872), this celebrating had been a celebration of life in accordance with Nietzsche's elevation of the human condition, whereas in 1888 the celebrating spills over to include self-congratulatory reflections and formulations.

Further indications of a revised state of mind after 1887 are furnished by Nietzsche's temporary enthusiasm for and work on a philosophical *magnum opus* (German *Hauptwerk*), which he referred to in his notes as "The Will to Power: Attempt at a Revaluation of All Values." Alan D. Schrift explains that this planned book "would appear to have been one of Nietzsche's overriding intentions from summer 1885 until early fall 1888," and "following the publication of *On the Genealogy of Morality*, Nietzsche worked diligently on this text."[1] Plans for "The Will to Power" were abandoned, but material from that project was published as *Twilight of the Idols*. For a brief time, a new major work was envisioned in four parts with the title "Revaluation of all Values"; this project was also abandoned soon after the appearance of the first part, which Nietzsche published as *The Anti-Christian*.[2]

Beyond Good and Evil

There is a close relationship between this title and *Thus Spoke Zarathustra*, as Nietzsche succinctly explained in *Ecce Homo*. Zoroaster, or Zarathustra, as he is known to Germans, "is the first to see in the battle of good and evil the actual wheel that drives things — the translation of morality into the metaphysical, as force, cause, purpose in itself, is *his* work. [. . .] Zarathustra *created* this most disastrous of errors, morality: consequently, he must also be the first to *acknowledge* it" (*EH* "Why I Am A Destiny" 3). Here we have Nietzsche's unequivocal statement on the motivation behind selecting Zarathustra as his modern prophet — the old Zarathustra set the machinery of good and evil in motion, so to speak, spawning the metaphysics of morality as the "most disastrous of errors" that needs to be recognized and remedied. While *Zarathustra* as the "book for all and none" does not engage in philosophizing as such, observe what Nietzsche had to say about *Beyond Good and Evil* in *Ecce Homo*: "After the Yes-saying part of my task had been fulfilled came the turn of the No-saying, "*not-doing*" half: the revaluation of the former values themselves, the great war — the summoning up of a day of decision. This includes

1. Alan D. Schrift, "Nietzsche's *Nachlass*," in *A Companion to Friedrich Nietzsche: Life and Works*, ed. Paul Bishop (Rochester, NY: Camden House, 2012), 410, 413.

2. Ibid., 418.

the slow look round for relatives, for those who, out of strength, would lend me a hand *in destroying*" (*EH* BGE 1). On this reasoning the significance of the subtitle of *Beyond* is most clear: Nietzsche created a new ground zero in moral terms with *Zarathustra*, and the subsequent works designed to explicate and clarify *Zarathustra* are part of a larger project to revalue all values — a phrase Nietzsche used frequently in his published and unpublished writings to indicate the undoing of metaphysics based on good and evil. Observe as well that Nietzsche at this point does not see himself working alone; whether they are called free spirits or new philosophers, these individuals are those who will extend a hand to him — they have the strength to contribute to the task of revaluation, and a glance at the chapter titles for *Beyond* gives us valuable clues regarding the identity of such people.

"On the Prejudices of Philosophers" stakes out the ground Nietzsche will cover in philosophical terms; after their prejudices are exposed, we can infer that philosophers will be in a stronger position to philosophize in the Dionysian manner that calls for destruction and creation. With their blinders removed, philosophers will be free to engage in work that makes a difference to the species and involves a certain degree of danger, as indicated by §23, where he concludes that "psychology is now once again the way to the fundamental problems." If philosophers have the courage of what we know about the human psyche, Nietzsche maintains, we can use the findings of psychology to motivate and inspire an intrepid species for whom the earth is new and unexplored (cf. *Joyful Science* 76, 124, 283, 289, 335, 343, 377). Part Two on the "free spirit" is the positive restatement of Part One, and in fact it contains numerous direct references to philosophers and to the new community of spirits to whom Nietzsche addresses himself: "Our highest insights must — and should — sound like follies, and in some cases like crimes when heard without permission" (§30). That the free spirits are philosophers, and Dionysian philosophers in particular, is signaled here by §40, where a profound spirit is described as needing a mask. This theme is elaborated on in §§41–44, where Nietzsche lays out a kind of code of conduct for a "new species of philosopher": "After all this do I still need to expressly say that they will also be free, *very* free spirits, these philosophers of the future?" (§44). Of course there may be other free spirits who "extend a hand" to Nietzsche and are not philosophers as such—leaving open the question as to whether the "new" and "coming" philosophers will be recognizable at all as philosophers in the traditional and esoteric sense.

"The Religious Character" may seem at first an unlikely ally for Nietzsche's new philosophical task, but on closer examination it makes perfect sense that religion must play a role in his task, and on a variety of levels. At the most primal level Nietzsche claims (and continues to claim in *On the Genealogy of Morality*) that much that passes for philosophy is in fact traceable to the metaphysical, ascetic impulses of religious types. The "religious neurosis" he discusses in §47, which was instrumental in launching Schopenhauer's career as a philosopher, gets a thorough and unforgiving treatment in *Genealogy*, Third Treatise, where Schopenhauer, Wagner, and entire peoples are treated as its symptoms. In this part of *Beyond* Nietzsche wants to render up to philosophy and psychology what is theirs and yet also credit religion for its benefits. The religious hierarchies in particular are useful for cultivating the notion of rank among human beings, and for providing a spiritual alternative to politics (cf. *JS* 358, where the Church is "under all circumstances a *nobler* institution than the state"). Moreover, religion provides solace and meaning to the masses, who are taught how to feel content and dignified despite their harsh lives (§61). But the "religious character" is perhaps most useful to the new philosopher as a warning and a motivation to remain vigilant: "Christianity has been the most disastrous kind of arrogance to date" (§62). It is over and against the great religions that Nietzsche and his spiritual kin will make their own way, serving the species as exemplars who would otherwise be wiped out by the anti-exceptionalism and pro-mediocritization campaigns of the major religions. Nietzsche is adamant that the religions must never be allowed to rule sovereign, but must instead be used by philosophers as their tools.

Even Part Four's "Epigrams and Interludes" suggests a function to be adopted by new philosophers, in this case levity as well as brevity of expression. Nietzsche is also reminding himself after three "chapters" in which he has treated some of the weightiest issues in the history of philosophy that aphoristic writings are his first love because they give voice to what is light and creative in the human spirit. This is the same strong message of *The Joyful Science*, which is as much a style as it is a title; the intellect becomes "an awkward, gloomy, creaking machine" whenever people "take something seriously" — this dismal view of knowledge must be countered by *joyful science* (*JS* 327). This spirit is masterfully embodied in *Beyond* 154: "Objections, wayward strokes, cheerful mistrust, and delight in mockery are signs of health: everything unconditional belongs to pathology."

"On the Natural History of Morality" calls for a more rigorous stance on morality itself rather than the traditional acceptance and representation of morality that even the philosophers have claimed to put on a "scientific" footing. This part revisits the prejudices of the philosophers with respect to morals in particular, singling out Kant, Schopenhauer, Plato, and Socrates. Obedience is examined as a powerful enforcer of morality, and herd morality is the diagnosis Nietzsche assigns to the socialist, democratic, leveling, and revolutionary spirits who constitute the fabric of modern values. Here, too, Nietzsche urges new philosophers to step forward to take up the task of revaluation and commanding; the danger he proclaims here, as at the conclusion of Part Three, is that if left unchallenged, modern morality could in fact achieve its vision of the human of the future — a degenerate, atrophied, and shrunken human being: "this animalization of human beings to dwarf animals of equal rights and claims is *possible*, there is no doubt!" (§203; cf. also Z, Part 3, "On the Virtue that Diminishes"). The antipode of the self-effacing morality is that of Cesare Borgia, that predatory "tropical human being" whom we have to discredit "at any cost," even though the morality of "temperate human beings" leads only to mediocrity (§197).

"We Scholars" might also puzzle some readers who are familiar with Nietzsche's critique of the scholar/scientist begun in *The Birth of Tragedy* and sustained in every subsequent work, but we must not overlook the fact that Nietzsche was a scholar by training, and that his closest model in terms of philosophizing was Schopenhauer, one of the most scholarly and widely read individuals of his age. What seems to concern him most in Part Six is the loose manner in which modern society fails to distinguish between scholarship and philosophy. Whereas scholars are abundant and quite predictable, a symptom of the leveling values of modern democratic society, "[t]he dangers to the development of a philosopher are in truth so manifold that we could doubt whether this fruit can even ripen anymore" (§205). He carefully lays out the differences between scholars or what he also calls scientific men and the genius, the philosopher who is a "Caesarian cultivator and brute of culture" (§207). Once again the philosopher is placed at the top of the hierarchy, as we observed in the relationship between religion and philosophy; of course a philosopher may have to experience a scholarly stage in his own development, during which he uses a range of skills to perform "philosophical labor," but Nietzsche insists that the scholar can no longer serve when it comes to creating values, and to commanding and legislating (§211). These new philosophers will be independent to the point of living in painful isolation (reminiscent of Schopenhauer's fate, as well as Nietzsche's), and their ability to assert themselves beyond good and evil will be the test of whether greatness is still possible in the modern age (§212). Judged by this standard, with the very possibility of greatness as a human concept hanging in the balance, Nietzsche draws the sharpest possible distinction between scholarly-scientific work and the value-creation that only philosophers can deliver.

"Our Virtues" underscores again how Nietzsche speaks in *Beyond Good and Evil* from a sense of community: "We Europeans of the day after tomorrow, we first born of the twentieth century" (§214). The future demands a radical break with the past in terms of what is regarded as virtue, as if Nietzsche were warning his spiritual peers that much baggage from the past will have to be abandoned. Maintaining "order of rank" among human beings and things generally will be the new criterion, such that "disinterested" observation and "unegoistic" morality, trendy but hollow expressions, will have to be interrogated in light of great differences between human beings and values (§§220, 221). Our virtues (and often our tastes) are those of a "hybrid European" who likes to dress up, to wear costumes found in the historical closets of a multitude of peoples and ages, enabling us to enjoy Homer and Shakespeare at the same time: "Like the rider on a steed champing to move on, we drop the reins before the infinite, we modern human beings, we semi-barbarians" (§§223, 224). Against the modernist mantra of abolishing suffering, Nietzsche claims that only great suffering "has created all the enhancements of humans" so far (§225), making it necessary to reflect seriously on whether pity can have the last word in matters of philosophy. As if to underscore the need to reflect on the long-term effects of pity, cruelty is defended (§229) and discussed in its various cultural manifestations throughout the ages; in the past, cruelty was understood strictly in terms of the suffering of others, but Nietzsche is serious about delving into the cruelty we practice on ourselves physically and emotionally, concluding "in every wanting-to-know there is a drop of cruelty" (§229). This theme of knowing in proximity to cruelty is pursued in the next section, where "*very* free spirits" are described as cutting through the surface noise and ornamentation of ideals such as honesty, love of truth, love of knowledge, and sacrifice for knowledge; beneath this moral finery lies "the terrible basic text of *homo natura*," and the new philosophers must work to translate humankind back into *this* nature, this "terrible" but scribbled-over nature whose basic text has been obliterated by idealists of the old virtues. If these ideas remind us of Zarathustra's speeches both in content and tone, then all the more so once Nietzsche begins in §231 to write about women, a favorite topic with which he closes out Part Seven. We have deceived ourselves about women, he insists, and again lampooning Goethe's "eternal feminine," as he did in *Zarathustra* "On Poets," Nietzsche does the historical arithmetic and concludes: "Since the French Revolution the influence of woman in Europe has *decreased* in proportion to the increase in her rights and claims" (§239). When it comes to "our virtues," Nietzsche chides "the scholarly asses of the male sex" who support the defeminization of women, inasmuch as their support of women in this venture amounts to giving her an equal right to the same stupidity that afflicts "European 'manliness'" (§239). Not to be forgotten is the larger context in which Nietzsche launches his critique of women: patriarchy has contributed richly to the old virtues and values that Nietzsche and his free spirits must revaluate—it is inconsistent to judge him a misogynist without simultaneously pointing out that patriarchy has failed dismally in his view.

Of course unless Nietzsche was speaking only in metaphorical terms about the free spirits and the new philosophers, they would have to take up residence somewhere. Part Eight, "Peoples and Fatherlands," is a geography of the free spirit, with Nietzsche weighing in on those peoples who are likely to extend a hand for his new task, as well as those who are not. Conspicuously, Germans draw the shortest straw, and by far most of his criticism is directed at them while he speaks to his "good Europeans." The Germans of today are paradoxically *not of today*, but like Wagnerian music they are rich in past and in future (§240). Nationalism, or "fatherlandishness and sod-hugging," resulted in a modern Germany that amounts to "a new tower of Babel or some monstrosity of empire and power" that the masses call "great" (§241). German profundity is deconstructed beginning again with Goethe, whose Faust laments that two souls dwell in his breast—a claim Nietzsche insists would "fall short of the truth by many souls" (§244). Using music as the standard, Nietzsche bemoans the loss of European echoes as they resounded around Mozart, Beethoven, Rousseau, Schiller, Shelley, Byron, and Napoleon. German Romanticism, incarnated in Robert Schumann, was "already a mere *German* event, no longer a European one as Beethoven was, as Mozart had been to an even more encompassing extent," such that "German music was threatened by its greatest danger, that of losing *the voice for the soul of Europe* and sinking to a mere fatherlandishness" (§245). In matters of style, German prose is tone deaf, and only Germany's preachers mastered the art of rhetoric: "The masterpiece of German prose is therefore, viewed fairly, the masterpiece of its greatest preacher: the *Bible* has so far been the best German book" (§247).

A good number of sections are devoted to the concept of the good European, who is often spoken of in terms reminiscent of the free spirit. As strong as the currents of nationalism were in Nietzsche's day, he gauged the strength of Europe's peoples according to their capacity to embrace a broader European identity and cultural agenda. Sometimes Nietzsche sounds prophetic, as for example when he writes that a process of similarization is at work among Europeans, whereby the unintended consequences of democratization include rising anarchism and favorable breeding grounds for tyrants (§242); or how German anti-Semitism flourishes because, unlike the Italians, the British, and the French, Germans cannot culturally "digest" their Jewish population, and German instincts lash out in fear of their own obliteration (§251). The basic fact that "Europe wants to become one" is masked and muted by nationalism, and even Germany's best cultural exemplars only became "fatherlanders" in their tired old age (§256).

England will not provide fellow free spirits; the English are "an unphilosophical race" addicted to Christianity and alcohol, and they also lack musicality (§252). Even worse, the "modern ideas" with which Europe is awash are of English origin and were merely filtered through and aped by the French: "European *noblesse*—of feeling, of taste, of custom, in short taking the word in every elevated sense—is *France's* work and invention" (§253). At the top of Nietzsche's cultural pyramid are the French, "the most spiritual and sophisticated culture in Europe and the preeminent school of taste" (§254). There are three reasons the French constitute the most promising repository of European cultural value, on the basis of which they have effectively resisted Germanization: artistic passion with devotion to form; diverse moral perspectives and psychological sensitivity; and a successful synthesis of north and south (§254). The fortunes of Nietzsche's writings throughout the twentieth century map well with these observations he made in 1886.

The final part of *Beyond Good and Evil* elaborates on a favorite concept of Nietzsche, namely, "what is noble." Always critical of the notion of progress as it is tied to Enlightenment smugness concerning the advance of knowledge and the alleged superiority of modernity, and likewise critical of what he called the "morality of improvement," whereby human beings are seen to be deficient from a variety of viewpoints, Nietzsche's writings attempt to define a property of human beings that is more difficult to explain and is also in serious decline in the modern era. Nobility, or *das Vornehme*, is not defined strictly on the basis of class, but Nietzsche insists that any elevating of the type "human being" is the work of aristocratic society, and "barbarians in every terrible sense of the word" have been the starting point of every noble caste (§257). This reasoning becomes clearer when he explains that society cannot exist for the sake of society but only as the infrastructure from which a higher type of human being arises (§258). This closely resembles the ideas Zarathustra expounds when he claims that the human is something that must be overcome (or superseded: *überwunden*) to make way for the superhuman. Recall that in its current state the species is heading for what Zarathustra calls "the last human being," which is the opposite of the superhuman: if our species does not have a goal or a desire that might shape its amorphous and constantly stalled potential, there will be no distinguishing between us and herd animals.

If nobility is supposed to function as this shaping force, it will first have to be rescued as a concept from the trash bin of history, to which it has been relegated by a modern ethos that refuses to acknowledge the necessity of exploitation, which for Nietzsche is the "*essence* of what lives" (§259). Viewed without sentimentality and of course from a standpoint "beyond good and evil," "life itself is *essentially* appropriation, injury, overpowering of what is foreign and weaker, oppression, harshness, imposition of one's own forms, incorporation and at least, at its mildest, exploitation—but why should we always have to use precisely those words on which from time immemorial a slanderous intention has been stamped?" (§259). Life's essence seen through this biological lens is harsh and brutal, indifferent to human ideals and aspirations, but the moment we begin to think in this manner, we are indeed engaging in the use of "words with slanderous intention." This phenomenon of life described unsentimentally is also the will to power, and it is also nature (unromanticized)—what obviously concerns and vexes Nietzsche is that we have a generally negative and pejorative way of thinking and speaking about life, whereas we might be predisposed to speak glowingly of our anthropomorphized and romanticized delusions about life. Historically speaking, the space of our lives, the earth, has indeed become a place of opprobrium, a prison of sorts that must be denied and eventually escaped in favor of a better "eternal" world. The point here is not that humans must engage in exploitation—we do this quite independently of anything Nietzsche thinks—instead, it is time to reconsider and to do something about the imbalance between what he calls master morality and slave morality.

These two moralities are not absolutes, and there is slippage between them. Noble types determine and create their own values; their sense of fullness and power projects outwardly as a "consciousness of wealth that would bestow and give of itself" (§260; cf. *Z* "On the Virtue of Gifting"). The dominating power holders who decree themselves to be good show "deep reverence for age and for one's background," in contrast to modern peoples who place their trust in ideas such as progress and the future. What makes this noble morality vulnerable in our time is "the severity of its principle that one has duties only to one's peers." The slave morality, on the other hand, is motivated by the realities of people who are oppressed, violated, unfree, and suffering; Nietzsche asks us to consider what their moral values must inevitably look like and what their consequences are. The whole human condition would be suspect to them, and humankind would be condemned; there is resentment of the virtues of the powerful, and mistrust of all that is good (as good is defined by the masters). By projecting their resentment onto the nobles, slave moralities create the classification of evil and brand themselves good; this notion of good resting on a foundation of victimization tends to conflate notions of goodness and stupidity (§260).

The argument for facing the reality of exploitation and assigning it to what is noble closely resembles the argument for the preservation of suffering (§225); whereas a society based on the value of pity strives to abolish suffering, Nietzsche's contention is that great suffering has been the very engine of enhancement of the human type. In both cases he is arguing in favor of suffering and exploitation, but in each case his endgame is a higher, enhanced human being. If we were to agree with Nietzsche that suffering and exploitation are inevitable in the human condition, is there a scenario according to which we would be willing to sublimate these drives and instincts that currently have only a negative connotation? The goal or endgame is not to create more suffering or to encourage and enable more exploitation but to ensure the enhancement of the species, which, on its current course, appears headed for a herdlike existence under the tutelage of slave morality. This point is made once again when Nietzsche describes the aftermath of the "tropical tempo" (cf. the discussion of Borgia in §197): "The dangerous and uncanny moment has been reached when the greater, more diverse, more comprehensive life *lives over and beyond* the old morality" (§262). At such time the only species of human being who can survive is "the incurably mediocre," and thus arises a morality of mediocrity (§262).

Distinguishing features of the noble include an "instinct for rank" (§263), a sound, unabashed egoism that would rechristen itself "justice" (§265), the experience of great suffering (§270), not sharing one's duties and privileges (§272), the ability to cultivate and live in solitude (§§273, 284), a need for the mask (§§278, 289, 290), and a capacity for "golden laughter" (§294). Laughter is richly in evidence throughout *Zarathustra*, where it is a symbol of affirmation, health, and defiance of gravity. The transformation of the shepherd into a *laughing* being whose laughter is not human suggests that Zarathustra has experienced a vision of the superhuman ("On the Vision and Riddle"). Similarly, Zarathustra's speeches on the "higher man" disclose a vital role for laughter, this time in direct contradiction of Christ's condemnation of laughter, in Luke 6:27–28: "Woe to you who laugh now, For you shall mourn and weep." Zarathustra reverses this warning: "Did he himself find no reasons to laugh on earth? Then he searched badly. Even a child finds reasons here" ("On Superior Humans" 16). The placement of the "golden laughter" section in this final part of *Beyond Good and Evil* is significant for its rhetorical effect.

Nietzsche's references in §294 to the rehabilitation of laughter, and specifically to its liberation from the bad reputation it appears to suffer among philosophers, are reminiscent of Zarathustra's elevation of laughter, but he gives even stronger clues that he has Zarathustra on his mind. After stating that golden laughter will be the sign of the highest-ranking philosopher, he writes: "And supposing that gods, too, philosophize, something to which many a conclusion has driven me to believe—then I do not doubt that they also know how to laugh in a superhuman and innovative way—and at the expense of all serious things!" This cryptic wording points to Zarathustra's teaching of the superhuman, while at the same time it signals the presence of Dionysus, the god "who philosophizes," as Nietzsche reveals in §295. Laughter, the superhuman, and Dionysus are connected by the fact that Dionysus is the god of tragedy and comedy. Whereas Nietzsche had emphasized the tragic (sublime) dimensions of the Dionysian in *The Birth of Tragedy*, his first book, he has by now transformed himself into a "Dionysian philosopher" whose appreciation of laughter allows him to accentuate both the tragic and the comic (absurd) dimensions of the Dionysian. *Birth of Tragedy* was a Dionysian work written by a scholar who considered the artist to be humankind's highest representation, whereas *Zarathustra* was a Dionysian work written by a philosopher, namely, the first "Dionysian philosopher."

Call it laughter, humor, levity, the comic—Nietzsche clearly considers these to be qualities of the noble, and at the conclusion of *Beyond Good and Evil* he invokes the name of Dionysus and speaks in cryptic, dithyrambic tones about this god's qualities, and about the god's relation to Nietzsche himself as well as to philosophy: "Even the fact that Dionysus is a philosopher and that gods therefore also philosophize seems to me a novelty that is not innocuous and will arouse suspicion" (§295). With great fanfare Zarathustra had proclaimed, "dead are all gods, now we want the superhuman to live" ("On the Virtue of Gifting" 3), but here he is calling on Dionysus, the life-affirming demigod to whom he had offered his first work as a sacrifice, as if to instate Dionysus and Dionysianism into the pantheon of figures and forces who will "extend a hand" to him for his new philosophical task. Dionysus makes more sense here than Zarathustra because the Dionysian is bigger than Zarathustra, subsuming Zarathustra, or, in the lexicon of tragedy, Zarathustra, like all tragic heroes, is a mask of Dionysus. And Dionysus's divine properties notwithstanding, Nietzsche elevates this figure because he is the *Versuchergott*, the tempter and experimenter and attempter god, who is known as the god of the mask and whose proximity signals danger. Since the work Nietzsche must perform as a new kind of philosopher is contrary in every way to the principles and articles of faith of Christianity, then working in his typically polarized style he will counter the Christian with the Dionysian, though not as one religion against the other but, as I argue elsewhere, as antifaith.[3] When he dons the mask and voice of Dionysus, as he does at the conclusion of *Beyond Good and Evil*, he knows that he is no longer speaking with the esoteric authority of the philosopher of tradition, and he knows that he is alienating his readers, leaving them behind in a very important sense. But that is the point—philosophy will not be "done" in the old school manner, nor by the philosophers of yesterday.

Metaphorical expression of the difficulty, indeed, impossibility, of engaging his philosophical task while maintaining friendships at the same time is found in Nietzsche's poem "From Lofty Mountains," with which he crowns his "prelude to a philosophy of the future." This "aftersong" as opposed to "afterword" speaks in the medium of the Dionysian, namely, music, and it appears here for reasons similar to those that motivated Nietzsche's use of "Dionysian dithyrambs" in the

3. Adrian Del Caro, *Grounding the Nietzsche Rhetoric of Earth* (Berlin: de Gruyter, 2004), 153–61. The conclusion of *BGE* on a Dionysian note is repeated more dramatically in the concluding sentence of *Ecce Homo*: "Have I been understood?— *Dionysus versus the Crucified.* . . ."

fourth and final part of *Zarathustra*. The setting of the poem, as well as its semantic field, is reminiscent of *Thus Spoke Zarathustra* and the prophet's failed attempts to find companions; however, the overarching metaphor here, as in *Zarathustra*, is the incommunicability of language for the expression of philosophy. Nietzsche turns to Dionysian forms of expression in the final part of *Zarathustra* because ultimately his message cannot be translated — words fail. This is what the older, more philosophical Nietzsche was saying in 1886 when he attached an "Attempt at a Self-Critique" to the second edition of *The Birth of Tragedy* and claimed: "It should have *sung*, this 'new soul' — and not spoken!" (*BT* "Attempt" 3). This "singing" in Nietzsche's texts is not limited strictly to poems that are set off and readily identifiable as poems but often includes entire sections and aphorisms that are Dionysian in their musicality and suggestiveness, such as those immediately preceding the "aftersong." Part of this reliance on musicality when words begin to let him down can be traced to Nietzsche's "fear of the inarticulate," as Erich Heller describes it.[4] It is quite clear, however, that at times Nietzsche wants us to transition from prose and its relative gravity and sobriety to a heightened Dionysian state of awareness, in which case poems take over and musicality becomes the locus of a shifted attention. It is therefore significant in the poem "From Lofty Mountains" that the singer/narrator is joined at the end by Zarathustra, this most Dionysian of "philosophers," the teacher of the eternal recurrence of the same. There is a distinct dithyrambic quality to the poem, despite its rhyme scheme and perhaps even enhanced by it, when we consider that dithyrambs were votive songs to Dionysus.

4. Erich Heller, "Nietzsche and the Inarticulate," in *Nietzsche: Literature and Values*, ed. Volker Dürr, Reinhold Grimm, and Kathy Harms (Madison: University of Wisconsin Press, 1988), 6, 11, 13.

On the Genealogy of Morality

Unlike *Beyond Good and Evil*, whose composition began in 1885 and concluded in the early months of 1886, *Genealogy* was written between July 10 and July 30, 1887. We know that *Beyond* drew on materials Nietzsche had written beginning already in 1881, but we do not have a detailed history of the preparation of *Genealogy* because, as Montinari points out, "with the exception of a few pages and fragmentary notes and their print manuscript in Nietzsche's handwriting—all the drafts of this 'polemic' have been lost" (see Montinari's Editor's Note, p. 406). However, as Nietzsche himself tells us in the Preface, the first expressions of his interest in the origin of moral prejudices are to be found in *Human, All Too Human* (1878–80), and of course aphorisms on the origin of morals are found in all the works beginning with *Human*. The reverse side of the title page of *Genealogy* contained this statement in the first printing: "Provided as a supplement and clarification of my recently published 'Beyond Good and Evil'."

Genealogy is the most expository of Nietzsche's late works, consisting of three treatises each devoted to a specific theme. The sections are consistently longer and more expansive than those of *Beyond*, the focus is much tighter, and generally the writing resembles the essayistic style of the *Untimely Meditations* (1873–76). We should bear in mind what Nietzsche wrote in *Ecce Homo* (see above) about *Beyond* and the post-*Zarathustra* works collectively, namely, that they constitute the no-saying and no-doing part of his philosophical task, whose yes-saying component had been *Zarathustra*. There is therefore a destructive and "deconstructive" dimension to the philosophy of the future as envisioned by Nietzsche, and nowhere is this more evident than in *Genealogy*, where his celebrated and long-practiced genealogical method drills down to the very core of morals and values, revealing their roots as well as the nature of the material in and out of which they have grown. He claims to speak more precisely about these issues now than ten years ago, and in the Preface he expresses the hope that his thoughts display coherence for having "originated in me not in isolation, not arbitrarily and sporadically, but from a common root, from a *fundamental will* of knowledge commanding from the depths" (P2).

He attributes a certain motivation for himself to his deep and abiding interest in the problem of the value of compassion — what he experienced on the basis of his exploration of its transformative effect on him: " — a tremendous new vista opens up for him . . . faith in morality, in all morality falters . . . we need a *critique* of moral values, *the value of these values must itself be questioned first*" (P6). The epiphany he describes here resembles the effect produced by his inquiry into the conditions that gave rise to the value judgments good and evil; he worked on this problem over the years, "until finally I had my own land, my own ground, an entire unmentioned, growing, blossoming world, secret gardens as it were, of which no one could have an inkling" (P3). Now placing the emphasis on *us* as if mindful of Voltaire's "*il faut cultiver notre jardin*," he went on to explain that ever since the vista opened up for him, he looked around for "bold and industrious comrades," as the job of traversing the "hidden land of morality" (cf. his formulation of a "morally round earth" in *JS* 289) is simply too big for one man (P7). He would speak in very similar terms in *Ecce Homo* about the task that lay ahead for new philosophers, for those who would "extend a hand" to him in his work of dismantling the old philosophical infrastructure.

Nietzsche issues a caution to readers of *Genealogy*: if they find the book incomprehensible or dissonant, it is because they haven't done their homework. In this case, the homework consists of Nietzsche's earlier writings, including *Zarathustra* and the earlier aphoristic works of which he says: "these are in fact not easily accessible" (P8). In his day the aphorism is "*not taken seriously enough*," and in order to demonstrate how much can and should be done by way of deciphering and interpretation, he points to an aphorism that he places at the beginning of *Genealogy*'s Third Treatise; the entire Third Treatise, he maintains, is "a sample" of what he means by interpretation, insofar as it serves as the interpretation of the "aphoristic" first section (P8).[5] Hyperbole aside, Nietzsche remained a philologist throughout his career, and he championed the values of good hermeneutics. *Genealogy* in this sense is the result of years of writing aphorisms and "ruminating" on them until the works of 1886 and 1887 were ready to assume their place in the dismantling phase of the new philosophy.

The treatise begins with questions regarding the motives, methods, and findings of moral inquiry as conducted by the English in particular. While he is generally appreciative toward them for pursuing research on the origin of morals, a neglected field of inquiry, they seem bent on tracing the origins to the "shameful" or "private" parts of humanity, as if to satisfy a desire to belittle our species somehow, or perhaps to settle a score of which they are not consciously aware. Potentially their psychological methods, their "microscopics" of the psyche, could lead to the discovery of truths of all kinds, even the most undesirable, but the psychologists themselves must be courageous and capable of reining in their own passions (§1). The main objection to their genealogy is the equation of good with useful, or with utility; Nietzsche maintains that "good" is of different origins and should not be traced to unegoistic deeds and motivations (§2). Instead, he sought the meaning of "good" in comparative etymology, not surprisingly since he was a philologist, concluding that "everywhere in the context of classes 'noble,' 'lordly' is the basic concept from which 'good' in the sense of 'noble of soul,' 'lordly,' of 'superior of soul,' 'privileged of soul' necessarily develops" (§4). This he

5. See John T. Wilcox, "What Aphorism Does Nietzsche Explicate in Genealogy of Morals, Essay III?," *Journal of the History of Philosophy* 35, no. 4 (1997): 593–610. Wilcox demonstrates that contrary to the long-held view that Nietzsche was referring to the *Zarathustra* epigraph at the top of the opening page of the Third Treatise, he was in fact referring to §1 of the Third Treatise.

does also with the opposite of "good" when he foregrounds words designating lowly, common, and base as the origin of notions of "bad," drawing on usages from German, Slavic, Iranian, Greek, Celtic, and Latin (§§5, 6). Here Nietzsche is firmly on the ground of his much earlier observation in *Human*, chapter 2, "On the History of the Moral Sensations" (§45), where he derives the origin of good and evil from the interplay between noble and base types; originally there are only good and bad corresponding to noble and base, but eventually the bad invent a category called "evil" in order to avenge themselves on the good, whereby they revaluate values in order to ascribe "good" to themselves. This genealogy of the terms *good* and *evil* stands of course in stark contrast to modernist efforts to situate the origins of "good" in notions of "utility" and "unegoistic" actions, which just happen to flatter and reflect the taste of Nietzsche's contemporaries (especially in Britain).

A dimension of "purity" is added to notions of the good by the priestly caste, this most intriguing and dangerous form of human being who is responsible for making humans "an interesting animal" (§6). In fact, so pervasive and so formidable is this type of "priest" that it poses a serious challenge to the knightly and aristocratic morality of the noble-good, who are opposed using every manner of *ressentiment* and vengeful, impotent spirit. While he credits the spirit of the impotent for enhancing humankind, in accordance with his views from *Human* detailing how the powerful succumb through stupidity to the intellectually and spiritually more motivated but impotent people who need to use their wits, he proceeds immediately to the greatest historical example of the triumph of the impotent: "Everything that has been done on earth against the 'noble,' 'the mighty,' 'the masters,' 'the power holders' is not worth mentioning in comparison with what *the Jews* have done against them; the Jews, that priestly people who in the end were only able to achieve satisfaction from their enemies and conquerors through a radical revaluation of their values, hence through an act of the *most spiritual revenge*" (§7). This language is striking because it singles out the ancient Jews as the quintessentially "priestly" people, and it does so during a period of flagrant political anti-Semitism, which Nietzsche abhors and against which he speaks out in his works. We must be mindful and respectful of the sweeping context in which Nietzsche makes these juxtapositions; there are priestly types in all cultures at all times, but historically speaking, the Jews ushered in the greatest revaluation of noble values so far, since they were able to "bring down" imperial Rome. Note, also, that the priestly type is humankind's "most interesting" and "most dangerous" type, as opposed to the sword-wielding conquerors who excel by virtue of brute strength, and note again that human history has been enriched and enhanced by the spirituality of the impotent, priestly type—we cannot ignore these tremendous boons to humankind. And even more important, before we affix the label of anti-Semitic to Nietzsche's genealogical findings, let us throw in anti-Christian as well, because Christianity "*inherited* this Jewish revaluation" (§7), and Christianity is a much larger, more diverse, and more powerful force than the relatively tiny Jewish people. Thus "the slave revolt in morality" that begins with the ancient Jews and is victorious today with its two-thousand-year history (§7) is in fact a Judeo-Christian-Platonic triumph over the master morality of the noble. This point is underscored in §8, where Nietzsche explains how the vengeful hatred of the ancient Jews toward their masters transforms into the gospel of love represented by Christ: "This Jesus of Nazareth as the incarnate gospel of love, this 'redeemer' who brought blessedness and victory to the poor, sinners, and the sick—was he not precisely seduction in its most uncanny and irresistible form, seduction and a detour to precisely those *Jewish* values and revisions of their ideal?" (§8).

By dramatizing this revaluation of noble values as a world-historical slave revolt, Nietzsche is using familiar language and a familiar point of departure—the ancient pre-Socratic culture gave way to a Socratic, theoretically optimistic, and metaphysically delusional worldview, such that Socrates became the "single turning point and vortex of so-called world history" (*BT* 15). Now Nietzsche transfers the struggle from Greece to Europe proper and expands the context to include not only the triumph of knowledge and Socratic optimism over tragedy but slave morality over master morality as well: "Let us acquiesce to the facts: the common people have won — or 'the slaves,' or 'the rabble,' or 'the herd' or whatever you prefer to call it — if this happened through the Jews, so be it! then never has a people had a more world-historical mission" (§9). On my reading, this places the Jews in good company. Moreover, recall that since Nietzsche refers to *his* task and *his* work as a "revaluation of all values," how laudatory and complimentary it is for him to model his revaluation on these historical revaluations he found to be simultaneously calamitous and exemplary for the spiritualization of our species.

Characteristic of the slave morality driven by *ressentiment* is its reliance on external stimuli. Noble types affirm themselves and project this confidence into the world, whereas base types take action only as a reaction: "His soul *squints*; his spirit loves hiding places . . . he knows the skill of keeping silent, not forgetting, waiting, temporarily belittling himself, humbling himself. A race of such human beings of *ressentiment* will in the end be necessarily *more clever* than any noble race" (§10). The more cerebral, spiritual life of the base types, while resulting in superior intellect relative to the nobles, has a downside in its inability to let go of emotions and especially in its encumbering manner of dealing with enemies. Nobles have the ability to forgive and forget misdeeds — they are "full natures in whom there is an excess of plastic, reconstructive, healing and even forgetting-inducing power" — but base people do not immediately purge themselves of negative emotions, and so their relations with others become poisoned. Indeed, Nietzsche here elevates the enemy in the same laudatory spirit he invoked in *Zarathustra* ("On Friends," "On War and Warrior-Peoples"); one must be able to love and honor one's enemies as the noble do, out of strength and solidarity, whereas the base *despise* their enemies as "evil ones" and are consumed by this hatred (§10).

Inasmuch as the noble are the ones who act and act out, the doers as opposed to the brooders and thinkers, their "predatory ground" must always emerge. "What constitutes the ground of all these noble races is the predator, the magnificent *blond beast* roaming about lustily after prey and victory; a discharging of this hidden ground is needed from time to time; the animal must emerge once more, must return to the wilderness: — Roman, Arabic, Germanic, Japanese nobility, Homeric heroes, Scandinavian Vikings — they are all the same in this need" (§11). The infamous "blond beast" is not exclusively Germanic and includes Homeric heroes and Roman nobility just as it includes Germanics and Vikings. The "blond" does indeed refer to the color of the lion, Zarathustra's companion in Part Four and the second figure in "On Three Transformations," but it is also clear from the context that Nietzsche is rather typically glorifying the warrior at the expense of the warrior's opposite, the "domestic animal" human, the tamed humans who embrace a slave morality. He does not dispute our need to fear the blond beast, but at the same time, "who would rather not fear a hundred times more if he could admire at the same time, than *not* fear but then no longer be able to escape the nauseating sight of the deformed, dwarfed, atrophied and poisoned?" (§11, continued in §12) The point is that for Nietzsche "greatness" in human beings is an endangered trait; it does not manifest in the tamed specimens but, rather, in the noble, warrior types who inspire fear but also admiration. The tamed human being represents degeneration, diminution of the species, and leveling, all qualities exposed and challenged by Zarathustra ("Zarathustra's Preface" 3–5, "On War and Warrior-Peoples," "On the New Idol," "On Flies of the Market Place," "On Loving Thy Neighbor," "On the

Compassionate," "On Priests," "On the Rabble," "On Virtue that Diminishes," etc.). Nietzsche's argument sounds far more reasoned when we consider that the "tamed" humans also represent sublimation, spiritualization, and danger; he typically works himself into a minor rhetorical frenzy by focusing on the extreme poles, when in fact he is describing the cultural consequences of the proverb "the pen is mightier than the sword."[6]

Speaking specifically to the later, *ressentiment*-powered "good" of the oppressed, we are invited to consider one of Nietzsche's favorite metaphors. "It does not seem strange that lambs bear a grudge against the great birds of prey; only this is no reason to hold it against the great birds of prey that they snatch themselves little lambs" (§13). What follows this statement of fact is a detailed analysis of how we ascribe a false choice to humans when we would never think to ascribe such a choice to lesser predators, such as eagles, hawks, and owls. "To demand of strength that it *not* express itself as strength, that it *not* be a will to overwhelm, a will to topple, a will to become master, a thirst for enemies and obstacles and triumphs is just as absurd as demanding of weakness that it express itself as strength" (§13). We are capable of acknowledging the necessity of this relationship in nature, but in the realm of human nature, specifically in the realm of morals, we rather fall apart, according to Nietzsche, and resort to denial. The weak, instead of admitting weakness as a consequence of impotence, claim to embrace weakness voluntarily in order to simultaneously claim the mantle of morality—the weak elevate their weakness to a merit, to a virtue (§13). This extremely clever inversion, or revaluation, is a kind of magic that turns impotence into kindness, fear into humility, misery into "selection by God," and spittle-licking into "honor the authorities."

6. Heinrich Heine, N's favorite poet, claimed the superiority of his pen, as poet, over the guns and force of the censors of Metternich-era Europe. See the conclusion to his *Deutschland: A Winter's Tale*, Caput XXVII.

By the end of their lives, the weak have consoled themselves for their suffering in the here and now by a "phantasmagoria of anticipated future blessedness" (§14). In fact, however, the profound, resentful denial of the base types spawns their ideals, many of which serve to masquerade as strength in the absence of strength. Nietzsche deconstructs this "blessedness" by quoting from Thomas Aquinas, whose schadenfreude is anything but saintly, and he follows this with an even longer quote by Tertullian.

The last two sections of the First Treatise pull together the major threads of the argument. "Good and bad" and "good and evil" are two different systems of valuation; the latter has been preponderant for millennia, but the struggle between them goes on and is symbolized as " 'Rome against Judea, Judea against Rome':—so far there has been no greater event than *this* struggle, *this* formulation of the question, *this* deadly contradiction" (§16). The Jews, meanwhile, "were the priestly people of *ressentiment* par excellence, endowed with a popular-moral genius without peer" (§16); except for a brief resurgence in the Renaissance, Rome and its classical ideal have succumbed, though the French did what they could in the seventeenth and eighteenth centuries, resulting in the appearance of Napoleon, "this synthesis of an *inhuman* and a *superhuman*" (§16). Nietzsche expresses the hope that the opposition is not over, not finished—and of course his *Genealogy* is an investment in reigniting the "terrible flaring up of the old fire." He wants it to be understood that his phrase "beyond good and evil" is *not* synonymous with "beyond good and bad" (§17). And he underscores how serious he is about his task by calling for an academic essay contest on the history of the development of moral concepts: "*All* the sciences from now on must work in advance on the philosopher's task of the future: this task understood to be that the philosopher has to solve the *problem of values*, that he has to determine the *rank-order of values*" (his note to §17).

The Second Treatise begins with a bold formulation on the nature of human being—nature's task has been to breed an animal that is allowed to make promises—Nietzsche asks, "Is this not the genuine problem *of* human beings?" (§1). Animals that we are, our "faculty of repression" has enabled us to mentally digest our experiences so as to forget and go on living, unhindered by memory: "Precisely this necessarily forgetful animal in whom forgetting represents a force, a form of *strong* health, has now bred in itself a counter-faculty, a memory with whose help forgetfulness is exempted for certain cases—namely, for those cases where promises are to be made" (§1). Memory was made, produced, and created in us through the long practice of "morality of custom," which throughout prehistoric times (and Nietzsche reckons in *Genealogy* in terms of the prehistory of human beings, our longest period to date) imposed a ritual of obedience that made us "predictable with the help of the morality of custom and the social straightjacket" (§2). At the end of this long and "tremendous process" we find modern humankind, "the autonomous, supermoral individual who has liberated himself from the morality of custom," but this was an arduous road paved with cruelty, the main tool used for making memory. Here Nietzsche is literally talking about making or building in the human species a capacity for memory, not speaking metaphorically of "making" a memory of a specific experience or event in a given person. This was messy work: "It never got done without blood, torture, sacrifice when humanity considered it necessary to make a memory for itself; the most horrific sacrifices and pledges (which include the sacrifice of the firstborn), the most repulsive mutilations (for example, castrations), the cruelest ritual forms of all religious cults (and all religions at their deepest foundations are systems of cruelty)—all of this has its origin in that instinct that intuited pain to be its most powerful mnemonic aid" (§3). The teaching of memory through torture and cruelty has a rich and long history, of which he provides specific examples from German medieval society; "reason, seriousness, mastery over the affects, this whole gloomy business we call reflection, all these prerogatives and showpieces of the human being: how dearly they have been bought! how much blood and horror are at the bottom of all 'good things'!" (§3).

Nietzsche wants next to account for the emergence of "guilt" and "bad conscience," more "gloomy things" in the manner of reason and reflection. Modern genealogists of morality do not go back far enough in time: "Have these previous genealogists of morality allowed themselves even to dream from a distance that, for example, the major moral concept 'guilt' has its origin in the very material concept 'debt'?" (§4). German *Schuld,* and, more commonly, its plural, *Schulden,* mean debt in the economic sense and guilt in the moral sense; the ubiquity and proximity of actual debts must surely precede the development of "guilt," of "moral debt" so to speak. Punishment, on this reasoning, developed first on the basis of "the idea that every injury has its *equivalent* somewhere and can be paid off, even if only through the *pain* of the offender," rather than on the basis of a much later and more refined notion that "a criminal deserves punishment *because* he could have acted differently" (§4). We must look to the "contractual relationship between *creditor* and *debtor*, which is as old as the existence of 'legal subjects,'" for the notion that every debt has its price, every debt can be discharged (§4). As he does throughout *Genealogy*, Nietzsche warns his readers that the details of prehistoric and even later trade and commerce are not for the squeamish: "Precisely here *promising* takes place; precisely here what matters is *making* a memory for the one who promises; precisely here, we may suspect, there will be a trove of harsh, cruel, painful things" (§5). For example, in order to persuade another of the solemnity of his promise to pay, a debtor "pledges something by virtue of a contract to the creditor in the event he does not pay, something that he otherwise 'owns' or over which he otherwise still has power, for example, his body or his wife or his freedom or even his life"

(§5). In the absence of these "collaterals," a substitute is sought for the goods that cannot be repaid: "The equivalence is provided by the fact that in place of an advantage that pays directly for the injury (thus in place of compensation in money, land, or possession of any kind) the creditor is granted a kind of *pleasure* as repayment and compensation—the pleasure of being allowed to vent his power uninhibitedly on someone powerless . . . [b]y means of 'punishment' of the debtor the creditor partakes of a *master's right*" (§5).

This punishment that brings pleasure to the creditor and therefore discharges the debt contributes to the blossoming of a culture of torture and cruelty. "[M]*aking* someone suffer felt good in the highest degree, insofar as the injured one traded an extraordinary counter-pleasure for the loss, including the displeasure over the loss: *making* someone suffer—a real *festival* . . . was priced more highly the more it contradicted the rank and social standing of the creditor"(§6). Nietzsche admits that he is conjecturing on the issue of price in relation to social standing, but it makes sense that deriving pleasure from a debtor's pain has the side effect of upward social mobility when the punishment is publicly celebrated, when even a commoner can play "the master," and when spectacles of cruelty contribute to the festivity of social events: "In any case it was not all that long ago that people could not imagine royal weddings and folk festivals on a grand scale without executions, torturings or perhaps an auto-da-fé" (§6). The suggestion is that even in contemporary spectacles of punishment "there is so much that is *festive!*" (§6).

Counterintuitively, Nietzsche claims that life was more cheerful during this "longest period of human history," during human prehistory "when humankind was not yet ashamed of its cruelty" (§7). For that matter, "it is even permitted to entertain the possibility that the delight in cruelty really need not have died out: in relation to how pain hurts more today, it merely needed a certain sublimation and subtilization" (§7). It is the supposedly pleasing sight of watching others suffer

that led to the prehistoric notion that "every evil is justified, if
the sight of it uplifts a god" (§7), a concept Nietzsche had
treated in *Dawn* 18 where he came to a similar conclusion:
cruelty is still with us. At this point Nietzsche ventures a guess
at the origin of the philosophical notion of free will. "Was not
that so audacious, so fateful invention of the philosophers,
which was first made at the time for Europe, that of 'free will,'
of the absolute spontaneity of human beings in good and evil,
not made above all in order to create a right to the idea that
the gods' interest in humans, in human virtue *could never
exhaust itself*? . . . a completely deterministically conceived
world would have been predictable for gods and consequently
also tiresome after a brief while" (§7). This notion of human
suffering as a spectator blood sport of the gods motivates the
need for early philosophers to speculate on free will, a concept whereby humans become responsible for their own actions and therefore unpredictable and *interesting* to gods. We
recall that in the First Treatise human beings first become an
interesting animal on account of "the priestly caste, this most
intriguing and dangerous form of human being" (§6). The
line here between philosophers and priests is very thin, and
not surprisingly, since Nietzsche ascribes ascetic impulses to
philosophers; this is a problem we will deal with in the Third
Treatise (cf. §§ 7–12 in particular).

The ancient buyer–seller relationship is deeply ingrained in
the psyche: "Setting prices, measuring values, thinking up
equivalents, exchanging—this preoccupied the very first
thinking of human beings to such an extent that in a certain
sense it is *the* thinking per se" (§7). This thinking is shared by
communities, adopted by them, as individuals agree to abide
by the community's morals and customs in exchange for security and protection; when the community intercedes on behalf
of its individuals, it "will get whatever repayment it can, we
can count on this. What is least at stake here is the direct injury caused by the offender; aside from this, the lawbreaker is
above all a 'breaker,' a breaker of his contract and word *to the*

whole" (§9). When the community is injured, moreover, it is not sufficient for the offender to merely lose the benefits of the community; "rather, he is now reminded of *what these goods are worth.* The anger of the injured creditor, of the community restores him to the wild and outlaw condition from which he was previously protected; it pushes him away—and now every manner of hostility may be vented on him" (§9). Pressing ahead to more modern times, Nietzsche explains that once the community becomes powerful it no longer feels an existential threat from a dangerous offender—the evildoer is no longer declared an outlaw, and penal law will treat his violations as dischargeable. In fact, the creditor-community begins to practice "humane" treatment when it wishes to demonstrate its wealth and strength by tolerating impairment: "Justice that began with 'everything is dischargeable, everything must be discharged' ends by looking the other way and allowing the one who is incapable of paying to go free—it ends like every good thing on earth, by sublating *itself.* This self-sublation of justice: we know by what beautiful name it calls itself—*mercy*" (§10). Thus the origin of mercy is no more or less mysterious, or divine, than the origin of punishment and the "justice" from which it arises. Observe, however, that the suspension of repayment, the "turning of the other cheek" in the language of humility, is not performed here out of altruistic motives—the community (and conceivably an individual) of supreme and sovereign power demonstrates its power through indifference to the offender.

So far Nietzsche has described a system of justice based on exchange, and he has pursued the thread of this justice from the relationship of the creditor to the debtor, where the notion prevails that all transgressions, all debts, are dischargeable, whether in terms of payment in goods or payment in pleasure at the sight of the debtor's pain. But his contemporaries, among them Eugen Dühring, seek the origin of justice on the ground of *ressentiment*, and this Nietzsche refutes in the next two sections, drawing mainly on his doctrine of the will to power. It is not the resentful, impotent, and furtively vengeful who invent justice; it is not here in the "soil of reactive feelings" "that the homeland of justice must be sought"; instead, "The active, attacking, infringing individual is always a hundred paces closer to justice than the reactive; it is simply not necessary at all for him to appraise his object falsely and with prejudice in the way the reactive person does, and must do" (§11). For demonstrations of this, he asks us to look around in history for the home of legal administration and the need for law, which will be found "in the sphere of the active, strong, spontaneous and aggressive." It is the powerful who intervene *against* reactive feelings; the strong powers assert their will over subordinates "to make an end of the senseless raging of *ressentiment* among them." Accordingly, "justice" and "injustice" come about only "once law is established (and *not*, as Dühring wants, beginning with the injurious act)" (§11). At this point Nietzsche relies on his naturalistic style of argumentation, cautioning that "from the highest biological standpoint legal circumstances can always be only *exceptional circumstances*, as partial restrictions of the actual will to life that aims at power, and subordinate themselves as individual means to its overall goal: namely as a means to create *greater* units of power" (§11). Thus for Nietzsche justice serves as a means in the continuing struggle for power, not as a neutralization or an attenuation of this necessary struggle.

Sections 12–15 refine the argument concerning the origin and purpose of punishment, separate issues that are too often conflated. Genealogists naïvely "discover some 'purpose' in punishment, for instance, revenge or deterrence, then they blithely place this purpose at the beginning, as *causa fiendi* of punishment, and — they're finished" (§12). However, "all purposes, all utilities are only *signs* that a will to power has become master over something less powerful and has impressed its own functional meaning onto it" (§12). This he explains by challenging another commonly held belief regarding evolution; there is no *progressus* toward a goal in evolution; "instead, it is the succession of more or less profound, more or less mutually independent processes of overpowering playing themselves out" in an organ. Even more striking, atrophy, degeneration, and death also "belong to the conditions of actual *progressus*: which always appears in the form of a will and a way to *greater power* and is always asserted at the expenses of numerous smaller powers." In *Zarathustra* we have a similar description, albeit in the elevated prophetic language that favors the use of parables. Zarathustra finds the will to be master even in those who serve; they serve the stronger because they want to be master of what is even weaker than they. The small give way to the great, but the greatest also gives way "and for the sake of power—bets its life." There is no will to existence, no will to life, but the proximity of will and life is underscored by Zarathustra: "Only where there is life, there, too, is will: not will to live but rather——so I teach you——will to power! / Much is valued by the living more highly than life itself; yet out of this valuing itself speaks——the will to power!" (*Z* "On Self-Overcoming"). This line of reasoning is also used to deflate the concept of adaptation as it is attributed to Herbert Spencer, who defines life "as an increasingly purposive inner adaptation to external circumstances" (§12). What is primary according to Nietzsche is "the principal superiority of the spontaneous, attacking, infringing, reinterpreting, reordering and shaping powers, upon whose effect 'adaptation' first follows" (§12). He made a very similar argument in *Beyond*, where he cautioned the physiologists against positing self-preservation as the cardinal drive of an organism; self-preservation is indeed present, but only as an indirect and frequent consequence of the organism's discharging of its strength (*BGE* 13).

The meaning of punishment is fluid, even indefinable, and this Nietzsche demonstrates by reciting a litany of "purposes" ranging from punishment as repayment to the injured party all the way to punishment as a compromise with the natural state of revenge (§13). One thing he desires to make clear is that punishment does *not* have the utility commonly ascribed to it, "of awakening the *feeling of guilt* in the guilty party," of triggering the bad conscience or the sting of conscience (§14). On the contrary, punishment "makes people hard and cold; it concentrates, it sharpens the feeling of alienation; it strengthens the power of resistance," thereby actually hindering the development of feelings of guilt. Add to this, he argues, the hypocrisy of the authorities who use underhanded and violent techniques in prosecuting offenders and administering punishment, and we must conclude that bad conscience, "this most uncanny and interesting plant of our earthly vegetation, did *not* grow from this soil" (§14). The actual effect of punishment would be more modest; for example, in humans and animals it can achieve "an increase of fear, a sharpening of prudence, a mastery of one's desires: this is how punishment *tames* a human being, but it does not make him 'better'" (§15). As usual, Nietzsche drills down far enough to expose the ugly roots of ideals; we desire that punishment stem from "noble" or altruistic motives and that it function as the trigger to bad conscience, but neither is the case.

The hypothesis he offers for the origin of bad conscience boldly frames its ramifications for ancient humankind. Recall that in §13 of the First Treatise, Nietzsche used the metaphor of the bird of prey feasting on little lambs; we do not side morally with the lamb in this struggle, that is, we do not ascribe "evil" to the bird of prey, because we understand that it cannot do otherwise. The morality of *ressentiment*, however, does ascribe the term *evil* to people of power, expecting their strength to express itself in terms of weakness. Let us say this is Nietzsche's metaphor from above, from the sky. In the case of bad conscience, he reaches down for a metaphor from the sea. Bad conscience is a "deep sickness to which humans had to succumb under the pressure of that most fundamental of all changes they could ever experience — that change of finding themselves locked once and for all under the spell of society and peace" (§16). We must imagine what it must have been

like "for aquatic animals when they were forced either to
become land animals or to perish," since these human semi-
animals had already adapted to warfare, roaming, and life in
the wilderness and now "all at once all of their instincts were
devalued and 'disconnected'" (§16). This is indeed difficult to
imagine, especially since the dramatic effect of this time-
consuming transformation allegedly occurs "all of a sudden,"
but Nietzsche stays the course: "I believe that never on earth
had such a feeling of misery, such a leaden uneasiness, existed—and what's more those old instincts had not all of a
sudden ceased to make their demands!" So it is an extremely
conflicted, extremely burdened human being who is in the
throes of coping with a forced curtailment of the instincts,
such that "subterranean gratifications" had to be sought. "All
the instincts that do not discharge themselves externally now
turn inward—this is what I call the *internalization*[7] of human
beings: now for the first time human beings grow what later is
called the 'soul'" (§16). Call it soul or psyche, what is in the
process of forming here does so under the strain of repression
or obstruction: "Those terrible bulwarks with which the state
apparatus protected itself against the old instincts of freedom—punishments above all belong to these bulwarks—managed to turn all those instincts of the wild, free, roaming
human being backward *against human beings themselves*" (§16).
Lacking external enemies and outlets, humans begin to tear at
themselves like caged animals.

This transformative event in the prehistory of humankind,
the emergence "of an animal psyche turning against itself,
taking sides against itself, brought about on earth something
so new, profound, unheard of, enigmatic, contradictory *and
full of future* that the aspect of the earth changed essentially as

---

7. N's term here is *Verinnerlichung*. It bears remarking that Freud uses the
term *verinnerlicht* in an identical fashion in chapter 7 of *Civilization and Its
Discontents* when explaining civilization's responsibility for the emergence
of the superego in terms of the internalization of aggression.

a result" (§16). Indeed, such a spectacle is involved here that Nietzsche once more raises the issue of the human spectacle seen from the point of view of gods, which provides an inspiration if not motivation for the invention of the concept of free will (§16). Here, however, it could almost go unnoticed that he is insisting on the linkage between the enormity of the event (forced herding into communities; animal psyche turning against itself) and its fitness to serve as food for the gods: "Indeed, it required divine spectators to appreciate the spectacle that began here and whose end is by no means foreseeable — a spectacle too subtle, too wonderful, too paradoxical for it to play out senselessly and unnoticed on some ridiculous planet!" (§16). It is a curious perspective, to say the least, that shows interest in this spectacle *and* considers the earth "some ridiculous planet." This is Dionysus speaking, or Nietzsche speaking through the mask of Dionysus as a "divine spectator." The clue to this interpretation is found in the Zarathustran conclusion to this section, where Nietzsche invokes Heraclitus, Zeus, and chance in speaking hopefully of this new and transforming humanity, "as if something new were announcing and preparing itself in him, as if humanity were not a goal, but only a way, an episode, a bridge, a great promise" (§16). In the prologue of *Zarathustra* we read: "What is great about humans is that they are a bridge and not a goal: what can be loved about humans is that they are a *crossing over* and a *going under*" (*Z* "Zarathustra's Preface" 4).

Two important stipulations are reiterated and elaborated on when Nietzsche insists that the change was not gradual and not voluntary; it must have occurred as a leap and a break, "an unavoidable disaster against which there was no struggle and not even *ressentiment*." Second, it took place as a sheer act of force perpetrated by the oldest and most tyrannical "state" with its "oppressive and ruthless machinery" of conformance. The executors of this deed are none other than the blond beasts, "some pack of blond beasts of prey, a race of conquerors and masters which, organized in a warlike manner and with the strength to organize, does not hesitate to lay its terrible paws on a perhaps tremendously superior population in terms of numbers, but one that is still shapeless, still roaming about" (§17). As he has on other occasions in *Genealogy*, here too he warns readers against reacting negatively to his message because "it is ugly and painful." What is at stake here is the eventual emergence of an "instinct of freedom" that Nietzsche prefers to call will to power, "only the material on which the formative and violating nature of this force vents itself is precisely humanity itself, its entire animal ancient self" (§18). Bad conscience, like *ressentiment*, is inventive; "a sickness as pregnancy is a sickness" (§19). We understand why Zarathustra speaks: "You who create, you superior humans! No one is pregnant for the sake of someone else's child" (*Z* "On Superior Humans" 11). At this point he is not yet done with the creative potential of bad conscience. The debtor-creditor relationship, already discussed in terms of individuals and the communities that intervene on behalf of individuals, is next applied by the present generation to their ancestors: "Here the conviction prevails that the tribe absolutely *exists* only through the sacrifice and achievements of the ancestors" (§19). The more stable and prosperous the community, the more guilt, the more debt feeling piles up in the present generation, until "ultimately the ancestors of the *mightiest* tribes must have grown to prodigious proportions through the imagination of growing fear, and they must have been pushed back into the darkness of a divine uncanniness and inconceivability:—in the end the ancestor is necessarily transfigured into a *god*" (§19). Here Nietzsche has traced the invention or, let us say, the motivation to invent gods, to extreme fear of one's ancestors, in turn motivated by extreme feelings of guilt, indebtedness, and bad (guilty) conscience.

From here we scroll forward to the modern era, to the apex of monotheism or to the period of the "maximal god," as Nietzsche calls him; its rise "also brought to the fore a maximum of guilt feeling on earth." However, if this maximal

Christian God is in decline, if he is dead, as Zarathustra proclaims, then "we can infer from the inexorable decline of faith
in the Christian God that now we also have a considerable
decline in the human consciousness of guilt." What will we do
with this new freedom, this atheism that functions as a "second innocence"? (§20). Unfortunately, with the moralization
of guilt and duty, which effectively stuffs them back into bad
conscience, the new opportunity for a second innocence is
stymied; even worse, this moralization pessimistically dictates
that the debt, the guilt, can never be discharged (enter "eternal
punishment"); now all humans are afflicted with a curse (enter
"original sin"); now humankind's womb, nature, is pronounced
evil (enter "demonization of nature"); now life on earth is
worthless (enter "nihilism and oblivion"). The way out, the
escape route, is the *redeemer*—"God sacrificing himself for
the guilt of humanity, God himself making payment to himself" (§21). There is a ghastly irony to this "redemption," symbolized first by the torture of humanity redeemed through the
physical torture (Crucifixion) of God's son but culminating in
"the creditor sacrificing himself for his debtor, out of *love* (can
you believe it?—) out of love for his debtor!" (§21).

The ideal of the "holy God" has brought forth "this insane
sad beast human being" (§22). We are sick, mad to the point
of psychic cruelty against ourselves, and Nietzsche asks us to
imagine "how in this night of torment and absurdity the cry
of *love* rang out" (§22). But he hastens to add that there have
been healthier, more uplifting conceptions of gods, such as
those of the ancient Greeks (§23). Here we are reminded of the
strong praise of polytheism in *Joyful Science* 143, where human
ingenuity, freedom, inventiveness, and free-spiritedness were
set in motion by donning the protective masks of manifold
gods and fictive beings, whereas monotheism exerts a choking,
reductive effect. But today we are "wedded to bad conscience,"
habituated to regarding our "natural inclinations with an 'evil
eye,'" and perhaps we are not strong enough to perform a reversal of this circumstance, "namely to wed to bad conscience

the *unnatural* inclinations, all those aspirations to the Beyond, to what is counter to the senses, instincts, nature, animal" (§24). Nietzsche leaves his questions unanswered at this point, but he suggests an alternative spirit in language remarkably reminiscent of Zarathustra's speeches and exhortations, until he can contain himself no longer: "But what am I saying here? Enough! Enough! At this point only one thing befits me, to be silent: otherwise I would profane what only a younger man is at liberty to do, a 'more future one,' a stronger one than I—what *Zarathustra* alone is at liberty to do, *Zarathustra the godless*" (§25). The figure of Zarathustra is used here in a manner very similar to Nietzsche's use of the Dionysian musical lyrical voice when expository prose ceases to meet his needs; Nietzsche claims he must be silent because Zarathustra has already spoken, and *Genealogy*, like *Beyond*, constitutes the nay-saying and nay-doing portion of his work, of which *Zarathustra* had been the yes-saying and yes-doing part. In the Second Treatise we are taken by the hand back to those times and places where the madness, the sickness, began, long before Judeo and Christian conceptions of God, but we are also taken through this period of moralization of the concepts guilt and bad conscience, until we are given a glimpse of the exit, a way out.

The Third Treatise is preceded by an epigraph from *Zarathustra*. It is significant that this treatise, like the second one, concludes on a Zarathustran note, though not as explicitly as the Second Treatise. The phrase "ascetic ideals" is used interchangeably with "the ascetic ideal"; what we learn about them is their place in the development of the human being to date as reflected in humankind's higher types, such as artists, philosophers, scholars, and priests. Wagner and Schopenhauer carry most of the weight for the artists and the philosophers, and it is with them that Nietzsche begins his inquiry.

The question of the meaning of ascetic ideals is rephrased: Why did Richard Wagner in old age pay homage to chastity? Why did he switch over to his opposite? He had planned an opera based on "the wedding of Luther," which would have bridged chastity and sensuality, or "animal and angel," but instead he created the *Meistersinger*. Instead of going the way of Hafiz and Goethe, who bridged these realms and this contradiction to the glory of their art, Wagner opted for chastity (§2). Parsifal, for instance, this "country bumpkin"—is he supposed to be taken seriously, or is he perhaps (through wishful thinking) a "mischievous parody of tragedy"? What he represents is a "curse on the senses and the spirit," a "return to Christian-pathological and obscurantist ideals," and for Wagner himself, "self-denial and self-effacement" (§3). Of course we must distinguish between an artist and his work; Homer would not have created an Achilles if he had been an Achilles, so in creating his Parsifal, Nietzsche implies, Wagner created something not of himself, and therefore turned on himself, so to speak (§4).

If artists are too mercurial, too inscrutable to help explain the meaning of the ascetic ideal, perhaps we can gain from examining philosophers. Schopenhauer, "a man and knight with a steely gaze," nonetheless paid homage to the ascetic spirit (§5). Schopenhauer subscribed to the Kantian understanding of aesthetics that foregrounds impersonality and universality and merely reflects on art as opposed to engaging it from the standpoint of the artist's experience. Kant's definition of the beautiful is "what pleases *without interest*" (§6), a hideous error for Nietzsche, who elevated art to a stimulus for living and was critical even of the modernist notion of art for art's sake. What Schopenhauer found appealing in this was the emphasis on disinterestedness; he used aesthetic contemplation to break free of sexual interestedness, which is a powerful manifestation of the will, and therefore to be resisted (§6). This rather coy, ascetic stance on the will and on sexuality betrays Schopenhauer's preference, to be sure, but Stendhal's insight that "the beautiful promises happiness" is closer to Nietzsche's heart. For the philosopher Schopenhauer (and perhaps for Kant as well?), the meaning of the ascetic ideal is "to break free of a torture" (§6).

Philosophers everywhere share a combination of "irritability and rancor" against sensuality and "prejudice and cordiality" for the ascetic ideal (§7). For instance, philosophers do not marry: "A married philosopher belongs in *comedy*" (§7). The ascetic ideal gives philosophers a way out, a free pass from all constraints, "so many bridges to *independence*" (§7). Thus Schopenhauer could use the ascetic ideal to free himself from sex, the will, and women. What the ideal means in philosophers, then, is "an optimum of the conditions of highest and boldest spirituality" (§7) — it is compatible with their needs. Far from thinking of the saint when they contemplate the value of the ascetic ideal, philosophers think of themselves, of their freedom, clarity of mind, and peace and quiet to work. This selfishness notwithstanding, philosophers "know the three great slogans of the ascetic ideal: poverty, humility, chastity," and all the inventive spirits will have all three of these to some extent (seclusion, distance, avoidance of fame, princes and women, no false martyrdom, and sexual abstinence) (§8). Philosophy lacked the courage to stand on its own in the beginning, therefore it clung to the *apron strings* of the ascetic ideal. Given the drives of the philosopher, which include doubting, negating, prudent decisions, analyzing, exploring, seeking, venturing, comparing, and balancing, his work ran "counter to the first demands of morality and conscience" (§9); in *Dawn* Nietzsche had discussed how the earliest contemplative human beings had to contend with enormous pressure because they were feared and despised (§10). No wonder, then, that the aloof, world-denying, and life-inimical stance of philosophers in recent times has become the default for philosophy—it had to "cloak itself" with an ascetic wrap in order to survive (§10). Now the relevant question for Nietzsche is whether the ascetic caterpillar has transformed into a daring spirit that could make philosophers possible, as if for the first time (§10).

But it is only in the ascetic priest that we can truly explore the question of the meaning of ascetic ideals. This "life-inimical species" prospers everywhere in all times, leading to the conclusion that it must serve the interest of life (§11). The priest's contradiction of life represents "*ressentiment* without equal," "insatiable instinct and power-will" (§11), which seeks out and identifies error "precisely where the actual life-instinct most unconditionally posits truth" (§12). On closer examination, the ascetic principle of "life against life" makes no sense physiologically, and Nietzsche is skeptical of clumsy psychological explanations. What is at stake is "*the protective and healing instinct of a degenerating life*," which resorts to ascetic means to counter the physiological sickness, weariness, and exhaustion of life. Counterintuitively, the work of the life-negating ascetic priest is a force for conserving and creating life in the face of sickliness. "Where does it come from, this sickliness? For humankind is sicker, more uncertain, more changing, more indeterminate than any other animal, there is no doubt of this—he is *the* sick animal" (§13). Humans are challengers of fate, experimenters with themselves, insatiable in struggling for mastery: "how should such a brave and rich animal not also be the most endangered, the one sickest for the longest time?" (§13). The denial of life turns to life stimulus: "when he *wounds* himself, this master of destruction and self-destruction—afterward it is the wound itself that compels him *to live*" (§13). Throughout history humankind has experienced malaise, weariness of existence, a "desire for the 'end,'" and this sickliness is overcome or diverted, perhaps even transformed, when the species *as a body* has to rally from self-inflicted wounds, such that biological forces are now activated.

Sickliness in the species is so pervasive, so normal, that we should do everything possible to honor humans who turn out well. "The sick are the biggest danger to the healthy; *not* from the strongest does harm come to the strong, but from the weakest" (§14). Those who do not turn out well, the "deformed" and the "failures," as Nietzsche refers to them, constitute a powerful force: "They stroll among us as incarnate reproaches, as warnings to us—as if health, turning out well, strength, pride, feeling of power were depraved things in themselves" (§14). We recall that these practitioners of *ressentiment* have invented the category of evil and apply it to the strong; their will to power expresses itself in devising ways to tyrannize the healthy (§14). Those who turn out well and are happy with themselves and with life are pressured to doubt their right to happiness, and here Nietzsche's fear (or, worse, paranoia) takes on a brittle edge; "That the sick should *not* make the healthy sick . . . that should of course be the supreme viewpoint on earth:—but this would require above all things that the healthy remain *separated* from the sick, protected against even the sight of the sick" (§14). So fragile, so endangered, are the healthy, the ones who turned out well (*die Wohlgeratenen*) that Nietzsche demands quarantine. He argued a similar point less stridently in *Twilight of the Idols* ("Forays of an Untimely One," 14, titled "Anti-Darwin"), where he cautioned that the strong *do not* survive—they are outnumbered by the weak, and the weak are also smarter. But here, where he actually speaks of quarantine, we are witnessing what Henry Staten refers to as "fear of the power of the weak, a power against which he must fortify and rigidify the boundaries of strength."[8] After all, this is the same thinker who gave us a compelling argument for "Refinement through degeneration" (*HAH* 224), which contains his theory of increasing strength based on inoculation; and the famous slogan "[w]hat does not kill me makes me stronger" (*TI* "Sayings and Arrows" 8). In any case, the strong must not be enlisted as nurses or caretakers of the weak; there must be observance of "pathos of distance" (cf. *GM* I 2 and *BGE* 257), which is not

---

8. Henry Staten, *Nietzsche's Voice* (Ithaca, NY: Cornell University Press, 1990), 108.

physical distance and partition as in the case of quarantine (§14).

The sickly and the weak, since they cannot be served and nursed by the strong, are instead served and treated, in the medical sense, by priests, that is, by physicians who are themselves sick, and the priest has a "tremendous historical mission: His realm is *dominion over the suffering*" (§15). If *ressentiment* were allowed to pile up indefinitely, it would have the power of an explosive; the priest's job, therefore, is to "discharge this explosive in such a way that it does not blow up the herd or the shepherd . . . the priest is the *direction-changer* of *ressentiment*" (§15). This the priest manages to do by convincing his charges, his patients, that *they are to blame* for their circumstances, for their suffering (§15). Now it becomes a matter of prescribing the proper medications and cures, even though the priest is not really a physician but a would-be "savior" (healer) who works only on the malaise of the sufferer, not its causes (§17). By Nietzsche's reckoning, religion itself is a sickness, "*a physiological feeling of inhibition*" that descends on the masses throughout history but whose remedy is always attempted by moral and psychological means (§17). So what the priest is able to administer for this depressed condition amounts, in psychological and moral terms, to "un-selfing" and "sanctification," while in physiological terms it amounts to hypnotization, a kind of hibernation or estivation for humans who are kept barely alive (§17). When hypnosis is not used to suppress sensitivity to pain, then an easier means is used: mechanical activity (§18), which is supplemented by "the joy of *giving* joy," of loving one's neighbor. In prescribing this "joy of *giving* joy," "the ascetic priest at bottom is prescribing a stimulation of the strongest, most life-affirming drive, even if in the most cautious dosage—of the *will to power*" (§18). Mutual benevolence, the will to mutuality, and community then achieve a fuller outburst in the previously triggered will to power, which contributes to "formation of a herd," an "essential step and victory in the battle with depression" (§18). By these standards the power and the subtlety of the priest as he wields his ascetic cures are unmistakable, and so too is the priest's service in redirecting the *ressentiment* of the oppressed, a class or cohort that is effectively *perpetuated* by his efforts but never cured.

The means just described for the treatment of malaise are innocent, and the priest has "guilty" means in his medicine cabinet as well, all of them involving "some kind of *excess of feeling*" (§19). Provided they are discharged suddenly, the affects have the potential to liberate the sick from malaise and depression: "anger, fear, lustfulness, revenge, hope, triumph, despair, cruelty . . . the ascetic priest has unscrupulously taken into his service the *whole* pack of wild dogs" (§20). We recall that the moralization of debt and bad conscience is the work of priests, so it does not surprise us that they are experts in exploiting guilt, to the point where his patients no longer protest against pain but crave it (§20). This long history of "emotional excess under the aegis of holy intentions" is indelibly inscribed on humanity, and the ascetic ideal is "*the genuine catastrophe* in the history of the health of European humanity" (§21). Not only the health of the psyche is ruined, but artistic and literary taste as well, along with the tact required for reverence. Nietzsche's favorite case in point is Martin Luther, "the peasant," who was "annoyed by the *good etiquette* of the Church" and its hierarchy, and insisted on speaking directly with his God (§22). Rather than credit Luther with liberating people from their priests, Nietzsche sees the appearance and actions of Luther as consequences of priestly activity; to the extent that Luther propped up and rescued the Church at the point where it should have collapsed from its own internal rot (cf. *BGE* 48, 50; *EH* "The Case of Wagner" 2), he reinvigorated the Church and Christianity, thereby contributing to the vicious circle of religious malaise that is never cured.

The Third Treatise takes stock of the ascetic ideal in terms of its extraordinary power and influence, prompting Nietzsche to ask: "*where* is the counterwill in which a *counterideal* expresses itself?" (§23). His objective here is to evaluate any existing alternatives, challengers, and competitors of the powerful ascetic ideal. He had earlier pointed in this direction when he discussed in §24 of the Second Treatise how "bad conscience" needs now to be wedded to all things *unnatural*, since thus far all things natural have been viewed with the evil eye. The counter will is not found in science, a likely enough contender, because "science today has absolutely *no* faith in itself . . . it is not the opposite of that ascetic ideal, but rather *its latest and most noble form*" (§23). Nor is it found among the philosophers and scholars, who believe themselves to be unbelievers; they are merely free thinkers, not free spirits (cf. *BGE* 44), because "*they still believe in truth*" (§23). Working with the Assassins' watchword of "nothing is true, everything is permitted," Nietzsche asks rhetorically: "Has any European, any Christian freethinker ever strayed into this proposition and its labyrinthine *consequences*? does he know the minotaur of this case *from experience*?" (§23). Note the Dionysian imagery ascribed to the experience of one who becomes lost in the labyrinth of truthlessness; labyrinth invokes Ariadne, the minotaur, and Dionysus the rescuer of Ariadne. Philosophers have never problematized truth; they have instead treated it like God, and for those who need more evidence of this, Nietzsche refers to *Joyful Science*, Book Five.

Artists are more likely to oppose the ascetic ideal, but we know this proposition is fraught because Nietzsche began his treatise with an examination of Wagner and Schopenhauer. Still, in art, "the *will to deception* has good conscience on its side," at least, and art was maligned by Plato as "the great slanderer of life" (§25). But when it comes to subservience to the ascetic ideal, "nothing is more corruptible than an artist" (§25), and we are back pondering why Wagner paid homage to the ascetic ideal in his older days. What about modern historiography then? Historiography has standards—it rejects teleology, has nothing to prove, is objective, suspends judgment, and so on, but here too we are disappointed; historians are lounging in their rotting armchairs; their "cowardly contemplativeness" and "lascivious eunuchry" have them "ogling at ascetic ideals" out of impotence (§26). Historians are not the heroes of the counter will and the counter ideal. He appears ready to conclude his search for a counter by claiming he will treat the issue in a work in preparation called "The Will to Power," but of course there would be no such work because Nietzsche gave up on that project—he instead wrote the works of 1888, which were obviously his priority.[9] One more contender is dismissed before he really abandons the search; atheism, which is still burdened by its will to truth. But atheism is not the counter either; rather, it is "that ideal itself in its most rigorous, most spiritual formulation, esoteric through and through, stripped of all outworks and thus not so much its remnant as its *core*" (§27). Stated differently, atheism "is the awe-inspiring *catastrophe* of a two-thousand-year training in truth, which in the end forbids itself the *lie of believing in God*" (§27). With all roads leading back to the will to truth, Nietzsche calls on his "unknown friends" to continue the exploration of the problem, *their* problem, namely, "that in us the will to truth came to consciousness of itself *as a problem*" (§27). The "unknown" or as yet unidentified friends, the "helping hands" he invoked in *Beyond*, will have to represent the counter ideal, build it, promulgate, and nourish it.

The importance of the ascetic ideal and the urgent need for its counter are brought together succinctly and pointedly in the final section. The very existence of human beings and the animal human had no meaning except for the meaning of the ascetic ideal itself, whose meaning is "that something was *lacking*, that a tremendous *void* surrounded humanity—he

9. Nietzsche's decision to give up the project of a work titled "The Will to Power" is discussed by Mazzino Montinari in "Nietzsche's *Nachlaß* 1885–1888 and the 'Will to Power,'" which appears as an editorial afterword to *CW* 9. See also Schrift, "Nietzsche's *Nachlass*" in *A Companion to Friedrich Nietzsche*, 405–28.

did not know how to justify, to explain, to affirm himself, he *suffered* from the problem of his meaning" (§28). The suffering suits us well as a species, but we want a reason for the suffering, a meaning and a purpose for suffering, "*and the ascetic ideal offered it a meaning!*" (§28). Humanity was poisoned by this ascetic ideal, to be sure, but also saved by it, because after all a wrong meaning or an unhealthy meaning is better than none at all; "*the will was saved*" (§28). The message here is that the will is paramount in humans, and as long as it can be active, there is hope. Nietzsche completes the circle when he reiterates his point of departure for the Third Treatise: "And, to say once more at the end what I said at the beginning: humanity would rather will *nothingness* than *not* will" (§28, cf. §1).

The challenge of a counter will that wills something affirmative, that effectively breaks out of the prison of nihilistic, ascetic willing, will require nothing less than heroics. Nietzsche signals the need for heroics and the means of these heroic efforts at key points in his narrative when he switches from expository prose and appears to interrupt his argument with Dionysian singing, with Dionysian bodied communication. We see this in *Beyond*, and we see it again in *Genealogy*, whether the transition is signaled by the mention of *Zarathustra*, his most Dionysian work, or by mentions of the labyrinth and minotaur and Ariadne—the Dionysian is the counter will, the counter ideal of the ascetic. But we should not kid ourselves about "heroics." For Nietzsche the concept of the hero is inextricably tied to tragedy as the chief function and meaning of the Dionysian, so we can expect any future heroics to be tragic, even as tragedy in *The Birth of Tragedy* is lauded as the most life-affirming expression. At the same time, the new "philosopher" Nietzsche is more attuned to the comic side of the Dionysian equation, the need to deal with the absurdity of existence through Dionysian means, which include music, playfulness, and defiance of gravity, both in physical and spiritual terms. *Thus Spoke Zarathustra* gave us a sense of the merits and faults of this new counter to the ascetic ideal—as heroes go, Zarathustra is not likely to sweep us off our feet, and he is more antihero than heroic as he struggles mightily, alternating between tears and laughter, to be affirmative.

Zarathustra is a start, a sign in the direction of growing into the counter ideal, the work Nietzsche considered his greatest very possibly because it was his most experimental, most tempting, and most "at-temptive." We recall that at the conclusion of *Beyond* he debuts Dionysus "the tempter god" (*Versucher-Gott*) as the philosopher god. All of the meanings of *versuchen* apply to *Zarathustra*: in it Nietzsche attempts, he experiments, he tempts, and he also visibly and repeatedly *fails*—Zarathustra's fortunes are ambiguous, his triumphs short-lived and limited—Zarathustra does not resolve or reconcile the contradictions of existence, but he is a bold experimenter of life affirmation, and perhaps his greatest service is that of midwifery. The works of 1886 and 1887 do indeed explicate *Zarathustra*, and they also attempt to explain, using the genealogical method, how formidable and extensive are the challenges to an affirmative habitation of the earth.

Problems of Translation

When we analyze the semantic fields of those virtues Nietzsche prizes, we find they are related to movement, defiance of gravity, and subtlety in taste and expression. Dance, music, and laughter are favorite guiding metaphors for Nietzsche's style, making him elusive for any translator. His pithy one-liners, the maxims and proverbs, are hard enough to render in their ambiguity and frequent wordplay, but even harder are the long, protracted sentences consisting of clauses that build to a crescendo or trail off into uncertainty. The complexity, indeed, musicality and muscularity, of Nietzsche's sentences should be visible on every page by the profusion of punctuation symbols—if these are missing, the translator has poured Nietzsche's prose into a blender, hoping in the end to give us something readable, something comprehensible, something familiar to the target language—and that is how Nietzsche's style gets lost in translation.

As Nietzsche's translator I have to assume that he knew how to punctuate a sentence, and I have to respect his choices for using a comma, a semicolon, a colon, an exclamation point, an ellipsis, quotations marks, and the all-important dash, known in German as the *Gedankenstrich*—literally the thought dash. It is potentially diminishing to remove these from his speech. To be sure, these tools of punctuation make it *different* to read Nietzsche, perhaps harder too, but are we not supposed to be reading Nietzsche? There is a tempo, a "time" in the sense of musical time, to Nietzsche's prose, and this is a quality he coaxed from the German language more effectively than most. Recent translators of Nietzsche have made important strides in capturing his style, understanding that quality of the thought is intimately related to its manner of presentation.

There are always certain German words and expressions whose equivalent is difficult to find in English. *Zurecht gefälscht and zurecht gedichtet,* from *BGE* 24, combine *zurecht,* roughly the state of modifying or arranging something in order to suit oneself, with the verbs *fälschen*—to forge or falsify—and *dichten*—to create or compose through writing; thus Nietzsche claims that our world is something we have "composed and forged into shape," basically to suit ourselves; there are other times when I use the verb "contrive" to indicate this kind of manipulation, depending on the verb that accompanies *zurecht. Der Erkennende* and *ein Erkennender* are verbal nouns formed from *erkennen,* to know or to recognize; literally we are referring to a knower, someone who knows, but this fails to convey the uncompleted nature of the activity of knowing. Some translators have used "seeker of knowledge" or "lover of knowledge," but these are too strong and specific, and when Nietzsche wants to use those qualifiers, he adds them: *Liebhaber der Erkenntnis* (*BGE* 26) means, literally, "lover of knowledge." Our connoisseur, borrowed from French, might apply in a few cases, but it refers to an expert and again lacks the ongoing quality of a verb. I mostly use "knowing one" for *Erkennender*. The noun *Not* most often means need, but it takes on nuances depending on the context; when it is not rendered as "need," it becomes, for example, "adversity" (*BGE* 44), "distress" (*BGE* 207, *GM* I 12), or "plight." The verb indicating that something turns out well or evolves successfully is *geraten*; "*ein Ding gerät*" means "a thing turns out well." Nietzsche frequently refers to human beings who turn out well, and to those who do not (§§62, 203). While *geraten* (to turn out well) and *missraten* (to turn out badly) are relatively straightforward, problems arise when he uses the participial forms of the verb to create nouns. *Halb-Mißratenen* (Part Nine, note 1) I shorten to "semi-misfits," but in *Genealogy*, where Nietzsche uses *die Missratenen* consistently to indicate people who have turned out badly, I use "the deformed," a strong expression but one that corresponds to its opposite, *Geratenes*, something well formed (cf. the conclusion of *GM* I 11).

Care must be taken in translating German to English around expressions used for human being. *Der Mensch* can mean human being, mankind, humankind, humanity, man, a person, or people, but because it is the word denoting the species human being, it is misleading to simply translate it as "man." *Mensch* is rendered as "human being" for the most part, but a specialized usage accompanied by a suffix, such as *Menschlichkeit* (*BGE* 263), must be rendered "humanity," to express humaneness. Similarly, in *Genealogy*, Nietzsche uses the noun *Menschheit* more than in any other work, and this I have rendered as "humankind" in order to distinguish it from his more common use of *Mensch* (human being). The important point to keep in mind is that Nietzsche is an ecumenical thinker whose concern is for the species human being; the concept *Übermensch* proclaimed by Zarathustra therefore rightly should be translated as "superhuman" (being).

In *Genealogy*, Third Treatise, two words are used synonymously for the psychic state of being depressed — *Verstimmung*, which ranges from "out of sorts" to "annoyed" to psychic "depressed," and *Depression*, whose meaning is indeed "depression." Some translators try to soften *verstimmt*, and its noun *Verstimmung*, to distinguish it from *Depression*, but here I think Nietzsche is describing people with a serious mental problem requiring priestly treatment, not merely people who are annoyed, displeased, or out of sorts. Where on one occasion Nietzsche uses both *Verstimmte* and *Deprimierte* (III 21), these are translated as "dejected" and "depressed," as opposed to interpreting this exception to mean that Nietzsche always assigns a different value to *verstimmt*. The verb *verunglücken* means to suffer a mishap, meet with an accident, or fail, hence when referring to humans, the noun *Verunglückte* is given as "failures," since these are not literally persons who have been involved in an accident. *Ausschweifung* can be "excess" or "dissipation," but I opt for the former to give a physical as opposed to a moral slant. *Unlust* is from the noun *Lust*, or "joy," which also carries the nuance of being in a good mood, being upbeat and happy, even motivated. It is a common expression for indicating like or dislike, as in *ich habe keine Lust*, "I don't feel like it" (or feel like doing anything). I use the word "malaise" for the condition Nietzsche describes as *Unlust* (at one point he uses *Depressions-Unlust* (III 20).

Other words posed problems, but the ones I just discussed required more compromise than most. *Beyond Good and Evil* and *On the Genealogy of Morality* elaborate in detail on thoughts and ideas Nietzsche had expressed with greater metaphoricity in *Zarathustra*. Something resembling a lexicon of technical terms emerges in *Genealogy*, where there is great focus on *die Seele*, the soul, or its Greek equivalent, *psyche*, more familiar to English speakers when the context turns to the psychological. Yet even in *Genealogy*, his most "technical" work, he avoids creating a jargon of his own, something later thinkers seem to find impossible.

A final word about how Nietzsche's works stand up to translation over the years. The more translations there are of a

work, the better, generally speaking, but the longer a translation has been in existence the greater our reliance on and our
familiarity with it. New translations of Nietzsche make the
original text seem strange to us, because we have grown accustomed to previous translations — but this "new" quality is
as it should be. For over half a century now, people in the English speaking world who take Nietzsche's writings seriously
have formed an impression of his thought based on previous
versions, most often those of Walter Kaufmann or R. J. Hol-
lingdale; this impression has influenced their thinking and
writing on Nietzsche — no later translator remains unaware
of this habituation and its profound effects. Still, every new
translation is a new opportunity, with fresh eyes possibly seeing nuances for the first time, and the current edition offers
not only the published writings but all of the notes, the so-
called *Nachlass* that has informed the best Nietzsche scholarship in the German- and English-speaking worlds.

Index of Persons

Subject Index

Page numbers followed by n and nn indicate notes.

Library of Congress Cataloging-in-Publication Data

Nietzsche, Friedrich Wilhelm, 1844–1900, author.
    Beyond good and evil ; On the genealogy of morality / Friedrich
Nietzsche ; translated, with an afterword, by Adrian Del Caro.
        pages cm — (The complete works of Friedrich Nietzsche ;
volume 8)
    "Translated from Friedrich Nietzsche, Sämtliche Werke: Kritische
Studienausgabe, ed. Giorgio Colli and Mazzino Montinari, in 15 vols.
This book corresponds to Vol. 5."
    Translation of: Jenseits von Gut und Böse ; Zur Genealogie der
Moral. München : Deutscher Taschenbuch Verlag ; Berlin ; New York :
De Gruyter, 1980.
    Includes bibliographical references and index.
    ISBN 978-0-8047-2880-5 (cloth : alk. paper) —
    ISBN 978-0-8047-8898-4 (pbk. : alk. paper)
    1. Ethics. I. Del Caro, Adrian, 1952– translator. II. Nietzsche,
Friedrich Wilhelm, 1844–1900. Jenseits von Gut und Böse. English.
III. Nietzsche, Friedrich Wilhelm, 1844–1900. Zur Genealogie der Moral.
English. IV. Title. V. Title: On the genealogy of morality. VI. Series:
Nietzsche, Friedrich Wilhelm, 1844–1900. Works. English. 1995 ; v. 8.
    B3313.J42E5   2014
    193—dc23

                                            2013046593